The Combat Myth According to Mark:
From Ancient Near Eastern Genre to Apocalyptic Gospel

Brendan Graham Dempsey

TABLE OF CONTENTS

ABBREVIATIONS

ABD	*Anchor Bible Dictionary*. Edited by D. N. Freedman (6 vols). New York: Doubleday, 1992.
ANE	Ancient Near East.
ANET	*Ancient Near Eastern Texts Relating to the Old Testament*. Edited by J. B. Pritchard. 3rd ed. Princeton: Princeton University Press, 1969.
ANRW	Aufstieg und Niedergang der römischen Welt.
1 Chron	1 Chronicles.
1 Cor	1 Corinthians.
2 Cor	2 Corinthians.
CAT	See *KTU*.
CTA	*Corpus des tablettes en cunéiforms alphabétiques*. Edited by A. Herdner. 2 vols. Paris: P. Geuthner, 1963.
Dan	Daniel.
Eph	Ephesians.
Est	Esther.
ESV	English Standard Version.
Ezek	Ezekiel.
Ex	Exodus.
Gal	Galatians.
Gen	Genesis.
Hab	Habakkuk.
Heb	Hebrews.
HTR	*Harvard Theological Review*.
Is	Isaiah.
Jas	James.
JBL	*Journal of Biblical Literature*.
Jer	Jeremiah.
Jn	John.
JNES	*Journal of Near Eastern Studies*.
Josh	Joshua.
JSNT	*Journal for the Study of the New Testament*.
JSS	*Journal of Semitic Studies*.
JTS	*Journal of Theological Studies*.
Judg	Judges.
1 Kgs	1 Kings.
KJV	King James Version.
KTU	*Die Keilalphabetischen Texte aus Ugarit. Teil 1*

	Transkription, Alter Orient und Altes Testament 24/1. Edited by M. Dietrich, O. Loretz, and J. Sanmartín. Kevelaer: Butzon und Bercker; Neukirchen-Vluyn: Neukirchener Verlag, 1976.
LSJ	*A Greek-English Lexicon*. Edited by Henry George Liddell and Robert Scott. Revised by Henry Stuart Jones and Robert McKenzie. Oxford: Clarendon Press, 1968.
LXX	Septuagint.
Mk	Mark.
NASB	New American Standard Bible.
Neh	Nehemiah.
NRSV	New Revised Standard Version.
NTS	*New Testament Studies*.
Num	Numbers.
OT	Old Testament.
OTP	*The Old Testament Pseudepigrapha*. Edited by J. H. Charlesworth (2 vols). Doubleday: Garden City, 1983.
1 Pet	1 Peter.
Phil	Philippians.
Ps	Psalm.
Pss	Psalms
RB	*Revue Biblique*.
Rev	Revelation.
Rom	Romans.
1 Sam	1 Samuel.
2 Sam	2 Samuel.
SVT	*Saint Vladimir's Theological Quarterly*.
T. Ash	*Testament of Asher*.
T. Sim	*Testament of Simeon*.
T. Naph	*Testament of Naphtali*.
T. Zeb	*Testament of Zebulun*.
1 Thess	1 Thessalonians.
2 Thess	2 Thessalonians.
2 Tim	2 Timothy.
UF	*Ugarit-Forschungen*.
VT	*Vetus Testamentum*.
Zech	Zechariah.
ZNW	Zeitschrift für die Neutestamentliche Wissenschaft.

PREFACE

This monograph began as an undergraduate honors thesis at the University of Vermont, which I defended in May of 2011. It was subsequently revised and expanded during a three month stay at the Albright Institute in 2012. Throughout its development, I have been aided by a number of individuals, foremost among them my thesis advisor and mentor, Dr. John Curtis Franklin. His consistently helpful feedback and extensive knowledge of the ancient Near East have benefited this work in innumerable ways; for all of his time and assistance I am extremely grateful. I am similarly indebted to the other members of my committee, professors Anne Clark and Andrew Barnaby, and to all of the helpful faculty in the departments of Classics and Religious Studies at UVM. Finally, I would like to thank the library services at Hebrew University and the National Library of Israel for their assistance during my stay in Jerusalem, as well as Sy Gitin and the W. F. Albright Institute of Archeological Research for housing me as an assistant to Dr. Franklin.

Regarding the biblical texts cited in this work, all translations are from the NRSV unless otherwise noted. Sometimes, however, I have emended the NRSV to better reflect some aspect of the original text— particularly when the mythic resonances have been lost in translation. In most cases, simple capitalization is enough to highlight the presence of a divine agent versus a natural entity (e.g., "Death" instead of "death"). Other alterations may serve to highlight specific and/or recurrent terminology of special interest (e.g., translating Heb. *měsillâ* as "processional road" instead of the NRSV's imprecise "highway"). Translations of the Septuagint are those of Sir Lancelot Brenton, modified for similar reasons and slightly modernized.

All translations from the Gospel of Mark are my own, following the 27th edition of the Nestle-Aland Greek text. With Mark, I have generally prioritized fidelity over aesthetics in an attempt to preserve, as much as possible, the author's original style and wording (e.g., maintaining changes of tense from past to historical present, etc.). For convenience, Greek and Hebrew verbs are cited by their lexical forms (first principal part and Qal perfect 3ms, respectively).

INTRODUCTION

Over the past half century, increased scholarly attention has been paid to the role of the ancient Near Eastern combat myth in the Hebrew Bible/Old Testament.[1] Indeed, these investigations have shed substantial light on the nature of early Israelite religion, enhancing our appreciation of Israel's place in its ancient Near Eastern milieu. However, despite such a plethora of studies, relatively little attention has been paid to the myth's significance in the New Testament, particularly in the four gospels. Here, though commentators and exegetes have acknowledged its presence, analyses have been invariably haphazard and undeveloped. The myth is superficially addressed where echoes of it are most obvious, but otherwise completely ignored.

This tendency is best exemplified by commentaries on Jesus' "calming of the storm" (Matt 8:23-27; Mk 4:35-41; Lk 8:22-25). In that event (as I shall examine in greater depth below), Jesus demonstrates his power over the Sea, rebuking its raging waters just as Yahweh the divine warrior had in the ancient Hebrew combat myth. Commentators typically note this mythological background and will often cite various OT passages describing Yahweh's battle with the Sea for comparison. This in turn may lead to a brief contextual nod to comparable ancient Near Eastern myths. However, while many *note* this mythological background, few actually probe for broader thematic significance, or seek to answer the questions naturally raised by its presence. These questions, however, are crucial, and include (but are not limited to):

> 1) *How* exactly did such an ancient mythic pattern find its way into a Christian work of the first century CE?

---

[1] Inaugurated by Hermann Gunkel, *Schöpfung und Chaos in Urzeit und Endzeit: Eine Religionsgeschichtliche Untersuchung über Gen 1 und Ap Joh 12* (Göttingen: Vandenhoeck und Ruprecht, 1895), the subject has since been extensively explored in works such as Mary K. Wakeman, *God's Battle with the Monster: A Study in Biblical Imagery* (Leiden: Brill, 1973); Foster R. McCurley, *Ancient Myths and Biblical Faith: Scriptural Transformations* (Philadelphia: Fortress Press, 1983), 12-71; John Day, *God's Conflict with the Dragon and the Sea: Echoes of a Canaanite Myth in the Old Testament*, University of Cambridge Oriental Publications No. 35 (Cambridge: Cambridge University Press, 1985); Carola Kloos, *Yhwh's Combat with the Sea: A Canaanite Tradition in the Religion of Ancient Israel* (Leiden: Brill, 1986); Neil Forsyth, *The Old Enemy: Satan and the Combat Myth* (Princeton: Princeton University Press, 1987), esp. 90-146; and Bernard Frank Batto, *Slaying the Dragon: Mythmaking in the Biblical Tradition* (Louisville: Westminster/John Knox Press, 1992).

2) *Why* is the evangelist employing ancient mythic material, specifically of battle?
3) Does he employ this myth, or related material, elsewhere?
   a) If so, where and to what end?
   b) If so, what do these allusions, taken together, communicate? Can they help elucidate anything about the gospel's
      i) message,
      ii) structure,
      iii) audience (etc.)?

Surprisingly, such avenues have been only scantly explored, and—until now—no critical scholarship has presented a reading of any gospel which attempts a *comprehensive* analysis of the combat myth's significance.

Of course, the reason why the Old Testament should receive more attention than the New with regard to the combat myth is by no means a mystery. The chronological and cultural proximity of the ancient Near Eastern material to the Hebrew Bible invites comparison. The New Testament, however—given its temporal and cultural separation from these older traditions—does not immediately demand the same kind of analysis. However, a reappraisal of this assumption is necessary, since it is now widely recognized that the authors of the New Testament, despite their chronological remove from the ancient Near East, remained connected to many of its mythic traditions by a crucial ideological bridge: *apocalypticism*.

It has long been acknowledged that Jewish apocalypticism significantly drew from, and found articulation through, the combat myth pattern of the ancient Near East.[2] Indeed, of all traditional mythic genres which most influenced Jewish apocalypticism, *"the most important by far is the combat myth,"* asserts Richard J. Clifford, "for it provided not only imagery but also a conceptual framework for explaining divine rule over the world."[3] This connection is crucial when we consider that early Christianity arose directly out of

---

[2] See e.g.,, Stanley Brice Frost, *Old Testament Apocalyptic: Its Origins and Growth* (London: Epworth, 1952), 12-15, 33-45; Paul D. Hanson, *The Dawn of Apocalyptic* (Philadelphia: Fortress Press, 1975), 299-324; Day, *God's Conflict*, 141-78; Forsyth, *The Old Enemy*, esp. 122, 142-146, 147ff, 248-57. For connections with the Persian Zoroastrian combat myth specifically, see Norman Cohn, *Cosmos, Chaos, and the World to Come: The Ancient Roots of Apocalyptic Faith* (New Haven: Yale University Press, 1993), 105-16.

[3] Richard J. Clifford, "The Roots of Apocalypticism in Near Eastern Myth," in *The Encyclopedia of Apocalypticism*, ed. John J. Collins (New York: Continuum, 1998), 4; emphasis mine.

apocalyptic Judaism. In fact, "[s]ince the beginning of the twentieth century," notes Richard Horsley, "Jesus and the Gospels have been interpreted as 'apocalyptic,' even as direct expressions of Jewish apocalypticism."[4] Given the substantial role of the combat myth in Jewish apocalypticism, it seems likely that the combat myth played a similarly significant role in early Christianity. As an outgrowth of Jewish apocalyptic thought, early Christianity inherited that worldview's conceptions, beliefs, and intellectual paradigms—including those based on the combat myth pattern of the ancient Near East.

The goal of this monograph is to investigate this issue by examining the Gospel of Mark and its use of that myth pattern. While Mark is a text worthy of consideration in its own right, it also serves as a logical starting place for any further investigation into the role of the combat myth in the Synoptic Gospels (assuming "Markan priority" and the three-source hypothesis). In the pages which follow, I shall argue that, via apocalypticism, the ancient Near Eastern combat myth became one of the key narrative frameworks through which the early church understood Jesus' ministry, as old mythological ideas were employed to articulate the eschatological hopes of Christians in the first century. It is within this framework, I posit, that *Mark portrays Jesus as the eschatological divine warrior who repeats Yahweh's primordial acts of battling the evil forces of Chaos: Sea and Dragon. Victorious, he then enters Jerusalem in a triumphant procession modeled on ancient Israel's cultic enshrinement of the combat myth, the New Year festival. There, still following the mytho-cultic paradigm, he re-purifies the Temple and its environs, assumes kingship at his enthronement on the cross, and battles the final chaos-enemy, Death.*

To provide the context for these mythic transformations, Part One offers an overview of the combat myth genre, followed by a survey of different combat myths from across the temporal and geographical span of the ancient Near East. The myths from Ugarit are considered last and given special attention, for they provide the best insight into the Canaanite mythological milieu out of which ancient Israel (and its combat myth) arose. In Chapter 2, I examine the glimpses that the Hebrew Bible offers of that ancient Israelite myth, then consider its development in Jewish thought after the Exile. Chapter 3 then looks at

---

[4] Richard Horsley, "The Kingdom of God and the Renewal of Israel: Synoptic Gospels, Jesus Movements, and Apocalypticism," ibid., 303.

the process by which the combat myth came to inform Jewish apocalypticism, and, from there, early Christianity.

The history and context established, Part Two specifically investigates Mark's utilization of the myth. After some brief introductory considerations in Chapter 4, Chapter 5 examines Mark's prologue, which sets up the presentation of Jesus as the eschatological divine warrior in terms of the traditional combat myth. I then consider these combats topically: first, Jesus' victories over Satan in Chapter 6, then over the Sea in Chapter 7. Given his success in all of these confrontations, Chapter 8 looks at Mark's depiction of Jesus' journey to/activities in Jerusalem *qua* the combat myth's chief cultic expression, the ancient Israelite New Year festival, while Chapter 9 concludes with a consideration of Jesus' victory over the final chaos-enemy, Death.

Part I: Contexts of the Combat Myth

CHAPTER 1
COMBAT MYTHS OF THE ANCIENT NEAR EAST

The Combat Myth Genre

In Genesis 1, Creation is presented as a series of differentiations, each one more minute than the last, until our own familiar world is, as it were, whittled into being from the formless, cosmic *tohu wa-bohu*. So God makes Order out of Chaos, and sense out of confusion—a process of paramount importance to human communities from the creation of Genesis to today. Indeed, to compare great things with small, the modern scholar engages in a similar task when approaching the disparate, sometimes bewildering, but ever fascinating texts which have come down to us from the ancient Near East. To make sense of them likewise requires differentiation: separating similar sorts from the whole, and forming categories of like types. When we do so, the dizzying blur is focused somewhat and we can see, if only a bit more clearly, through the eyes of the peoples who produced them.

The genre of "combat myth" is one such type or category, into which scholars place those ancient stories sharing the same basic plot of battle between two supernatural adversaries.[1] In rudimentary terms, such myths narrate a god's fight with a monstrous villain who threatens order and life in the cosmos. The champion "divine warrior" is invariably the storm-god, while his destructive adversary typically takes the form of a dragon or sea monster. After a struggle for dominance in which the dragon initially proves victorious, the divine warrior ultimately vanquishes his foe, thereby ensuring order and fertility in the cosmos. For this he is granted kingship and, his triumph festively celebrated, the storm-god processes to his newly-constructed palace (i.e., temple) for enthronement as king.

Versions of this myth are attested throughout the ancient Near East in Egyptian, Sumerian, Babylonian, Ugaritic, Hurro-Hittite, Assyrian, and Israelite texts. To the west, its variations appear in such Greek tales as the battle of Zeus with Typhon, and Apollo with Python;[2] further east, it underlies the Indian tale of Indra's battle with

---

[1] Other designations for the genre are sometimes used, such as "the myth of *Chaoskampf*" (struggle with Chaos) or the "conflict myth." Less common designations also occur.

[2] Joseph Fontenrose, *Python: A Study of Delphic Myth and Its Origins* (Berkeley: University of California Press, 1959). Cf. Carolina López-Ruiz, *When the Gods Were*

Vritra.[3] This attestation across such vast expanses of geography, time, and culture suggests that, to many ancient peoples, the myth maintained a considerable importance. However, to appreciate this significance we must more fully understand the myth itself.

Of course interpreting such myths in any definitive sense is impossible; they are multivalent stories with resonances in various semantic registers (some of which have no doubt been lost to history). Nevertheless, from our vantage point, the combat myth does seem to have at its core one appreciable, overarching concern, whose fundamental importance to human life helps to explain its broad popularity. That concern is *order* itself: where it comes from, how to maintain it, and what to do when it goes away. Viewed in this light, the enduring popularity of the combat myth would have owed largely to its success at providing a means by which ancient peoples could make sense of their world—to know *why* and *how* the world was structured. Thus Richard J. Clifford astutely notes that

> the combat myth was a customary ancient way of thinking about the world. Ancient Near Eastern "philosophical" thinking was normally done through narrative. …To do philosophy, theology, and political theory, modern thinkers employ the genre of the discursive essay rather than the narrative of the combat myth. Despite the differences, one should not forget that ancients and moderns share an interest in ultimate causes and both are intent on explaining the cosmos, the nature of evil, and the validity and the functions of basic institutions.[4]

Once one appreciates this fundamental concern with the establishment of *order*, the combat myth's specific relationship to 1) agricultural, 2) cultic, 3) political, and 4) philosophical/theological aspects of life in the ancient Near East becomes more clear. Examining these diverse yet interrelated realms of experience reveals an equally complex set of semantic interrelationships, all of which bear heavily on the present study:

1) *Agricultural.* An interpretation with nearly universal acceptance among scholars holds that most combat myths reflect the transitions of the agricultural calendar, its narrative progression mirroring seasonal changes and their effect on fertility. In this sense,

---

Born: Greek Cosmogonies and the Near East (Cambridge: Harvard University Press, 2010), 84-129.

[3] Fontenrose, *Python*, 194-209.

[4] Clifford, "The Roots of Apocalypticism," 28.

the divine warrior is principally the god of the storm and rainfall, and thus the bringer of fertility, sustenance, and life itself. Conversely, the enemy of the divine warrior represents sterility and death: the forces of destruction and Chaos embodied as a monstrous creature such as a dragon or serpentine beast. Every year these cosmic forces—fertility/sterility, the growing season/the barren summer—battle for supremacy. The lack of rain and relative dearth of summer signaled the temporary victory of the chaos-monster, but fall rejuvenation heralded the ultimate success of the storm-god, whose autumnal rains then came to revive the land yet again.

This agricultural interpretation provides perhaps the most basic and obvious sense of the combat myth—one whose universal significance would in itself justify the broad popularity of the narrative in the ancient world. The order of the seasons—so important to agricultural societies—is explained, its origin made clear, and assurance given that, even in the harsh dearth of the barren season, life *will* spring again; such is the order of things.

2) *Cultic*. Linking the mythic narrative to agricultural realities allows us to appreciate the actual material contexts of the myths themselves, since most seem to have had a cultic *Sitz im Leben* at a (usually springtime) New Year festival. As a celebration of new life and the return of fertility, it is not surprising that such a setting occasioned the myth's chief cultic realization (given the basic agricultural interpretation just considered).

Yet the relationship of the combat myth to the New Year is still more fundamental. Indeed, because the combat myth is essentially about *order* and the imposition of order onto Chaos, the creative act lies at the heart of the myth. For this reason, the combat myth is often a cosmogony, the victory of the divine warrior resulting in the actual Creation of the world. Since Creation provided the paradigmatic model for the New Year festival—the "Beginning" as archetype for the new beginning—the role of the combat myth at the festival is further elucidated.

However, to say that Creation provided the archetype for the New Year is not to suggest that the first was a kind of metaphor for the second, or that the New Year was somehow "modeled" on Creation. Rather, the New Year *was* Creation: each New Year was a new Creation. As Mircea Eliade has shown, ritual activity in ancient religious cult did not merely *recall* sacred deeds of the primordial past—it *re-created* them. Thus, ancient Near Eastern New Year festivals were celebrated as a return to the beginning of time itself; indeed, each New Year was a re-Creation of the cosmos. This "eternal return" helps to explain one chief concern of ancient New Year ceremonies: *purification*. Eliade writes:

> Since the New Year is a reactualization of the cosmogony, it implies *starting time over again at its beginning*, that is, restoration of the primordial time, the "pure" time, that existed at the moment of Creation. This is why the New Year is the occasion for "purifications," for the expulsion of sins, of demons, or merely of a scapegoat. For it is not a matter merely of a certain temporal interval coming to its end and the beginning of another (as a modern man, for example, thinks); it is also a matter of abolishing the past year and past time. Indeed, this is the meaning of ritual purifications...[5]

This semantic association of the New Year with renewal, re-purification, forgiveness of sins, and ablution is critical, and I shall note particular examples as they appear. In terms of specific rites, however, the notion that these festivals were fundamentally re-creations and not simply recollections or commemorations elucidates why the combat itself is thought to have been ritually reenacted at such New Year festivals, as well as why the texts of these myths were recited as part of the celebrations. Through these enactments, participants in the cult actually helped facilitate the new Creation.

Eliade's notion of eternal return may also shed light on the key cultic activity of these ancient Near Eastern New Year festivals. For central to all was *the festal procession of the storm-god's idol*, which was taken from its temple and ceremonially paraded with majestic pomp and fanfare before the people as it traveled to some different cultic site(s). Since sheltered for the rest of the year within its holy precincts, out of sight, this was the god's chief presentation before the people—that is, his chief *epiphany*. The New Year was the time when the god revealed himself in all his glory. So Eliade:

> Symbolically, man became contemporary with the cosmogony, he was present at the creation of the world. In the ancient Near East, he even participated actively in its creation (cf. the two opposed groups, representing the god and the marine monster). It is easy to understand why the memory of that marvelous time haunted religious man, why he periodically sought to return to it. *In illo tempore* the gods had displayed

---

[5] Mircea Eliade, *The Sacred and the Profane: The Nature of Religion* (New York: Harcourt, 1959), 77-8; emphasis original.

their greatest powers. *The cosmogony is the supreme divine manifestation, the paradigmatic act of strength, superabundance, and creativity.*[6]

The presentation of the deity concluded, the god returned through the city gates to his great temple in the main city. With the reinstallation of the idol, the cultic rites of the New Year festival were essentially concluded.

In the interaction of myth and ritual, the orderly cycle of Nature's seasonal changes has its counterpart in the human realm of religious rite, each one dialectally informing the other: myths *about* order are actively embodied as actions which *give* a sense of order to human life. Patterned behavior and religious time impose order on the bewildering Chaos of personal experience and, as players in the cosmic drama, human beings themselves help facilitate rejuvenation of the cosmos through ritual.

3) *Political.* On the level of human communities, social hierarchy and institutions were structural givens of ancient life in need of explanation as much as those of the natural world. In practical terms, the maintenance of social order required strong political leadership, and in the ancient Near East it was the king who filled this vital role—a position of immense social, cultic, and even philosophical importance. For this reason *kingship* is a central concern in nearly all combat myths. The divine warrior, consequent to his mighty deeds, is granted kingship over the cosmos, and a palace is built for him (the palace of the god being in fact his temple: the god's abode on earth).

Though, since divine kingship was itself a reflection of earthly practices and perceptions of kingship, historical/political realities also played a role in various combat myths. As the god's representative on earth, the human king was also associated with the storm-god's battles against the negative forces of Chaos and destruction. The king's battles with his earthly enemies mirrored the god's battles with his supernatural enemies. On this level, then, combat myths had clear political and historical overtones; myth and history informed one another.

4) *Philosophical/Theological.* Finally, seeing the combat myth as a vehicle for "philosophical" or "theological" thinking allows us to consider broader ways in which the myth articulates assumptions about the nature of the world, and what kinds of conclusions its draws. When

---

[6] Ibid., 79-80; emphasis original.

we do so, a particular worldview emerges—one which, though realistic about the struggles and trials of life, is ultimately optimistic about the underlying workings of the cosmos. The divine warrior is a god of order, while the dragon represents all that is destructive and disorderly—that is, Chaos. Because of this dichotomous conflict, the combat myth is often referred to as the myth of *Chaoskampf*: the battle with Chaos. But Chaos *is* defeated (if only cyclically), which in itself seems to assert a basic confidence in the life-affirming workings of the cosmos, thus offering hope in times of death, dearth, and loss.

The god of order and fertility is the rightful king, whose power was both theologically important (i.e., indicative of/justifying the god's central place in the pantheon) but also of a broader "philosophical" significance. That the divine warrior is proclaimed king entails more than just neat narrative closure to such myths. Rather, it says something about the cosmos: the good god of order and fertility is in control. He is powerful over the forces of Chaos; he can defeat them, and has. In the ever-uncertain lives of men and women in the ancient world—so much at the whim of death, disease, war, and a host of other uncontrollable forces—such narratives no doubt provided a sense of reassurance and stability. Though the fields go barren and chaotic forces take hold of the world for a time, the god of order and prosperity is in charge; he is king.

Additionally, the association of the combat myth and *purification* outlined earlier should also be considered in light of its broader philosophical implications. In a similar way to the existential threats just cited, spiritual degradation and corruption no doubt presented their own anxieties. Impurities resulting from moral and/or ritual failures, personal or public, required purgation. With the return to the pure, original state of the cosmos, the New Year offered fresh assurance of a clean slate. Thus, by extension, the victory of the storm-god and the defeat of Chaos could inspire private, psychological comfort in addition to general, philosophical confidence.

All of these aspects of the combat myth form a complex of interrelated themes. Rejuvenation, divinity, kingship, and justice interweave in a rich tapestry of association—each informing the other, each but one element in a broader, holistic worldview. The totality, however, is best understood as one cosmic myth of *order*.

Having considered the crucial themes and associations common to all ancient Near Eastern combat myths, our task now turns to examining the common structure they share. However, Clifford cautions, "One must be careful methodologically about describing the elements of the genre of combat myth in the ancient Near East. There is no ideal form of the myth but only diverse realizations."[7] Unique elements in any regional combat myth should not be looked upon as divergences from some pure and original form; each version of the myth reflects the specific concerns of the people telling it.[8] Though, given this important caveat, Clifford does ultimately conclude that "a consistent plot line can be abstracted."[9] Indeed, some useful attempts have already been made at outlining the basic plot of the combat myth and abstracting its core narrative elements.

The first major attempt to do so was put forth by Joseph Fontenrose in his comprehensive study of ancient combat myths.[10] His outline proved a crucial first step, though not without its flaws (as subsequent critique by Neil Forsyth has demonstrated).[11] Forsyth subsequently proposed an alternative schema, applying to the combat myth those narrative functions developed by the Russian Formalist Vladimir Propp.[12] His schema identifies the following fundamental narrative elements:

1. Lack/Villainy
2. Hero emerges/prepares to act
3. Donor/Consultation
4. Journey
5. Battle
6. Defeat
7. Enemy ascendant
8. Hero recovers
9. Battle rejoined
10. Victory
11. Enemy punished
12. Triumph

---

[7] Clifford, "The Roots of Apocalypticism," 28.

[8] For an insightful analysis of this process see Fontenrose, *Python*, 5-9.

[9] Clifford, "The Roots of Apocalypticism," 7.

[10] Fontenrose, *Python*, 262-4. He presents the following components as key elements: (1) The Dragon Pair, (2) Chaos and Disorder, (3) The Attack, (4) The Champion, (5) The Champion's Death, (6) The Dragon's Reign, (7) Recovery of the Champion, (8) Battle Renewed and Victory, (9) Restoration and Confirmation of Order. Adela Yarbro Collins made use of this schema in Adela Yarbro Collins, *The Combat Myth in the Book of Revelation*, Harvard Dissertations in Religion (Eugene: Wipf and Stock Publishers, 1976), 59-61.

[11] Forsyth, *The Old Enemy*, 441-4.

[12] Vladimir Propp, *Morphology of the Folktale* (Austin: University of Texas Press, 1928).

Thus the conflict begins with an initial dilemma: (1) A monstrous villain poses a challenge. (2) The heroic warrior god appears to meet this challenge. (3) At this point, he may be aided by some counsel, a "donor" supplying him with either a helpful gift or merely some important advice. (4) The storm-god sets out on his mission. (5) The battle ensues, usually with (6) the god's initial defeat by the monster. Consequently, (7) the monster's power and strength increase. However (8) the god soon recovers from his initial defeat and (9) the second round of the cosmic battle ensues. (10) This time the god is victorious and (11) he punishes the monster (usually by mutilating the corpse in some way). (12) Finally, the storm-god exults in a triumphant celebration, such as a feast or glorious procession (thus reflecting the cultic New Year setting). Forsyth notes that some of these elements are always present in combat myths (e.g., Villainy, Battle, Victory) "for without them the narrative would not be a combat," but adds that "others may at times be absent or attenuated without changing the basic structure and character of the narrative."[13] Though not without its own flaws, Forsyth's narrative schema is helpful for providing a consistent framework for the genre, and I shall adopt it in this monograph.[14]

Having thus considered the myth's basic themes and structure, a few specific motifs warrant attention, since certain motifs and images reoccur in different combat myth traditions with a regularity suggestive of generic composition. Indeed, since these are often employed outside of a strictly narrative context (particularly in later texts, whose allusions assume familiarity with the myth), their recognition can be crucial for appreciating less explicit applications of the *Chaoskampf* myth.

The most important of these include the following: (1) Because the hero is god of the storm, anthropomorphized meteorological phenomena provide common images: thus the winds are his chariot, lightning-bolts are his arrows, and, most importantly, thunder is his

---

[13] Forsyth, *The Old Enemy*, 446. Those which may not always appear, and are therefore less essential, include functions 7-9.

[14] As does Clifford, "The Roots of Apocalypticism," 28-31. It is important to note, however, that I am only making use of Forsyth's schema and not attempting any kind of Proppian/functional analysis. Though Forsyth roots his schema in Proppian terminology, he does so with a critical eye to Propp's weaknesses and methodological shortcomings (see Forsyth, *The Old Enemy*, 446, 447, 450). Moreover, his schema is comprehensive, synthesizing Propp, Fontenrose, as well as the Aarne and Thompson folktale index (ibid., 446). This schema will be helpful for the majority of ancient Near Eastern texts, though it becomes problematic in examinations of the Hebrew material (see Chapter 2).

battle cry or *mighty voice*. At the sound of his *mighty voice*, the storm-god's enemies quake, flee, or submit. (2) Whether in the context of battle or punishment, *binding* of the enemy is a recurrent topos, either with a rope or, more specifically, a muzzle. (3) After defeating the chaos-monster, *trampling* of the body, or any form of stepping/stomping/standing upon the body are common punishments (thus humiliating the victim, and exalting the victor). (4) So too is a) *dividing/dismembering* the body, which is usually followed by b) *scattering* of the corpse. Though distinct actions, the latter requires the former to have first taken place, and so I consider these as two parts of the same motif.

While many of these actions no doubt reflect common features of actual battle in the ancient world, in myths of combat they become essentially formulaic deeds of the victorious storm-god, with a regularity typical of generic composition. Still, one must be cautious about positing allusions to the combat myth based on such imagery. Imagery alone is rarely enough to establish a connection; obviously not every instance of binding or trampling recalls the myth of *Chaoskampf*. However, one is on sounder ground certainly the more such motifs are found together, while a true convergence of themes, structure, and imagery will provide the strongest case for arguing a text's dependence on the combat myth.

Finally, with regard to the history of the combat myth pattern, we find that its origins, transmission, and influence are complex and fairly unclear. Fortunately, however, these considerations are not relevant to the present study since we are not attempting any kind of in-depth history of the ancient Near Eastern combat myth genre. Rather, our interests are limited to that's genre's application in one text of the first century CE, the Gospel of Mark. The following survey of select combat myths from the ancient Near East is meant therefore only to flesh out the above narrative schema and highlight the recurrent themes and motifs so that one can recognize their ultimate presence in the Gospel of Mark. Accepting a genetic relationship of these texts while ignoring more complicated issues of origin and lines of dependence, the following survey is organized more or less chronologically[15]—a presentation which may obfuscate the complexity of transmission

---

[15] With the deliberate exception of the Ugaritic material, which is considered last and at greater length given its importance for the Hebrew combat myth.

history, but nonetheless allows for a general sense of evolution. To these specific examples of the combat myth we now turn.

Ninurta vs. Azag

Perhaps the oldest extant combat myth from the ancient Near East is the Sumerian text *Lugal-e,* which describes the battle between Ninurta (god of the thunderstorm and fertility) and the dragon Azag. The version we possess was originally composed around 2150 BCE.[16] The conflict begins as Ninurta sits on his throne at feast. Sharur, his trusty battle mace (which acts as an independent agent in the story), enters and informs him of a terrible and unprecedented new threat: the "fearless warrior, Azag," who was "nursed by wild beasts."[17] This Azag has spawned a host of evil helpers—the Stone Things, which serve the villain as an army of warriors—and has been treacherously proclaimed king over the highland by the plants there. Sharur warns Ninurta that Azag now seeks a decisive confrontation:

> It has given instructions concerning you for an encounter,
> Warrior, there have been consultations with a view to *taking away your kingship.*
> …It is slapping faces, relocating dwelling-places,
> Daily the Azag is turning the border (district) over to its side![18]

Thus roused to action by this encroaching threat, Ninurta sets off to battle the rebellious beast. He mounts his storm-chariot, riding the seven gales and casting a tempest in front of him as he hurries onward.

---

[16] Thorkild Jacobsen, *The Harps That Once…: Sumerian Poetry in Translation* (New Haven: Yale University Press, 1987), 234. However, notes Forsyth, *The Old Enemy,* 55, the first known copies of this myth date only from c. 1800 BCE.

[17] Jacobsen, *The Harps That Once,* 237-8, lines 27, 28. The text is not clear about the nature of Azag. Jacobsen has suggested that it may be some kind of "tall hardwood tree," but notes that there are "any number of possibilities" (234, 237 n. 8). Other commentators, such as William J. Hamblin, *Warfare in the Ancient Near East to 1600 BC: Holy Warriors at the Dawn of History* (London: Routledge, 2006), 124, refer to it simply as a dragon. Indeed, ninth-century BCE reliefs erected by Assyrian king Assurnasirpal II depict a god carrying thunderbolts and attacking a dragon-lion. These are thought to depict Ninurta attacking Azag, as is a similar scene found on Neo-Assyrian seals. See Jeremy A. Black and Anthony Green, *Gods, Demons and Symbols of Ancient Mesopotamia: An Illustrated Dictionary* (London: British Museum Press, 1992), 36.

[18] Jacobsen, *The Harps That Once,* 239, lines 52-53, 55-56.

As he drives, he slaughters countless couriers of the enemy, and victories over various draconic and serpentine beasts are recalled:

> O Ninurta, may the names of the warriors slain by you be mentioned:
> The Kulianna, *the Basilisk*, the Gypsum…
> …the Thunderbird, and *the "Seven-headed Serpent"*
> you verily slew, (o) Ninurta, in the highland.[19]

Though successful against the helpers of the enemy, perhaps even *trampling* them all before him,[20] Ninurta is eventually cautioned by Sharur not to attack Azag. Ninurta disregards Sharur's counsel, however, and as the sun stops and darkness covers the earth he confronts the dragon:

> The Azag rose to attack in the front line of the battle,
> The sky it pulled down as a weapon for its hip, took it in hand,
> into the earth it struck the head snakelike…
> The Azag was going to crash like a wall (down) on Ninurta, Enlil's son;
> as were it a day of doom, it screamed wrathfully,
> like a formidable serpent, it hissed from among its people…[21]

Against Ninurta's attack, Azag raises a dust storm and thereby defeats the overconfident storm-god. The divine warrior overcome, Sharur flees to Enlil for counsel in the matter, where he learns that Enlil will muster a rainstorm to clear the dust that Azag is raising. Enlil does just this, and Ninurta—no longer choked by the dust—is able to vanquish the dragon. In a rage, Ninurta sends forth his *battle cry* and *tramples* Azag, then *dismembers/divides* its body. This done, he then "*scattered* it over the mountain" and "strewed it like flour."[22]

After thus vanquishing Azag, Ninurta then judges its helpers, the Stone Things, turning them into a massive irrigation system by heaping up large quantities of the rocks. Each receives a unique punishment or reward, depending on whether or not it defected to his side. Where dispersed lakes had formed on mountaintops, he now builds dams to combine their waters and direct them down from the mountaintops to water the fields. So his combat results in a fertilizing, creative, and order-bringing act, whereas before the forces of Chaos had threatened

---

[19] Ibid., 243, lines 128-9, 133.
[20] The text is unclear. This interpretation accords with ibid., 235, line 4.
[21] Ibid., 245, lines 168-170, 173-5.
[22] Ibid., 249-250.

to encroach and destroy. After this, Ninurta makes his way to his barge which, piled with riches, then festively processes down the waters to songs and praise. Finally, for all of his accomplishments, Enlil affirms the kingship of Ninurta, and the gods praise his kingly glory.

This text is exemplary of the combat myth as outlined above. The usual themes are prominent: Ninurta must defend his just and orderly kingship from the would-be usurper dragon. The storm-god's victory results in greater order in the cosmos, both because the depredations of Azag have been neutralized, but also because the battle itself leads to an act of creation. Moreover, all of this is connected with the agricultural calendar, as the summer dust winds of Azag are defeated and Ninurta's irrigation system waters the fields. The barren season is over and the abundance of the growing time begins.

All the imagery typical of the combat myth is likewise employed here. We see the god's *mighty voice* in the form of his battle cry, as well as the *trampling* of the enemy, the *dividing/scattering* of its body, and even the *binding* of the Stone Things.

In its basic elements, the narrative rather neatly fits Forsyth's combat myth schema: (1) *Lack/Villainy*: The dragon Azag has arisen and challenges Ninurta's kingship, hoping to usurp the throne of the storm-god himself. (2) *Hero emerges/prepares to act*: Ninurta hears of this threat and is compelled to battle the beast. (3) *Donor/Consultation*: Sharur counsels Ninurta on the danger and strength of his foe. (4) *Journey*: Ninurta rides forth on storm clouds to fight Azag. (5) *Battle*: The two foes meet; Ninurta attacks, but Azag raises a giant dust storm in counter-attack. (6) *Defeat*: The dust storm overwhelms Ninurta. (7) *Enemy ascendant*: Consequently, Azag appears victorious in his rebellion. (8) *Hero recovers*: Sharur goes to Enlil, however, from whom he secures assistance.[23] (9) *Battle rejoined*: With the aid of Enlil's rainstorm, the battle begins anew. (10) *Victory*: This time, Ninurta is victorious, and he slays Azag. (11) *Enemy Punished*: In a rage, Ninurta sounds his battle cry and tears the Azag apart, then scatters the body over the mountains. (12) *Triumph*: Ninurta festively processes down the waters in his barge. His kingship is asserted and his power is again uncontested as a result of his victory.

As intimated above, this final event, the procession of the god, reflects cultic practices—perhaps even a festal event specific to this very myth (though in this instance we cannot be certain). William

---

[23] This may also be seen as a double of Donor/Consultation.

Hamblin observes that Ninurta's battle here represents an ideal form of warfare in the ancient Near East, and that such a triumphal procession would have taken place after the defeat of an historical enemy. The "Hymn to Innana," he says, provides evidence of such, whose text describes a triumphal procession complete with music from tambourines and lyres.[24] Generally, procession of a god's idol from one cultic site to another was a phenomenon practiced in the ancient Near East, sometimes by barge (as in Egypt), and it seems likely that this text reflects just such a cultic procession. Moreover, given the agricultural underpinnings of the myth, it is very plausible that it was associated with a seasonal festival celebrating the triumph of fertility (Ninurta) over barrenness and Chaos (Azag).

Ninurta vs. Anzu

Ninurta is the hero of another extant, though incomplete, combat myth. In this myth, the storm-god battles the monster Anzu: a composite beast with lion- and bird-like features. This Anzu has been appointed the guardian of the chief god Enlil's chambers—chambers which house the Tablet of Destinies: a sacred tablet which confers on its possessor the authority to rule over the cosmos. After being entrusted with guarding it, Anzu comes to covet the Tablet and dreams of usurping power:

> The exercise of his Enlilship his eyes view.
> The crown of his sovereignty, the robe of his godhead.
> His divine Tablet of Destinies Anzu views constantly.
> As he views constantly the father of the gods, the god of Duranki,
> *The removal of Enlilship he conceives in his heart.*
> "I will take the divine Tablet of Destinies, I,
> And the decrees of the gods I will rule![25]

Finally, seizing the opportunity while Enlil is disrobed and bathing in the holy waters, Anzu steals the Tablet of Destinies and flies away to his mountain. With the Tablet controlling the Norms of the cosmos now under the control of the monster Anzu, order is destroyed and Chaos assumes dominance over the cosmos.

---

[24] Hamblin, *Warfare in the Ancient Near East*, 125-6.
[25] ANET 112-13, Lines 5-9, 12-13.

Ultimately, the task falls to Ninurta to battle the beast, retrieve the Norms, and thereby reassert order. His mother Mami counsels Ninurta, advising him to use the powers of the storm to subdue Anzu and then slit his throat. Then,

> When the hero heard the speech of his mother,
> He was wroth, he raged (and) departed for [Anzu's] mountain.
> My lord hitched the Seven-of-Battle,
> The hero hitched the seven ill winds,
> The seven whirlwinds which stir up the dust,
> He launched a terrifying war, a fierce conflict.
> While the gale at his side shrieked for strife,
> Anzu and Ninurta met on the mountainside.[26]

The two then battle one another in single combat as darkness overtakes the mountain. Ninurta unloads the power of the storm on Anzu, then fires an arrow at the beast. But his arrows prove ineffective so long as Anzu has the Tablet. Temporarily defeated, Ninurta has the god Hadad report his failure to Ea, the trickster god, in hope of some assistance. As a result, Ea provides Ninurta with a plan to use the South Wind against Anzu's wings; after this, he is to cut them, then slit the beast's throat. Unfortunately, the remainder of the text is too fragmentary to say precisely what follows. However, it is clear that Anzu is defeated, his throat slit (presumably by Ninurta), and order reinstated with the reacquisition of the Tablet of Destinies.

Again, themes and motifs common to the combat myth reappear. The central concern is again kingship. When Anzu steals the Tablet of Destinies, he has effectively usurped Enlil's kingship over the cosmos. The good god of order has been defeated by a monstrous beast of disorder. Now, Ninurta must go forth to battle Anzu. To do so, he employs all of his meteorological weaponry.

Plot-wise, this story also fits well the combat myth schema: (1) *Lack/Villainy*: The chaos-monster Anzu steals the Tablet of Destinies. (2) *Hero emerges/prepares to act*: After other gods refuse the challenge, Ninurta emerges to conquer Anzu. (3) *Donor/Consultation*: Ninurta's mother, Mami, counsels him before his departure. (4) *Journey*: Ninurta heads to Anzu's mountain. (5) *Battle*: Ninurta and Anzu engage in their initial combat. (6) *Defeat*: The arrow Ninurta launches is ineffective. (7) *Enemy ascendant*: Anzu is seemingly insurmountable so long as he possesses the Tablet. (8) *Hero recovers*:

---

[26] ANET 515, Tablet II, lines 28-35.

Ninurta is taught by Ea how to defeat Anzu using the South Wind. Due to the fragmentary nature of the sources, however, we cannot speak definitively about narrative functions 9 through 12, though we assume that (9) the battle is rejoined, because (10) Anzu is ultimately defeated. The punishment of Anzu (11) and Ninurta's triumph (12) cannot be identified with certainty.

The Storm God vs. the Serpent

A very compact version of the combat myth has survived from the Hurro-Hittite tradition. It relates the conflict between the Storm God and the Serpent, also known as Illuyankas. The text goes back to at least the Old Hittite Period (c. 1750-1500 BCE), but our surviving copies date to sometime between 1500 and 1190 BCE.[27] The action begins:

> When the Storm God and the serpent fought each other in Kiskilussa, the serpent defeated the Storm God.
> Then the Storm God invoked all the gods: "Come together to me." So Inara prepared a feast.[28]

A grand banquet is then prepared, teeming with alcoholic drinks. The goddess Inara then enlists a man named Hupasiya to aid her in a scheme. She dresses in her finest clothes and lures the serpent from his lair, saying, "I'm preparing a feast. Come eat and drink!"[29] The serpent obliges her, comes up from his lair and drinks heartily at the banquet until he is incapacitated. This done, Hupasiya emerges and *binds* the serpent with a rope. The dragon thus ensnared, "The Storm God came and killed the serpent, and the gods were with him."[30]

Though rather brief compared to the Ninurta myths, this ancient story still exhibits most of the core elements of the combat myth. Functions 1, 2, and 5 are quickly combined,[31] as the villain Illuyankas and the hero Storm God are introduced in the same breath relating the

---

[27] Harry A. Hoffner and Gary M. Beckman, *Hittite Myths*, 2nd ed., Writings from the Ancient World (Atlanta: Scholars Press, 1998), 11.

[28] Ibid., 11, A i 9-11.

[29] Ibid., 12, B i 7-8.

[30] Ibid., 12, B i 17-18.

[31] (1) Lack/Villainy, (2) Hero emerges/prepares to act, and (5) Battle.

battle. Function 4 seems entirely lacking, however.[32] (5) The two battle, (6) with the initial defeat of the Storm God. (8)The Storm God recovers after (3) Inara aids him. (9) The second battle then occurs once Hupasiya has bound the Serpent. (10) This time the Storm God is victorious. (12) The hero's triumph is recognized and celebrated by his fellow gods, who gather together with him at the battle's conclusion.

With regard to imagery, the *binding* motif is notable, particularly for such a compact telling of the conflict. Its presence demonstrates that the *binding* topos was more than a superfluous narrative detail, recurrent in such combat myths simply for its prevalence in actual warfare tactics. Rather, it was an important formulaic motif—a persistent element in the combat myth genre.

Now, compared to those already considered, far more can be said about this myth regarding its agricultural significance and related cultic context. For the account we have of this Hittite combat myth is prefaced by a note explaining it as "the text of the Purulli (Festival)."[33] This *Purulli* Festival was the annual New Year's festival that celebrated the regeneration of life and re-confirmed the kingship.[34] As we have noted, the defeat of the chaos-monster and the victory of the storm-god symbolized the destruction of disorder and infertility and the cyclical ascension of fertility and life. Thus the myth was recited at the annual festival, when the earth became fertile and green again:

> ...[T]hey speak thus—
> "Let the land prosper (and) thrive, and let the land be protected" –and when it prospers and thrives, they perform the Purulli Festival.[35]

It was only at this special cultic event that the statue of the Storm God was brought out from its temple and wheeled on an ox-drawn carriage in a festive procession.[36] Trevor Bryce paints a vivid picture of this scene:

> We can retrace the path of a festival procession as it leaves the palace gate and proceeds along the ceremonial way, exiting the city through the so-

---

[32] (4) Journey.

[33] Hoffner and Beckman, *Hittite Myths*, 11, A i 1.

[34] Trevor Bryce, *Life and Society in the Hittite World* (Oxford: Oxford University Press, 2002), 195.

[35] Hoffner and Beckman, *Hittite Myths*, 11 A i 4-8.

[36] Charles Allen Burney, *Historical Dictionary of the Hittites* (Lanham: Scarecrow Press, 2004), 86.

called King's Gate, and passing outside the walls before again entering the city through the Lion Gate. We can imagine the processional way lined with the city's inhabitants and foreign visitors, awaiting the spectacle soon to pass by them. In the distance, the songs of musicians, the pounds of the drums, cymbals, tambourines, and castanets can be heard, growing ever louder as the procession approaches. …Various cultic calls are made by designated performers and attendants—'aha!', 'kasmessa!', 'missa!'.[37]

Hittite processions led to a *ḫuwasi* stone outside the city: an altar-propped stele housed in a sacred shrine which represented the deity's presence.[38] At the New Year, the Storm God traveled even farther, all the way to the city of Nerik, where the story of his defeat of the dragon Illuyankas was probably ritually re-enacted.[39] After this, the icon of the Storm God was returned to its usual residence within the city temple until the next great festal procession.

Marduk vs. Tiamet

The *Enûma Eliš* is the best-documented combat myth to survive from the ancient Near East. Composed in the latter part of the second millennium BCE,[40] it recounts the battle between the storm-god Marduk and the serpentine goddess Tiamet,[41] whose name means "Sea." The narrative begins with an account of the creation of the gods by Tiamet and Apsu (Sea and Sky). Soon after their creation, however, this younger generation of gods grows too noisy and disruptive for their parents. Tiamet and Apsu therefore plan to destroy their boisterous offspring. However, the god Ea, hearing of the plot, intervenes and preemptively slays Apsu. This only temporarily neutralizes the threat, however, since Tiamet continues with her plan to destroy the other gods—now as an act of vengeance for the murder of her consort. To aid

---

[37] Bryce, *Life and Society*, 189, 190.

[38] See Burney, *Historical Dictionary of the Hittites*, 87, 255-6.

[39] Bryce, *Life and Society*, 195.

[40] Benjamin R. Foster, *Before the Muses: An Anthology of Akkadian Literature*, 3rd ed. (Bethesda: CDL Press, 2005), 436. The precise date is much debated.

[41] While the *Enûma Eliš* does not explicitly describe Tiamet as a serpent or dragon, it does make reference to her "tail," and a Neo-Assyrian cylinder seal (c. 900-750 BCE) showing a warrior with lightning in his hands treading upon the back of a long dragon may represent the slaying Tiamet (Clifford, "The Roots of Apocalypticism," 17).

her in this fight, she forms and dispatches great helper beasts including "monster serpents," "the Viper" and "the Dragon."[42]

Ea hears of this new plotting too, and brings the news to the Divine Council. At first, the gods who might dare challenge Tiamet are either unable or too afraid to do so. Eventually, however, the young storm-god Marduk steps up to battle Tiamet. Marduk requests that in return for this service he be declared the ultimate king over the cosmos. To this the gods readily oblige:

> Joyfully they did homage: "Marduk is king!"
> They conferred on him scepter, throne, and *vestment*.[43]

Marduk then mounts his storm-chariot, harnesses the winds, and readies lightning-bolt arrows as his weapons. Finally, sea-god and storm-god engage in single combat:

> The lord spread out his net to enfold her,
> The Evil Wind, which followed behind, he let loose in her face.
> When Tiamet opened her mouth to consume him,
> He drove in the Evil Wind that she close not her lips.
> As the fierce winds charged her belly,
> Her body was distended and her mouth was wide open.
> He released the arrow, it tore her belly,
> It cut through her insides, splitting her heart.
> Having thus subdued her, he extinguished her life.
> He cast down her carcass to stand upon it.[44]

So is the cosmic Sea defeated and her body *trampled*. Tiamet's allies are terrified by the defeat and seek to escape, but Marduk rounds them up and *binds* them all:

> The whole band of demons that marched on her right,
> He cast into fetters, their hands he bound.
> *For* all their resistance, he trampled (them) underfoot.
>   ...valiant Marduk
> Strengthened his hold on the vanquished gods,
> And turned back to Tiamet whom he had bound.
> The lord trod on the legs of Tiamet,
> With his unsparing mace he crushed her skull.[45]

---

[42] ANET 62, Tablet I, lines 133 and 140.
[43] ANET 66, Tablet IV, lines 29-30; italics original.
[44] ANET 67, Tablet IV, lines 95-104.
[45] ANET, Lines 116-118, 127-30; italics original.

Marduk then picks up the corpse of Tiamet and, "like a fish" *divides* the body in two. Thus he fashions the heavens and the earth out of the defeated Sea, literally creating life and order out of the dead embodiment of sterility and Chaos. He then sets the proper boundaries for the raging waters and fashions humanity. The combat myth thus becomes a cosmogony. Marduk takes the Tablet of Destinies from the wrongful gods and fastens it on his own breast. The Norms have come to an orderly and just ruler. A palace/temple is constructed and the throne granted to him; his victory validates the gods' proclamation of him as eternal king over the cosmos.

Again, the themes of kingship and order are fundamental to this combat myth. Only Marduk is able to slay Tiamet, making him uniquely qualified to rule as king. The rule of Tiamet was cruel and destructive, while the accession of Marduk inaugurates the prosperous reign of the beneficial storm-god.

Nearly all of the typical images reoccur: Marduk wields the weapons of the storm, *binds* Tiamet and her serpentine helpers, and *tramples* the carcasses of his enemies. Finally, the body of the chaos-monster is *divided*, becoming the fertile material for creation.

Plot-wise, the myth fits well into Forsyth's schema. Briefly: (1) *Lack/Villainy*: Tiamet seeks to destroy the gods. (2) *Hero emerges/prepares to act*: Marduk emerges at the Divine Council. (3) *Donor/Consultation*: Marduk is promised kingship at the Council and prepares his weapons for battle. (4) *Journey*: Marduk sets out to confront Tiamet. (5) *Battle*: Marduk and Tiamet engage in single combat. (10) *Victory*: Marduk is triumphant. (11) *The enemy punished*: Marduk binds and tramples upon the conquered, then tears Tiamet in two. (12) *Triumph*: Marduk receives his kingship, a palace/temple is built for him, and all the gods chant his glorious names in the Divine Council. Interestingly, functions 6 through 9 (Defeat, Enemy ascendant, Hero recovers, Battle rejoined) are lacking here—an omission which may have served to heighten the philosophical/theological implications of the myth: Marduk is so powerful he needs but one attempt to defeat the forces of Chaos. Such zealous propaganda for the god, while emphasizing the power of the divine warrior, implicitly emboldens the religious participant: the greater Marduk is, the greater assurance one can have in the ultimate triumph of order over Chaos.

Like the Hittite combat myth's connection with the New Year *Purulli* Festival, recitation of the *Enûma Eliš* was a key liturgical element in the Babylonian *Akītu* Festival: the twelve-day Babylonian New Year festival celebrating agricultural rejuvenation. Marduk's victory over Tiamet was assured, and his reign meant the renewal of the world. While Chaos and death had for a time asserted themselves over the cosmos, the festival allowed for the turning back of the clock—indeed, all the way back to the creation of the world. To ritually enact this re-creation, on the fourth day of the festival the *sesgallu* priest would recite the *Enûma Eliš* to the temple statue of Marduk.[46] The following day, the priests would purify the temple of all spiritual pollution, thus ridding the sacred precincts of the contamination which had accumulated throughout the year. Recalling that the New Year meant a return to the completely pure state of the first Creation, this necessitated that all pollution be cleansed. So Julye Bidmead notes that the *Akītu* was a time of general ablution, when demons were expelled, diseases cured, and sins forgiven.[47] So too was the kingship renewed, as the king was ritually humiliated by the priest in the temple to show his ultimate subservience to Marduk.

On either the eighth or ninth day of the festival the great procession began. At this time, the statues of the gods were removed from their temples and processed through the streets of the city on jeweled chariots in great pomp and fanfare. Accompanied by singers, dancers, and musicians, the statue of Marduk traveled the processional way, the Babylonian *via sacra*, from the main gate of the Esagila (Marduk's temple) out of the city's Ishtar Gate to the *bīt akīti* (the "house of the *Akītu*").[48] Like the *ḫuwasi* stone of the Hittite processions, the *bīt akīti* was a small cultic structure just outside the city. It served to house the gods during the festival, where they would remain for a few days before ultimately returning to their usual temples until the next New Year festival.

---

[46] Julye Bidmead, *The Akītu Festival: Religious Continuity and Royal Legitimation in Mesopotamia*, Gorgias Dissertations Near East Series (Piscataway: Gorgias Press, 2002), 60.

[47] Ibid., 72.

[48] Ibid., 96.

At last we come to the Ugaritic texts, the so-called Baal Cycle, consisting of Baal's battles with Yamm (Sea), the seven-headed dragon Litan (sometimes written as Lotan), and Mot (Death). Though likely composed earlier than some of the myths already considered (c. 1400 BCE), I consider them here for more in-depth analysis, and as the most applicable segue into the Hebrew texts of the following chapter. For, since it is generally accepted that the West Semitic mythology preserved in these texts is exemplary of the broader Canaanite mythology which influenced the Hebrew Bible, these combat myths are our closest extant parallels to those of the early Israelites and thus provide crucial material for comparison.

The Baal-Yamm conflict is a rich example of the combat myth genre. Unfortunately, due to the fragmentary nature of the recovered materials, our knowledge of these myths is incomplete and our understanding of the Cycle's narrative progression reliant on scholarly reconstructions. Nevertheless, we can still glean a more or less coherent series of events.

The first conflict begins, as we have it, *in medias res*: Yamm, the chaos-monster—who, like Tiamet, represents the raging Sea (and is himself some kind of dragon)—has sent messengers to the Divine Council, demanding that the storm-god Baal be taken captive and that Yamm's kingship be acknowledged. As head of the Council, El consents to their demand and gives Baal over to Yamm as his prisoner. The rebel Yamm is thus made king.

However, the craftsman god Kothar-wa-Hasis constructs two clubs for Baal with which he might slay Yamm and reassert his own kingship. Baal takes the first and attacks Yamm, but the weapon proves ineffective. After this initial defeat, Kothar presents Baal with the second club, and with this Baal is finally able to slay Yamm:

> The weapon leaps from Baal's hand,
> [Like] a raptor from his fingers.
> It strikes the head of Prince [Yamm,]
> Between the eyes of Judge River.
> Yamm collapses and falls to the earth,
> His joints shake,
> And his form collapses.
> Baal drags and dismembers (?) Yamm,

Destroys Judge River.[49]

For this victory over Yamm, Baal is thus proclaimed king:

> So Yamm is dead!
> [Baal reigns! (?),]
> So he rules![50]

Now recognized as king, Baal demands of El that a palace/temple be built for him. Eventually El consents and allows one to be built on the storm-god's holy mountain, Zaphon. He announces this to Anat, Baal's consort, who then carries the news to Baal as a messenger and joyously proclaims El's decree:

> Adolescent Anat laughed,
> She raised her voice and declared:
> "Receive the good news, O Baal,
> Good news I bring to you!
> 'Let a house be given you like your brothers',
> A court, like your kin's.
> Call a caravan into your house,
> Wares inside your palace.
> Let the mountains bring you abundant silver,
> The hills, the choicest gold.
> And build the house of silver and gold,
> The house of purest lapis lazuli.'"[51]

With his temple complete, Baal then travels (presumably in a triumphal procession) through the towns of the surrounding country, concluding finally with the victorious god's entry into his temple. Once enthroned within, the storm-god sounds his *mighty voice*—his thunder that reverberates throughout the land:

> Baa[l] gave forth his holy voice.
> Baal repeated the is[sue of (?)] his [li(?)]ps,
> His ho[ly (?)] voice covered (?) the earth,
> [At his] voice…the mountains trembled.
> The ancient [mountains?] leapt [up?],
> The high places of the ear[th] tottered.

---

[49] *CTA* 2.iv.25-27 = Mark S. Smith and Simon B. Parker, *Ugaritic Narrative Poetry*, Writings from the Ancient World (Atlanta: Scholars Press, 1997), 104.
[50] *CTA* 2.iv.34-35 = ibid., 105.
[51] *CTA* 1.4.v.25-35 = Mark S. Smith, *The Ugaritic Baal Cycle Vol. 1*, Supplements to Vetus Testamentum, (Leiden: E.J. Brill, 1994), 539.

The enemies of Baal took to the woods,
The haters of Hadd to the mountainsides.
And Mightiest Baal spoke:
"O Enemies of Hadd, why do you tremble?
Why tremble, you who wield a weapon against the Warrior?"
Baal looked forward;
His hand indeed shook,
The cedar was in his right hand.
So Baal was enthroned in/returned to his house.[52]

Thematically, concerns of fertility and kingship are clearly evident in this myth, while, with regard to specific images, the god's *mighty voice* is clear from the above passage, and the *dividing/dismembering* of the defeated corpse may be attested at the battle's close (though the condition of the text makes a definite translation impossible). In terms of plot, the narrative represents a fairly complete combat myth: (1) *Lack/Villainy*: Yamm dethrones the storm-god Baal. (2) *Hero emerges/prepares to act*: Baal moves to attack Yamm's messenger, but is stopped by either Anat or Asherah.[53] The text becomes fragmentary, however, so that we do not know precisely about Baal's next action(s). (3) *Donor/Consultation*: Kothar counsels Baal and gives him two clubs with which to defeat Yamm. Function 4 is not attested. (5) *Battle*: Using the first of Kothar's clubs, Baal attacks Yamm. (6) *Defeat*: The first club proves ineffective against Yamm. (7) *Enemy ascendant*: Yamm stands strong after this first attack, Baal's efforts having had little effect. (8) *Hero recovers*: Kothar gives Baal the second club. (9) Battle rejoined: Baal attacks Yamm with the second club. (10) *Victory*: The second attack proves successful, and Yamm collapses. (11) *Enemy Punished*: Uncertain, though according to Smith and Parker's tentative translation, Baal dismembers Yamm. (12) *Triumph*: Baal goes through many towns, presumably on a triumphant procession, concluding ultimately with his enthronement in his palace/temple.

Many scholars believe that a cultic procession of the god's idol is reflected in this final event.[54] Indeed, given the broad attestation of

---

[52] *CAT* 1.4.vii.29-42 = Mark S. Smith and Wayne Thomas Pitard, *The Ugaritic Baal Cycle Vol. 2*, Supplements to Vetus Testamentum (Leiden: E.J. Brill, 2009), 650.

[53] The text is corrupt here and the names of either goddess are possible restorations. See ANET, 130.

[54] See Oswald Loretz and Manfried Dietrich, *Mythen und Epen IV* (Gutersloh: Gutersloher Verlagshaus, 1997), 1168 n. 112; Johannes Cornelis de Moor, *An Anthology of Religious Texts from Ugarit*, vol. 16, Religious Texts Translation Series (Leiden: E. J.

such practices throughout the ancient Near East, it seems likely that Ugarit too had its processional ceremonies, at which time the victorious storm-god—fresh from victory over the forces of Chaos—traveled amongst the people before being led back to his temple. Indeed, some have posited a Ugaritic New Year festival similar to the *Purulli* and *Akītu* festivals; though celebrated at the harvest-time rather than at spring, this festival would have shared similar characteristics as a celebration of fertility's return.[55] While more cautious on the notion of an autumnal Ugaritic New Year festival, Mark Smith nevertheless acknowledges that "both the Baal-Yamm and Baal-Mot conflicts lead up to the autumn rains,"[56] and that

> each major part of the cycle uses the imagery of the fall interchange period... This period witnesses the alternation of the eastern dry winds of the scirocco with the western rain-bringing winds coming off the Mediterranean Sea until the western winds finally overtake the eastern winds... The meteorological phenomenon of Baal's coming in the storm over Yamm could be correlated with the coming of the fall rains. Scholars have long viewed Baal's battle with Yamm as inspired by the eastward procession of the rain-storm from the Mediterranean Sea to the coast.[57]

Such a backdrop for the Baal Cycle certainly supports the idea that its combat myths had some role in a fall Near Year harvest festival. At this festival, the Baal Cycle would have likely served as a key cultic text, perhaps even as a sort of script for the religious pageant. So Arvid Kapelrud writes, "The arrival of the god to the temple, his enthronement and the hieros gamos are all acts that were not told for enjoyment; they represent cultic performances."[58] Given what we know from other New Year festivals, such a conclusion is very compelling, and suggests that the enthronement of Baal was a chief ritual of the

Brill, 1987), 62 n. 277; Gregorio del Olmo Lete, *Canaanite Religion: According to the Liturgical Texts of Ugarit* (Bethesda: CDL Press, 1999) 139-41, 282-91; Dennis Pardee and Theodore J. Lewis, *Ritual and Cult at Ugarit*, Writings from the Ancient World (Leiden: Brill, 2002) 69-72. Smith, *The Ugaritic Baal Cycle Vol. 1*, more cautiously concludes, "This seems plausible, although it cannot be confirmed."

[55] The best presentation of the thesis is Johannes Cornelis de Moor, *New Year with Canaanites and Israelites*, 2 vols., Kamper Cahiers (Kampen: Kok, 1972). He has interpreted some extant texts (describing celebratory dancing and music to lyres, tambourines, and cymbals) in light of this cultic rite (specifically *U 5 V*, no. 2: Obv.3-5).

[56] Smith, *The Ugaritic Baal Cycle Vol. 1*, 63.

[57] Ibid., 97-8.

[58] Arvid Schou Kapelrud, *Baal in the Ras Shamra Texts* (Copenhagen: G.E.C. Gad, 1952), 29-30.

festival. While such enthronements may have played a part in other New Year festivals—since the storm-god's accession to kingship is a ubiquitous theme in ancient Near Eastern combat myths and likely had a ritual counterpart (presumably connected to his re-installation within his temple/palace)—of the New Year festivals *thus far considered*, evidence for the ritual enthronement of the deity is strongest at Ugarit.[59] As we shall see, however, ancient Israel likely shared this practice.

Baal/Anat vs. the Dragon

In addition to Yamm, Baal is also said to have slain the seven-headed dragon Litan, which is either a helper of Yamm, or another designation for Yamm himself:[60]

> When you killed Litan, the Fleeing Serpent,
> Annihilated the Twisty Serpent,
> The Potentate with the Seven Heads,
> The heavens grew hot, they withered.[61]

A parallel tradition depicts Anat as the slayer of Yamm and his Dragon (Ugaritic "Tunnan"). She boasts:

> Surely I fought Yamm, the Beloved of El,
> Surely I finished off River, the Great God,
> Surely I bound Tunnan and destroyed (?) him.
> I fought the Twisty Serpent,
> The Potentate with the Seven Heads.[62]

Elsewhere we read:

> She sets a muzzle on Tunnan.
> She binds him on the heights of Lebanon.

---

⁵⁹ For the idea of the Ugaritic New Year festival as an "enthronement festival," see ibid., 117, 123, 128, 143; Sigmund Mowinckel, *The Psalms in Israel's Worship* (Oxford: Blackwell, 1962), 125, 132-4; L. R. Fisher and F. B. Knutson, "An Enthronement Ritual at Ugarit," *JNES* 28 (1969): 156-7; Moor, *New Year with Canaanites and Israelites*, vol. 1, 4-10.

⁶⁰ For the former interpretation, see Kapelrud, *Baal in the Ras Shamra Texts*, 101-2. The latter interpretation is favored by Day, *God's Conflict*, 14.

⁶¹ *KTU* 1.5.i.1-4 = Smith and Parker, *Ugaritic Narrative Poetry*, 141.

⁶² *CAT* 1.3.iii.38-42 = ibid., 111.

> "Toward the desert (*or*: Dried up), shall you be scattered, O Yamm!
> To the multitude of *ḥt*, O Nahar!
> You shall not see (or: Indeed shall you see); lo! you shall foam up!"[63]

Here we reencounter the slaying of the sea dragon, which is said to have seven heads (cf. Ninurta's enemy, the "Seven-headed Serpent"). In addition, we see again the *binding* motif encountered in other combat myths, such as Ninurta's binding of the Stone Things, the binding of Illuyankas, and Marduk's binding of Tiamet. Here the manner of binding is specified as *muzzling*. Finally, according to Wayne Pitard's translation, Anat *scatters* him in the desert—by now a very familiar motif, as the chaos-monster's body is *divided/dismembered* and then strewn.

Because these passages are only fragmentary allusions to a combat elsewhere unattested, they do not provide us with a narrative complete enough for a generic analysis based on plot. Beyond the obvious fact that they narrate a battle with a monstrous villain, only their scattered images—so recognizable now from the genre—allow us to suppose a more developed combat myth which once framed them.

Baal vs. Death (Mot)

Fresh from his victory over Yamm and the building of his temple, Baal is confronted by his ultimate enemy: Death ("Mot" in Ugaritic). Like Yamm, Mot is a representative of Chaos and destruction—indeed, as the very negation of life and fertility, he is the chaos-enemy *par excellence*. "The progression in the myth is logical," notes E. Theodore Mullen. "To insure the fertility and stability of the cosmos, [Baal] must first make the universe secure from Yamm and the chaotic forces of the sea. Next he must overcome the forces of death and sterility, an equally important conflict."[64] Indeed, I should say *more* important. With the threat of Mot, there is a progression in magnitude: the Dragon and Sea were formidable; Death is existential. Yamm was antagonistic; Mot is antithetical.

---

[63] *KTU* 1.83:9-13 = Wayne T. Pitard, "The Binding of Yamm: A New Edition of the Ugaritic Text KTU 1.83," *JNES* 57, no. 4 (1998): 273.
[64] E. Theodore Mullen, *The Divine Council in Canaanite and Early Hebrew Literature*, Harvard Semitic Monographs (Chico: Scholars Press, 1980), 75-76.

This final conflict begins after Baal, newly enthroned within his temple, sends messengers to Mot to communicate word of his kingship. But Mot responds by announcing his own insatiable appetite, and threatens to devour Baal. Indeed, Baal succumbs, and accepts submission to Mot, who then directs Baal to his underworld domain, commanding:

> And you, take your clouds,
> Your winds, your bolts, your rains;
> …Lift the mountain on your hands,
> The hill on top of your palms.
> And descend to Hell, the House of "Freedom,"
> Be counted among the inmates of Hell;
> And you will know, O God, that you are dead.[65]

Lifting up the mountain, Baal is to descend into the pit and so enter Hell. His defeat is also depicted in more anthropomorphic terms by Mot, who elsewhere recounts:

> Then I approached Mightiest Baal;
> I took him like a lamb in my mouth,
> Like a kid crushed in the chasm of my throat.
> Dead is mightiest Baal,
> Perished the Prince, Lord of the Earth.[66]

Baal, the god of rain and fertility, is thus killed by the chaos-enemy Death—eaten by the voracious consumer of life. Like Sea before him, Death now assumes his temporary dominance over the cosmos as the life-bringing rains cease. The gods can only mourn Baal's end, lamenting a future ruled by bareness and sterility.

Eventually, however, Anat goes to retrieve Baal from Death. She finds Mot and attacks him. The two battle and Anat proves victorious. She *divides/dismembers* Mot, then *scatters* his body like seed, letting the birds eat his limbs. Mot overcome, Baal is thus restored to life, and upon his return is re-enthroned as king. Rain and fertility return to the world as a result of his resurrection, and El himself rejoices:

> "I can sit and I can rest,
> And my spirit within can rest.

---

[65] *KTU* 1.5.v.6-8, 14-17 = Smith and Parker, *Ugaritic Narrative Poetry*, 147.
[66] *KTU* 1.6.ii.21-23; 149, *KTU* 1.5.vi.9-10 = ibid., 156.

> For Mightiest Baal lives,
> The Prince, Lord of the Earth, is alive."[67]

After his resurrection, Baal seeks Mot, who—despite his confrontation with Anat—nevertheless remains undefeated. The two then engage in battle:

> They eye each other like fighters,
> Mot is fierce, Baal is fierce.
> They gore each other like buffalo,
> Mot is fierce, Baal is fierce.
> They bite each other like serpents,
> Mot is fierce, Baal is fierce.
> They drag each other like runners,
> Mot falls, Baal falls.[68]

The fight is evenly matched; both gods rage until mutual defeat or exhaustion. Eventually, though, El steps in to arbitrate and calls on Mot to withdraw. He does, and Baal is once again proclaimed king over the cosmos, having proved victorious over the great forces of Chaos: Sea, his associate Dragon, and Death.

Most of the themes of the combat myth are starkly illustrated here. The reflection of agricultural changes, for example, is clearly evident. As the parched, barren summer corresponds to Mot's ascendency and the death of the storm-god, Mot's defeat means agricultural rejuvenation. That his defeat by Anat is described as the sowing of new crops makes the association even more explicit. The return of fertility is celebrated as Baal's resurrection, while the rather indecisive conclusion to his battle with Mot suggests the endless nature of the agricultural cycle. Mot is not annihilated; the battle is perennial.

Having already discussed the relationship of the Baal Cycle with Ugaritic religious cult, it is noteworthy that the conflict with Mot strengthens the hypothesis that a New Year festival existed at Ugarit and celebrated agricultural renewal through Baal's victory over Sea and Death. At this time the statue of Baal was likely taken from its temple and brought through the surrounding towns before ultimately being processed back to the temple for a ritual re-enthronement of the deity.

Though more tenuous, we may even read philosophical and theological significance in the myth's presentation of Death. Not

---

[67] *KTU* 1.6.iii.18-21 = ibid., 158.
[68] *KTU* 1.6.vi.16-22 = ibid., 162.

surprisingly, Death is a malevolent force, its insatiable appetite serving as an apt metaphor for the ubiquity of the mortal condition and the transience of all life. Moreover, the fact that Death is never ultimately killed, and that Baal's battle with him essentially ends in a draw, reflects a realistic reflection on the nature of mortality. Death is an intractable element of life; even mightiest Baal is subject to it.

Finally, all of these ideas (i.e., seasonal change, the ordering of the cosmos, mortality) are expressed as contests for kingship. Thus the myth intimately links natural order with political order, as different qualities and states of existence are presented as different kingdoms/kingships. The kingdoms of Yamm and Mot are destructive, bleak, and tyrannical. The kingdom of Baal, by contrast, is generally bountiful, joyous, and just.

The clearest generic motif attested in this combat myth is the *dividing* and *scattering* of Mot's body. That Anat scatters the body like seed (to be eaten by birds) is reminiscent not only of her battle with the Dragon (whom she also scatters in uncultivated/desert places), but also of Ninurta strewing the defeated body of the dragon Azag like flour over the mountains. The similarities suggest a coherent topos: the defeated chaos-monster is divided, its body serving as nourishment in a once-barren place.

In Baal's battle with Mot, we find again the fundamental plot progression of the combat myth: (1) *Lack/Villainy*: Mot contests the kingship of Baal. Functions 2 through 4 are absent,[69] and Baal appears to acquiesce immediately to the threat. (5) *Battle*: Mot devours Baal. (6) *Defeat*: Baal is killed. (7) *Enemy ascendant*: With Baal dead, the rains stop and the powers of death and sterility overshadow the world. (8) *Hero recovers*: Baal returns to life. (9) *Battle rejoined*: Baal and Mot engage in single combat. (10) *Victory*: While the actual result of the battle seems like more of a stalemate, El declares Baal the victor. (11) *Enemy Punished*: Baal does not appear to punish Mot, and in fact Mot is never actually killed. (12) *Triumph*: Baal re-ascends his throne, and Mot is now subject to his kingship. The forces of Chaos have been defeated.

---

[69] (2) Hero emerges/prepares to act, (3) Donor/Consultation and (4) Journey. Function 2 would be redundant, since Baal has already emerged to defeat Yamm. Additionally, one could see Anat's help in reviving Baal as fulfilling the role of function 3, the way Inara can be seen as the Donor in the Illuyankas combat myth.

To conclude, we have surveyed in this chapter some of the extant combat myths from the ancient Near East. These myths pit warrior storm-gods against the forces of Chaos, embodied variously as a dragon, the raging Sea, or even Death itself. The divine warrior rises to meet this challenge, and battles his enemy with the weapons of the storm. His first attempt ends in defeat, however, and in this temporary failure the forces of Chaos become dominant over the cosmos. Eventually, the warrior god revives and in his resurgence slays the enemy. Such victories often include the *binding/muzzling*, *trampling*, and *dividing/scattering* of the chaos-monster. With his victory, the storm-god sounds his *mighty voice* (thunder) and assumes kingship over the cosmos—an achievement celebrated at a New Year festival which included a triumphal procession of the god and perhaps a ritual enthronement of the deity within his temple.

In the next chapter, I shall show how these ancient Near Eastern combat myths—particularly those from Ugarit—provide insight into the combat myths the ancient Israelites. From there I shall demonstrate how and why later apocalyptic Jewish authors articulated their eschatological ideas in terms of the Hebrew combat myth, and trace these ultimately to their presence in the Gospel of Mark.

CHAPTER 2
THE HEBREW COMBAT MYTH

As a kingdom in the ancient Near East, Israel had its own combat myths and associated cultic traditions. In the Hebrew version, Yahweh is the storm-god warrior who subdues the Sea and its associate dragon; there is even evidence that, like Baal, he too battled Death. To these myths, their contexts, and the various uses to which they were put diachronically I now turn.

For the history of Yahwism—from ancient Israelite cult to Second Temple Judaism and beyond—the importance of the combat myth and the depiction of Yahweh as divine warrior can hardly be overstated. Indeed, Theodore Hiebert well summarizes this enduring significance when he writes:

> The understanding of God as a warrior is grounded in the origins of biblical religion. The image of the divine warrior dominates the oldest Israelite poetry, remains a frequent characterization of God throughout the biblical period, and gains a new prominence in the apocalyptic literature of both Jewish and Christian communities.[1]

Understanding the evolution of this conception from ancient myth to crucial apocalyptic framework is necessary for an appreciation of its ultimate role in the Gospel of Mark.

So far, we have identified and analyzed various ancient Near Eastern combat myths by means of their thematic, motivic, and structural similarity. However, considerations of narrative progression become appreciably more difficult as we move into the Hebrew material since, as Andrew Angel has rightly noted, combat myth motifs are mostly found outside the context of strict narrative in Hebrew texts:

> A definition [of the Hebrew combat myth] by plot would be very difficult as the tradition uses images frequently but it never places these images within a connected narrative... For example, the use of the *Chaoskampf* image in Isa. 17.12-13 can hardly be deemed a story, and the narrative is partial even where elements of story are present, e.g. Ps. 18.4-15.[2]

---

[1] *ABD*, "Warrior, Divine," 876.

[2] Andrew R. Angel, *Chaos and the Son of Man: The Hebrew Chaoskampf Tradition in the Period 515 BCE to 200 CE*, Library of Second Temple Studies (London: T & T Clark, 2006), 25 n. 177.

Indeed, the hints that we get of the Hebrew combat myth from the Prophets and Psalms, for example, presume the story rather than tell it. For this reason we must largely set aside our narrative schema in this chapter, and instead rely primarily on the knowledge gleaned from the previous investigation of the combat myth genre, particularly its common themes and imagery. Later, we may return to the narrative schema when appropriate.

Yahweh vs. Sea (Yam)

Like Baal, Yahweh's chief enemy in the Hebrew combat myth is Yam, the raging Sea. As a representative of Chaos, Sea must be defeated if order and fertility are to be secured in the cosmos. So we read, in scattered allusions from the Psalms and Prophets, how the Israelite storm-god battles the chaos-enemy. One text reads:

> Was your wrath against River, O Yahweh?
>   Or your anger against River,
>   or your rage against Sea,
> When you drove your horses,
>   your chariots to victory?
> You brandished your naked bow,
>   sated were the arrows at your command.
> ...You *trampled* the Sea with your horses,
>   churning the mighty waters. (Hab 3:8-9a, 15)

Yahweh's conflict with Sea/River is clearly analogous to Baal's enemy Prince Sea/Judge River—both "Yam(m)" and "Nahar" in the Semitic languages, and both frequently noted in poetic parallelism.[3] Here the *trampling* of the chaos-enemy is attested, particularly reminiscent of how Marduk trampled the primordial Sea after sating *his* lightning-bolt arrows.

Again, the roaring thunder that accompanies such lightning was understood as the storm-god's *mighty voice*, and so Yahweh's chief battle weapon is often described simply as his voice, roar, or, most frequently, his *rebuke* (Hebrew *g'r*):

> He rode on a cherub, and flew; he came swiftly upon the wings of the wind.
> He made darkness his covering around him,

---

[3] Frank Moore Cross, *Canaanite Myth and Hebrew Epic: Essays in the History of the Religion of Israel* (Cambridge: Harvard University Press, 1973), 140.

> his canopy thick clouds dark with water.
> Out of the brightness before him
> > there broke through his clouds hailstones and coals of fire.
> Yahweh also thundered in the heavens,
> > and the Most High *uttered his voice*.
> And he sent out his arrows, and *scattered* them;
> > he flashed forth lightnings, and routed them.
> Then the channels of the Waters were seen,
> > and the foundations of the world were laid bare
> *at your rebuke*, O Yahweh,
> > at the blast of the breath of your nostrils. (Ps 18:10-15)

Here, in addition to the *scattering* of the raging Sea waters, we find all anthropomorphic characterizations of the storm-god's weapons: his lightning as arrows and his thunder as his *rebuking voice*. At his rebuke the Sea recoils and reveals the foundations of his creation.

We find similar examples of Yahweh rebuking the chaos-waters in Psalm 106:9, Isaiah 17:13 and 50:2, and Nahum 1:4. All relate the basic idea that at his *rebuke* (i.e., his *mighty voice*, the thunderous crash of his lightning) the Sea, like a defeated enemy, hurries away and recedes to its rightful boundaries. Thus order is established and the chaotic waters are contained. Another psalm draws all of these aspects together:

> ...You have laid the beams of your chambers on the Waters,
> You make the cloud your chariot,
> > you ride on the wings of the wind...
> ...You set the earth on its foundations,
> > so that it shall never be shaken.
> You cover it with the Deep as with a garment;
> > the Waters stood upon the mountains.
> At your *rebuke* they flee;
> > at the sound of your thunder they take to flight.
> ...You set a boundary that they may not pass,
> > so that they might not again cover the earth. (Ps 104:3, 5-7, 9)

Here Yahweh is none other than the storm-god in his cloud-chariot who tames the chaotic Sea by his imposition of order. Indeed, as in other combat myths, his defeat of Sea is intricately linked to cosmogony and creation. Ninurta created an irrigation system that stopped the waters from remaining upon the mountains; Marduk created heaven and earth out of Sea's body. So Yahweh likewise keeps the waters from flooding the mountaintops and establishes an ordered, differentiated cosmos.

Though most prevalent in the Psalms (for reasons considered below), references to this cosmic battle are found elsewhere in the

Hebrew Bible. In poetic terms, the author of Job makes use of Yahweh's contention with Sea as he reflects on the unthinkable power of Yahweh and the futility of fighting against him—as Sea had tried, but failed:

> If one wished to contend with him,
> > one could not answer him once in a thousand.
> He is wise in heart, and mighty in strength
> > —who has resisted him, and succeeded?—
> ...[he] who alone stretched out the heavens
> > and *trampled* the waves of Sea. (Job 9:3-4, 8)

So we encounter the *trampling* of the Sea and its connection with Creation. Elsewhere, feeling that God is now contending against *him*, Job laments:

> Am I Sea, or Dragon,
> > that you set guard over me?
> ...Why have you made me your target?
> > Why have I become a burden to you? (Job 7:12, 20)

This Dragon to which Job refers is another enemy that Yahweh slays in his battles against the Sea and the forces of Chaos.

Yahweh vs. the Dragon

Like Baal and the other storm-gods, Yahweh does battle with the draconic helpers of chief chaos-enemy. Thus the seven-headed sea dragon Litan from the Baal Cycle reappears, with its name only slightly changed, as the many-headed sea dragon Leviathan:

> Yet God my King is from of old,
> > working salvation in the earth.
> You *divided* Sea by your might;
> > you shattered the heads of Dragons in the Waters.
> You crushed the heads of Leviathan;
> > you gave him as food for people in the wilderness.
> You cut openings for springs and torrents;
> > you dried up ever-flowing streams.
> Yours is the day, yours also the night;
> > you established the luminaries and the sun.
> You have fixed all the bounds of the earth;
> > you made summer and winter. (Ps 74:12-17)

Here, the thematic concerns with both kingship and agricultural regularity are present, while, with regard to motifs, we encounter the *dismembering/dividing* of the enemy Sea. Indeed, the relationship of combat and cosmogony is particularly pronounced in the Hebrew tradition. After Yahweh crushed the heads of the dragons in primordial time (cf. Marduk and Baal crushing the heads of their draconic Sea nemeses), he established the celestial objects, the boundaries of the Earth, and the seasons. In perhaps the most fascinating similarity, however, Yahweh casts Leviathan's corpse in the desert to serve as food—just as Anat scattered the Dragon/Yamm in the desert, as well as the body of Mot (which was then eaten by birds). Thus we find the topos present in the Hebrew tradition as well, in which the defeated chaos-monster is divided, its body serving as nourishment in a once-barren place.

An extensive description of Leviathan occupies Job 41. Here, Yahweh boasts to Job about his conquest of the sea monster:

> Can *you* draw out Leviathan with a fishhook?
> Or press down his tongue with a cord?
> Can *you* put a rope in his nose
> or pierce his jaw with a hook?
> …Will you play with him as with a bird,
> or will you *bind him* for your maidens?
> …Lay your hand on him; Remember the battle;
> *you* will not do it again! (vv. 1-2, 5, 8, NASB).

Again we find the *binding* motif, as Yahweh himself boasts of ensnaring Leviathan—even specifically *muzzling* the Dragon just as Anat muzzled Tunnan. Elsewhere, Yahweh makes a similar boast:

> The Lord said: "I stifled the Serpent, muzzled the Deep Sea. (Ps 68:23)[4]

Thus, similar to the Canaanite combat myths, Yahweh is said to have *muzzled* the Dragon/Sea in the course of their battle.

Other passages speak of the slaying of Rahab, whose name means "The Boisterous One" and thus, as John Day observes, "an apt term for

---

[4] For this translation, see Mitchell Dahood, *Psalms* (Garden City: Doubleday, 1966), 131. Though this reading is debated, many scholars translate this passage similarly, likewise reading the Hebrew verb *šbm* here. Cf. Patrick D. Miller, "Two Critical Notes on Psalm 68 and Deuteronomy 33," *HTR* 57 (1964): 240, who translates, "The Lord said, 'I muzzled the Serpent, I muzzled the Deep Sea.'" He cites Frank Moore Cross for additional authority, n. 3. For a critique of this reading, see Day, *God's Conflict*, 113-19.

the personified raging sea."[5] Rahab is certainly a chaos-monster, and may in fact be simply another name for Leviathan.[6] Psalm 89 links the taming of the Sea, the crushing of Rahab, and Creation:

> You rule the raging of the Sea;
>> when its waves rise, you still them.
> You crushed Rahab like a carcass;
>> you *scattered* your enemies with your mighty arm.
> The heavens are yours, the earth is also yours;
>> the world and all that is in it—you have founded them. (Ps 89:9-11)

Similarly, Job meditates on the unrelenting anger of Yahweh in considering his own plight:

> God will not turn back his anger;
>> the helpers of Rahab bowed beneath him.
> …How then can *I* answer him,
>> choosing my words with him? (Job 9:13-14)

The thought again echoes the *trampling* motif: the helpers of the sea-dragon Rahab lie in submission beneath Yahweh's feet as defeated enemies of the angry divine warrior. So Ninurta trampled Azag's helpers, Baal Yamm's helper(s), and Marduk Tiamet's.

Yahweh vs. Death (Mot/Sheol)

It is debatable whether explicit mention is made in the Hebrew Bible of any battle between Yahweh and Death (Hebrew "Mot"). However, given Israel's traditional continuity with the Canaanite combat myths of Baal vs. Sea/River and the Dragon, the existence of such a myth is quite plausible. Indeed, investigating such a hypothesis yields intriguing and suggestive evidence that such a myth did exist, and even persisted for centuries in tradition despite its scarcity within canonized texts.

Even in canonical Hebrew texts, however, the personification of Death as a pernicious supernatural agent often transcends mere poetic expression. Indeed, the ancient Israelites clearly shared many mythic

---

[5] *God's Conflict*, 6.
[6] Ibid., 6, 39.

conceptions of Death and the underworld with the Canaanite tradition.[7] So, for example, Psalm 49:14 speaks of foolish men in these terms:

> Like sheep they are appointed for Sheol;
>> Death shall be their shepherd;
> straight to the grave they descend,
>> and their form shall waste away;
>> Sheol shall be their home.

This idea of Death as shepherd may relate to a tradition attested in the Ugaritic texts. In *KTU* 1.6.ii.21-23, Death boasts of taking Baal as a kid in his mouth and carrying him away like a lamb.[8]

As the passage illustrates, Death is often paired with Sheol, the underworld, and indeed the two often appear to be essentially synonymous. Sheol is thus a kind of periphrasis for Death/Mot himself, as the poetic parallelism of Habakkuk 2:5 suggests:[9]

> …The arrogant do not endure.
> They open their throats wide as Sheol;
>> like Death they never have enough.
> They gather all nations for themselves,
>> and collect all peoples as their own.

This verse exemplifies the most notable Israelite continuity with the Canaanite conception of Death: his rapacious appetite. We saw that, in the Ugaritic texts, Death is characterized by his insatiable appetite, and even swallows Baal himself. The same is true of Death in ancient Israelite conceptions. Thus Proverbs 27:20 declares, "Sheol and Abaddon [Destruction] are never satisfied," and Proverbs 30:15c-16 reads:

> Three things are never satisfied;
>> four never say, "Enough":
> Sheol, the barren womb,
>> the earth ever thirsty for water,
>> and the fire that never says, "Enough."

---

[7] For an extensive comparison, see *Yahweh and the Gods and Goddesses of Canaan*, Journal for the Study of the Old Testament. Supplement Series (Sheffield: Sheffield Academic Press, 2002), 185-225.

[8] Ibid., 186.

[9] Wakeman, *God's Battle with the Monster*, 107.

Sheol is even depicted as the swallower, whose consumption leads the dead into "the Pit":

> Like Sheol let us swallow them alive
> and whole, like those who go down to the Pit. (Prov 1:12)

Likewise Isaiah 5:14:

> Therefore Sheol has enlarged its appetite
> and opened its mouth beyond measure;
> the nobility of Jerusalem and her multitude go down,
> her throng and all who exult in her.[10]

Seeing that Death was often understood as a supernatural agent with the same characteristics as the Canaanite god, some scholars have posited the existence of a combat myth between Yahweh and Death similar to the combat between Baal and Death. Indeed, W. F. Albright sees the myth reflected in Habakkuk 3:8-14, translating the text:

Is Thy wrath, O Yahweh, against River —Against River is Thy Wrath <directed ?>
Or is Thine anger against Sea ;
That Thou dost ride Thy horses, Thy chariot <which bringeth>victory ?
Bare dost Thou strip Thy bow, Sated by the fight which Thou hast decreed.
The mountains saw Thee and quaked, The Deep gave forth its voice ;
The clouds streamed with water, The rivers, which cleave the earth.
The exalted one, Sun, raised his arms, Moon stood<on>his lordly dais ;
By the light of Thine arrows they move, By the lightning sheen of Thy spear !
In anger dost Thou tread the earth, *In wrath dost thou thresh the nations,*
Going forth to save Thy people, *To save<the people>of Thine Anointed.*
Thou didst smite the head of wicked Death, *Destroying (him) tail-end to neck ;*
Thou didst pierce <his>head in the fight, *While his followers (?) stormed...?*[11]

---

[10] Of course, death does not always have these mythical resonances. Often in the Hebrew material death is simply the expiration of life. Like the sea, which was also understood devoid of its supernatural agency, death's mythological overtones must be assessed contextually.

[11] W. F. Albright, "The Psalm of Habakkuk," in *Studies in Old Testament Prophecy*, ed. Harold Henry Rowley (Edinburgh: T. & T. Clark, 1957), 12-13. On reading "Death" in v. 13, Albright declares in note oo on 17: "The θάνατον of [the LXX] is obviously original, as seen by Cassuto, *Annuario di Studi Ebraici, loc. cit."* Wakeman, *God's Battle with the Monster*, 108, seems to accept Albright's translation, but notes, "Should this reading be accepted, it would be the only direct reference to a conflict between Yahweh and Mot." Day, *Yahweh and the Gods and Goddesses of Canaan*, 192, rejects it, positing that "nothing in the text previously has led one to expect that 'death' is actually the name of the enemy. How exactly the verse should be translated is uncertain." However, as we have seen, the text is brimming with *Chaoskampf* imagery, as Yahweh's battles with Sea

Clearly, this passage is rife with *Chaoskampf* imagery, beginning with allusions to Yahweh's battles against Sea and River, then turning to the battle with Death: the same progression, it should be noted, as the Ugaritic material. Albright states that here "we have a vivid sketch of the prostrate body of a dragon,"[12] suggesting that Death too was understood as a chaos-monster.

This translation is given additional weight by two aspects not noted by Albright. First, verse 14 in the Masoretic text refers to the enemy's desire to devour (Heb. *'kl*). So the NRSV describes the enemies "gloating as if *ready to devour the poor...*" The idea is retained in the Septuagint with the participle *esthiōn*. Albright however does not translate the line, thinking it corrupt. Though this is possible, should the presence of the enemy's desire to devour reflect any aspect of the original, it would be entirely fitting with the nature of Death, *the swallower*, who is characterized by his insatiable appetite. Secondly, when we appreciate that Death/Sheol and the underworld are often referred to as "the Earth,"[13] it is possible to read the treading of Earth as a part of Yahweh's battle with Death. The *trampling* of Earth would thus be similar to the punishment of Sea,[14] as would the smiting/piercing of his head (cf. Baal crushing Yamm's head).

Recognizing Earth as another name or epithet for the underworld deity, Mary Wakeman has proposed the existence of a chaos-monster whose associations were primarily terrestrial, rather than oceanic (as they are with Leviathan/Rahab). While Behemoth has long been understood as the terrestrial land monster, her association of this chaos-monster with Mot is novel.[15] If correct, Mot was understood as a terrestrial chaos-monster which Yahweh defeated as he defeated Yam, the chaos-monster of the sea. Such an interpretation would fit very well

---

and River are recalled. Even the Sun and Moon appear with their mythological associations here. Thus the context certainly suggests a mythological interpretation of Death as the final enemy in the Canaanite combat myth. Moreover, Day admittedly cannot provide a better, alternative translation.

[12] Albright, "The Psalm of Habakkuk," 17 n. qq.

[13] See, e.g., Is 14:12; 1 Sam 28:13; Ps 71:20, 143:6; and Job 4:23, 15:29. See Wakeman, *God's Battle with the Monster*, 108.

[14] The trampling of Death may also be at work in Micah 1:3: "For lo, Yahweh is coming out of his Place, and will come down and tread upon the back of the Earth," though the broader context of the verse makes this interpretation dubious. However, the idea that Yahweh would come forth from his Temple to battle the forces of Chaos is entirely in keeping with the primary cultic context which celebrated his victories over the chaos-monsters: the New Year festival. This shall be considered in greater depth below.

[15] Wakeman, *God's Battle with the Monster*, 106-17.

here with the description of Death's draconic presentation and the mention of his tail.

Later evidence for a battle between Yahweh and Death is found in the book of Isaiah. The prophet addresses Yahweh:

> For you have been a stronghold to the poor,
>   a stronghold to the needy in his distress,
>   *a shelter from the storm and a shade from the heat*;
> for the breath of the ruthless is like a storm against a wall,
>   like heat in a dry place.
> You subdue the noise of the foreigners;
>   *as heat by the shade of a cloud*,
>   so the song of the ruthless is put down.
> On this Mountain, Yahweh of Hosts will make for all peoples
>   a feast of rich food, a feast of well-aged wine,
>   of rich food full of marrow, of aged wine well refined.
>   And he will swallow up on this Mountain
>   the covering that is cast over all peoples,
>   the veil that is spread over all nations.
> *He will swallow up Death forever*. (Is 25:4-8, ESV).

Here the prophet seems to draw on the Levantine agricultural underpinnings of the combat myth—between the fecund autumn of the storm-god and the barren, hot summer of Mot. We recall that, as Mark Smith puts it, "both the Baal-Yamm and Baal-Mot conflicts lead up to the autumn rains"[16] and that

> each major part of the [Baal] cycle uses the imagery of the fall interchange period... This period witnesses the alternation of the eastern dry winds of the scirocco with the western rain-bringing winds coming off the Mediterranean Sea until the western winds finally overtake the eastern winds.[17]

Here this seasonal interchange becomes a metaphor for Yahweh's salvation of his people: the storm-god's rainclouds overcome the oppressive heat of summer, i.e., Death. This metaphor is continued with the image of the feast. The abundant feast of Yahweh on the citadel of Jerusalem recalls a first-fruits or harvest festival. We have seen that just such a festival likely provided the cultic context for the Ugaritic combat myths—including Baal's battle with Death—and, as we shall see, the Israelite combat myths as well. Finally, behind the last verse

---

[16] Smith, *The Ugaritic Baal Cycle Vol. 1*, 63.
[17] Ibid., 97.

undoubtedly lies not only the mythological motif of Death as the swallower, but indeed the whole combat myth in which Death swallows the storm-god Baal.[18] Here, the prophet has reversed the idea: it is the storm-god Yahweh who will swallow Death! That the author could draw upon such a tradition suggests that the mythic battle likely had a place in the Hebrew tradition too, wherein Yahweh defeats Death.

Additional evidence for the existence of a combat myth between Yahweh and Death will be considered later in light of apocalyptic texts which may, like the above passage from the so-called "Isaianic Apocalypse," allude to such a myth. Briefly, however, we shall note that in Revelation 20, after defeating the Dragon, Christ defeats Death and Hades by throwing them into a lake of fire—a likely reflex of the ancient combat myth progression. Likewise, some of Paul's letters seem to evince a knowledge of such a myth.[19] Again, these aspects shall be considered in greater detail in later chapters. For now, we may simply conclude that, though evidence is limited for a combat myth between Yahweh and Death in our oldest extant sources, it is quite plausible that such a myth existed. In it, Yahweh, not Baal, battled Death as the rain-bringing storm-god, and proved victorious.[20]

Yahweh vs. Israel's Enemies

As noted in Chapter 1, the thematic significance of divine kingship in ancient Near Eastern combat myths obliged associations with earthly kingship, since the former both reflected and idealized the latter. For this reason, historical and political realities often inform combat myths or, rather, there is a kind of dialectic of myth and history: history informed myth, while myth was employed to interpret and articulate history. Until now, we have not considered instances in which specific historical contexts are reflected this way, though Clifford assures that this historical element is indeed present in most ancient Near Eastern *Chaoskampf* myths. For example, Ninurta's enemies, Azag and Anzu, reside in the northeastern mountains, which

---

[18] See the analysis of Day, *Yahweh and the Gods and Goddesses of Canaan*, 186.

[19] For example, in 1 Cor 15 and Rom 5.

[20] Such a myth would also explain other biblical authors' more subtle allusions to Yahweh's battles with Death. See e.g., Alan J. Hauser, "Yahweh Versus Death: The Real Struggle in 1 Kings 17-19," in *From Carmel to Horeb: Elijah in Crisis*, ed. Alan J. Hauser and Russell Inman Gregory (Sheffield: Almond Press, 1990), 11-83.

were in fact the homeland of the Gutians and other enemies of the Mesopotamian plain dwellers.[21] Thus, historical conflicts are sublimated to the realm of myth; the Gutians are equated with chaos-monsters, the Babylonian king with Ninurta. Similar historical/political interpretations have been applied to the Baal Cycle, though such readings are often more conjectural.[22]

Again, these associations were dialectical. Myth and history informed one another; dependence went both ways. Thus historical powers drew as much from myth as myth from historical powers. In the process, both were reaffirmed. In Canaan and Egypt, for example, the powers of the mythic storm-god were applied to the ruling kings. Strikingly, *the associations draw specifically from generic motifs of the combat myth*. Thus, in one text, the Egyptian pharaoh is said to "give forth his cry in the sky like Baal," a clear reflection of the god's *mighty voice* motif.[23] Likewise, the victory stele of Tutmosis III "renders this king in terms reminiscent of Baal-Haddu," according to Mark Smith and Wayne Pitard.[24] It reads in part:

> I have come that I may cause You to *trample* on the eastern land and *tread down* those who are in the regions of Tonuter; that I may cause them to see Your Majesty as a lightning flash, strewing its levin-frame and giving its flood of water...I have come that I may cause you to *trample* on the Islanders in the midst of the sea, who are possessed with *your war shout*...[25]

The meteorological imagery is obvious, but most remarkable here is the presence of motifs drawn directly from the combat myth: the *trampling* motif (which equates "the Islanders" with the chaos-monster "in the midst of the sea"), and the allusion to the storm-god's war-cry—his *mighty voice* which causes the enemy to quake and surrender. The earthly king thus mirrors not just Baal, but triumphant Baal from the combat myth. Myth provides a crucial framework through which history is interpreted.

This historicizing tendency is particularly pronounced in the Hebrew tradition.[26] In one respect, its presence in royal propaganda and

---

[21] Clifford, "The Roots of Apocalypticism," 17, 19; cf. Hamblin, *Warfare in the Ancient Near East*, 122.
[22] See Smith, *The Ugaritic Baal Cycle Vol. 1*, 87-96.
[23] Ibid., 108.
[24] Ibid., 108.
[25] Quoted in Ibid., 108; emphases mine.
[26] Clifford, "The Roots of Apocalypticism," 29.

ideology is comparable to other kingdoms of the ancient Near East. So Smith compares the above texts to Psalm 89:26, where Yahweh invests the Davidic king with the powers of the divine warrior:

And I shall set on Yamm his hand, and on River(s) his right hand.[27]

So the Israelite king was presented as a reflection of the victorious storm-god. However, in another respect, the pronounced inclination to historicize the combat myth stems from a rather unique theological conception. Ancient Israelites emphasized their god as acting *within history*—not only in the sacred, primordial past—in a way that invited poets to construe historical events in terms of the combat myth.[28]

Indeed, this was the use to which the myth was put in the earliest Hebrew traditions, when poets articulated Yahweh's defeat of the Egyptian pharaoh's forces in the language of the combat myth.[29] So Exodus 15:[30]

> *Yahweh is a warrior*;
>   Yahweh is his name.
> Pharaoh's chariots and his army he cast into the Sea;
>   his picked officers were sunk in the Red Sea.
> The Deep covered them;
>   they went down into the depths like a stone.
> Your right hand, O Yahweh, glorious in power—
>   your right hand, O Yahweh, shattered the enemy.
> In the greatness of your majesty you overthrew your adversaries;
>   you sent out your fury, it consumed them like stubble.
> *At the blast of your nostrils* the Waters piled up,
>   the Floods stood up in a heap;
>   the Deep congealed in the heart of the Sea.
> …You brought [the people] in and planted them on the Mountain of your
>   possession,
>   the Place, O Yahweh, that you made your abode,
>   the Sanctuary, O Yahweh, that your hands have established.
> *Yahweh will reign forever and ever.* (vv. 3-8, 17-18)

---

[27] Smith, *The Ugaritic Baal Cycle Vol. 1*, 109.

[28] For an intriguing view on apocalypticism's development in light of the evolving dynamic between myth and history in ancient Israel (and, briefly, the combat myth), see Paul Hanson, "Jewish Apocalyptic against Its Near Eastern Environment," *RB* 78 (1971): 31-58.

[29] Clifford, "The Roots of Apocalypticism," 31-32.

[30] For the dating of Exodus 15, see Cross, *Canaanite Myth and Hebrew Epic*, 121-3. Cross calls it "one of the oldest compositions preserved in biblical sources" and suggests a "tenth-century date or earlier for its being put first into writing," 123.

Here, Yahweh's defeat of the Sea is artfully combined with and reflective of his defeat of Egypt. Indeed, the defeat of Sea is the means of Egypt's ruin, for it is the *dividing* of Sea at the "blast from his nostrils" that allows Israel to cross and Egypt to be consumed. Thus, the common images of the combat myth infuse the "historical" account of a political victory. Moreover, Yahweh's victory in this combat at sea concludes with his declaration as king: the expected progression of the combat myth. He even guides Israel up his mountain to his "Place" and "Sanctuary," leading his people in procession to his house (i.e., Temple).

Finally, as we have seen, ancient Near Eastern combat myths were sometimes cosmogonies, and this was certainly true in the case of the Hebrew myth. Now, because the Exodus tradition was Israel's primary foundation story—the creation account, as it were, of the ancient Israelites' world—it is not surprising that we find the Exodus articulated in terms of the combat myth.[31] Indeed, this is an essential aspect of the Exodus story. The Exodus is, in fact, but a variation of the combat myth—an historicized version of the combat myth genre. Appreciating this point will be critical in our eventual assessment of Exodus typology in the Gospel of Mark.

Moving beyond the earliest poetic material, we see the combat myth employed throughout the Hebrew tradition in order to help frame specific political/historical situations. Indeed, various prophets liberally apply its imagery in attempts to heighten their political denouncements of rulers or enemies of Israel. So, for example, Isaiah 14:12-19 paints the king of Babylon as the cosmic adversary of the combat myth:

> How you are fallen from heaven, O Day Star, son of Dawn!
>> How you are cut down to the ground, you who laid the nations low!
> You said in your heart, "I will ascend to heaven;
>> *I will raise my throne above the stars of God*;
> I will sit on the Mount of Assembly *on the heights of Zaphon*;
> I will ascend to the tops of the clouds,
>> I will make myself like the Most High."
> But you are brought down to Sheol, to the depths of the Pit.
> Those who see you will stare at you, and ponder over you:
>> "Is this the man who made the earth tremble, who shook kingdoms,
> who made the world like a desert and overthrew its cities,
>> who would not let his prisoners go home?"
> All the kings of the nations lie in glory, each in his own tomb;
>> but *you are cast out*, away from your grave, *like loathsome carrion*,

---

[31] For a more extensive treatment of Exodus 15 and the combat myth see ibid., 112-144.

> clothed with the dead, those pierced by the sword,
> who go down to the stones of the Pit,
> *like a corpse trampled underfoot.*

The shamed king is described with language steeped in mythological imagery, particularly *Chaoskampf* imagery. He is presented as an attempted usurper, a challenger to Yahweh's throne in the same way that Yamm and Mot challenged Baal's kingship; or Anzu, Enlil's; or Azag, Ninurta's. He would enthrone himself above Yahweh, on the traditional mountain of the Canaanite storm-god (Zaphon). But instead, the king is defeated, hurled into the "the depths of the Pit" for his offense and cast out from his grave to be eaten (perhaps reflecting the *scattering* motif). Certainly the combat myth *trampling* motif is employed here. Such is the fate of rebels who stand against the true cosmic king, Yahweh.

The prophet Ezekiel employs very similar imagery in his prophecies of the imminent destruction which Yahweh will bring upon Israel's hubristic political enemies. So Yahweh summons Ezekiel to deliver his ominous message regarding the presumptuous kings:

> Mortal, say to the Prince of Tyre, Thus says the Lord God:
> Because your heart is proud and you have said, "I am a god;
> I sit in the seat of the gods, *in the heart of the seas,*"
> yet you are but mortal, and no god,
> though you compare your mind with the mind of God.
> …Therefore thus says the Lord God:
> Because you compare your mind with the mind of a god,
> therefore, I will bring strangers against you, the most terrible of the nations;
> they shall draw their swords against the beauty of your wisdom
> and defile your splendor.
> They shall thrust you into the Pit,
> and you shall die a violent death in the heart of the seas. (Ezek 28:2, 6-8)

Again, the cosmic language of the combat myth is employed in this political execration. As above, the ruler boasts of his enthronement as a god. While the references to the seas are ostensibly due to Tyre's geographical position as a city jutting out into the Mediterranean, they may also reflect a subtle equation of the Prince with the oceanic chaos-enemy, the monster "in the midst of the sea." Like the combat myth adversaries, however, the would-be king is defeated by Yahweh, and hurled into the Pit.

Equation of the king with the chaos-monster is more explicit in the prophecies directed at the Egyptian pharaoh, the first of which comes a few verses later, presented in parallel form to the last denunciation:

> Mortal, set your face against Pharaoh king of Egypt, and prophesy against him and against all Egypt; speak, and say, Thus says the Lord God:
>
> I am against you,
> > Pharaoh king of Egypt,
>
> *the great Dragon sprawling*
> > *in the midst of its channels,*
>
> saying, "My Nile is my own;
> > I made it for myself."
>
> I will put hooks in your jaws,
> > and make the fish of your channels stick to your scales.
>
> I will draw you up from your channels,
> > with all the fish of your channels
> > sticking to your scales,
>
> I will fling you into the desert,
> > you and all the fish of your channels;
>
> you shall fall in the open field,
> > and not be gathered and buried.
>
> To the animals of the earth and to the birds of the air
> > I have given you as food. (Ezek 29:2-5)

The Pharaoh, like the King of Tyre, is guilty of unchecked hubris that challenges the supremacy of Yahweh. In his pride he rebels against the true supreme deity, viewing himself as equal to the true Lord of Creation. To this Yahweh responds with the imagery of the combat myth. The Pharaoh is nothing more than the Dragon that Yahweh triumphantly vanquished. He is no greater than Leviathan, the dragon in the sea which Yahweh has slain and cast into the desert as food. Thus is the traditional topos reemployed, in which the chaos-enemy is made food in the desert. Here, the topos provides a metaphor for the punishment of the Egyptian pharaoh.

Indeed, the association of the arrogant rebel king with the chaos-monster Leviathan seems clear. Compare the above passage with those texts which elsewhere describe the Dragon:

I will put *hooks in your jaws*, and make the fish of your channels stick to your scales.	Can you put a rope in its nose, or *pierce its jaw with a hook?*"
I will *draw you up* from your channels… (Ezek 29:4)	"Can you *draw out* Leviathan with a *fishhook*, or press down its tongue with a

	cord?
	(Job 41:2,1)
The great *dragon sprawling in the midst of its channels…*	
…I will fling you into the desert… You shall fall in the open field, and not be gathered and buried. *To the animals of the earth and to the birds of the air I have given you as food.*	…you broke the heads of *the dragons in the waters.* You crushed the heads of Leviathan; *you gave him as food for the people in the wilderness.*
(Ezek 29:3, 5)	(Ps 74:13-14)

The specific imagery of the combat myth is even more explicit in the denouncement of the Pharaoh in chapter 32:

> You consider yourself a lion among the nations,
>> but *you are like a Dragon in the Seas*;
> you thrash about in your streams,
>> trouble the water with your feet,
>> and foul your streams.
> Thus says Yahweh God:
>> In an assembly of many peoples
>> *I will throw my net over you*;
>> and I will haul you up in my dragnet.
> I will throw you on the ground,
>> *on the open field I will fling you,*
> *and will cause all the birds of the air to settle on you,*
>> *and I will let the wild animals of the whole earth gorge themselves wit*
>>> *you.*
> I will *strew your flesh on the mountains,*
>> and fill the valleys with your carcass.
> I will drench the land with your flowing blood
>> up to the mountains,
>> and the watercourses will be filled with you.
> When I blot you out, I will cover the heavens,
>> and make their stars dark;
> I will cover the sun with a cloud,
>> and the moon shall not give its light. (vv. 1-7)

The Pharaoh is the raging chaos-monster, the Dragon in the Sea, whom Yahweh *binds* in his net, then *divides* and *scatters*—specifically over the mountains here, in remarkable similarity to the way Ninurta scatters and strews Azag over the mountains. All of this is done in the context of the storm theophany, as Yahweh covers the sky with his clouds, casting the scene of this *Chaoskampf* (as in others) into darkness.

So is history interpreted in light of the combat myth. Israel's political enemies are the chaos-monsters; Yahweh—acting through Israel generally, or her king specifically—is the mighty storm-god who shall vanquish them. Such historicization of the combat myth was employed in the earliest Hebrew poetry, particularly in characterizations of the Exodus. However, it continues throughout the biblical period, especially in the Prophets. Eventually, interpretations of political conflict through the framework of the combat myth become a vital feature of Jewish apocalypticism, as we shall see in Chapter 3.

The Combat Myth in Hebrew Cult

Until the turn of the twentieth century and the achievements of comparative scholarly studies, Yahweh's battle with Leviathan and the raging Sea remained largely opaque—a theme seemingly scattered haphazardly throughout the Psalms or the occasional prophetic passage in enigmatic references. Even today, the idea of Yahweh battling a giant sea dragon remains quite foreign to many. To suggest then that it once provided perhaps the most crucial mythic narrative for ancient Israelite religious practice may sound presumptuous to say the least. Nevertheless, there is ample reason to believe that it once lay at the heart of ancient Israelite religion.

The insights of Paul Hanson are a helpful starting place for mitigating this discrepancy between the myth's apparent infrequency in biblical texts and its ancient cultic significance. According to Hanson, the Bible we have to today is not representative of the ancient cult of Yahweh as practiced at the Jerusalem Temple, but rather reflects the minority views of certain prophetic circles which ultimately came to dominance after the Exile. In Hanson's analysis, most of the prophets make relatively scant use of the Hebrew combat myth because their theological programs often stood in marked contrast to the royal theology of the Jerusalem court and cult, where the combat myth played a primary role. However, at the court and Temple cult, argues Hanson,

> the visionary element of myth was safeguarded against the rival theology of prophecy, and although later developments led to a canon dominated by prophetic Yahwism, the royal psalms preserve examples of the type of theology which was in a real sense the national orthodoxy.[32]

Thus, as liturgical texts from the cult, the Psalms provide us with insight into the nature of Israelite religion as practiced "officially" at

---

[32] Hanson, "Jewish Apocalyptic against Its Near Eastern Environment," 43.

the Jerusalem Temple, and not the idiosyncratic views of the rival prophetic circles who generally diluted the mythological element. In the temple liturgy, writes Hanson, "the ritual pattern of the conflict myth not only survived, but flourished."[33]

Though imperfect, Hanson's analysis is helpful in at least two respects. First, it draws attention to the fact that the Prophets are not necessarily the best representatives of ancient Israelite religion. Consequently, if the combat myth does not appear to play a dominant role in prophetic literature—which, indeed, now dominates the biblical canon—this does not mean that it did not play such a role in the more prevalent conceptions and rites of the cult. Secondly, the combat myth *did* play a central role in the "official" Israelite cult. This is demonstrated by an analysis of the Psalms, which I present below. Since the cult was the primary means by which most ancient Israelites would have engaged with and enacted shared religious conceptions, one is justified in saying that the combat myth was a central aspect of religious life in ancient Israel.

While this analysis of Hanson's might be enough to justify hypothesizing a particular prominence of the combat myth in popular religious practice, a necessary critique actually strengthens the argument. For Hanson argues that, contrary to the *Chaoskampf*-dominated cult, Yahwistic prophecy downplayed the mythological element and thus made scant use of the combat myth. Yet, as we have seen (and shall have ample opportunity to cite in further detail), the combat myth *also* flourished in prophetic circles. To be sure, its application in prophetic literature is less explicit (leading to a canon *seemingly* limited in *Chaoskampf* material). But this is not because the theological agenda of classical prophecy necessarily sought to downplay mythological material. Rather, the myth appears more diluted because the role it plays in prophetic literature is essentially different: as *allusion* and poetic *reference*, not strict presentation.

The combat between Yahweh and the chaos-monsters appears nowhere in the Hebrew bible as a pure narrative. We have, as it were, no Yahweh Cycle as we have a Baal Cycle. While the Psalms indeed come closest to this (probably because they also reflect a liturgical origin), even they are essentially allusive. Indeed, whether a strict narrative of Yahweh's battles with Chaos ever existed as such, we cannot now know (barring, of course, some new archeological

---

[33] Hanson, *The Dawn of Apocalyptic*, 304.

evidence). Thus, we acquire our sense of the story through metaphor, suggestion, and allusive images coupled with recurrent themes. This is particularly true in the prophetic literature, where the allusive and metaphorical use of *Chaoskampf* imagery constitutes its primary mode of presentation.

However, having reconstructed the general story (primarily through the more explicit imagery of the Psalms as well as in comparison with other ancient Near Eastern combat myths), a host of hitherto unrecognized allusions to the Hebrew combat myth in the Prophets come to light. Many of these allusions are considered below, and are employed, sometimes extensively, by Isaiah, Jeremiah, Ezekiel, Amos, Habakkuk, Zechariah, and Malachi. In this sense then, the combat myth has in fact always played a considerable role in *most* biblical texts, we had simply lacked the central conception upon which these more subtle allusions were predicated. With careful analysis, however, we see that the combat myth is common to and pervasive in both the Psalms *and* the Prophets.

Indeed, appreciating the dominance of the combat myth in the cult puts the prophetic material in context: the Prophets *assume* this dominance in order to allude to it. Prophetic applications of the combat myth could be so subtle and allusive precisely because the myth was a given. In this sense, the seemingly diluted role of the myth in prophecy—far from being rooted in a fundamental tension between prophecy and "orthodoxy"—provides additional testimony to the myth's general popularity. Just as a jazz musician relies on his listener's knowledge of a popular tune in order to riff on it and add harmonic color, the prophets could presume familiarity with the myth in order to adapt and augment it.

All of this helps to highlight the fundamental role the combat myth played in the religious life of ancient Israel. The story of Yahweh's battles with the forces of Chaos clearly undergirds both the national cult, represented in the canon essentially by the Psalms, but *also* the Prophets, albeit less perceptibly.

With this important qualification, I return to Hanson's analysis of the official Jerusalem cult through its extant liturgical literature, the Psalms. Here, we recall, Hanson says that the combat myth "flourished," appearing frequently in a traditional form he calls the "Divine Warrior Hymn." Remarkably, this form follows essentially the same progression as the combat myth schema we have been using. Thus, we often see:

1) Threat
2) Combat – victory over enemy
3) Salvation of his people
4) Manifestation of universal reign
5) Victory shout
6) Procession
7) Shalom (return to fertility – new creation)

In Hanson's terminology, the "shalom" represents the bounty and abundance consequent to Yahweh's victory over Chaos. This is the agricultural rejuvenation which occurs because of the storm-god's victory. The "victory shout" is the *mighty voice/battle cry* of the divine warrior while the "manifestation of universal reign" is analogous to the storm-god's accession to kingship.

These essential elements of the Divine Warrior Hymn, he says, "can be recognized in numerous psalms from various periods in the biblical psalter."[34] I present his extensive list below:

Psalm 2

1-3   Threat: Conspiring of the nations
4-5   Combat – victory over enemy
8-11b Manifestation of universal reign
11c   Victory shout

Psalm 9

6-7   Combat – victory over enemy
8-9   Manifestation of universal reign
10-11 Salvation of his people
12-13 Victory shout

Psalm 24

1   Manifestation of universal reign
2   Combat vs. seas/rivers- victory
(3-6 Entrance Torah)
7-10 Victory shout
      Procession after victory to temple

Psalm 29

3-9a Combat vs. waters- victory
9b   Victory shout
10   Manifestation of universal reign
11   Shalom (abundance) of the restored order

Psalm 46

2-7   Threat: Chaos and nations
      Combat – victory over enemy
8   Salvation of his people
9-12 Manifestation of universal reign

Psalm 47

2-4   Combat – victory over enemy
5   Salvation of his people
6   Procession
7-8   Victory shout
9-10 Manifestation of universal reign

Psalm 48

5   Threat: Kings assemble vs. Zion
6-8   Combat – victory over enemy
9   Salvation of Zion
10-12 Victory shout
13-14 Procession around the city
15   Yahweh's universal reign

Psalm 65

6   Salvation of his people
7-8   Combat vs. seas and nations – victory
9   Manifestation of universal reign
10-13 Shalom (return to fertility – new creation)

---

[34] Ibid., 305.

Psalm 68
A) 1-2 Combat – victory
3   Victory shout
B) 7-8 Combat of Divine Warrior (ritual
      conquest)
9-10 Salvation of his people
11-14 Victory over enemy
15-18 Procession to Zion
19-20 Victory shout
C) 21 Combat – victory over enemies
22-23 Salvation of his people
24-27 Procession to sanctuary – victory
      shout
28-35 Manifestation of universal reign

Psalm 77:17-21
17-19 Combat vs. sea – victory
20   Procession
21   Salvation of his people

Psalm 97
1-2   Yahweh reigns
3-5   Combat – victory over enemies
6-7   Manifestation of universal reign
8-9   Victory shout

Psalm 104
1-9   Combat – victory (creation myth)
10-30 Shalom (return to fertility – new
      creation)
31-35 Victory shout

Psalm 110
1.4   Yahweh establishes his king
2   Manifestation of king's reign
3   Procession to Zion
5-7   Combat – victory

Psalm 76
4-8   Combat – victory over enemies
9-10 Salvation of oppressed
11-12 Procession to brings gifts to
      Yahweh
13   Manifestation of universal reign

Psalm 89
6-9   Yahweh's universal reign
10-13 Victory over enemies
11-19 Procession – victory shout

Psalm 98
1-2   Combat – victory
3a   Salvation of his people
3b   Manifestation of universal reign
4-9   Procession

Psalm 106:9-13
9-10a Combat vs. sea – victory
10b   Procession
11-13 Salvation of his people

In his seminal works on the psalter,[35] Norwegian scholar Sigmund Mowinckel proposed a comprehensive interpretation for these texts. Given the psalms above, some of which comprise a subset of a distinct corpus dealing with Yahweh's kingship (the so-called "Enthronement Psalms"),[36] Mowinckel proposed a *Sitz im Leben* within the liturgy of a

---

[35] Sigmund Mowinckel, *Psalmenstudien*, 6 vols. (Oslo: J. Dybwad, 1921-1924), vol. 2 = *The Psalms in Israel's Worship*, 106-92.
[36] Pss 47, 93, 95, 96, 97, 98, 99, 100.

festival similar to the Babylonian *Akītu* Festival or the Hittite *Purulli* Festival. Such would have been, for the Israelites, *the Feast of Tabernacles*, also called the Feast of Booths and Sukkot: Israel's (originally New Year) harvest festival.[37] It was at this time, as the agricultural year came to its end, that infertility, death, and disorder became most salient. The forces of Chaos would assume their temporary dominance over the cosmos, and the Israelites looked to Yahweh's autumn rains which would herald the return of fertility and life.[38] In anticipation of such rejuvenation, and akin to other ancient Near Eastern New Year festivals, the festival celebrated (and, in Eliadean terms, *enacted*) Yahweh's defeat of the raging Sea and its associate Dragon,[39] as well as his victory over Death.[40]

Mowinckel argued that the central cultic event of this festival was the triumphal procession of Yahweh.[41] In this procession, Yahweh—symbolized by his holy shrine, the ark—was carried amidst singing and dancing to the Temple, where the god was then ritually enthroned.[42] Such processional rituals were, as we have seen, integral parts of other ancient Near Eastern New Year festivals, while it is possible that such a ritual enthronement had also existed at Ugarit.

It is in the context of such an event that antiphonal processional hymns like Psalm 118 become clear:

> There are glad songs of victory in the tents of the righteous.
> "The right hand of Yahweh does valiantly..."
> ...*Open to me the Gates of Righteousness,*
>   *that I may enter through them*
>   *and give thanks to Yahweh.*
> This is the Gate of Yahweh;
>   the righteous shall enter through it.
> ...*Save us, we beseech you, O Yahweh!*
>   O Yahweh, we beseech you, give us success!
> *Blessed is the one who comes in the name of Yahweh.*
>   We bless you from the House of Yahweh.
> Yahweh is God,
>   and he has given us light.

---

[37] Sigmund Mowinckel, *He That Cometh* (New York: Abingdon Press, 1956), 131-45; *The Psalms in Israel's Worship*, 106-192.

[38] *The Psalms in Israel's Worship*, 130, 134-5, 163-4.

[39] Ibid., 108, 135, 143-6, 167.

[40] Ibid., 152.

[41] As the above list shows, the procession was an important element in the Divine Warrior Hymns, no doubt reflecting their cultic setting.

[42] Mowinckel, *The Psalms in Israel's Worship*, 115, 130, 170-82.

> Bind the festal procession with branches,
> up to the horns of the altar. (vv. 15, 19-20, 25-27)

The "victory" here alluded to is none other than Yahweh's triumph over the forces of Chaos, celebrated as the procession makes its way to the inner gates of the Temple.[43] The "tents" were likely the ritual booths, and the branches those the Israelites cut in celebration of the Feast of Tabernacles:

> On the fifteenth day of this seventh month, and lasting seven days, there shall be the Festival of Booths to Yahweh.
> ...On the first day you shall take the fruit of majestic trees, branches of palm trees, boughs of leafy trees, and willows of the brook; and you shall rejoice before Yahweh your God for seven days.[44]

Like the cultic icons of the gods at the other ancient New Year festivals, the ark no doubt followed along a fixed processional road, a *via sacra*, on its way to the Temple. Mowinckel posits that this was the *měsillâ*: the ascending "paved road" often citied in related psalms.[45] Indeed, in an article entitled "No Highway! The Outline of a Semantic Description of *Mᵉsillâ*," N. L. Tidwell provides an in-depth analysis of the nature and function of this kind of road in ancient Israel. He independently concurs that the *měsillâ* indeed acted as the processional *via sacra* of ancient Israel, particularly during the Feast of Tabernacles:

> The Old Testament portrait of ancient Israel's "road that ascends" consistently maintains an unbreakable bond between *mᵉsillâ* and sacred sites, specifically the tabernacle/tent/Ark-sanctuary cities...In fact, the evidence suggests that *the "road that ascends" to the city gate and continues beyond the gate as the main, paved route to the city's temple was on certain festival occasions, notably at Sukkot, a significant part of a sacred way whose two termini were the temple within the city and a natural sacred site outside the city walls.*[46]

Given the nature of this processional road, Tidwell draws comparisons with the processional road at Hattusa, "which extended from the sanctuary within the city to the *ḫuwasi* stone outside the city," as well as with the processional road at Babylon which linked Marduk's temple

---

[43] Ibid., 180-2.

[44] Lev 23:34, 40.

[45] Mowinckel, *The Psalms in Israel's Worship*, 171.

[46] N. L. Tidwell, "No Highway! The Outline of a Semantic Description of Mesillâ," *VT* 45 (1995): 263; emphasis mine.

to the *bīt akīti* outside the city. [47] Like these other processional roads principally associated with the New Year festival, the Sacred Way in Jerusalem likely ascended from a "natural sacred site" just outside the city up to the Temple in the city proper. From this suburban site, the ark would have been processed up the Jerusalem *mĕsillâ* into the Temple during the New Year festival.

Again, these findings corroborate Mowinckel's assertion that the procession to the Temple was understood as the "ascent" or "going up" to Jerusalem/the Temple, expressed in numerous psalms by the Hebrew verb *'ālâ*.[48] Likewise, Tidwell finds that

> the verb most distinctly and, among the road-words of the Old Testament, uniquely associated with *mᵉsillâ* is *'ālâ*; *mᵉsillâ* alone, of all the biblical road words, is ... the only road word which functions as the grammatical subject of *'ālâ*.[49]

So, for example, Psalm 24, which describes the cultic "ascent" to the gates of the Temple and the following antiphonal exchange between celebrants, who bear the ark and petition entry from the gate-keeper:

> The earth is Yahweh's and all that is in it,
>   the world, and those who live in it;
> for he has founded it on the Seas,
>   and established it on the Rivers.
> Who shall ascend (*'ālâ*) the Mountain of Yahweh?
>   And who shall stand in his Holy Place?
> Those who have clean hands and a pure heart,
>   who do not lift up his soul to what is false,
>   and do not swear deceitfully.
> They shall receive blessing from Yahweh,
>   and vindication from the God of his salvation.
> Such is the company of those who seek him,
>   who seek the face of the God of Jacob.
> Lift up your heads, O gates!
>   and be lifted up, O ancient doors!
>   that the King of (the) glory may come in.[50]
> Who is the King of (the) glory?
>   Yahweh, strong and mighty,
>   *Yahweh, mighty in battle.*

---

[47] Ibid., 263-4.

[48] This phrase thus has a specifically cultic meaning, as the "Songs of Ascent" (Psalms 120-34) reflect. See Mowinckel, *The Psalms in Israel's Worship*, 171 n. 171.

[49] Tidwell, "No Highway," 259-60.

[50] The "glory" (*kbôd*) of Yahweh is explicitly associated with the ark in 1 Sam 4:21-22.

> Lift up your heads, O gates!
>> and be lifted up, O ancient doors!
>> that the King of (the) glory may come in.
> Who is this King of (the) glory?
>> Yahweh of Hosts,
>> he is the King of (the) glory.[51]

Yahweh, who is proclaimed King at the New Year festival, is here represented by his ark, which has arrived at the Temple gates and awaits cultic installation within the Holy of Holies.

Concerning the details of the processional road, its location and starting-point, Mowinckel conjectures:

> On the basis of the story told in 2 Sam. 6 as to how David took Yahweh's ark to Jerusalem, we may guess that the processional way started from a place called the house of Obed-Edom, outside the oldest part of the town, the 'castle of David', and from there it ran on the outside (to the east) of, or through the royal castle and into the temple court through the eastern gate...[52]

Based on a convergence of evidence given above, I posit here that *the House of Obed-Edom was probably the "natural sacred site" at the starting point of the mĕsillâ*. This correlation matches the comparative data well: as the *ḥesti* house marked the starting point of the Hittite processions, and the "*Akītu* house" the Babylonian processions, so the House of Obed-Edom began the Israelite processional way.

Leaving the House of Obed-Edom and traveling along this Sacred Way, Yahweh (as the ark) would then pass by the festive crowds excitedly clamoring for a glimpse at their deity. As noted in Chapter 1, it was for this reason that the New Year procession was also the premier cultic *epiphany* of the god. Mowinckel too argues this idea, noting that this was the time when Yahweh's shrine was presented to be seen before all of Israel, not hidden in the darkness of the Holy of

---

[51] Frank Moore Cross also suggests that this "psalm is an antiphonal liturgy used in the autumn festival. The portion of the psalm in verses 7-10 had its origin in the procession of the ark to the sanctuary at its founding... On this there can be little disagreement." He also points out the psalm's connection with the combat myth, noting, "We may see reflected in this liturgy the reenactment of the victory of Yahweh in the primordial battle and his enthronement in the divine assembly or, better, in his newly built (cosmic) temple." See Cross, *Canaanite Myth and Hebrew Epic*, 93. Later, he notes the similarity between the festal shout, "Lift up, O Gates, your heads!" and the triumphant shout of Baal after defeating Yamm in the Ugaritic texts, "Lift up, O Gods, your heads!" (97-99).
[52] Mowinckel, *The Psalms in Israel's Worship*, 171.

Holies. "The festival is, then," he notes, "a festival of *the epiphany of Yahweh* in the literal meaning of the word."[53] Moreover, Mowinckel argues, "It is this appearance and enthronement day of Yahweh which originally was called 'the day of the Lord', 'the day of the feast of Yahweh'."[54] The Day of the Lord is thus the same as the day of Yahweh's procession during Sukkot—the day of his epiphany.

Finally, with much singing and dancing, the ark arrived at the Temple, where it was re-installed. This was understood as the god's *enthronement*. Indeed, Yahweh was imagined as "enthroned between the Cherubim" of the ark in the Temple.[55] Like the triumphant announcement of Baal's kingship after his defeat of Yamm, and that of Marduk before his defeat of Tiamet, Yahweh was then declared king after his defeat of Sea, Leviathan, and Death. So Enthronement Psalm 93:[56]

> *Yahweh has become king!* he is robed in majesty;
>   Yahweh is robed; he is girded with strength.
> He has established the world; it shall never be moved.
>   *Your throne is established from of old;*
>   you are from everlasting.
> The Rivers have lifted up, O Yahweh,
>   the Rivers have lifted up their voice;
>   the Rivers lift up their roaring!
> *But mightier than the voices of many Waters,*
>   *than the waves of Sea,*
>   *is Yahweh on high.*
> Your decrees are very sure;
>   holiness befits your House,
>   O Yahweh, forevermore.[57]

Yahweh has become king after defeating the chaos-forces and creating the world. The chaos-waters—here "the Rivers" and "Sea," and thus parallel to Baal's enemies (Judge) River and Sea—opposed him, lifting up their thunderous voice in challenge to his power. But *his mighty*

---

[53] Ibid., 119; emphasis mine. Earlier, he writes that "the fundamental thought in the festal experience and the festal myth is that Yahweh is coming...and 'revealing himself', 'becoming revealed' and 'making himself known'... This is not a mere idea, it is reality, visibly expressed through the symbols and rites of the feast... The festival, in short, is the festal epiphany of Yahweh," 142.

[54] Ibid., 116.

[55] 1 Sam 4:4; 2 Sam 6:2; 2 Kings 19:15; 1 Chron 13:6; Ps 80:1; Ps 99:1; Is 37:16.

[56] Mowinckel, *The Psalms in Israel's Worship*, 144-5.

[57] Following Mowinckel's interpretation of "*Yahweh mālakh.*" Cf. Ibid., 107-9.

voice (thunder) is mightier than theirs, and so he rules assuredly and forevermore from his house (Temple) as king. As Baal's voice was said to issue forth from his temple at the celebration of his enthronement, so is Yahweh's voice praised at his.

These aspects are highlighted in Psalm 29, which many scholars maintain was originally "a Canaanite psalm taken over wholesale, with the simple substitution of the name of Yahweh instead of Baal for the deity concerned."[58] Regardless, it too presents Yahweh enthroned after vanquishing the chaos-waters, emphasizing the power of his *mighty voice*:

> The voice of Yahweh is over the Waters;
> the God of glory thunders,
> Yahweh, over many Waters.
> The voice of Yahweh is powerful;
> the voice of Yahweh is full of majesty.
> The voice of Yahweh breaks the cedars;
> Yahweh breaks the cedars of Lebanon.
> He makes Lebanon skip like a calf,
> and Sirion like a young wild ox.
> The voice of Yahweh flashes forth flames of fire.
> The voice of Yahweh shakes the wilderness;
> Yahweh shakes the wilderness of Kadesh.
> The voice of Yahweh causes the oaks to whirl,
> and strips the forest bare;
> and in his temple all say, "Glory!"
> *Yahweh sits enthroned over the Flood;*
> *Yahweh sits enthroned as king forever.*
> May Yahweh give strength to his people!
> May Yahweh bless his people with peace! (vv. 3-11)

Ingenious, comprehensive, and placing ancient Israel appropriately in its ancient Near Eastern milieu, Mowinckel's theory has found widespread acceptance—though also its share of detractors.[59]

---

[58] Cross, *Canaanite Myth and Hebrew Epic*, 151-152; Day, *God's Conflict*, 60.

[59] A survey of the scholarly debate is provided by J. J. M. Roberts, "Mowinckel's Enthronement Festival: A Review," in *The Book of Psalms: Composition and Reception*, ed. Peter W. Flint, et al. (Leiden: Brill, 2005), 97-115. Miller draws on J. J. Stamm's extensive survey of Psalms research up to 1955 and notes that "Mowinckel's theory was accepted, even if with some reservations, by [F. M. Th.] Böhl, [Johannes] Pedersen, [Aage] Bentzen, [Ivan] Engnell, [Aubrey R.] Johnson, and [Geo] Widengren" and counts "[Paul] Humbert, [Elmer A.] Leslie, and [Gerhard] von Rad among those who accepted some form of Mowinckel's enthronement festival." However, "it was rejected, *but with hardly any argument*, by [Jean] Calès, [Heinrich] Herkenne, [Edward J.] Kissane, [Friedrich] Nötscher, [Emanuel] Podechard, [Alphons] Shulz, [Raymond J.] Tournay,

I side with recent defenders of the theory[60] and accept the outlines of Mowinckel's hypotheses as stated above. Indeed, as we shall see in Chapter 7, Mowinckel's reconstruction is crucial for understanding Mark's handling of Jesus' ministry, particularly the triumphal entry and crucifixion, and even informs the very structuring of the gospel narrative.

Drawing all of these strands together, from traditional motifs of the combat myth to reconstructions of its crucial festival, I close this examination of the combat myth in its original ancient Israelite cultic context with a look at Psalm 68. As a liturgical text of the New Year festival, it is dense with *Chaoskampf* material, and includes within its cluster of imagery the *mighty voice, binding, trampling,* and *scattering* motifs; traditional epithets and descriptions of the Canaanite storm-god; allusions to the battles with Sea and Death; as well as vivid descriptions of the New Year procession to the Temple:

> Let God rise up, *let his enemies be scattered*;
>> let those who hate him flee before him.
> ...Sing to God, sing praises to his name;
>> lift up a song to *the Rider of the Clouds*;
> his name is Yahweh—
>> be exultant before him.
> ...Rain in abundance, O God, you showered abroad;

[W. Emery] Barnes, [Bernardus Dirks] Eerdmans, [Otto] Eissfeldt, [Johnnes] de Groot, [Robert Henry] Pfeiffer, [Ernst] Sellin-Rost, and [Moses] Buttenweiser. The *only scholars to make a sustained argument against Mowinckel's reconstruction* were [Lásvló István] Pap, [Norman H.] Snaith, [Sverre] Aalen, and [Hans-Joachim] Kraus, and of those, according to Stamm, the only one to make a persuasive case was Krause" (101-4); emphasis mine. However, Miller then states, "One may question whether Kraus has made a persuasive case" (104). Cf. Johann J. Stamm, "Ein Vierteljahrhundert Psalmenforschung," *Theologische Rundschau* 23 (1955): 1-68. For a similarly sympathetic overview of the debate, see Ben C. Ollenburger, *Zion, the City of the Great King: A Theological Symbol of the Jerusalem Cult*, Journal for the Study of the Old Testament Supplement Series (Sheffield, England: JSOT Press, 1987), 22-33. More recently, a sustained critique has been offered in Allan Rosengren Petersen, *The Royal God: Enthronement Festivals in Ancient Israel and Ugarit?* Ibid. (Sheffield: Sheffield Academic Press, 1998). This is presented almost as a general indictment of the entire Myth-and-Ritual School's methods, and is ultimately unpersuasive. Indeed, Miller posits that the recent lack of consensus about Mowinckel's view owes more to shifting interests of the field than to any successful counter-argumentation, 109.

[60] Day, *God's Conflict*, 18-38, 123-4, 180ff, 165, and reaffirmed in *Yahweh and the Gods and Goddesses of Canaan*, 100; Patrick D. Miller, "Israelite Religion," in *The Hebrew Bible and Its Modern Interpreters*, ed. Douglas A. Knight and Gene M. Tucker (Philadelphia: Fortress Press, 1985), 220-22; John Gray, *The Biblical Doctrine of the Reign of God* (T & T Clark, 2000); and Roberts, "Enthronement Festival," 113.

> you restored your heritage when it languished;
> your flock found a dwelling in it;
> > in your goodness, O God, you provided for the needy.
> …With mighty chariotry, twice ten thousand,
> > thousands upon thousands,
> > Yahweh came from Sinai into the Holy Place.
> You *ascended the high Mount,*
> > *leading captives in your train*
> > and receiving gifts from people,
> even from those who rebel against Yahweh God's abiding there.
> …Our God is a God of salvation,
> > and *to the God Yahweh belongs escape from Death.*
> But God will shatter the heads of his enemies,
> > the hairy crown of those who walk in their guilty ways.
> Yahweh said, "*I stifled the Serpent,*
> > *I muzzled the Deep Sea!*"
> …Your *solemn processions are seen*, O God,
> > *the processions of my God, my King, into the Sanctuary—*
> *the singers in front, the musicians last,*
> > *between them girls playing tambourines:*
> "Bless God in the great congregation,
> > Yahweh, O you who are of Israel's fountain!"
> There is Benjamin, the least of them, in the lead,
> > the princes of Judah in a body,
> > the princes of Zebulun, the princes of Naphtali.
> Summon your might, O God;
> > show your strength, O God, as you have done for us before.
> …*Rebuke* the Beasts that live among the reeds,
> > the herd of bulls with the calves of the peoples.
> *Trample under foot* those who lust after tribute;
> > *scatter* the peoples who delight in war.
> …O Rider in the heavens, the ancient heavens;
> > listen, he sends out *his voice, his mighty voice.*
> > > (vv. 1, 4, 9-10, 17-18, 20-22, 24-28, 30, 33)

Developments of the Hebrew Combat Myth

No doubt owing to its significance in cultic life, the Israelite combat myth became an extremely potent topos in Hebrew literature. It was one configuration that later prophets and writers could count as a given for their audience, be they commoners or kings. Moreover, the whole complex of almost archetypal meanings informing the myth provided an infinitely rich treasure-trove of images from which to draw. Power, hubris, victory, death, defeat, revival, celebration, triumph—all had their place in the combat myth; all could be employed to heighten the semantic and expressive levels of one's message.

Of course, such images were not taken indiscriminately, outside the demands of context; essentially, it was the chief *themes* of the myth which provided the basis for association and metaphor. Thus, the full range of agricultural, cultic, political, and philosophical interconnections are brought to bear. Re-creation, renewal, feast, purification, epiphany, procession, victory, kingship, and the assertion of justice—all interwoven in the combat myth—likewise interweave in allusion. Some theme or image may be more prominent in one writer's metaphor, some in another, but all are at least latent and implicit, none is far from the surface. Thus, reading of restoration one minute, we should not be surprised if the author then alludes to a procession or enthronement. Though a seeming *non sequitur*, familiarity with the combat myth and its cultic context makes the connection logical and even expected. This said, we can begin to examine some of the most important applications and revalorations of the combat myth in Israel's history.

After the fundamental significance of the *Chaoskampf* myth in the cult, the most important by far is the one it took in times of national persecution or disaster. In particular, concerns over renewal/restoration and the assertion of lapsed justice help to explain its relevance in moments of defeat. In such crises, the myth was invoked as part of a divine call to action.[61] Thus, Yahweh's past victories against the chaos-forces were consulted as the archetype for his salvific work, to which men in later times of trial could harken back. If Yahweh had defeated the enemy *then*, surely he could do it again.

To be sure, the most disastrous event in Israel's history before the first century CE was the Babylonian Exile, when Nebuchadnezzar II invaded Judah, ended the monarchy, destroyed the Temple, and deported a great number of Jews to Babylon. In the wake of such tragedy, many struggled to make theological sense of what had happened. In their desperate prayers and lamentations, some in exile turned to the *Chaoskampf* tradition from old Israelite myth and cult as a reminder (and perhaps, in some sense, a reenactment) of Yahweh's power to overcome great foes. Indeed, the cosmogonic aspect of the myth—that is, the Creation of Israel's world, whose fundaments had been the Temple and Davidic Monarchy—became particularly salient for a people still smarting from the recent destruction of those national

---

[61] See Jon Levenson, *Creation and the Persistence of Evil: The Jewish Drama of Divine Omnipotence* (San Francisco: Harper & Row, 1988), 17-26.

pillars. Recollections of Yahweh's great victory thus became an impassioned plea for him to repeat that epic battle—to become the divine warrior yet again and rescue his people from the destructive grips of a great enemy. As before, this victory would bring about the creation of a new Israel, a new king and a new Temple. As ever, the combat myth became the framework for interpreting political realities: Babylon was the beast, Yahweh the vanquishing storm-god.

We find an example of such use in Psalm 74, where the author examines his people's suffering despite Yahweh's supposed power and Israel's former glory. He pleads with Yahweh to vindicate his humiliated people, and thus his own name, by coming again as the divine warrior:

> How long, O God, is the foe to scoff?
>> Is the enemy to revile your name forever?
> Why do you hold back your hand;
>> why do you keep your hand in your bosom?
> Yet God my King is from of old,
>> working salvation in the earth.
> You divided Sea by your might;
>> you broke the heads of the Dragons in the waters.
> You crushed the heads of Leviathan;
>> you gave him as food for the people in the wilderness. (vv. 74:11-14)

Likewise Psalm 77:

> Will the Lord spurn forever,
>> and never again be favorable?
> Has his steadfast love ceased forever?
>> Are his promises at an end for all time?
> ...I will call to mind the deeds of Yahweh;
>> I will remember your wonders of old.
> I will meditate on all your work,
>> and muse on your mighty deeds.
> ...When the Waters saw you, O God,
>> when the Waters saw you, they were afraid;
>> the very Deep trembled.
> The clouds poured out water;
>> the skies thundered;
>> your arrows flashed on every side.
> The crash of your thunder was in the whirlwind;
>> your lightning lit up the world;
>> the earth trembled and shook.
> Your way was through the Sea,
>> your path, through the mighty Waters;
>> yet your footprints were unseen. (vv. 7-8, 11-12, 16-19)

Of all the writers to employ the combat myth in this way, one in particular demands special attention. He is the author of Isaiah 40-55 (called Second or Deutero-Isaiah), and he employs *Chaoskampf* traditions extensively to this end. Indeed, fundamental to his entire prophetic message is the metaphorical comparison of Israel's impending restoration from exile with the rejuvenation which followed Yahweh's victory over the forces of Chaos. So we read:

> Awake, awake, put on strength,
>   O arm of Yahweh!
> Awake, as in days of old,
>   the generations of long ago!
> Was it not you who cut Rahab in pieces,
>   who pierced the Dragon?
> Was it not you who dried up Sea,
>   the Waters of the Great Deep;
> who made the depths of Sea *a road*
>   for the redeemed to cross over?
> So the ransomed of Yahweh shall return,
>   and *come to Zion with singing*;
> Everlasting joy shall be upon their heads;
>   they shall obtain joy and gladness,
>   and sorrow and sighing shall flee away.
> I, I am he who comforts you;
>   why then are you afraid of a mere mortal who must die,
>   a human being who fades like grass?
> You have forgotten Yahweh, your Maker,
>   who stretched out the heavens
>   and laid the foundations of the earth.
> You fear continually all day long
>   because of the fury of the oppressor,
> who is bent on destruction.
>   But where is the fury of the oppressor?
> The oppressed shall speedily be released;
>   they shall not die and go down to the Pit,
>   nor shall they lack bread.
> For I am Yahweh your God,
>   who troubles the Sea so that its waves roar—
>   Yahweh of Hosts is his name.
> I have put my words in your mouth,
>   and hidden you in the shadow of my hand,
> stretching out the heavens
>   and laying the foundations of the earth,
>   and saying to Zion, "You are my people." (Is 51:9-16)

The prophet begins by pleading with his god, literally attempting to rouse him as though he had fallen asleep and thus become inattentive to

the calamities befalling Israel. He harkens back to the "days of old,"
when Yahweh was still a warrior fighting for his people. He
demonstrated his power then by defeating the Dragon Rahab and the
roaring Sea, whom he divided so that Israel might cross into the
Promised Land. With this connection, Deutero-Isaiah highlights the
fact that the Exodus tradition is itself based on the combat myth.
However, in an imaginative and bold move, he adds to the traditional
topos (present even in Exodus 15) which linked Yahweh's
dividing/dismembering of the Sea and Israel's crossing of the Red Sea.
Indeed, he relates this salvific passage to the Sacred Way of the New
Year festival. Thus, in a crucial metaphorical linkage, *Deutero-Isaiah
makes the Exodus crossing the via sacra of the New Year procession.*
With this brilliant relationship, the *dividing* and *trampling* motifs are
combined: the Sea itself is the Way trampled by the faithful en route to
the Temple.

Deutero-Isaiah continues the metaphor: after Yahweh defeated
Sea, he established Creation ("stretching out the heavens..."); now he
is urged to fight again, not Sea but Babylon. He is compelled to create
again, not the first Monarchy and Temple—which lie in ruins—but new
ones. Then his chosen people shall return to Zion a saved and redeemed
nation, not sent to Death's Pit as through the famine of barren summer.
Rather, in abundance, they shall march to Zion "with singing" as they
had during the New Year procession. For sorrow and sighing will flee
away just as the chaos-waters were said to flee at God's rebuke.

As this passage demonstrates, the language used to articulate the
future hope of Yahweh's intervention and restoration could be drawn
not only from the combat myth generally, but the New Year festival
specifically as the cultic enshrinement of that myth. Writing during the
Babylonian Exile, Deutero-Isaiah draws frequently from the festival as
a powerful metaphor for Israel's eventual renewal. Mowinckel
summarizes this succinctly, writing:

> Interpreters have always been aware of the close relationship between the
> enthronement psalms and Deutero-Isaiah...[who is] dependent on the
> ideology and style of the enthronement psalms. That is to say, he has
> consciously imitated and used them as a pregnant expression of the message
> he is bringing.[62]

---

[62] Mowinckel, *The Psalms in Israel's Worship*, 116-17.

So the festival's processional road features prominently. Such, we recall, was the *měsillâ*, the paved road, which indeed permeates the book of Isaiah as a kind of leitmotif. Here it is reimagined as the road which will run from Babylon to Zion, carrying the exiles home:

> Then the eyes of the blind shall be opened,
>   and the ears of the deaf unstopped;
> then the lame shall leap like a deer,
>   and the tongue of the speechless sing for joy.
> For waters shall break forth in the wilderness,
>   and streams in the desert;
> the burning sand shall become a pool,
>   and the thirsty ground springs of water;
> the haunt of jackals shall become a swamp,
>   the grass shall become reeds and rushes.
> *A processional road (měsillâ) shall be there,*
>   *and it shall be called the Sacred Way;*
> the unclean shall not travel on it,
>   but it shall be for God's people;
>   no traveler, not even fools, shall go astray.
> No lion shall be there,
>   nor shall any ravenous Beast come up on it;
> they shall not be found there,
>   but the redeemed shall walk there.
> And the ransomed of Yahweh shall return,
>   and come to Zion with singing;
> everlasting joy shall be upon their heads;
>   they shall obtain joy and gladness,
>   and sorrow and sighing shall flee away. (Is 35:5-10)

The return of the captives is here pictured as Yahweh's cosmic rejuvenation (the divine warrior's "Shalom" in Hanson's terms), and the path of the exiles as the Sacred Way, the processional road of the New Year festival. Only the redeemed shall walk there, as only the righteous/purified could enter the Gate of Righteousness,[63] and no Beast will any longer be a threat. The exiles shall return to Zion with singing and celebration along this "eschatological *via sacra,*"[64] and here again, "sorrow and sighing" flee away like the rebuked chaos-waters.

Indeed, even the language of physical healing recalls the festival. As Eliade observed, the New Year was indeed a re-creation, a return to the pure time of origin. All accumulations of stain or imperfection were

---

[63] Cf. Pss 24, 118.
[64] Mowinckel, *The Psalms in Israel's Worship*, 171.

abolished. All Nature returned to a state of original purity. For this reason, the New Year was not only a time of ritual ablution, but also associated with healing. Eliade writes that

> since ritual recitation of the cosmogonic myth implies reactualization of that primordial event, it follows that he for whom it is recited is magically projected *in illo tempore*, into the "beginning of the World"; he comes contemporary with the cosmogony. What is involved is, in short, a return to the original time, the therapeutic purpose of which is to begin life again, a symbolic rebirth.[65]

The "eschatological *via sacra*" described in Isaiah 35 reappears in Isaiah 40, which likewise leads the exiles back to Zion through the desert:

> A voice cries out:
> "In the wilderness, clear the Road of Yahweh!
>   Make straight in the desert a processional way (*mĕsillâ*) for our God!
> Every valley shall be lifted up,
>   and every mountain and hill be made low;
> the uneven ground shall become level,
>   and the rough places a plain.
> Then the glory (*kbôd*) of Yahweh shall be revealed,
>   and all people shall see it together,
>   for the mouth of Yahweh has spoken."
> ...Ascend (*'ālâ*) a high mountain,
>   O herald of good tidings to Zion;
> lift up your voice with strength,
>   O herald of good tidings to Jerusalem,
>   lift it up, do not fear;
> say to the cities of Judah,
>   "Behold your God!"
> *See*! Lord God comes with might,
>   and his arm rules for him. (Is 40:3-5, 9-10a)

This passage is brimming with imagery from the procession of the New Year festival. Of special interest, however, is the processional herald, crying out to the people, "Clear the Road of Yahweh!" This figure is not simply a poetic construction. Evidence shows that actual heralds were responsible for leading ancient cultic processions. So, for example, in the eleventh book of *The Golden Ass*, Apuleius notes in his description of the Isis procession: "And there were many whose job it

---

[65] Eliade, *The Sacred and the Profane: The Nature of Religion*, 82.

was to cry out, 'make the road clear for the sacred objects'."[66] Compare also the description of the *Akītu* procession and its emphasis on clearing the processional road for the passing deity:

> From Hostile Elam [Nabu] entered upon a road of jubilation, a path of rejoicing … of success to Su-an-na. The people of the land saw his towering figure, the ruler in (his) splendor. Hasten to go out (Nabu), Son of Bel, you who know the ways and the customs. *Make his way good, renew his road, make his path straight, hew him out a trail.*[67]

Such heralds would certainly have been part of the New Year procession in ancient Israel when, as the people excitedly clamored to glimpse the deity—when his glory (the *kbôd* of his ark) was revealed in cultic *epiphany* (explaining the prophet's reiterations of "Behold your God!" and "See!")—a clear path was needed for passage. Such would have been the role of the processional herald.

However, the herald's proclamations were more than simple calls for room. Indeed, in Deutero-Isaiah's scene, after "ascending" (*ālâ*) the processional road (*měsillâ*) up the Temple mount, the herald was also to proclaim the "good news." These are not mere general exultations, however, as the Hebrew verb *bśr* usually means "to report good news" in a very specific sense—namely "to report the good news from the battlefield." Indeed, this association with military triumph renders it an almost technical term: the *bśwrh* is the good news proclaimed by a messenger/herald after victory in battle (so e.g., 2 Samuel 18:20-27; 2 Kings 7:9;). So we find that *bśr* is the verb used to announce the death of enemy kings (e.g., 1 Samuel 31:9; 2 Samuel 1:20; 4:10; 18:19-32). Used in the context of the New Year festival—the cultic celebration of the storm-god's defeat of the chaos-monsters—the term thus refers specifically to Yahweh's victory in battle against the forces of Chaos. The enemy king (Yamm or Mot) is dead; Yahweh, instead, has become king.

Such, indeed, was the significance of *bśr* and its cognates even in the Baal Cycle. There we read how, after Baal slew Yamm, Anat comes as a herald from El to Baal with message that, since he is now king, a palace/temple can be built for him:

---

[66] *Met.* 273.13-14, as noted in *ABD*, "Processions," 472.
[67] Paul Volz, *Jesaia II*, Kommentar Zum Alten Testament (Leipzig: Deichertsche, 1932), 4.

<blockquote>
Adolescent Anat laughed,
She raised her voice and declared:
"Receive the good news (bšr), O Baal,
Good news (bśwrh) I bring to you!
'Let a house be given you like your brothers',
A court, like your kin's.[68]
</blockquote>

Sigmund Mowinckel observes that "[t]he term 'glad tidings' (bšrt) was already used in Ugarit about the announcement that Baal had again become alive, and in the same terms the cultic festival announced to Israel the appearance of Yahweh as king and his enthronement."[69] Such appears to be the significance of "reporting the good news" (the Hebrew verb bśr) in the New Year Enthronement Psalms:

<blockquote>
Sing to Yahweh, bless his name;
   report the good news (baśśĕrû) of his salvation from day to day.
…Say among the nations, "Yahweh has become king!" (Ps 96:2, 10a)
</blockquote>

Such was the task of the New Year festival herald, about whom we may briefly conjecture further, since a survey of the usages of bšr in the Hebrew Bible reveal an intimate connection with a specific figure: the son(s) of the high priest of the ark. So, for example, Ahimaaz, son of Zadok, high priest of the ark, bears the "good news" to David that the would-be usurper Absalom is dead (2 Samuel 18). Likewise, in 1 Kings 1:42, Jonathan, son of the other high priest of the ark, Abiathar, relates the "good news" to the would-be usurper Adonijah that Solomon has become king. Notably, in 1 Sam 4:17, an unnamed Benjaminite must report the good news from the battlefield (of the ark's capture), since Hophni and Phineas, the sons of the high priest of the ark, Eli, have themselves been killed in the battle. These, and other passages, suggest that the traditional herald/messenger of the good news was the son of the high priest of the ark—a fitting designation, given the ark's importance in the New Year festival. The would-be usurper king, Sea or Death, was defeated, and the son of the high priest could march triumphantly at the fore of the procession, proclaiming the good news and demanding, "Clear the Road of Yahweh!"

---

[68] CTA 1.4.v.25-9 = Smith and Pitard, The Ugaritic Baal Cycle Vol. 2, 539.

[69] Mowinckel, The Psalms in Israel's Worship, 142.

It is from just this festal scene that Deutero-Isaiah draws the basis for his cosmic vision in the earlier passage above and again a few verses later:

> How beautiful upon the mountains
> > are the feet of *the herald of the good news* (*mĕbaśśēr*),
> > *who announces peace*,
> > *the herald who brings good news* (*mĕbaśśēr ṭôb*),
> > *who announces salvation*,
> > who says to Zion, "Your God has become king!"
> Listen! Your sentinels lift up their voices;
> > together they sing for joy;
> For in plain sight they see
> > the return of Yahweh to Zion. (Is52:7-8)[70]

The "good news," originally the proclamation of Yahweh's ultimate victory over the chaos-forces by the herald, is here imagined as Yahweh's victory over the nations which brings his people home. "Yahweh has become king!"—the exclamation of the festival—is now used to symbolize Yahweh's re-assumption of power once Israel is restored. Peace is at hand now that Yahweh's war with the Dragon (Babylon) is over. Now the people can sing just as they sang at his procession, since now they see Yahweh return to Zion, just as he used to process up his hill and into his Temple for enthronement. Such is the role of the combat myth and the New Year festival in Deutero-Isaiah.

Though, while Deutero-Isaiah was the most important prophet to employ the combat myth and its cultic festival in this way, he was certainly not the first. Even before the Exile, Nahum's prophetic message spoke to the late seventh century downfall of Assyria in terms of the primordial battle:

> A jealous and avenging God is Yahweh,
> > Yahweh is avenging and wrathful;
> Yahweh takes vengeance on his adversaries
> > and rages against his enemies.
> ...His way is in whirlwind and storm,
> > and the clouds are the dust of his feet.
> *He rebukes the Sea and makes it dry,*
> > *and he dries up all the Rivers*;
> ...Yahweh is good,
> > a stronghold in a day of trouble;
> he protects those who take refuge in him,

---

[70] For the translation "Yahweh has become king," see ibid., 107-9.

Nahum is certainly similar to the later prophet in his metaphorical utilization of the combat myth and the New Year festival. Yahweh is again the cloud-rider storm-god, whose mighty *rebuke* subdues the traditional enemies of the *Chaoskampf*: Sea and River. In an interesting boast, the prophet even alludes to the traditional progression of the combat myth in which the storm-god's first attack would prove ineffectual, thus allowing the adversary to "rise up twice." Like Marduk, however—whose immense power demanded only one attempt to slay the Sea—Yahweh can likewise boast that the first battle with his enemies shall prove the last. Finally, and in very similar language to Deutero-Isaiah, the herald of the festival is mentioned. The herald tops the Temple mount and declares the good news of Yahweh's ultimate victory (here, over Assyria), allowing Judah to celebrate the Festival of Booths without fear of invasion. As Isaiah shows, of course, this assurance proved misplaced, since the very power that destroyed Assyria then came and subjugated Judah. Yahweh's enemies did indeed rise twice, or, rather, the Yamm of Assyria fell, only to be followed by the swallowing Mot of Babylon. So could the message of Nahum become the message of Deutero-Isaiah—only now writ larger.

Eventually, however, Isaiah's long hoped-for Restoration did occur. With the Persian defeat of Babylon, the Jewish exiles were indeed allowed to return to their homeland and begin rebuilding the national pillars which war had destroyed decades earlier. In a basic sense, then, the expectant visions of Isaiah were fulfilled. Babylon, the chaos-monster, was destroyed and Israel had traveled the desert Way back to a new Temple. With this apparently successful conclusion, one might expect a cessation of grand visions for return and the renewal of Israel. However, various historical developments following the

Restoration led to precisely the opposite: rather than ceasing, prophetic visions of rejuvenation and re-creation actually *intensified.*

In part, this was justified by the very real disappointments and frustrations of reconstruction. On the other hand, and not without irony, the continuance of yearning for cosmic renewal was a product of its own indulgence: it was a dissatisfaction with reality engendered by an over-exuberant hope. Given the lofty, cosmic language used so poetically and with such power by Isaiah and other visionaries, no restoration could ever have matched the rhetoric. With every frustration, delay, false-start, and failure to return Israel to its imagined former glory, disappointment grew, and the prophetic visions of a Second Paradise now but served as a foil to the lackluster realities on the ground. Surely *this* was not the promised rejuvenation, some must have thought. Surely it is still to come.

With these developments, it is not surprising that the hoped-for event comes to lose its moorings in historical reality. Since presumably unfulfilled, the idea of restoration continued to be developed and, with time, took on a truly cosmic scope. So, as Mowinckel puts it, "The salvation to come is looked upon as *an enthronement day of Yahweh with cosmic dimensions*—such in short is the substance of the prophecy of re-establishment and later also of eschatology."[71] This is why the combat myth and apocalypticism are so intricately linked. The language of the New Year poetically employed by prophecy becomes infinitely enlarged. In this way, the temporary dominance of the Chaos at the end of the year is transformed into world cataclysms at the End of Time. The storm-god's defeat of these forces and the return of original fertility is transformed into Yahweh's final battle with the forces of Evil and the ultimate restoration of the earth back to the Edenic Paradise of the Beginning. The apocalypse is essentially the cosmic New Year.

Such cosmic aggrandizement of the New Year likely provides the background for the so-called Isaianic Apocalypse (chapters 24-7), written probably a century or more after Israel's return from captivity and later embedded into earlier prophecies. It reads in part:

> Your dead shall live, their corpses shall rise.
> > O dwellers in the dust, awake and sing for joy!
> For your dew is radiant dew,
> > and the earth will give birth to those long dead.

---

[71] Ibid., 189; emphasis mine.

> Come, my people, enter your chambers,
>   and shut your doors behind you;
> hide yourselves for a little while
>   until the wrath is past.
> For Yahweh comes out from his Place
>   to punish the inhabitants of the earth for their iniquity;
> the earth will disclose the blood shed on it,
>   and will no longer cover its slain.
>
> On that Day, Yahweh with his cruel and great and strong sword will punish Leviathan, the fleeing serpent, Leviathan the twisting serpent, and he will kill the Dragon that is in the Sea. (Is 26:19-27:1)

"The Day of the Lord," the epiphany day of Yahweh at his harvest New Year festival, becomes the day of impending restoration of the entire cosmos, and the judgment for Israel's enemies.[72] So the combat myth, notably the themes of rejuvenation and the assertion of justice, undergirds apocalyptic expectation. Of particular note in this passage, however, is the antiquity of the mythic traditions employed despite the relatively late date of the text.[73] The language describing Leviathan here in Isaiah 27:1 is so similar to that describing Baal's defeat of Litan that scholars propose direct dependence on a common West Semitic tradition:[74]

Isaiah 27:1	*KTU* 1.5.i.1-4
...punish Leviathan the fleeing serpent, Leviathan the twisting serpent...	...killed Litan, the Fleeing Serpent, Annihilated the Twisty Serpent...

This late use of particularly ancient mythic traditions becomes a recurrent tendency in apocalyptic literature (and one I shall further explore in the following chapter).

---

[72] For the original motif of "judgment" and Yahweh's epiphanic festival, see ibid., 146-50.

[73] Many scholars have proposed a late date for the Isaiah Apocalypse. In his commentary on Isaiah 1-39, Joseph Blekinsopp notes, "Study of the language, vocabulary, themes, and tone of these chapters persuaded practically all critical readers as early as the first half of the nineteenth century…that they come to us from the time of the Second Temple," Joseph Blenkinsopp, *Isaiah 1-39: A New Translation with Introduction and Commentary*, The Anchor Bible (New York: Doubleday, 2000), 347-8. However, others have proposed an earlier composition in the sixth century BCE, including Cross, *Canaanite Myth and Hebrew Epic*, 135, and Blenkinsopp himself, 348. Either way, the temporal distance from the Ugaritic material is substantial.

[74] Day, *God's Conflict*, 142; Angel, *Chaos and the Son of Man*, 5.

While the resurrection imagery in this passage could simply be metaphorical for Israel's expected renewal as a nation, it may represent the apocalyptic expectation of bodily resurrection in the radical new world order after Yahweh's epiphany and judgment—a utopian world where there shall be no more death for Israel's faithful. In this sense, we see the apocalyptic reflex of the storm-god's defeat of Death. The prophet writes similarly in a passage a few verses earlier:

> And he will destroy on this mountain
> > the shroud that is cast over all peoples,
> > the sheet that is spread over all nations;
> > he will swallow up Death forever.
> Then the Lord God will wipe away the tears from all faces,
> > And the disgrace of his people he will take away from all the earth,
> > For Yahweh has spoken.
> It will be said on that day,
> > Lo, this is our God; we have waited for him, so that he might save us.
> > This is Yahweh for whom we have waited;
> > let us be glad and rejoice in his salvation. (Is 25:7-9)

As noted before, we find here an ironic reversal of the Baal/Mot (or rather Yahweh/Mot) combat myth. Whereas Death conquered Baal by swallowing him, here Yahweh swallows Death. Thus Yahweh is the divine warrior who defeats the forces of death and destruction—not just at the end of the year, but *forever*. The victory has a decidedly eschatological tone, as his success over those forces inaugurates a radically new era of divine intimacy, joy, forgiveness, and deliverance from oppression. Day notes that these sections of Isaiah are best understood as "proto-apocalyptic or late prophecy," and posits, quoting G. W. Anderson, that they belong "to that phase in prophecy in which *the sharp contours of the here and now begin to be lost in more spacious visions of a transformation of all things.*"[75]

Nowhere is this tendency more pronounced than in chapters 9-14 of Zechariah, usually attributed to an author called Second Zechariah. Though these post-Exilic texts are notoriously difficult to date,[76] they are clearly at home in the "proto-apocalyptic" tradition, if not representative of full-blown apocalypticism. So we read:

---

[75] G. W. Anderson, "Isaiah XXIV-XXVII Reconsidered," *SVT* 9 (1963): 126, quoted in Day, *God's Conflict*, 144; emphasis mine.

[76] Cf. Carol L. Meyers and Eric M. Meyers, *Zechariah 9-14: A New Translation with Introduction and Commentary*, The Anchor Bible (New York: Doubleday, 1993), 15-16, who argue a fifth-century setting (18-26).

> See, the Day of Yahweh is coming, when the plunder taken from you will be divided in your midst. For I will gather all the nations against Jerusalem to battle, and the city shall be taken and the houses looted and the women raped; half the city shall go into exile, but the rest of the people shall not be cut off from the city. (Zech 14:1-2)

So the world descends into utter Chaos. The deprivations and decay of the closing year are eschatologized into the ultimate ruin of the city of Jerusalem. However, this moment of Chaos' triumph does not last long. As in the combat myth, this is the cue for the glorious divine warrior. So we read in the next verse:

> Then Yahweh will go forth and *fight against those nations as when he fights on a day of battle*. On that Day his feet shall stand on the Mount of Olives, which lies before Jerusalem on the east; and the Mount of Olives shall be split in two from east to west by a very wide valley; so that one half of the Mount shall withdraw northward, and the other half southward. And you shall flee by the valley of the mountain, for the valley between the mountains shall reach to Azal; and you shall flee as you fled from the earthquake in the days of King Uzziah of Judah. (14:3-5b)

The battle won, so follows the rejuvenation and assumption of kingship:

> Then Yahweh my God will come, and all the Holy Ones with him. On that Day there shall not be either cold or frost. And there shall be continuous day (it is known to Yahweh), not day and not night, for at evening time there shall be light. On that Day living waters shall flow out from Jerusalem, half of them to the eastern sea and half of them to the western sea; it shall continue in summer as in winter. And *Yahweh will become King over all the earth*; on that Day Yahweh shall be one, and his name one. (14:5c-9)

Finally, as if to make all of these connections with the New Year festival and the combat myth explicit, the prophet concludes:

> Then all who survive of the nations that have come against Jerusalem *shall go up* (*'ālâ*) year after year to worship the King, Yahweh of Hosts, and *to keep the Feast of Tabernacles*. ...And there shall no longer be traders in the House of Yahweh of Hosts on that Day. (14:16, 21b)

The language of the prophet is certainly far beyond "the here and now," describing rather scenes of truly cosmic restoration and transformation. His use of the combat myth—and, more specifically, the New Year Feast of Tabernacles—is notable. Again, the festival's

"Day of the Lord" is projected as a cosmic event: Yahweh is revealed, not in the epiphany of his ark during the procession, but *in person* as it were—as the wrathful divine warrior himself appearing to the entire world. So Yahweh will fight, bestriding like a colossus the divided Mount of Olives. Entering Jerusalem from the east—echoing the ark's festal procession through the Temple's eastern gate—he then defeats Israel's enemies, whose typical association with the chaos-monsters is assumed. His (re)assumption of kingship is the consequence of this victory, and Yahweh is proclaimed king over the cosmos. Finally, the Temple is cleansed of impurity (the "traders" being expelled) in a ritual re-purification expected of the New Year, and all the nations of earth go up year after year to celebrate *the Feast of Tabernacles*.

From here it is not too difficult to see the contours of later, full-blown apocalypticism, as well as the role which the combat myth and the New Year festival will play within that emerging tradition. Such developments are the focus of the next chapter and are crucial for understanding the role and importance of the combat myth in the Gospel of Mark.

CHAPTER 3
APOCALYPTICISM AND THE COMBAT MYTH

Despite the lofty hopes of the prophets, the return from exile in Babylon did not end Israel's woes. Except for their relatively brief independence after the Maccabean revolt, the Jews were never again the true proprietors of their own territory, but rather played the vassal state to a succession of far more powerful empires—Persian, Ptolemaic, Seleucid, and then Roman. Thus subjugated, hopes of reconstituting the Davidic monarchy dwindled. The Temple, however, was indeed rebuilt (albeit after much delay and frustration)—only to become a lightning rod of criticism, as zealous groups lambasted the religious authorities with charges of corruption, hypocrisy, Hellenizing, and the like. So, while the exiles had returned, it could hardly be said that Israel's world had been securely reset upon her former national pillars.

The Exile thus created fundamental difficulties for Israelite religion that were never fully resolved, even after return from Babylon in the late sixth century. Commenting on the prevailing post-Exilic sentiment from the return to the first century CE, N. T. Wright concludes:

> Most Jews of this period, it seems, would have answered the question 'where are we?' in the language which, reduced to its simplest form, meant: we are still in exile. They believed that, in all the senses which mattered, Israel's exile was still in progress. Although she had come back from Babylon, the glorious message of the prophets remained unfulfilled.[1]

As Mowinckel observed, the tendency to project Israel's future restoration "as an enthronement day of Yahweh with cosmic dimensions" becomes a core tenet of Jewish eschatology.[2] Indeed, as the frustrations which preoccupied late prophecy continued unanswered into the post-Exilic period, this tendency and its cosmic scope only grew. The prophetic outlook became increasingly pessimistic, until all hope for the possibility of reform through human means had eroded. Only divine intervention could right the myriad wrongs which Israel now suffered. Like a barren land in the dead of summer, Israel was withered and weltering, the oppressive heat of foreign domination still

---

[1] N. T. Wright, *The New Testament and the People of God* (Minneapolis: Fortress Press, 1992), 268-9.
[2] Mowinckel, *The Psalms in Israel's Worship*, 189.

stinging and the Davidic monarchy still a corpse. Only Yahweh's victorious coming—his slaying of Death and Dragon in salvific rejuvenation—could truly restore the people and bring about the radical transformation promised by the prophets. Thus, with the rise of apocalypticism, the combat myth retained its immense significance in Jewish thought, as writers turned in ever heightened zeal to its reassuring framework of divine victory over Chaos.[3]

However, sheer enlargement of scope was hardly the most important modification to the combat myth occasioned by these events. Rather, key theological developments during this period would serve to truly transform the myth from a powerful metaphor of restoration into the all-encompassing worldview of apocalypticism. Of these developments, certainly the most important was *the Devil*.

Despite the importance of the rise of the Devil in post-Exilic thought, it is not my intention to attempt here a full-scale examination of the Devil's historical evolution, as that task is both beyond the scope of the present study and has already been tackled quite effectively by other authors besides.[4] What does warrant investigation, however, is the Devil's connection to the combat myth, since it is profound and fundamental. Indeed, the very conception of Satan as he appears in early Jewish and Christian texts owes largely to apocalyptic transformations of the ancient Near Eastern combat myth. Appreciating this continuity with the *Chaoskampf* tradition is crucial for understanding the role of that tradition in apocalyptic texts, including the gospels.

Persistence of Myth: The Devil as Chaos-Enemy

The centrality of myth and mythic frameworks to apocalypticism has long been noted by scholars. So Frank Moore Cross, for example, speaks of "a second era of the recrudescence of myth in the rise of proto-apocalyptic."[5] Indeed, the general impression from surveying the

---

[3] See e.g., Hanson, *The Dawn of Apocalyptic*, 299-324; Forsyth, *The Old Enemy*, 124-211.

[4] See Jeffrey Burton Russell, *The Devil: Perceptions of Evil from Antiquity to Primitive Christianity* (Ithaca: Cornell University Press, 1977), 174-220; Elaine H. Pagels, *The Origin of Satan* (New York: Random House, 1995), 35-62.

[5] Cross, *Canaanite Myth and Hebrew Epic*, 135-6.

relevant extant texts is of emphatic return to mythic paradigms with the advent of apocalyptic eschatology.

While this basic significance of myth is clear, the idea of *revival* or, to use Cross's term, "recrudescence," is a bit more tenuous. This would suggest that, at some point (presumably during the height of classical prophecy), the popularity of myth declined or lapsed in some way, allowing for this later *return* to mythic frameworks. However, when we appreciate Hanson's point that the works of the classical prophets, far from representing Israelite "orthodoxy," in all likelihood but showcase the rather idiosyncratic derivations of a vocal, albeit poetic, but nevertheless marginal group, the notion that myth "went away" becomes considerably problematic. Indeed, in all likelihood the traditional mythic narratives as safeguarded by the Jerusalem court and cult remained more or less the dominant frame of reference for common Israelite piety.

In fact, the only time that would present a likely break with this tradition is the Exile itself—or, since those who went into exile would have carried the traditions, the generation born *after* the defeat of 587. Yet it is precisely around this generation and the return from exile that we see this supposed "recrudescence" of myth. This leaves a very short time indeed for the whole mythic framework of traditional Israelite religion to be forgotten or dismissed and subsequently revived—and, besides, is certainly not what is usually meant by such a recrudescence of myth in apocalypticism. Moreover, given the commonly accepted idea that the Exile itself provided the very impetus for *preservation* and *codification* of Israelite religion, this last position strains the basic credibility of such a notion.

Rather than positing a "return" to myth with the rise of apocalypticism, it seems far more likely that *mythic frameworks and narratives remained potent and vital aspects of popular Israelite religion both during and after the Babylonian Captivity*. The sense of decline or depreciation owes rather to the prominence of extant prophetic texts in the canon—which, as we have seen, even in themselves do not necessarily dilute mythical material, but generally *seem* to place less emphasis on myth because its role is more referential, poetic, and allusive than liturgical texts such as the Psalms.

This seemingly pedantic distinction is in fact of some importance, as accepting continuity rather than discontinuity for the central role of myth in Israelite religion more adequately explains one aspect of myth in apocalypticism: its *antiquity*. Indeed, the mythic resonances we encounter in apocalyptic texts reveal a familiarity with particularly ancient traditions. In some cases, the only precedent available for comparison is, by the time of the apocalyptic text, over a thousand years old, and comes to us only from the Ugaritic material. So, for example, we saw that the language describing Leviathan in the Isaianic Apocalypse (c. 500 BCE or even later) is so similar to that describing Baal's defeat of Litan (c. 1400 BCE) that scholars propose direct dependence on a common West Semitic tradition:[6]

Isaiah 27:1	KTU 1.5.i.1-4
...punish Leviathan the fleeing serpent, Leviathan the twisting serpent...	...killed Litan, the Fleeing Serpent, Annihilated the Twisty Serpent...

This employment of very ancient traditions is a recurring element in apocalyptic texts. Such antiquity suggests enduring lines of transmission whose living and unbroken connection with the past adds further weight to the notion of myth's persistence in Israelite religion.

For transforming the combat myth rebellion into a complete eschatological worldview, apocalyptic writers had a host of traditional material from which to draw. However, we often lack the original sources of this material, since by no means would all become canonical, and therefore preserved. Thus, ancient traditions—both cultic and mythic—inform apocalyptic texts which, though still current in some form at the time of composition, have since been lost to history. In short, says Collins, "the apocalyptic writers had at their disposal a much fuller mythology than is now extant in the Hebrew Bible."[7]

Yet the same must be stressed about cultic expressions: religious *praxis* too lay at the disposal of apocalyptic writers. Inherently perishable, its interaction with apocalyptic literature would be less apparent than literary influences (even of reconstructed or hypothetical texts), yet is equally important. To the extent then that ancient ritual practice can be reconstructed, its bearing on apocalyptic texts must be considered. This is of special importance because, as demonstrated in the previous chapter, the rites of the New Year festival were central to proto-apocalyptic texts. As I shall show, this tendency continues into apocalypticism.

---

[6] Day, *God's Conflict*, 142; Angel, *Chaos and the Son of Man*, 5.
[7] *ABD*, "Apocalypses and Apocalypticism," 283.

Though this will become more important in the pages to follow, for now, the recognition that mythic frameworks were securely entrenched in Israelite religious conceptions allows us to appreciate a vital aspect of the Devil's development in apocalypticism. Namely, *the Devil is described in the terms of the combat myth because he evolves out of the combat myth*. The *Chaoskampf* tradition is not so much revived to articulate the cosmic battle between Yahweh and Satan; rather, the cosmic battle between Yahweh and Satan is a direct development from the cosmicsization of the combat myth.

Such is essentially the thesis of Neil Forsyth's substantial work on the origins and development of the Devil, *The Old Enemy: Satan and the Combat Myth*. In it, Forsyth persuasively demonstrates that the conception of the Devil found in early Jewish and Christian works in fact evolved out of that persistent ancient myth. So he writes:

> One of the chief characteristics of Jewish apocalyptic literature is the revival, both during and after the exile, of ancient mythological modes of thought. Some of these mythological modes were no doubt learned fresh from Babylon itself, or borrowed from the successive oppressors, Persian, Greek, and Roman, but for the most part they had come from Canaanite sources and had been carried, whether as allusion or metaphor, within the sacred texts of Judaism itself. Those sacred scriptures must now be seen in the whole context, made available by the archaeologists, of ancient Near Eastern mythological systems. From these ancient systems, a continuous series of transformations leads to the various Christian efforts to tell the story of Christ's struggle with Satan.[8]

So it is that, from the original mythological systems of the ancient Near East, the Devil himself takes shape.

In apocalyptic transformations of the combat myth, says Forsyth, the Devil functions as a variant of the *Chaoskampf* rebel. We have encountered this rebellion theme before. While it is perhaps most evident in the Ninurta/Anzu myth, Forsyth suggests that "there are enough fragments and allusions in other contexts to encourage the assumption that the rebel plot was indeed a common variant of the

---

[8] Forsyth, *The Old Enemy*, 12-13. In light of the arguments made above, the only qualification I would give to this statement is a critique of the word "revival." Additionally, Forsyth exclusively speaks of "sacred scriptures," which, even interpreted in its broadest sense (to include pseudepigrapha and other texts that did not become canonical), does not give adequate attention to non-textual sources, such as oral traditions, cultic practices, etc., as lines of transmission for these ancient mythological modes.

combat pattern."[9] He points specifically to the *Enûma Eliš* and the Baal Cycle as possessing aspects of this common variation.[10] However, he says, examples are more striking in the Hebrew tradition.[11]

Indeed, more recently Hugh Rowland Page, under the guidance of Frank Moore Cross, has posited the existence of a West Semitic myth of cosmic rebellion.[12] Like Forsyth, he sees Athtar, a figure in the Baal Cycle, as a potential prototypical anti-hero for such a myth. This myth, argues Page, has reflexes in biblical literature, the most notable examples of which are Isaiah 14 and Ezekiel 28 and 29—texts whose mythological overtones we have already considered. He concludes his argument with a hypothetical reconstruction of the rebellion myth, based mostly upon the later biblical texts which may attest it:

> After having enjoyed primacy of place within the pantheon as one of the creator's most perfect entities—endowed with wisdom and beauty (cf. Ezekiel 28:3,-3, 12b, 15, 17)—Athtar conspired to make war against El and wrest control of the pantheon and the cosmos from him. He was corrupted by the very characteristics that made him unique among his divine peers (Ezekiel 28:2, 5, 15-17) and his hubris led him to claim equality with El (Ezekiel 28:2, 6, 9; Isaiah 14:14). He boasts of sitting in El's throne (Ezekiel 28:2), of being in possession of a wisdom comparable to that of his wise patron and benefactor (Ezekiel 28:5), and, indeed, of being El (Ezekiel 29:9). He had honorable status on El's mountain (Ezekiel 28:13) where he communed with other astral gods before corruption led to his demise (Ezekiel 28:13-18). He aspired to rise above the circumpolar stars, to set his throne on El's mountain in the far north, to mount the clouds like Baal, and to make himself like Elyon (El) (Isaiah 14:13-15). He declared war against El and pitched his battle encampment at El's tent-shrine (Daniel 11:45). He was defeated, driven from his place on the holy mount (Ezekiel 28:16), and exiled to the underworld (Psalm 82:7; Isaiah 14:9-11, 14-19; Ezekiel 28:8).[13]

Whether or not such a West Semitic myth ever existed in such a concentrated form is certainly debatable. Indeed, it seems more likely that rebellion was simply the principle undercurrent of various combat myths: any challenge to existing kingship—be it from an Azag, Anzu, Yamm, Mot, or other villain—was essentially an act of rebellion against the prevailing and proper rule of the storm-god. In this sense

---

[9] Ibid., 126.
[10] Ibid., 126-32
[11] Ibid., 134-42.
[12] Hugh R. Page, *The Myth of Cosmic Rebellion: A Study of Its Reflexes in Ugaritic and Biblical Literature* (Leiden: E. J. Brill, 1996).
[13] Ibid., 206.

then, Forsyth need not speak of a rebellion "variant," since rebellion in a broad way lies at the heart of every combat myth. Likewise, Page's reconstruction is helpful principally as an abstraction of the various expressions of this persistent rebellion theme. It is the ideal that, though it likely never existed in any "pure" form, finds partial representation in most of the combat myths we have considered.[14]

Taken up by later apocalyptic writers, this rebellion theme in the combat myth proved highly effective at explaining one of the fundamental difficulties in the post-Exilic theodicy. So Gregory Boyd observes:

> Assuming that there is one eternal Creator God who is all-good and all-powerful, it is illogical to posit a foundational structural evil within the cosmos (which is the main point of the Chaoskampf passages) without postulating a significant rebellion at some previous point that has corrupted the cosmos (which is the subsidiary point of the Chaoskampf passages). In short, if the all-powerful Creator is perfectly good but creation is largely evil, something must have interfered with creation.[15]

Indeed, philosophical reflection on the origin and nature of evil no doubt provided one of the chief catalysts for the Devil's development. Israel's former theodicy of 1) national sin, 2) consequent punishment, 3) repentance, and 4) eventual redemption/salvation was strained to breaking with the calamities of the Exile. The traditional notion, insofar as it was articulated in prophetic literature, that Yahweh alone was the cause of both good and evil became increasingly untenable after the unrelenting suffering of captivity and subjugation. It is because of these trials that the concept of a Devil figure became theologically attractive at all. This theodicean theory lies at the core of Russell's analysis, who writes:

> Both sins and punishments were so frequent and so great that they seemed disproportionate to the powers of puny man to displease the deity. And always at the back of their minds the Hebrews wondered how it was that the God, all powerful and all knowing as he was, would permit humanity to sin. The corrupt will of human beings seemed insufficient to explain the vast and terrifying quantity of evil in the world. For an answer, the Hebrews turned to another explanation: the instigator of evil was a malignant spirit whose power to offend was far greater than that of mere mortals. The

---

[14] For a comprehensive concordance of texts which developed the rebellion/combat myth from ANE material into the New Testament, see ibid., 35-45

[15] Gregory A. Boyd, *God at War: The Bible & Spiritual Conflict* (Downers Grove: InterVarsity Press, 1997), 101-2.

If this were the reasoning, it was the combat myth that supplied the material from which to realize such a theological conception. In this way, the combat myth, already enlarged to a cosmic scope, becomes the vehicle for developing a dualistic conception in Judaism. The cosmic chaos-enemy becomes the Devil.

Because of this direct link with the ancient myth pattern, *the central themes of the combat myth have clear reflexes in apocalyptic eschatology*. Indeed, the fundamental issue of *order* still lies at its heart, though now with a decidedly more "spiritual" and less materialistic focus. Put another way, the basic focus has shifted from agricultural/institutional concerns to theological/metaphysical ones. Rather than answering "Why do the fields go barren, and when will fertility return?" it seeks to answer "Why is there evil in the world, and when will justice return?" In any event, the agricultural, cultic, political, and philosophical/theological concerns all carry over in modified form—that is, aggrandized and given cosmic revalorizations:

Agricultural. Agricultural ideas certainly have their cosmic reflexes in the apocalyptic combat myth. First, simple *rejuvenation* becomes the endless bounty of *the eschatological New Eden/Paradise*. Yahweh retains his essential character as the creator god—an identity once intricately linked with being god of the storm: the bringer of rain, fertility, and life. As the defeat of Sea, Dragon, and Death had ushered in a new year of growth, so the defeat of the Devil shall usher in a new paradisal world of perpetual abundance. All shall return to the way it had been at the first creation of the world—that is, the world will become a second Eden.

We already saw early glimpses of this in proto-apocalyptic texts. So Isaiah 35:6 spoke of the cosmic rejuvenation, saying:

> For waters shall break forth in the wilderness,
> and streams in the desert;
> the burning sand shall become a pool,
> and the thirsty ground springs of water;
> the haunt of jackals shall become a swamp,
> the grass shall become reeds and rushes.

---

[16] Russell, *The Devil: Perceptions of Evil from Antiquity to Primitive Christianity*, 182-3.

Similarly, Second Zechariah wrote that, on the day of Yahweh's final battle, "there shall be neither cold nor frost," and "living waters shall flow out of Jerusalem" which "shall continue in summer as in winter" (14:7-9). These notions are expanded in full-blown apocalypticism, where the defeat of the Devil shall be the necessary event to bring it all about.

Secondly, the idea of *revival* has its cosmic reflex in the idea of *resurrection of the dead*. Just as Yahweh's defeat of Death allowed the fields to revive, so will his defeat of the Devil allow the faithful to revive. As the ultimate source of evil and Chaos, the Devil's end is analogous to Mot's. Indeed, we have also seen the initial stages of this idea in proto-apocalyptic passages. So, in the Isaianic Apocalypse, the prophet rejoices,

> Your dead shall live, their corpses shall rise.
> > O dwellers in the dust, awake and sing for joy!
> For your dew is radiant dew,
> > and the earth will give birth to those long dead. (Is 26:19)

This revival shall occur precisely because, as we read a few verses later, it is on that day that Yahweh shall slay Leviathan. Indeed, on that day, Yahweh shall swallow Death! With the rise of full-scale apocalypticism, these ideas are developed into a complete theology of *resurrection*.

Cultic. We have also seen clear examples of how proto-apocalyptic prophets employed the chief cultic setting for the combat myth: the Israelite New Year festival—the Feast of Tabernacles. This association is also developed in apocalyptic eschatology. The New Year and its cultic rites become the very archetype for the cosmic New Year. Just as Yahweh and his people celebrated with a feast the god's defeat of the chaos-monsters (which re-created the world and returned it to its initial state of purity), so shall Yahweh and his people celebrate with a feast at his defeat of the Devil (which will create a new world free from all impurity).

Indeed, the Feast of Tabernacles itself becomes the cosmic eschatological banquet. This cosmic feast is already mentioned in the Isaianic Apocalypse when, after he has swallowed up Death,

> On this Mountain, Yahweh of Hosts will make for all peoples
> > a feast of rich food, a feast of well-aged wine,
> > of rich food full of marrow, of aged wine well refined. (Is 25:6, ESV)

In apocalyptic texts, this festival, the celebration of Yahweh's defeat of Chaos, is aggrandized to the cosmic festival at the end of time, celebrating Yahweh's defeat of the Devil.

Indeed, in its original sense the "Day of Yahweh" meant the New Year festival's day of procession. Then was the ark paraded and *seen* by the people, representing the great *epiphany* of Yahweh. In the apocalyptic aggrandizement, this becomes the "Day of Judgment" or the Day of Wrath, when the whole world shall see Yahweh come as the divine warrior and reassert his kingship. So in the Isaianic Apocalypse we read, "*On that Day*, Yahweh with his cruel and great and strong sword will punish Leviathan the fleeing serpent..." Indeed, the phrase "on that Day" repeatedly punctuates Second Zechariah's apocalyptic vision of the end. In his vision, we recall, it is on that Day that the nations will celebrate the Feast of Tabernacles. This Day *is* the Feast of Tabernacles—the eschatological Day of Yahweh.

Additionally, the rites of purification, so important to the earthly New Year festival, are eschatologized into a full-scale purification of the world and Yahweh's people. As we saw, these New Year purifications had meant a return to the original, pure time of creation— a time without tint, evil, or sickness. For this reason, purification and healing are essentially connected, and healing too is a recurrent aspect in apocalypticism. Even in Isaiah 35:5-6b, we read that, at the cosmic New Year,

> Then the eyes of the blind shall be opened,
> and the ears of the deaf unstopped;
> then the lame shall leap like a deer,
> and the tongue of the speechless sing for joy.

There can be no sickness or ill health when the cosmic New Year has revitalized all things. Even so, once Yahweh has defeated the Devil, all shall be made pure and healthy again.

Political. As with the combat myths of the ancient Near East, including Israel's, the apocalyptic combat myth creates direct historical associations between the chaos-enemy and the political enemy of the people. Indeed, this tendency is emphatically continued in apocalypticism, as the political enemies of Israel are literally aggrandized to mythic proportions. So Israel's overlords are equated with the beasts and monsters of Chaos. In the apocalyptic period, these are her Greek and Roman oppressors.

But the apocalyptic transformation of the myth takes this idea even further. Perhaps in keeping with its tendency to emphasize the spiritual over the material, it posits that these earthly oppressors are really but underlings of the true, cosmic enemy: the Devil. In this sense, Israel's political oppressors play a similar role to the "helpers" of the chief chaos-enemy, such as Ninurta's Stone Things, Yamm's Dragon, Tiamet's monstrous helpers, or even "the helpers of Rahab" in the Hebrew combat myth. In apocalypticism, political authorities are the Devil's "helpers."

Like the original myth, apocalypticism sees played out in the world a *competition for kingship*. One king is the god of order and life, the other of Chaos and destruction. The result of the ensuing battle shall determine the state of the cosmos as one of abundance, order, and justice, or one of death, Chaos, and evil. As the rebel of the apocalyptic combat myth, it is the Devil who has challenged Yahweh's supreme reign. The Kingdom of the Devil has waged war against the Kingdom of God.

However, in a striking theological application of the myth, apocalypticists interpreted their current world of suffering and sin as signifying, in some sense, the temporary triumph of the Devil. In essence, the Devil has indeed usurped kingship from Yahweh, such that *he now rules the world*. This is why he is able to control the nations and oppress Israel. It is because of this usurpation that justice and peace for Yahweh's people has been so frustrated. Only with Yahweh's return and the second round of the battle can Israel ever be saved. In short, the earthly world of the apocalypticist exists between functions 7 and 8 in Forsyth's schema: *Enemy ascendant*, and *Hero recovers*. At any moment, the *battle may be rejoined*. Indeed, this is the most fervent hope of the apocalypticist. For after this comes Victory.

Philosophical/Theological. Even in the pre-apocalyptic understanding of the combat myth, the divine warrior's victory says something about the cosmos: the good god of order wins. He is powerful over the forces of Chaos; he can defeat them, and has. Thus, though the fields went barren and chaotic forces took hold of the world for a time, the god of order and prosperity was still in charge—he was king.

This same sense of assurance and ultimate optimism (if it may be so called) lies at the heart of the apocalyptic battle. Indeed, this is what Clifford means when he says that, of the ancient genres which most influenced apocalypticism, "the most important by far is the combat myth, for it provided not only imagery but also a conceptual framework for explaining divine rule over the world."[17] This conceptual framework posits that Chaos and its dominance *will* be defeated. Though in the apocalyptic transformation this Chaos has been enlarged from agricultural dearth to ultimate ruin, disaster, and catastrophe, so too has the rejuvenation been enlarged. The combat shall end in victory; the power and scope of the enemy is proportional to the totality of the renewal. Just as, when sterility and death had overtaken the land, Yahweh had arrived, beaten back the forces of Chaos, and ensured order and fertility in the cosmos—so too, when evil and suffering have utterly consumed Israel, shall Yahweh come, destroy the forces of the Devil, and ensure justice and eternal life for his people. Such are the ways in which the original themes and concerns of the combat myth revalorized with cosmic, eschatological significance.

Before moving forward now with a survey of some apocalyptic texts with clear links to the *Chaoskampf* tradition, it is pertinent to summarize the general assertions so far considered. 1) Mythic frameworks are a dominant aspect of apocalypticism. This probably owes to the general persistence of myth's significance in Israelite religion, from ancient times to the apocalyptic period. 2) This continuity of myth does well to explain the remarkable antiquity of mythic material in apocalyptic texts, which evince familiarity with particularly ancient traditions. 3) Unfortunately, given the nature of the sources, the specific lines of transmission which linked writers of the apocalyptic period with these very ancient traditions is not always clear. 4) The most important myth pattern for apocalyptic eschatology was the combat myth. Indeed, the Devil evolved out of, and for this reason found articulation through, apocalyptic transformations of this ancient myth. 5) Because of this genetic relationship, the combat myth's agricultural, cultic, political, and philosophical/theological concerns reappear in the apocalyptic transformation of the myth, though now projected to a cosmic level. There is similar continuity with the typical images and structure of the myth.

These points reiterated, I shall now present a brief consideration of apocalyptic texts which give some evidence for these assertions. From them one can glean the importance of the combat myth for the apocalyptic worldview, and, with this appreciation, start upon analysis of the Gospel of Mark.

---

[17] Clifford, "The Roots of Apocalypticism," 4.

As noted above, the theme of rebellion in the combat myth was crucial for developing a new theology of sin and evil centered upon a Devil figure. This idea of the Devil as cosmic rebel finds perhaps its earliest and most influential expression in the apocalyptic work *1 Enoch*. The text as we have it now is probably a composite of various material written between the fourth and first centuries CE.[18] In it, we get an early glimpse of the Devil evolving out of the combat myth as the rebel angel.

One of the work's earliest sections develops an enticingly brief story found in Geneses 6:1-4, in which the "sons of God" descend from heaven in order to copulate with mortal women in the antediluvian period. However, the author of *1 Enoch* strikingly adapts this older story by depicting the "sons of god" as the Watchers: angels in heaven who lust after women on earth. Led by the angels Azazel and Semjaza, these Watchers form a pact to transgress Yahweh's laws and eventually descend to earth to fulfill their evil desires.

As in Genesis, their intercourse with women produces Giants. Here, however, the Giants are not great men or heroes, but destructive abominations who eventually attack human beings and terrorize the earth. In addition to all of this, the Watchers also reveal forbidden heavenly knowledge to mortals, including divination, astrology, and the making of war materials. Through all of these acts, wickedness and suffering are introduced into the world—not by Yahweh, nor by man, but by rebellious angels.

Eventually, the chief angels alert Yahweh to these disasters, at which point the god intervenes to put an end to the evils. So he commands that Azazel and Semjaza be bound and imprisoned:

> And secondly the Lord said to Raphael, "*Bind Azaz'el hand and foot* (and) throw him into the darkness!" And he made a hole *in the desert* which was in Duda'el and *cast him there*; he threw on top of him rugged and sharp rocks. And he covered his face in order that he may not see light; and in order that he may be sent into the fire on the great Day of Judgment. (1 Enoch 10:4-6a)

Michael is ordered to do the same with Semjaza, binding him to be left captive in the earth until the Day of Judgment. Such means of defeat clearly employs the imagery of the combat myth. The *binding* motif is

---

[18] OTP 1.6-7.

obvious and recalls the fate of numerous chaos-enemies. Moreover, by being cast into a pit in the desert, recurrent elements of the *scattering* motif are present, as the bodies of Yamm/the Dragon, Leviathan, and the cosmic rebel in Ezekiel 29 were all cast into the desert after their defeat.

After subduing the rebellious angelic leaders is complete, a cosmic rejuvenation is promised for the world:

> And then shall the whole earth be tilled in righteousness, and shall all be planted with trees and be full of blessing. And all desirable trees shall be planted on it, and they shall plant vines on it: and *the vine which they plant thereon shall yield wine in abundance, and as for all the seed which is sown thereon each measure (of it) shall bear a thousand, and each measure of olives shall yield ten presses of oil. And cleanse thou the earth from all oppression, and from all unrighteousness, and from all sin, and from all godlessness: and all the uncleanness that is wrought upon the earth destroy from off the earth.* And all the children of men shall become righteous, and all nations shall offer adoration and shall praise Me, and all shall worship Me. And the earth shall be *cleansed from all defilement, and from all sin,* and from all punishment, and from all torment, and I will never again send (them) upon it from generation to generation and for ever. (1 Enoch 10:18-22)

So are the cultic revalorations of the New Year (already developed in late prophecy) clearly apparent here. The "Day of Judgment" is, we have seen, the eschatological aggrandizement of the Day of Yahweh—the god's cultic epiphany at his New Year procession. While in prophecy, it had been Israel's salvation from historical enemies that would occur "on that Day," here we see for the first time the idea that *the cosmic enem(y/ies)* shall be ultimately defeated on the Day of Yahweh. The cosmic New Year shall destroy all Devils and the evil they caused just as the seasonal New Year had destroyed Mot and the barrenness he had caused. The result is agricultural rejuvenation on a cosmic scale, while the ritual *re-purification* of the festival is transformed into a complete annulment of sin and defilement. The earth shall be completely cleansed of iniquity. Finally, as Second Zechariah prophesied a whole world celebrating one giant Feast of Tabernacles, so too does the writer of *1 Enoch* envision the whole earth worshiping Yahweh.

But this glorious end is still some time away. The Day of Yahweh still lies in the future. Until then, humanity must cope with the evils unleashed by the rebel angels. Indeed, while the Giants themselves were immediately destroyed, their spirits continue to exist upon the earth, attacking and oppressing humans just as the Giants had done:

> They will become evil upon the earth and shall be called evil spirits…And these spirits shall rise up against the children of the people and against the women, because they have proceeded forth (from them). (1 Enoch 15:9, 12.)

As with the Devils, these spirits will only be subdued on the "Day of the Great Conclusion" (1 Enoch 16:1-2). Only the cosmic New Year can truly eradicate these oppressive forces from the world.

This account of the Watchers is exemplary of the theological developments taking place during the apocalyptic period. In it, we glimpse one early attempt to flesh out a new spiritual figure, the Devil (or, in this case, Devil*s*), from traditional religious material—specifically the combat myth. Theodicean concerns are clearly one principal catalyst for such innovation, as the ancient workings of rebel angels helped to justify Israel's suffering with Yahweh's benevolence and power.[19] Indeed, it is by no means insignificant that the rise of evil spirits—which become prominent in Jewish theology only during the apocalyptic period—is explained *qua* the theodicy of the cosmic combat myth. Such evil spirits, of course, play a crucial role in the Gospel of Mark.

Another interesting aspect of this story, which we shall see reoccur in various apocalyptic combat myths, is that *Yahweh himself does not battle the Devil*. Rather, he delegates this "dirty work" to his chief angels, Raphael and Michael. Why the author (or the tradition which he records) opted for this vicarious conflict is not entirely clear. Nevertheless, we sometimes see in various texts of the apocalyptic period a Yahweh who is less the charging warrior god and more the ultimate Judge, sitting at the head of the Divine Council. Indeed, it is the Council itself (made up of those lesser spiritual beings such as the "sons of god") which preoccupies so much apocalyptic speculation. In this sense then, Yahweh assimilates more into the role of the Canaanite El, while his more active and aggressive doings (one might say his Baal-like characteristics) become the domain of his angelic underlings. In any event, it is clear that the rebel angels are defeated *at Yahweh's*

---

[19] 10:12 reads, "And the whole earth has been corrupted through the works that were taught by Azazel: *to him ascribe all sin*."

command, if not by his own hand. The role of "hero" is thus played by a kind of heavenly coalition.

The Watchers story of *1 Enoch* features many elements of the typical combat myth plotline: (1) *Lack/Villainy*: Semjaza and Azazel's rebel angels flaunt Yahweh's reign by transgressing his decrees. (3) *Donor/Consultation*: The archangels of heaven inform Yahweh of the evil and suffering on earth. (5) Yahweh orders Raphael and Michael to bind the rebel angels and cast them into desert prisons. (10) *Victory*: The enemies shall be completely destroyed on the Day of Judgment. (11) *Enemy Punished*: Their bodies shall be cast into the fire. (12) *Triumph*: As the earth blooms in cosmic abundance, Yahweh will be worshipped by all people.

One might also compare the progression of the story with Hanson's elements of the "Divine Warrior Hymn":

<pre>
6:1-9:11   1) Threat
10:1-16   2) Combat – victory over enemy
10:17   3) Salvation of his people
10:18-22   4) Shalom (return to fertility – new creation)
</pre>

Thus, while not exhibiting every narrative element of the combat myth pattern, the general progression is there, as are some of its common motifs.

With regard to themes, the agricultural and cultic reflexes are most apparent, while questions of kingship and historical/political associations seem largely lacking. However, the philosophical and theological component is, in many ways, fundamental here: the combat myth is clearly the chief means by which theodicean concerns are developed and Yahweh's ultimate sovereignty over the world affirmed.

Yahweh vs. Satan/the Serpent (The Life of Adam and Eve)

While *1 Enoch* was one early and particularly influential attempt to flesh out the Devil and the origin of evil, it was by no means the last word on the subject. The Devil continued to be developed and reimagined in other texts of the apocalyptic period, some of which present the rebellion theme in a manner that would eventually gain wide popularity (and so more familiar to us today). One such text seems to have been the *Life of Adam and Eve*, which, composed sometime between 100 BCE and 200 CE,[20] cements the connection between the Devil and the rebellious chaos-enemy from the combat myth.

Here, the Devil is called by his more familiar name, Satan, while the subject of his rebellion is drawn not from Genesis 6, but Genesis 2: the story of Adam and Eve. Interestingly, the account is written from Satan's perspective, who narrates his fall to Adam. Satan says that, after God made Adam, he ordered his angels to worship his new creation. When Satan refused, Michael compelled him further:

> And Michael asserted, 'Worship the image of God. But if now you will not worship, the Lord God will be wrathful with you.' And I said, 'If he be wrathful with me, *I will set my throne above the stars of heaven and will be like the Most High.'*
> And the Lord God was angry with me and sent me with my angels out from our glory; and because of you we were expelled into this world from our dwellings and have been *cast onto earth.*[21]

Again, the Devil is *cast out* with force and thrown to earth—probably a variant of the *scattering* motif, if now barely perceptible since stripped of its original components. More obvious in this account is the allusion to the cosmic rebel of Isaiah 14, which explicitly links Satan with the mythic enemy of Yahweh. Satan is the cosmic enemy who would depose Yahweh and enthrone himself on the Canaanite storm-god's mountain as king over the cosmos. Yet this rebellion does not succeed, and Yahweh hurls Satan headlong to the earth. In his analysis, Forsyth observes that "[t]he story is a resurgence of an old Near Eastern myth pattern. It is adapted now by scattered allusions to the Old Testament, but the plot itself has no canonical foundation."[22] The traditional combat myth informs this composition even more than do canonical biblical texts.

Out of jealousy and revenge, Satan then seeks to attack the man responsible for his expulsion. To do this, he tempts Eve as a serpent in the Garden. With this connection of Satan and serpent, the author links the Genesis account of mankind's expulsion—part of the traditional theodicy—to the combat myth of the rebel angel. The Devil is now the Serpent, uniting all the serpentine and draconic associations of chaos-

---

[20] OTP 2.252.
[21] *Life of Adam and Eve* 14:3-16:1 in OTP 1.262.
[22] Forsyth, *The Old Enemy*, 238.

monsters with God's cosmic enemy. *The Devil is the Dragon.* Forsyth notes:

> Here at last the serpent of Genesis is linked to the apocalyptic adversary, and his name is explicitly Satan. ...*Diabolos* [Devil], we have seen, was the word used generally in the Septuagint to translate the Hebrew *śṭn.* By now both words imply the whole apocalyptic combat myth. The tempter is the cosmic adversary.[23]

The Son of Man vs. the Beast of the Sea (Daniel)

Under the Persians (whose defeat of Babylon allowed their new subjects to return to Israel), Jews maintained a complex relationship with their imperial overlords, but certainly not one characterized by intractable hostility. However, after Alexander's defeat of Persia brought Israel under Greek control, this dynamic fundamentally changes. In 167 BCE, taking political advantage of internecine strife in Jerusalem, the Syrian military under the Seleucid King Antiochus Epiphanes intervened with a harsh hand. Antiochus then set to work on an intense Hellenization campaign, suppressing Jewish customs, forbidding circumcision, and setting up a foreign cult in the Jewish Temple. All of this was anathema to most Jews—even those who had supported various Hellenizing aspects before this intervention. Tensions aroused sentiments of enmity toward their foreign overlords not attested since the Babylonian Exile.

Eventually, these tensions exploded into open revolt and insurrection against their Greek oppressors and, influenced by the theological developments of apocalypticism, many understood the struggle in cosmic terms. The Devil himself was seen as waging war against God's holy ones via his earthly Greek commander, Antiochus. Like the Chaos and destruction occasioned by Yam or Mot's ascendency, the persecution owed but to the temporary ascendancy of the Devil over the world. However, God would soon step in as the divine warrior and fight for his oppressed people. The Beast would be destroyed, and justice would return with the final realization of the prophets' message of the cosmic New Year.

---

[23] Ibid., 232, 233.

Such thinking lies at the heart of the apocalyptic vision in the seventh chapter of Daniel:

> I, Daniel, saw in my vision by night the four winds of heaven stirring up the great Sea, and four great Beasts came up out of the Sea, different from one another. (Dan 7:2-3)

The beasts are undoubtedly chaos-monsters, arising out of a chaotic and raging Sea.[24] However, as we are later told, they also represent historical kingdoms of the earth (most likely the Neo-Babylonians, the Medes, and the Persians).[25] With this connection, the author continues the ancient tradition of linking historical enemies with mythic chaos-monsters. The last Beast to appear is apparently the worst, described as "terrifying and dreadful and exceedingly strong" as it had "great iron teeth and was devouring, breaking in pieces, and stamping what was left with its feet" (v. 7). This Beast has ten horns, and a small one that rises up with "a mouth speaking arrogantly" (v. 8). With this description, the author paints the final Beast, the Greek kingdom, as the most terrible. The little horn speaking arrogantly is Antiochus Epiphanes himself,[26] and his arrogance echoes the pride of the rebellious chaos-enemies of Isaiah 14, Ezekiel 28 and 29—texts we have seen apocalyptic writers use to flesh out the identity of the Devil.

The vision continues:

> As I watched,
> thrones were set in place,
>   and an Ancient of Days took his throne,
> His clothing was white as snow,
>   and the hair of his head like pure wool;
> His throne was fiery flames,
>   and its wheels were burning fire.
> A stream of fire issued
>   and flowed out from his presence.

---

[24] Interestingly, the first Beast, with its lion's body and eagle wings, recalls the Anzu bird: the chaos-monster from the Babylonian Ninurta/Anzu combat myth, which has both lion and bird-like features. For this connection specifically, and the relationship of Daniel 7 to the combat myth generally, see John H. Walton, "The *Anzu* Myth as Relevent Background for Daniel 7?" in *The Book of Daniel: Composition and Reception*, ed. John J. Collins and Peter W. Flint (Leiden: Brill, 2001). There is general consensus about the idea that the sea in Dan 7:2 recalls the Chaotic Sea of ancient Near Eastern combat myths. For this, see the bibliography in Angel, *Chaos and the Son of Man*, 100 n. 4.

[25] John J. Collins, *Daniel: A Commentary on the Book of Daniel*, Hermeneia (Minneapolis: Fortress Press, 1993), 295ff.

[26] Ibid., 278.

> A thousand thousands served him,
>   and ten thousand times ten thousand stood attending him.
> The Court sat in judgment,
>   and the books were opened. (Dan 7:9-10)

So the Divine Council convenes in judgment, with an *enthronement* of the head deity, here called the Ancient of Days. Strikingly, the description of this figure lacks precedent in the Hebrew Bible, as nowhere else in canonical texts is Yahweh described as an elderly figure. Indeed, the author seems rather to be drawing upon traditional mythology—probably Hebrew in source but, since lost, recognizable now only through comparisons with Canaanite sources. Thus, in Ugaritic conceptions of the head god, El—the "Father of Years"—is an old man with a gray beard, as mentioned in *CTA* 3.5.10 and *CTA* 4.5.65-66.[27] We shall consider these mythological reflexes in more depth momentarily.

Daniel's vision concludes with the defeat of the Beast:

> I watched then because of the noise of the arrogant words that the horn was speaking. And as I watched, *the Beast was put to death, and its body destroyed* and given over to be burned with fire. *As for the rest of the Beasts, their dominion was taken away*, but their lives were prolonged for a season and a time. As I watched in the night visions,
> > I saw one like a son of man
> >   coming with the clouds of heaven.
> > And he came to the Ancient of Days
> >   and was presented before him.
> > *To him was given dominion*
> >   *and glory and kingship*,
> > that all peoples, nations, and languages
> >   should serve him.
> > His dominion is an everlasting dominion
> >   that shall not pass away,
> > and *his kingship is one*
> >   *that shall never be destroyed*. (Dan 7:11-14)

So the chaos-monster is slain, while the slayer himself is introduced in the following lines as the "one like a son of man coming with the clouds of heaven."[28] The Beast's body is then destroyed—the usual fate of the defeated chaos-monster—here given over to be burned with fire.

---

[27] Ibid., 301 n. 216.

[28] While the text is ambiguous on this point, I side with Day, who writes, "Although not explicitly stated, we are probably to understand that the one like a son of man himself (under God) defeated the dragon." Day, *God's Conflict*, 162. Collins, less definite, at

Just who this "son of man" figure is, and the position he serves, has long been the subject of debate. He is undoubtedly a being of some divine status, but the idea of two ruling gods is foreign to the Jewish tradition. This has led commentators such as John J. Collins to posit that "[t]his configuration has no precedent in the biblical tradition. It is quite intelligible, however, against the background of Canaanite mythology."[29] In the Canaanite configuration, one does find an elderly god who sits as head of the Divine Assembly—El, the "Father of Years"—and a subservient god of the younger generation whose defeat of a chaos-monster initiates the head deity's conferment of kingship: Baal, the "Rider of the Clouds." In Daniel 7, this figure most likely symbolizes the archangel Michael: the heavenly representative of the Jewish people.[30] The vision is thus ultimately about Israel's final defeat of her adversaries, both earthly and cosmic, and the power that will soon be hers with God's intervention.

Again, however, it is important to stress that the author of Daniel 7 is not drawing from Canaanite mythology, and certainly not from the Ugaritic material specifically. Such dependence would be impossible, as Collins makes clear: "No one would argue that the extant Ugaritic texts were the actual sources on which the author of Daniel 7 drew. There is an interval of more than a thousand years between these texts and the composition of Daniel."[31] Rather, he asserts what I have been emphasizing throughout this monograph, that *the Canaanite tradition was transmitted down to the first century through sources, whether Jewish or pagan, that are no longer extant.*[32] Indeed, rather than turning to foreign sources, "the author of Daniel was using imagery that had long been at home in the religion of Israel."[33] Thus, the author of Daniel 7, writing around 165 BCE, gives concrete evidence that the Hebrew combat myth was still flourishing in the apocalyptic period, the

---

least challenges some scholars' assumptions that the dragon is *not* defeated in combat, for in fact, he defends, "we are not told how it meets its demise." See Collins, *Daniel*, 303-4 n. 237.

[29] *Daniel*, 290; cf. 291, 294. The idea was first proposed at length in J. A. Emerton, "The Origin of the Son of Man Imagery," *JTS* 9 (1958): 225-242. It has since gained increasing support. Cf. Clifford, "The Roots of Apocalypticism," 33; Day, *God's Conflict*, 157-77; Angel, *Chaos and the Son of Man*, 102-10.

[30] Collins, *Daniel*, 310; Day, *God's Conflict*, 167.

[31] Collins, *Daniel*, 291.

[32] Ibid., 288-289; emphasis mine. See also 59-60.

[33] Ibid., 292. Cf. Day, *God's Conflict*, 166.

myth itself having been transmitted from ancient times through sources now lost to history.

Indeed, it is clear that there was knowledge of such mythic conceptions up to the second century BCE and beyond. Andrew Angel has provided a survey of definite *Chaoskampf* imagery in use from 515 BCE all the way to 200 CE.[34] We can be fairly certain then that the traditional combat myth continued to flourish in Jewish religion and, though not emphasized in the texts that now comprise most of the Hebrew Bible, had long been kept alive in the tradition. We can assume that the author of Daniel 7 not only had knowledge of configurations that to us now seem more Canaanite than Hebrew, but that he could expect his Jewish audience to understand and appreciate these allusions as well.

Probing further into the principle means of transmission for this mythic pattern, some scholars have stressed the continuity of cult and ritual practice for the combat myth's persistence. Indeed, the durability of ritual action over time gives this theory some weight, while it also helps to explain the lack of written sources attesting clear transmission. So J. A. Emerton, following Aage Bentzen,[35] posited that *the author of Daniel inherited this complex of mythological motifs from Israel's autumnal New Year festival*. He writes:

> If Mowinckel's theory be accepted—and it must suffice here to express the opinion that it is essentially right, however much it may need to be modified in details—then it can hardly be denied that Dan. vii reflects the imagery of the festival. The beasts rising from the sea, the salvation of Israel, and the act of receiving kingship all suggest the complex of ideas of the enthronement festival. Dan. vii is an eschatological form of the situation of that festival. [...] Bentzen is no doubt right in connecting Dan. vii and the Israelite enthronement festival, and in thinking that *this was the channel by which Canaanite mythological imagery reached the apocalyptic writer*.[36]

If such a hypothesis is true in any meaningful way, it would mean that the core of the New Year festival's mythic underpinnings were alive and well even in the second century BCE. The continuity of Israelite cult would have provided a key means of transmission for the Hebrew combat myth. Indeed, in his consideration of the Enthronement Psalms and cultic continuity, Mowinckel writes:

---

[34] Angel, *Chaos and the Son of Man*.

[35] Aage Bentzen, *King and Messiah* (London: Lutterworth Press, 1955), 74ff., 109f.

[36] Emerton, "The Origin of the Son of Man Imagery," 230-1; emphasis mine.

Likewise, considering the eventual separation of the New Year festival into two separate festivals (that of Yom Kippur and the Feast of Tabernacles), he writes, "This did not make the latter lose its old character [as the New Year enthronement festival], on the contrary it remained still very much alive in the rites as well as psalms *till the fall of the Temple*, and was even known to the tradition of the Mishna."[38]

All of this is not to say, of course, that the New Year festival—as it had been celebrated in ancient Judah—continued unchanged into the first century CE. What it does show, however, is that the central myths and functions of that festival were still, at the very least, so much engrained in the cultural memory of Jews of the apocalyptic era that they could be employed in apocalyptic literature for the articulation of eschatological conceptions to an audience likewise familiar with such traditions. Cultural memory of the New Year festival, with so much of its mythic underpinning, had continued on through cult and oral tradition. Apocalyptic writers, just like the later prophets, had these traditions at their disposal to articulate the theological concerns of cosmic restoration.

To return to the text, however, we see that the traditional themes of the combat myth are here present in their apocalyptic transformations. The *cultic* reflexes are evident in their allusions to the New Year festival. Just as Yahweh was ritually enthroned at the festival, having processed to his temple after defeating the chaos-monsters, so do we see here a scene of enthronement and conferral of kingship after the defeat of the Beast of the Sea. This ties in well of course with the *political* aspect, as the whole conflict is understood in both historical and cosmic terms: the war between the Jews and the Greeks has its spiritual parallel in the heavens as a battle between the Rider of the Clouds and the Beast of the Sea. The Devil's kingdom is defeated, and his helpers are deprived of power, while the Kingdom of

---

[37] Mowinckel, *The Psalms in Israel's Worship*, 117.
[38] Ibid., 123; emphasis mine.

God is reasserted and the angelic slayer of the Beast given rule. Apart from the usual *philosophical* significance of Yahweh's ultimate victory over Chaos, the combat myth in Daniel proves *theologically* important for developing novel conceptions of the deity and the powers in heaven. We see now the angel, to whom Yahweh had delegated the task of slaying the chaos-enemy, gain particular prominence. In some ways, the emphasis has shifted away from Yahweh entirely, who now, in his more passive El-like position, merely presides over the action. Meanwhile the active Beast-slayer, this angelic "one like a son of man" (who may be Michael) comes to the fore as the more direct savior of Israel. In this way, the ancient Canaanite configuration of the combat myth is crucial for reimagining roles and relationships in the heavenly court. Indeed, this new emphasis on Yahweh's delegate in the combat becomes crucial for developments of the messiah figure in Jewish apocalypticism, and so ultimately in early Christianity.

Surprisingly little traditional imagery is used in this text. We see no binding, no trampling, no scattering of the body. The battle itself is not narrated, while the punishment of the body is not by dismemberment, but by the increasingly popular apocalyptic motif: destruction by fire.

Despite this dearth of traditional imagery, the story is notable for its strong adherence to the traditional structure of the combat myth. Indeed, until now we have not seen a complete narrative depiction of any Hebrew combat myth, but only its mythic imagery. Here, however, in this apocalyptic vision of Daniel, we see a full-fledged combat myth. With regards to Forsyth's plot schema, we find the main elements: (1) *Lack/Villainy*: Terrifying and destructive Beasts arise out of the raging Sea. The last Beast is the worst, and its little horn wages war against God's holy ones. (2) *Hero emerges/prepares to act*: The Ancient of Days comes into the Court and takes his throne. (3) *Donor/Consultation*: The Divine Council meets and the books are opened. The *Battle* (5) itself is not described. (10) *Victory*: The Beast and its haughty horn are put to death. (11) *Enemy Punished*: Its body is destroyed and given over to be burned in fire. The other Beasts lose their dominion. (12) *Triumph*: One like a son of man travels (cf. processes) to the cosmic Court (cf. Temple) and receives kingship from the Ancient of Days. His dominion over the cosmos is assured forever.

Again, however, in this text the "hero" role is not occupied solely by Yahweh—a configuration noted earlier with regard to the *1 Enoch* story, where Raphael and Michael are assigned the act of combat. In a similar way, the role of "hero" here seems to be filled by a kind of coalition between the Ancient of Days, the "one like a son of man," and also the "holy ones of the Most High." Indeed, the role of the "holy ones of the Most High" should not be overlooked, for they too are instrumental in this coalition. In the angelic explanation of the vision to Daniel, the triumph of the "one like a son of man" corresponds to the triumph of "the holy ones of the Most High":

Son of Man (vision)	The Holy Ones (explanation)
To him was given dominion and glory and kingship, that all peoples, nations, and languages should serve him. His dominion is an everlasting dominion that shall not pass away, and his kingship is one that shall never be destroyed. (v. 14)	The kingship and dominion and the greatness of the kingdoms under the whole heaven shall be given to the people of the holy ones of the Most High; their kingdom shall be an everlasting kingdom, and all dominions shall serve and obey them. (v. 26)

When we recognize this, even functions 6-9 are present, for preceding the explanation of the vision, the author recounts:

> As I looked, this horn made war with the holy ones *and was prevailing over them*, until the Ancient of Days came; then judgment was given for the holy ones of the Most High, and the time arrived when the holy ones gained possession of the kingdom. (Dan 7:21-22)

Thus we see (6) *Defeat*: The holy ones of the Most High fight the horn of the Beast but are not successful. (7) *Enemy ascendant*: The horn of the Beast is prevailing. (8) *The hero recovers* when the Ancient of Days comes, and then (9) *the battle is rejoined* when the son of man slays the Beast. Daniel 7 therefore represents a fairly complete apocalyptic combat myth.

Messiahs vs. Beliar (Testaments of the Twelve Patriarchs)

The Jewish revolt against the Seleucids ultimately proved successful and led to the establishment of an autonomous Jewish kingdom. This was the first time Jews ruled their own land since the Babylonian invasion over four hundred years earlier. However, once again it did not take long before many felt that the imperfections of this new kingdom did not reflect the utopian vision of the cosmic rejuvenation anticipated. Trial and disappointment did not end with the defeat of their Greek overlords, and so in many ways life continued on as usual despite this new autonomy.

Consequently, apocalyptic expectations and eschatological musings did not disappear, but continued with all the passion and ultra-certainty of the zealous. A composition called the *Testaments of the Twelve Patriarchs* is but one example of the evolving apocalyptic tradition in the centuries following the Maccabean revolt. While there is considerable debate over the date and provenance of its original composition, many scholars believe it to be a Jewish document written sometime in the last two centuries BCE which eventually saw minor Christian edits and interpolations.[39] As the purported last-words of the twelve sons of Jacob, the text also incorporates apocalyptic-style visions and is exemplary of the general apocalyptic perspective found in many works of this period.

Indeed, the author makes frequent though scattered allusions to the Hebrew *Chaoskampf* tradition in articulating his vision of the coming end times. These frequent allusions reveal a larger continuity with the combat myth tradition. We thus encounter the traditional themes in their apocalyptic transformations. Political concerns are pronounced, as the critique of current authorities and ruling powers is expressed in terms of the combat myth. Historical enemies continue to be presented as chaos-monsters and the raging Sea, as in the *Testament of Judah*:

> Those who rule shall be like sea monsters,
>> swallowing up human beings like fish.
> Free sons and daughters they shall enslave;
>> houses, fields, flocks, goods they shall seize.
> …Like a whirlwind shall be the false prophets:
>> They shall harass the righteous.[40]

Here we find a familiar scene: the sea monster and tempestuous winds stirring up ominous dangers for the righteous. The rapaciousness of the chaos-monster, specifically Death and his insatiable appetite, may also be at work here. Suffering, clearly, is not over, and the righteous will continue to experience the persecutions of those who have acquired their earthly power from the Devil.

---

[39] OTP 1.777-78.
[40] *T. Judah* 21:7, 9. All *Testaments* translations from OTP 1.782-828.

One notable aspect though is the inclusion of *religious* authorities in the camp of the chaos-enemy. False prophets, as well as evil rulers, are all helpers of the Devil. The idea of "the enemy" now includes not just foreign oppressors, but members of the Jewish community itself. The opposing camps are no longer construed along ethnic, political, or broadly religious lines (e.g., Israel against Babylon, *our* king against *their* king, Jew against Greek), but actually *within* Judaism itself. There can be righteous as well as unrighteous Jews. The latter are also classed with the Devil, for they too are deemed oppressive.

However, this unfortunate situation *will* change when God finally steps in to right the wrongs of the virtuous. So Asher shares with his children a "prophecy" of Israel's future troubles and eventual salvation:

> For I know that you will sin and be delivered into the hands of your enemies; your land shall be made desolate and *your sanctuary wholly polluted.* You will be scattered to the four corners of the earth; in the dispersion you shall be regarded as worthless, like useless water, *until such time as the Most High visits the earth.* [He shall come as a man eating and drinking with human beings,] *crushing the Dragon's head in the water.* He will save Israel and all the nations, [God speaking like a man].[41]

Here the final struggle is articulated using the cultic language of the New Year. At the end, the Temple shall be polluted and require re-purification, just as it did during the festival. Most striking in this passage, however, is the language that so clearly parallels God's primordial battle with the Dragon and his final eschatological battle with evil at the culmination of history. The text recalls Psalm 74:13-14, in which the psalmist reminds God, "You broke the heads of the Dragons in the waters. You crushed the heads of Leviathan." So will God crush Satan in the final apocalyptic battle. For the apocalypticist, the connection with the Devil and the Dragon of the combat myth is well-cemented. It is now a given that to slay Leviathan is to defeat Satan.

Indeed, apocalyptic warfare is a persistent and important theme in the *Testaments*. In the text, the Devil is called Beliar,[42] and he oppresses the righteous through the power he has over the world. It is

---

[41] *T. Ash.* 7:2-3. The bracketed elements are most probably later Christian interpolations.

[42] Though the name "Satan" is used a number of times to refer to God's cosmic adversary, by far the more popular designation is Beliar, which occurs no less than 29 times. See Harm W. Hollander and Marinus de Jonge, *The Testaments of the Twelve Patriarchs: A Commentary,* Studia in Veteris Testamenti Pseudepigrapha (Leiden: E.J. Brill, 1985), 49.

clear that the author envisions two warring camps—indeed, two kingdoms—of divine beings. On the one hand is God and all his host, and in opposition: Beliar and his evil spirits. As in the traditional myth, only one can claim kingship, while the identity of the king determines the nature of existence. Beliar must be defeated if the righteous are to prosper.

In the *Testaments* this ultimate victory is promised. Though, like the other apocalyptic combats thus far considered, Yahweh is not necessarily the specific agent of Beliar's defeat. Rather, two messianic figures, one royal and one priestly, shall be delegated the task of battling the Devil. We saw a similar configuration in analysis of Daniel 7. In some ways, the prominence of the son of man figure in that text prefigures the importance that the delegate of Yahweh would play in apocalyptic battle. Indeed, while we may take the bracketed sections in the previous passage as later Christian interpolations, it may be possible that they are indeed original and actually *anticipate/inform* the Christian conception of a divine-human figure who slays the Beast. In this sense, the ambiguous one *like* a son of man in Daniel 7, though probably an angel in that composition, is with time developed into an *actual* son of man figure: a human messiah figure who shall come and crush the heads of the Dragon at the end. However, given how much the identity of the messiah was then in flux, it is extremely difficult to draw any definite lines of dependence.

In any event, the *Testaments* mention two messianic figures of some sort who will, like the angelic warriors of the other apocalyptic combats, defeat the Devil and usher in the cosmic rejuvenation:

> And there shall arise for you from the tribe of Judah and (the tribe of) Levi
> the Lord's salvation.
> *He will make war against Beliar;*
> He will grant the vengeance of victory as our goal.
> And he shall take from Beliar the captives, the souls of the saints;
> And he shall turn the hearts of the disobedient ones to the Lord,
> And grant eternal peace to those who call upon him.
> *And the saints shall refresh themselves in Eden;*
> *The righteous shall rejoice in the New Jerusalem,*
> Which shall be eternally for the glorification of God.[43]

The messiah(s) shall battle the Devil and liberate those he has taken captive. This victory shall usher in a New Eden and New Jerusalem—

---

[43] *T. Dan* 5:10-12.

apocalyptic reflexes of the original New Year rejuvenation. The defeat of the Devil shall, like the defeat of the chaos-monsters, return the world to its original state of purity.

As in the Isaianic Apocalypse and the Book of Daniel, this cosmic rejuvenation is articulated specifically as apocalyptic *resurrection* in the *Testament of Judah* 25:3-4a:

> And you shall be one people of the Lord, with one language.
> There shall be no more Beliar's spirit of error, because he will be thrown
>   into eternal fire.
> And those who died in sorrow shall be raised in joy…

With the victory of these messianic figures, the Devil shall be destroyed and the earth consequently renewed to a sinless state (here expressed as a pre-Babel world). The Chaos-enemy slain, the dead shall rise. Mot shall have no more dominion.

As we just saw, this battle with Beliar will bring about the liberation of Beliar's "captives." These are the *aichmalōsia*. Derived from *aichmē* "spear" and *halōsis* "conquest," the word literally suggesting one taken captive by the spear. The captives of Beliar are thus like prisoners of war taken amidst the cosmic conflict. The *Testament of Dan* 4:7 elucidates the identity of such captives, noting that "when the soul is continually perturbed, the Lord withdraws from it and Beliar rules it." Thus, the prisoners over whom Beliar rules are those long-perturbed souls whom his spirit possesses. Since common belief at the time (evidenced in *1 Enoch* as well as such texts as *Jubilees* 10:7-12) also understood human illness as corruption by evil spirits, this group includes the sick as well. The "captives of Beliar" are thus spirit-possessed and diseased persons. At the end, on the Day of Yahweh, the divine warrior is expected to come and liberate these prisoners from the Devil. So we read in the *Testament of Zebulun* 9:8:

> And thereafter the Lord himself will arise upon you, the light of
> righteousness *with healing* in his wings. He will liberate every captive of
> the sons of men from Beliar, and every spirit of error will be *trampled*
> down.

The captives of Beliar will be healed by the Lord, and thereby set free from Satan's rule—liberated, one might say, from his oppressive kingdom. Then those evil spirits at fault will meet the typical fate of the chaos-monster: they will be *trampled*.[44]

As I noted at the outset of this chapter, healing is one important apocalyptic reflex of the combat myth. Originally, healing was an important aspect of the New Year festival, as New Year purifications meant a return to the original, pure time of creation—a time without tint, evil, or sickness. In in apocalyptic transformations of the combat myth, however, these rites of purification are eschatologized to a full-scale purification of the world and Yahweh's people. For this reason, purification and healing are essentially connected—an association already developed in proto-apocalyptic texts. So in Isaiah 35:5, we read that, at the cosmic New Year, "the eyes of the blind shall be opened, and the ears of the deaf unstopped; then the lame shall leap like a deer, and the tongue of the speechless sing for joy." There can be no sickness or ill health when the cosmic New Year has revitalized all things. Even so, once the messiah has defeated the Devil, all shall be made pure and healthy again.

One passage from the *Testament of Levi* combines many of these themes and images:

> And [the messiah] shall open the Gates of Paradise;
> He shall remove the Sword that has threatened since Adam,
> And he will grant to his saints to eat of the Tree of Life.
> The Spirit of Holiness shall fall upon them.
> And Beliar shall be *bound* by him.
> And he shall grant to his children the authority to *trample* on wicked
> spirits.[45]

Such passages evince a sustained articulation of the final eschatological battle in terms of the combat myth. Here we find the agricultural reflex of the New Eden, as well as the traditional *binding* and *trampling* motifs applied to the Devil and his evil spirit helpers. Though scattered throughout the *Testaments*, these intimations of the eschatological conflict and the coming cosmic New Year are well at home in the apocalyptic worldview. They show clearly how the revalorations of the combat myth and its cultic associations, begun in late prophecy, emphatically continued in the apocalyptic period.

---

[44] Cf. also *T. Sim.* 6:6.
[45] 18:10-12.

Yahweh vs. Belial (Qumran)

The apocalyptic combat myth also permeates a great deal of the literature which comes to us from the community at Qumran. Here too, though, it is used sporadically, with no full-fledged narrative of battle. Nevertheless, themes and imagery abound, and this survey would certainly be incomplete without at least a cursory look at the apocalyptic combat myth in the texts from Qumran. The following are broadly representative of its application in those diverse texts.

As an ultra-conservative sectarian group whose retreat to monastic living seems to have been occasioned by a sharp break with the traditional religious authorities, it is not surprising that we see a strong prominence in the political reflex of the combat myth. The traditional religious authorities are undoubtedly under the sway of the Devil (usually called Belial in the Qumran literature). I first noted this growing tendency to associate even fellow Jews with Satan in my consideration of the *Testaments*. For the ultra-righteous sectarians of Qumran, this association is commonplace. For this reason, all worldly authorities—religious and political—are deemed wicked, and represented as chaos-monsters.

For example, one hymn includes a prayer lamenting the power of the Devil and his wicked helpers:

> I have become a taunt-song for the rebellious, and the assembly of the wicked have stormed against me. They roar like a gale on the seas, when their waves churn, they cast up slime and mud...
> Brutal men seek my soul, while I hold fast to your covenant. They are the fraudulent council for the congregation of Belial, they do not know that my office is from You...
> Like the roar of many Waters is the uproar of their voice; a cloudburst and a downpour to destroy many. As catapults (?), wickedness and fraud burst out when their waves pile up.[46]

So are the wicked in power compared to the raging chaos-waters. As the floods lifted up their voice in challenge of Yahweh, so here do the wicked of Belial roar and lift up their voice.

Still, this dire situation will not last much longer. As we should well expect by now, the connection of the wicked oppressor with the chaos-monster sets up the fundamental expectation of the apocalyptic

---

[46] 11QH^a Col. X (Col. II) 11b-13a, 21b-22, 27-28a = Donald W. Parry and Emanuel Tov, *The Dead Sea Scrolls Reader*, 6 vols., vol. 5 (Leiden: Brill, 2004), 19-21.

combat myth: battle and victory. "For all their wisdom is swallowed up by the roar of the seas," reads another text, "when the ocean depths boil over the springs of water, and they are tossed up, Sh[eo]l [and Abaddon] shall open..."[47] The text concludes with a climax of all-out apocalyptic war:

> The torrents of Belial burst through into Abaddon, and the plotters from the deep make an uproar with the noise of those who belch forth slime. The earth shouts out, because of the disaster which comes about in the world, and all its plotters scream. All who are upon it behave as if mad, and they melt away in the gr[ea]t disaster. For *God thunders with the roar of His strength* and His holy dwelling roars forth in His glorious truth. Then the heavenly hosts shall raise their voice and the everlasting foundations shall melt and quake. The war of the heroes of heaven shall spread over the world and shall not return until an annihilation that has been determined from eternity is completed. Nothing like this has ever occurred.[48]

Thus, as in the psalms of the New Year festival, the raging waters (i.e., the forces of the Devil) lift up their voice to plunge the world into Chaos. But Yahweh thunders his own roar, the rebuke of his *mighty voice*. Here this is even matched by the roar of the heavenly hosts (another instance of a divine coalition), which cause the foundations of the world to tremble and melt away as apocalyptic battle rages over the entire world. Clearly, the language of the ancient combat myth is central to these apocalyptic conceptions. The ancient myth of storm-god versus sea monster has, through its dramatic apocalyptic revaloration, become a battle of Yahweh and his angelic army against the Devil and his demonic helpers.

Feast of the Chaos-Monsters (4 Ezra and 2 Baruch)

In apocalyptic revalorations of the combat myth, the festival itself is aggrandized to a cosmic celebration of Yahweh's victory over the Devil. In this sense, the Feast of Tabernacles itself becomes the cosmic eschatological banquet, at which Yahweh's reasserted kingship is gloriously praised and the cosmic rejuvenation of the earth indulged in. The chaos-monsters have been defeated and the righteous can now rejoice.

---

[47] 1QHᵃ Col. XI (Col. III + Frg 25) line 15 = ibid., 23.
[48] 1QHᵃ Col. XI (Col. III + Frg 25) lines 32-36 = ibid., 25.

Only with this appreciation of the fundamental relationship between the ancient Hebrew combat myth and the apocalyptic concept of the cosmic New Year festival can we understand an otherwise enigmatic idea in some apocalyptic texts. For we read that, after the defeat of the Devil, the chaos-monsters Leviathan and Behemoth will be served as food for the righteous at the messianic banquet. Whether or not this idea goes back to any ancient myth, available to apocalyptic writers but now lost to us, we cannot know. The idea that celebrants of the original New Year festival would eat the body of the chaos-monster does not appear in any of the texts we now possess, which would suggest that the idea is a unique innovation of the apocalyptic period. However, on closer inspection, I think we can posit that this idea has ancient roots. Indeed, it seems to have been, in a basic sense, a recurrent aspect of the combat myth genre: we have seen it in the *scattering* motif.

In the ancient Near Eastern combat myths, scattering the dead body of the defeated chaos-monster is often linked to sustenance. Ninurta is said to have taken the slain body of the Azag demon and "scattered it over the mountain" and "strewed it like flour."[49] Similarly, when Anat attacks Mot, she splits his body up and plants him like seed; his limbs are eaten by birds. Such traditions were clearly present in the Hebrew combat myth as well. So Psalm 74, for example, reads: "You crushed the heads of Leviathan; you gave him as food for the people in the wilderness." The basic idea that the chaos-monsters serve as sustenance is later referenced in Ezekiel 32:2-4, where the Egyptian pharaoh—in the form of a sea dragon—is caught by Yahweh and thrown into the open to be the food for birds and wild animals. All of this suggests a recurrent topos of the combat myth: *the defeated chaos-monster is divided, its body serving as nourishment in a once-barren place.*

In the apocalyptic combat myth, this topos is continued and creatively reimagined. Here, the chaos-monsters become nourishment for the righteous at the cosmic New Year. We find the idea expressed in *4 Ezra* 6:49-52, written at the turn of the first and second centuries CE:[50]

> Then you kept in existence two living creatures; the name of one you called Behemoth and the name of the other Leviathan. And you *separated* one

---

[49] Jacobsen, *The Harps That Once*, 250, lines 292, 296.
[50] OTP 1.520.

> from the other, for the seventh part where the water had been gathered
> together could not hold them both. And you gave Behemoth one of the parts
> which had been dried up on the third day, to live in it, where there are a
> thousand mountains; but to Leviathan you have the seventh part, the watery
> part; and *you have kept them to be eaten by whom you wish, and when you
> wish.*

That these chaos-monsters will be eaten specifically at the end-times is made explicit in the early second-century CE book *2 Baruch* 29:4:[51]

> And it will happen that when all that which should come to pass in these
> parts has been accomplished, the Anointed One will begin to be revealed.
> And Behemoth will reveal itself from its place, and Leviathan will come
> from the sea, the two great monsters which I created on the fifth day of
> creation and which I shall have kept until that time. *And they will be
> nourishment for all who are left.*

The relationship of the chaos-monsters to Yahweh and the righteous is rather unclear in both of these passages. In some senses, they seem to be acting more in Yahweh's service than as his enemy. Perhaps, as the Devil came to supercede the chaos-monsters proper as enemy of Yahweh, their role changed into one of passive subservience. On the other hand, they may retain their adversarial quality here, but, since subdued, are at Yahweh's will to do with them as he pleases (and, indeed, given over to be eaten does not necessarily evince a close relationship with the god). Indeed, we see the Sea submissive to Yahweh's will even in Exodus 15. In any case, we see continuity with the ancient combat myth tradition. In the apocalyptic transformation of the myth, the bodies of the chaos-monsters shall be consumed at the eschatological banquet. Their bodies, one can presume, shall be *divided* then like any meat from a carcass, and provided as nourishment to the righteous.

Christ vs. the Devil and Death (NT: Epistles)

By the first century CE, Jewish theology had seen dramatic transformations, the most important of which was the general acceptance of a cosmic evil figure who stood in opposition to Yahweh. The Devil—Satan, the ancient serpent—was in control of the world through his puppet gentile nations, and only God's direct intervention

---

[51] For dating of *2 Baruch* see OTP 1.616-17.

at the end of days could set things right. Indeed, Judaism had grown very concerned with eschatological matters, and by the first century apocalypticism seems to have been thoroughly entrenched in its popular worldview.

Given this rise of apocalyptic thought in Second Temple Judaism, it is hardly surprising that the early Christian church, which grew out of first century Judaism, was likewise steeped in apocalyptic thinking. So Dale C. Allison observes:

> The apocalyptic view of things was not just held by many Jews in general; it was also held by many of the first Christians in particular. Passages from a wide variety of sources leave little doubt that many early followers of Jesus thought that the eschatological climax was approaching.[52]

Indeed, there is a great deal of continuity between the perspectives of the New Testament and the apocalyptic worldview found in the pseudepigrapha. In fact, many New Testament authors evince familiarity with those works. The author of Jude, for example, cites *1 Enoch* 1:9 in his epistle (1:14-16), and elsewhere alludes to the rebellious Watcher angels. So he writes, presumably accepting that apocalyptic narrative:

> And the angels who did not keep their own position, but left their proper dwelling, [God] has kept in eternal chains in deepest darkness for the judgment of the great Day. (Jude 1:6)

Like apocalyptic authors before them, writers of the New Testament understood their historical circumstances as part of a cosmic war—a battle between the forces of good and evil, light and darkness, God and Satan. Like the persecuted sectarian community at Qumran, the political themes of the combat myth were very salient for persecuted Christians in the first century. The challenges and crises of the early church were thus envisioned and communicated in terms of cosmic warfare. Ephesians 6:11-12 reads:

> Put on the whole armor of God, so that you may be able to stand against the wiles of the Devil. For our struggle is not against enemies of blood and flesh, but against the Rulers, against the Authorities, against the cosmic

---

[52] Dale C. Allison, "The Eschatology of Jesus," in *The Encyclopedia of Apocalypticism*, ed. John J. Collins (New York: Continuum, 1998), 276. For examples, Allison cites Acts 3:19-20; Rom 13:11; 1 Cor 16:22; 1 Thess 5:1-11; Heb 10:37; Jas 5:8; 1 Peter 4:17; 1 John 2:8; Rev 22:20; and *Didache* 16.

This apocalyptic idea that the workings of both political and religious authorities were orchestrated by the Devil is prevalent in Pauline writings. Such thinking is explicit when Paul writes to the Corinthians about the cosmic battle lines:

> Do not be mismatched with unbelievers. For what partnership is there between righteousness and lawlessness? Or what fellowship is there between light and darkness? What agreement does Christ have with Beliar? (2 Cor 6:14-15)

The strict apocalyptic dualism is evident, and articulated in terminology quite at home in apocalyptic thinking. Light and Darkness were the principle designations used by the community at Qumran to refer to the righteous elect and the wicked helpers of the Devil. Interesting here as well is Paul's use of the name Beliar for the cosmic adversary—a common name for Satan in the intertestamental writings. In fact, Paul may be drawing directly from the *Testaments of the Twelve Patriarchs*. The *Testament of Levi* 19:1 reads, "Choose for yourselves light or darkness, the Law of the Lord or the works of Beliar." The language and dichotomies are common to both.[53] Elsewhere, in Romans 8:38, he refers to "angels," and supernatural "Rulers" and "Powers" that might try to separate the saints from God. The Devil is in control of the world through these and other forces, and one must take one's stand in one camp or the other.

Of critical importance for the present investigation, though, is the fact that *Paul and other early Christians were unique in understanding the ministry of Jesus as a battle with these demonic forces—one in which Jesus proved victorious.* Christianity distinguishes itself from other forms of Jewish apocalypticism in the assertion that Jesus of Nazareth was the hoped-for messiah-figure who would come and battle the Devil at the end of time. Indeed, as a movement grown out of Jewish apocalypticism, Christianity had at its core the belief that Jesus had in fact fulfilled the role of divine warrior through his ministry. *Through his ministry, death, and resurrection, Jesus performed the role of the long-awaited delegate of Yahweh: the messiah-figure who would*

---

[53] This possible allusions is made all the more intriguing for the fact that Paul seems to substitute "Christ" for "the Law of the Lord"—a rhetorical move quite in keeping with his theology.

come to crush the heads of the Dragon in the Sea, and swallow up Death forever. For the early Christians, Jesus was the apocalyptic divine warrior.

Thus Colossians 2:1 describes the salvific work of Jesus in terms of a victorious general, stating, "He disarmed the Rulers and Authorities and made a public example of them, triumphing over them in it." Boyd notes that this final phrase (*thriambeusas autous en autō*) is "a likely reference to a military general leading his captives through the streets of his kingdom to display his victory over the vanquished army."[54] Jesus is thus the victorious divine warrior in the eschatological battle, vanquishing the Satanic principalities who control the world—called the "Rulers and Authorities in the heavenly places" in Ephesians 3:10—and even *leading them in a triumphal victory procession*.[55] Such an image may indeed allude to the procession of the victorious divine warrior at the cosmic New Year festival.

Elsewhere, the language of the *Chaoskampf* myth is clearly employed by Paul to present Jesus as the victorious divine warrior of the apocalyptic combat myth. So 1 Corinthians 15:24:

> Then comes the end, when [Jesus] hands over the kingdom to God the Father, after he has destroyed every Ruler and every Authority and Power. For he must reign until he has *put all his enemies under his feet*. The *last enemy* to be destroyed *is Death*.

Theodore Hiebert writes: "Lying behind this Pauline perspective is the apocalyptic idea that the world is caught in a struggle between divine and diabolical forces which will one day be resolved by the conquest of Chaos and death."[56] Though Christ was indeed victorious over the forces of the Devil during his earthly ministry, the final culmination of his rule has not yet taken place. At the ultimate end, however, Christ will completely and finally destroy these evil supernatural rulers, *trampling* them under his feet in true divine warrior fashion. Elsewhere, he makes a similar allusion to the apocalyptic combat myth, writing, "The God of peace will shortly crush Satan under your feet" (Rom 16:20), thereby directly linking the Devil with the trampled chaos-monsters from Hebrew tradition.

---

[54] Boyd, *God at War*, 261.

[55] In 2 Cor 6:13 and 7:2 Paul announces to the Corinthians, "Be wide open for us…Make room for us," which may also reflect the herald's language at a sacred procession (*ABD*, "Processions," 472).

[56] *ABD*, "Warrior, Divine," 879.

Even Death's epithet, "the last enemy," seems to recall the progression of the traditional myth: first the Dragon is trampled, then comes the defeat of Death. So too in the Christian variant of the apocalyptic combat myth: first Jesus conquers the Devil and his various helpers, then he defeats Death. So does ancient Near Eastern myth become budding Christian dogma.

The theme of kingship and its transference expectedly follows the defeat of the chaos-monsters. However, the handing over of kingship to the Father seems to be an interesting reversal of the configuration presented in Daniel 7, where the *older* deity confers kingship on the *younger* "son of man." In an important sense, the growing dominance of the delegate of Yahweh (first encountered in *1 Enoch*, but continued with increasing emphasis on the lesser messianic figure in Daniel 7 and the *Testaments of the Twelve Patriarchs*) reaches its peak in Christian configurations of the myth. Indeed, Jesus comes to be accepted as completely co-equal with Yahweh in Christian thinking. Here, we glimpse the greatest exaltation of the delegate divine warrior: *it is he who transfers kingship onto Yahweh*. With the rise of Christianity, the figure delegated by Yahweh to fight the Devil and his chaos-monsters becomes assimilated to and in some senses supersedes Yahweh with the person of Jesus.

Christ vs. the Dragon and Death (NT: Revelation)

Revealing as these passages are, nowhere is the apocalyptic transformation of the combat myth so vividly and directly employed as in the only full-fledged apocalypse in the New Testament, the Book of Revelation. This composition has much in common with the other apocalyptic literature we have seen, drawing liberally from older visionary texts (especially the Book of Daniel) and ancient mythic patterns. In the Christian canon, notes Forsyth, it is the work "that most clearly establishes [Satan's] continuity with the cosmic adversary of the Near East."[57]

The entire work is in fact so rich with allusions to the *Chaoskampf* tradition, time and space do not allow for a full analysis. Indeed, one notable feature of Revelation is its comprehensive inclusion of virtually every incarnation of the chaos-enemy. Here we encounter the Dragon,

---

[57] Forsyth, *The Old Enemy*, 251.

his helper Beasts (including both Leviathan and Behemoth), the political helpers of the chaos-monster, the raging Sea, and Death/Sheol/Abaddon. It is as though the author were eager to include every representation of the chaos-monster, each one singularized and apocalyptically aggrandized in order to augment the finality of their destruction. While this comprehensive quality shall prove difficult to cover, hopefully a cursory look at selected passages should suffice for an appreciation of how the early Christian church understood and articulated the ministry of Jesus by means of the apocalyptic combat myth.

In the twelfth chapter, visions of a dragon's attack on a woman in labor are interwoven with a cosmic war in heaven. Beginning with the first vision, we read:

> A great portent appeared in heaven: a woman clothed with the sun, with the moon under her feet, and on her head a crown of twelve stars. She was pregnant and was crying out in birthpangs, in the agony of giving birth. Then another portent appeared in heaven: *a great red Dragon, with seven heads and ten horns*, and seven diadems on his heads. His tail swept down a third of the stars of heaven and threw them to the earth. (12:1-4a)

The ten horns of the Dragon in this vision recall those of the chaos-monster in Daniel 7:7, while the sweeping down a third of the stars probably alludes to the fall of rebellious angels (such as the Watchers in *1 Enoch*). That the dragon is said to have seven heads—a detail found here and of the "beast rising out of the Sea" in 13:1—is truly remarkable. In the extant Hebrew material, the great chaos-monster Leviathan is said to have multiple heads, but the texts never state exactly how many.[58] *The Ugaritic combat myths, however, explicitly enumerate seven heads for the chaos-monster Litan*[59]—that Ugaritic ancestor of the Hebrew Leviathan.[60] With this detail, the author evinces familiarity with archaic traditions that, though not preserved in the Hebrew Bible, must have continued into the first century CE and beyond as part of a more extensive mythology.[61] Indeed, like the author of Daniel, the apocalypticist may have received this ancient

---

[58] So Ps 74:14, which speaks of "heads" in the plural, but does not specify their number.
[59] Smith and Parker, *Ugaritic Narrative Poetry*, *KTU* 1.5.i.1-4.
[60] Cf. also the "Seven-headed Serpent" which Ninurta slays. Text in Jacobsen, *The Harps That Once*, 243, lines 128-9, 133.
[61] Forsyth, *The Old Enemy*, 252; Day, *God's Conflict*, 24; Collins, *Daniel*, 288.

information via cultic traditions for, as we shall see, he also employs the imagery of the ancient New Year festival.

Following a thwarted attack by the Dragon on the woman and her child, full-blown apocalyptic battle erupts in heaven. We read:

> And war broke out in heaven; Michael and his angels fought against the Dragon. The Dragon and his angels fought back, but they were defeated, and there was no longer any place for them in heaven. The great Dragon was thrown down, that ancient Serpent, who is called the Devil and Satan, the deceiver of the whole world—he was thrown down to the earth, and his angels were thrown down with him. (12:7-9)

Here—as in *1 Enoch* and, presumably, Daniel 7—it is the archangel Michael who fights the chaos-monster as the delegate of Yahweh. The chaos-monster is explicitly called the Devil and Satan here, who is "the ancient serpent" from Isaiah 27:1 (which originally referred to Leviathan), or, given the theological developments linking the Devil with the tempter in the Garden, Genesis 2.

However, though Michael and the heavenly host are the most immediate agents responsible for the Dragon's expulsion from heaven, we learn the ultimate cause immediately afterwards:

> Then I heard a loud voice in heaven, proclaiming, "Now have come the salvation and the power and the kingdom of our God and the authority of his messiah, for the Accuser of our comrades has been thrown down, who accuses them day and night before our God.
> But *they have conquered him by the blood of the Lamb* and by the word of their testimony, for they did not cling to life even in the face of Death.
> Rejoice then, you heavens and those who dwell in them! But woe to the earth and the sea, for the Devil has come down to you with great wrath, because he knows that his time is short!" (12:10-12)

It was thus ultimately *the sacrificial death of Jesus* that caused the Dragon's defeat. Indeed, this is the true and most basic opposition in Revelation's apocalyptic combat myth. Though Michael was the immediate heavenly delegate of Yahweh to battle the Devil, it was actually Jesus who was the essential messianic figure. Jesus is the hero whose salvific work on earth began the downfall of Satan. Such was the belief of the early Christians, and such, we shall see, was the message of another crucial, thoroughly-apocalyptic text from the early church: the Gospel of Mark.

However, by this point in the narration the Dragon has not been defeated—only expelled from heaven. Now on the earth, the Dragon's power actually increases. He seeks to attack the mother of the child again, but she is given eagle's wings and again flies away to the wilderness. To stop her, the Dragon spits water like a river out of his mouth. But "the earth came to the help of the woman; it opened its mouth and swallowed the river that the dragon had poured from his mouth" (12:16). So the Dragon attempts to use the destructive Waters as a weapon. Thwarted, the Dragon skulks away to war further against the righteous.[62]

At the opening of the thirteenth chapter, he takes his stand on the shore of the Sea:

> And I saw a Beast (*thērion*) rising out of the Sea having ten horns and seven heads; and on its horns were ten diadems, and on its heads were blasphemous names. And the Beast that I saw was like a leopard, its feet were like a bear's, and its mouth was like a lion's mouth. *And the Dragon gave it his power and his throne and great authority.* One of its heads seemed to have received a death-blow, but its mortal wound had been healed. In amazement the whole earth followed the Beast. They worshiped the Dragon, for he had given his authority to the Beast, and they worshiped the Beast, saying, "Who is like the Beast, and who can fight against it?" (13:1-4)

So Leviathan, the Beast of the Sea with his traditional seven heads, appears. With his entry, the political theme of the combat myth becomes particularly pronounced, as here the Beast symbolizes Rome: the oppressive historical power now persecuting the righteous. This association is made clear when, in 17:9, its seven heads are connected with the seven hills of Rome.[63] That the Beast (Rome) gets its power directly from the Dragon (Satan) is a hallmark of apocalypticism: political authorities derive their power from the Devil, the current king over the earth. This arrangement is presented in Revelation as a direct allusion to the ancient combat myth: Yam is Satan, and his Leviathan, Rome. The political authorities are Satan's helpers just as Leviathan was Sea's helper.

Thus, though the salvific work of Jesus has ousted the Dragon from heaven, the Dragon now reigns on earth via his political helper, the Roman Empire. Jesus' sacrificial death, though crucial to the apocalyptic battle, has at least temporarily led to the ascendency of the

---

[62] Cf. Ps 124, where the righteous one escapes "like a bird" from his enemies, here compared to "the Flood" (v. 4) and "the raging Waters" (v. 5).

[63] David Edward Aune, *Revelation*, 3 vols., Word Biblical Commentary (Dallas: Word Books, 1997), vol. 3, 944.

Dragon and his helpers on earth. With this rise of the Devil and his associate Beast, the righteous are defeated, and Satan becomes king over the cosmos:

> The Beast was given a mouth uttering haughty and blasphemous words, and it was allowed to exercise authority for forty-two months. It opened its mouth to utter blasphemies against God, blaspheming his name and his dwelling, that is, those who dwell in heaven. *Also it was allowed to make war on the saints and to conquer them.* It was given authority over every tribe and people and language and nation… (13:5-7)

Indeed, the Beast of the Sea is soon aided by another oppressor, the Beast of the Earth: Leviathan is thus joined by Behemoth.[64] However, recalling Wakeman's analysis, we may also see in this earth monster the figure of Death as chaos-enemy. If so, two of the principal enemies from the ancient combat myth are present: Leviathan and Mot.[65] These two continue to oppress and defeat the righteous, as tremendous suffering and calamity overtake the world. Indeed, the cosmos has descended into utter Chaos.

However, as we should expect, this is the very cue for the divine warrior and the rejoinder of battle. So, in chapter fourteen, we read:

> Then I looked, and there was the Lamb, standing on Mount Zion! And with him were one hundred forty-four thousand who had his name and his Father's name written on their foreheads. And *I heard a voice from heaven like the sound of many waters and like the sound of loud thunder*; the voice I heard was like the sound of *harpists playing on their harps, and they sing a new song before the throne* and before the four living creatures and before the elders. (14:1-3a)

Jesus, as the Lamb, is seen on the holy mountain in a scene whose imagery recalls the cosmic New Year festival. So a *mighty voice* rumbles like thunder, while the image of harpists around the throne is invoked, reminiscent of the singers and harpists at the enthronement of the ark at the New Year festival.

These connections with the ancient harvest festival are continued a few verses later:

> Then I looked, and there was a white cloud, and seated on the cloud was one like the Son of Man, with a golden crown on his head, and a sharp sickle in his hand! Another angel came *out of the Temple, calling with a*

---

[64] Day, *God's Conflict*, 83 n. 59; 141; Angel, *Chaos and the Son of Man*, 146 and n. 245.
[65] Following Wakeman, *God's Battle with the Monster*, 106-17

So is the end of the world related to the end of the agricultural year. To usher in the New Year, Jesus—as the "one like a son of man" figure from Daniel 7, the slayer of the Beast—comes as the storm-god rider of the clouds and himself reaps the harvest of earth. The call of the angel in the Temple may allude to the antiphonal psalms of the New Year enthronement, as priests of the Temple would call out to celebrants of the festival bearing the ark of Yahweh.

The succeeding chapters, fifteen through eighteen, then narrate the judgment meted out by Yahweh upon the followers of the Beast. But Satan's kingdom remains unshaken, and sends out demons to assemble a vast army for the final apocalyptic battle at Mount Meggido. So the chaos-monsters continue their oppressive reign until the climactic conclusion in chapter nineteen, when the resurrected Jesus himself finally rides forth as the dreadful divine warrior to slay the Beasts:

So Jesus emerges as the warrior, flanked by his heavenly host and armed with a sword to battle the Beasts. Immediately after this, the apocalyptist writes:

So we reencounter the cultic festival, eschatologized as the cosmic New Year banquet. The helpers of the Beasts—not as chaos-monsters but rather as political allies: kings and authorities—serve as food for wild animals. That the angel calls specifically to the birds is reminiscent of the ancient Canaanite motif in which Anat allows the birds to eat the limbs of the defeated Mot, later attested in the Hebrew tradition by Ezekiel 32:4.

Finally, the principal helper of the Dragon, the demonic Beast Leviathan, is slain by Jesus:

> Then I saw the Beast and the kings of the earth with their armies gathered to make war against the Rider on the Horse and against his army. And the Beast was captured, and with it the false prophet... These two were thrown alive into the lake of fire that burns with sulfur. *And the rest were killed by the sword of the Rider on the Horse*, the sword that came from his mouth; and *all the birds were gorged with their flesh*. (19:19-21)

So the Beast is captured, or "arrested" as the word *epiasthē* might be translated, which may allude to the traditional *binding* motif. Its body is then destroyed by fire, while the helpers of the Beast are likewise punished, their corpses eaten by birds in a variant of the *scattering* motif. The mention of Jesus' sword may recall Isaiah 27:1, which reads: "On that Day, Yahweh *with his cruel and great and strong sword* will punish Leviathan the fleeing serpent, Leviathan the twisting serpent, and he will kill the Dragon that is in the sea." Jesus thus fulfills the role of Yahweh himself, serving as the divine warrior on the Day of Yahweh, the cosmic New Year.

Next, with the helpers of the Dragon defeated, the Dragon himself is dealt with:

> Then I saw an angel coming down from heaven, holding in his hand the key to the bottomless Pit and *a great chain*. He seized the Dragon, that ancient Serpent, who is the Devil and Satan, and *bound him* for a thousand years, and threw him into the Pit, and locked and sealed it over him, so that he would deceive the nations no more, until the thousand years were ended. (20:1-3)

Here, the *binding* motif is far more explicit, as the Devil is once again emphatically identified with the Dragon, the ancient Serpent of the traditional combat myth. He is cast into the Pit, just as the cosmic rebel was, his body eventually destroyed by fire.

Having thus defeated the helper Beasts and the Dragon, Jesus then moves to defeat Death—thereby mirroring the progression of the ancient myth:

> And the Sea gave up the dead that were in it, Death and Hades gave up the dead that were in them, and all were judged according to what they had

> done. Then *Death and Hades were thrown into the lake of fire*. This is the
> second death, the lake of fire; and anyone whose name was not found
> written in the book of life was thrown into the lake of fire. Then I saw a *new
> heaven and a new earth*; for the first heaven and the first earth had passed
> away, and *the Sea was no more*. (20:14-21:1)

One striking aspect of this passage is the mention of "Death and
Hades," since the Greek "Hades" usually translated the Hebrew
"Sheol"—another name, as we saw earlier, for the Death god himself.
Conceptually then, it is not two different entities cast into the fire here,
but one: the old enemy from the combat myth, Mot/Sheol, referenced in
poetic parallelism just as they often are in the Hebrew literature.[66]
Coupling this with Forsyth's assertion that "[t]he sea here is not the
ordinary sea that sailors cross; it is the mythological enemy, the
Ugaritic Yamm blended with the hostile Red Sea of the Exodus,"[67] we
see that both of the traditional forces of Chaos are slain here. This is
final defeat of Sea and Death/Hades (that is, Yam and Mot/Sheol). The
order of the defeat here (Sea and then Death), and in the narrative more
broadly (Beasts, Dragon, Death), matches the progression of the
traditional combat myth. Jesus, like Baal and Yahweh, first defeats the
helper monsters (Leviathan/Behemoth), then the Dragon (Yam), then
Death (Mot).[68]

As in the traditional combat myth, these victories usher in the
cosmic New Year and the return to original purity. Thus a new heaven
and a new earth are born. The dead are resurrected, and a new, re-
purified world comes into being. With this great transformation comes
the typical conclusion to the combat myth pattern: the victorious divine

---

[66] The singularity of Death/Hades may even be reflected in manuscript variants, which
read: "And Death-and-Hades gave up (singular) the dead in him/it (singular)." See Aune,
Revelation, vol. 3 ns. 13.d-d and 13.e-e on 1075.

[67] Forsyth, *The Old Enemy*, 256.

[68] A separate allusion to the defeat of Death may be found in Rev 7:16-17. Here, the
martyrs stand in God's throne room with palm fronds (likely an allusion to the cosmic
New Year festival) and rest assured in his protection: "They will hunger no more, and
thirst no more; the sun will not strike them, nor any scorching heat; for the Lamb at the
center of the throne will be their shepherd, and he will guide them to springs of the water
of life, and God will wipe away every tear from their eyes." In the traditional myth,
Death was the summer sterility of the land—the "scorching heat" causing hunger and
thirst. Thus, here God has saved the righteous from Death. Moreover, Mot/Death was
also sometimes understood as a shepherd (e.g., *KTU* 1.6.ii.21-23; Ps 49:15). Here, the
role is reversed as Christ (as the Lamb—another irony) will be the shepherd leading them
to springs of *life*. These ironic reversals are capped by a final allusion to Is 25:8, which,
we have seen, ironically reveres the old myth by declaring *God* will swallow *Death*.

warrior can receive kingship over the cosmos. So both Yahweh *and Jesus* are enthroned to great praise, their kingship finally assured after slaying the chaos-monsters.

As this analysis makes clear (and, to be sure, more evidence could be presented, since this hardly exhausts the *Chaoskampf* material in Revelation), the combat myth was a crucial framework through which early Christians understood and articulated Jesus' ministry. Ancient mythic material appear in this first century apocalypse to be creatively revalorized into a distinctly Christian vision. Jesus is now the divine warrior, the storm-god of the ancient myth. It is his sacrificial death which expels Satan from heaven. It is his return as the resurrected rider which inaugurates the final defeat of Sea, Dragon, and Death.

We have undoubtedly seen the thematic reflexes of the apocalyptic combat myth: agricultural (e.g., resurrection), cultic (e.g., enthronement), political (e.g., Rome as Beast), and philosophical and theological (e.g., Jesus co-equal with Yahweh). So too are the *mighty voice*, *binding*, and *scattering* motifs employed.

The full narrative trajectory of Revelation is complex and convoluted, rendering any easy plot schematization impossible. Nevertheless, stepping back (quite a bit) and risking over-simplification, one might present the general outline as follows: 1) *Lack/Villainy*: The Dragon makes war on the righteous. 2) *Hero emerges/prepares to act*: A coalition of Yahweh, his angels, Jesus and his faithful fulfill the hero role. 3) *Donor/Consultation*: The sacrificial death of Jesus is the means by which the Dragon is cast out of heaven. 5) *Battle*: Michael and the angels battle the Dragon in heaven. 6) *Defeat*: The "defeat" of Jesus and his death on the cross precipitate the Dragon's fall from heaven. 7) *Enemy ascendant*: Thrown to earth, the Dragon, now with helper Beasts and kings of the earth, conquer the righteous. 8) *Hero recovers*: The resurrected Jesus appears, first as the rider of the clouds to reap earth's harvest, then on his horse, charging forth with his heavenly army. 9) *Battle rejoined*: Jesus and his army battle the Beast and the kings of earth. 10) *Victory*: The Beasts are slain; the Dragon is bound; Death and Sea give up their captives. 11) *Enemy punished*: The bodies of the Beasts, the Dragon, and Death are destroyed by fire; the bodies of the Beast's helpers are feasted upon by birds; the Sea is destroyed. 12) *Triumph*: In celebration at the cosmic New Year, Yahweh and Jesus take their thrones, praised for their assured kingship over the cosmos.

Before moving on to the primary concern of this monograph—an examination of the role of the combat myth in the Gospel of Mark—it is helpful to briefly summarize some of the key findings of Part One, particularly those which we are to encounter again in the following section.

Clearly the combat myth was a crucial mythic genre in the ancient Near East. Fundamentally a myth about *order*, it offered to many people of antiquity a philosophically optimistic framework for understanding the agricultural, cultic, and political realities of their time. Telling of the storm-god's victory over the draconic forces of Chaos and destruction, the myth assured that the god of fertility, order, and justice was in charge—he was king. In addition to such fundamental themes, these myths also employed certain generic motifs, including the storm-god's *mighty voice*, and the *binding, trampling,* and *dividing/scattering* of the defeated chaos-monster's body. It also followed a basic plot progression, whose abstraction by Forsyth I have employed throughout my analysis.

In the ancient Near East, these combat myths were usually a central liturgical aspect in a New Year festival. Celebrating the return of fertility after the barren season, the festival included a recitation or reenactment of the mythic narrative as an efficacious ritual to usher in the New Year. Also central to such New Year festivals was the procession of the storm-god's cultic idol, at which time the idol was removed from its temple and brought to a suburban cult shrine. With the idol removed, the temple of the storm-god was then re-purified as the ritual impurities accumulated throughout the year were cleansed. This done, the god's idol was then carried in a glorious procession from the sacred site back to his temple, accompanied by music and festal calls along the way. Since most of the year the idol remained unseen within the temple, this was the great *epiphany* of the god, the time when his people could look on his sacred glory. The idol of the god, having processed back to his temple along the city's *via sacra*—the fixed processional road—was then reinstalled in his shrine. In Ugarit, and perhaps in other kingdoms, this probably took the form of a ritual enthronement of the deity.

Like other ancient Near Eastern peoples, the ancient Israelites had their own combat myth traditions. By comparing extant Hebrew texts with other ancient Near Eastern mytho-cultic traditions, it is possible to glean a relatively clear picture of this ancient Hebrew myth. In it, Yahweh has as his enemy primarily the raging Sea and its associate Dragon, Leviathan/Rahab. Though Sea's waters rage and roar against him, Yahweh always proves mightier. Riding in upon the clouds and gales, he terrorizes the waters into submission by his thunderous *rebuke*: the Hebrew variant of the god's *mighty voice*. He *tramples* upon the back of Sea, and *divides* it in two, restoring the rebellious waters to their rightful place. As for Sea's Dragon, he *binds* it, specifically with a *muzzle*, and subdues the beast. Finally, though less prevalent in the Hebrew texts, it seems that, like Baal, Yahweh also battled Death after defeating the Sea and its Dragon. Death, with its rapacious appetite, may also have been conceived of as a dragon/beast and was the last enemy to be defeated by Yahweh.

In ancient Israel, these victories were also celebrated at a New Year festival: the harvest Feast of Tabernacles. At this festival, Yahweh's deeds of defeating the forces of Chaos were likewise recalled. Serving as the symbol of the god, the ark was removed from the Temple and placed in the House of Obed-Edom while the Temple was cleansed of the year's impurities. Then the ark was led in a celebratory procession back to the Temple, appearing before all the people. This was the god's chief cultic epiphany, the Day of Yahweh. Music and singing accompanied the procession as it made its way from the House of Obed-Edom back up to the Temple, traveling upon the Sacred Way: Israel's festal *via sacra*. All the while, clearing the Way for the ark and proclaiming Yahweh's "good news" of victory over the enemy, went the processional herald/messenger (probably the son(s) of the high priest). Finally, arriving through the eastern gate, the ark was reinstalled in a ritual enthronement of the deity.

The Hebrew combat myth and its associated festival clearly had a primary place in ancient Israelite religion. Many Psalms, presumably liturgical texts from the festival, describe Yahweh's battle with the chaos-monsters, his victorious procession, and his enthronement. Even in prophetic circles at odds with the Jerusalem court and cult, the myth was popular. However, because of the different uses to which they put the myth—primarily as metaphorical allusion—its presence is more subtle in prophetic texts.

After the Babylonian invasion destroyed the Temple and the monarchy, the combat myth and its cultic celebration continued on as potent conceptions in Israelite religion. Prophets in exile drew from the mytho-cultic complex for its powerful images to articulate their hopes for restoration. Indeed, much of the message of Deutero-Isaiah was predicated on metaphorical application of the myth to Israel's political situation. So the prophet imagines Babylon as the historical chaos-enemy whom Yahweh would soon slay. Then a new *via sacra*, a processional way running from Babylon to Zion, would appear, on which the exiles could return with singing and dancing as their god once again became their king. Truly cosmic rejuvenation would then occur, as the great defeat of the chaos-forces would usher in a kind of Second Eden.

However, after the return, continued frustrations, trials, and disappointments led many to feel that such prophetic messages remained unfulfilled. Consequently, fervent hope for restoration continued, becoming increasingly lofty and separated from reality in its expression. So in Zechariah, for example, Yahweh's salvation is articulated as the New Year festival's Day of Yahweh with cosmic dimensions. The divine warrior returns, standing upon the Mount of Olives as it splits in two and forms a road to save the righteous. The Lord then swoops into the city of Jerusalem, purifying it of evil forces, and inaugurates a utopian world where all the nations come up to celebrate the Feast of Tabernacles.

This tendency of cosmic projection of the combat myth and its festival was characteristic of late prophecy and proto-apocalyptic, culminating with the rise of full-blown apocalypticism. For this reason, the combat myth became central to apocalyptic ideas about Yahweh's impending salvation, and the ultimate evil which necessitated it. This source of evil was the Devil, the rebel of the combat myth who, with everything else, became cosmically aggrandized. In essence, he was Leviathan, writ large. The Day would come, however, when Yahweh would appear, defeat Israel's enemies, and slay the Dragon in the sea just as he had done before. Satan, Sea, and Death would be defeated once and for all. Then, as before, Yahweh would be enthroned, and at this cosmic Feast of Tabernacles, this eschatological banquet, the righteous would eat the carcasses of the chaos-monsters. Death would be no more, and glorious abundance would proliferate in the Second Eden.

Such is the essence of the apocalyptic combat myth. In its apocalyptic revaloration, the traditional themes of the myth each have their cosmic reflexes. So, for example, agricultural rejuvenation at the New Year becomes the miraculous fecundity of the cosmic New Year and bodily resurrection; the cultic realities of the festival are transformed into an eschatological feast and processional *via sacra*; the association of the chaos-monsters with political enemies becomes a vision of the world as the kingdom of the Dragon, whose helper beasts are the oppressive political powers (both Jew and gentile) of earth; and the general assurance that the god of fertility and order ruled becomes the fervent promise that Yahweh's victory over the Devil is imminent, his cosmic power assured. Such was the framework of Jewish apocalypticism, influenced as it was by the traditional Hebrew combat myth.

As an outgrowth of Jewish apocalypticism, however, early Christianity inherits this framework, adapting it of course to the ministry and identity of Jesus of Nazareth. With this re-imagination, Jesus becomes the divine warrior, the delegate messiah of Yahweh whose mission is none other than to slay the Dragon and thereby attain kingship. Indeed, his ministry on earth was the first crucial inauguration of this final cosmic battle between Yahweh and Satan. This connection of Jesus of Nazareth with the divine warrior of the apocalyptic combat myth underlies the theological message of Paul, and utterly permeates the apocalyptic visions of Revelation. So too, as we shall now see, does it lie at the heart of the Gospel of Mark.

Part II: The Combat Myth in Mark

CHAPTER 4
MARK AND *CHAOSKAMPF*: PREFATORY REMARKS

Transmission and Tradition: Hints at Provenance?

In my introduction, I listed but a few of the pertinent yet generally unanswered questions raised by the recognized *Chaoskampf* allusions in the gospels. Of these, the first two inquired *how* and *why* such an ancient mythic pattern found its way into a Christian work of the first century CE. After the surveys and analyses of Part One, hopefully the answers to these questions (or at least their contours) should by now be clear. Our brief examination of the New Testament which closed the previous chapter showcased some demonstrable evidence that the early church retained the apocalyptic perspective of late Second Temple Judaism, out of which the new movement arose. But of course the principle framework for Jewish apocalypticism itself derives in no small way from aggrandizement of the traditional Hebrew combat myth.

That Christianity arose as a movement within apocalyptic Judaism thus explains both *how* and *why* the ancient mythic pattern comes to be employed in a first century Christian text. The myth was a key framework in apocalypticism mainly for its philosophical implications of divine victory over the forces of Chaos—or, in its apocalyptic reflex, Yahweh's victory over the Devil. Early Christians shared this perspective with their Jewish neighbors, with one crucial distinction: they interpreted Jesus of Nazareth as the delegated divine warrior of Yahweh. For early Christians, the final cosmic war had been inaugurated by Jesus' ministry on earth. He was the messiah who would help usher in the great restoration and fulfill the unrealized message of the later prophets.

To be sure, this is the very core of Mark's message. To communicate it, he—like so many apocalyptic writers before him— turned to the still-pervasive, still-potent story of the combat myth. It is with this mythological palette that he colors so many elements of Jesus' ministry, painting a powerful divine warrior come to battle the forces of Chaos and destruction: Satan, Sea, and Death. Only after these cosmic victories can he take his throne and rule uncontested over the cosmos— his Kingdom without end.

It is more difficult, however, to be so precise about *how* the myth came to Mark specifically. As we saw, the exact lines of transmission of the myth itself are quite convoluted. The Psalms and authoritative Jewish texts were certainly one source, but there were undoubtedly other materials available in the first century which linked apocalyptic writers with the traditions of the past. Beyond mere general themes and imagery, it is clear that the Hebrew combat myth survived as a distinct and coherent story well into the Common Era. This longevity of the tradition is revealed piecemeal in extant sources. Specific details are preserved in texts hundreds of years removed from earlier textual attestations. Recall, for example, how Revelation specifically enumerates seven heads for Leviathan—a detail nowhere preserved in extant Hebrew texts, yet revealed through comparison with the ancient Ugaritic material; or the description of Leviathan in the Isaianic Apocalypse, whose similarities with Ugaritic traditions (anywhere from eight hundred years to as much as a millennium old at the time of the text's composition) demand direct dependence on shared poetic traditions:

Isaiah 27:1	KTU 1.5.i.1-4
...punish Leviathan the fleeing serpent, Leviathan the twisting serpent...	...killed Litan, the Fleeing Serpent, Annihilated the Twisty Serpent...

In the same way, we saw how the author of Daniel 7, writing in the mid-second century BCE, makes use of ancient mythological configurations which are unprecedented in extant Jewish texts, leading John J. Collins to conclude that such material "was transmitted down to the first century through sources, whether Jewish or pagan, that are no longer extant."[1] In all three cases, apocalyptic authors evince familiarity with archaic mythological material, separated from the closest surviving parallels by over one thousand years.

Such continuity suggests a durable line of transmission. Moreover, the dearth of surviving literary sources could suggest that this tradition may have been, in some cases, of a non-literary nature. Given these observations, one of the strongest candidates for the carrier of such traditions would be cultic practice. *The Feast of Tabernacles itself may thus have been the chief carrier of traditional mythic material through the ages.* Both J. A. Emerton and Aage Bentzen have posited just this with regard to the book of Daniel. In their view, such material was ultimately transmitted to Daniel by means of the New Year festival/Feast of Tabernacles, which would have preserved within

---

[1] Collins, *Daniel*, 288-289. Cf. 291-4.

cultic memory for later generations the more ancient stories.[2] Thus, a much fuller account of Yahweh's victories over his chaos-enemies was known even in the first century CE when Mark was writing. Mark would hardly be conspicuous then in his use of such material, and could count on his audience to appreciate his application of the myth just as much as Daniel could his.

As we shall see, Mark makes considerable use of the New Year festival both thematically and structurally. If Daniel (c. 165 BCE) indeed received his mythological configurations from the Tabernacles tradition, it seems plausible that Mark too was largely informed by echoes of ancient cultic practice. However, in Daniel's time, and even more so in Mark's, the celebration of Tabernacles was admittedly a very different festival than it had been during the Monarchy. Most conspicuous is the absence of the ark, which no longer played a role in the Temple cultus by the first century; this centerpiece of the New Year festival was gone. So too was the kingship itself, which was crucial to the festival, being renewed every year at the celebration.

Nevertheless, an appreciable amount of cultic continuity still existed between the harvest New Year festival of ancient Israel, and Sukkot of the Hellenistic and Roman eras. Josephus, for example, offers us an intriguing glimpse of Tabernacles circa 103 BCE, when Antigonus, brother of the Hasmonean king Aristobulus, celebrates the festival:

> But on one occasion when Antigonus had returned from a campaign with glory, as the season of the festival during which tabernacles are erected to God was at hand, it chanced that Aristobulus fell ill, and *Antigonus, arrayed in great splendour and with his heavy-armed soldiers about him, went up to the temple* to celebrate the festival and pray earnestly for his brother's recovery; thereupon the unscrupulous men who were bent on disrupting the harmonious relation between them, found in Antigonus' ambitious display and in the successes he had achieved, a pretext to go to the king and maliciously exaggerate the pomp of his appearance at the festival, saying that everything that had been done was out of keeping with the behavior of a private person and that *his actions rather had the indications of one who imagined himself a king…*[3]

---

[2] Emerton, "The Origin of the Son of Man Imagery," 225-42. For a recent defense of this idea, see Day, *God's Conflict*, 165.

[3] *Ant.* 13.304-6 = Flavius Josephus, *Jewish Antiquities*, trans. H. Thackeray, 10 vols., The Loeb Classical Library (Cambridge: Harvard University Press, 1926), 381.

This illuminating passage shows that various aspects of the festival persisted centuries after the Exile. First, we may read a procession to the Temple in Antigonus' actions: he "goes up" (*anabainō*) to the Temple "arrayed in great splendor" in the company of his soldiers. So would the Davidic kings at the New Year festival. Moreover, this appears to have been a kind of triumph for Antigonus, as he has returned from military campaign in glory. So too was the enthronement procession a triumph for Yahweh, who came fresh from his victories over the chaos-forces. The festival's royal associations are still very much alive in the people's minds, as Antigonus' actions allow some to convincingly depict him as a would-be king. His spectacular triumphal procession to the Temple during Tabernacles could all too easily be construed as projecting royal airs, even in 103 BCE—hundreds of years after the last Davidic king would have processed at the festival. The continuity of cultic ritual and the persistence of the festival's associated themes (e.g., victory in battle, kingship, etc.) even down to specific terminology (e.g., the "going up") are striking. Given this, it seems entirely plausible that Mark—writing only a few generations later— could still draw upon the enthronement festival/Tabernacles and its associated themes.

However, the traditional celebration of the Israelite New Year— with its procession of cultic objects, ritual ablution, etc.—may have had its closest living parallel not in the first century Feast of Tabernacles celebrated at Jerusalem, but rather in pagan counterparts. To be sure, cultic processions continued to lie at the heart of Greco-Roman cultus, but there is also considerable evidence that traditional ancient Near Eastern festivals were maintained into the first century CE. Indeed, the *Akītu* festival was still celebrated well into the Common Era in Syria, most notably at the city of Palmyra.[4] A Palmyran bas-relief depicts a scene of battle between a warrior god and a serpentine foe (half-snake, half-woman) which probably depicts Bēl (Marduk) and Tiamet. The inscription on the pedestal dates the dedication of the temple to a feast on Nisannu 6, 32 CE—the time of the spring New Year and Babylonian *Akītu* festival.[5] Many believe cultic processions continued to play their

---

[4] Bidmead, *The Akītu Festival*, 36-7.
[5] Ibid., 36. As we have seen, temple construction/renewal and New Year festivals often coincided.

crucial role in the religious practices here at the temple of Bēl,[6] as they certainly would have in any New Year *Akītu* festival.

All of this is particularly important since a growing number of scholars now posit a Syrian provenance for Mark's gospel.[7] If Mark was indeed writing in Syria, he would have been familiar with such pagan New Year festivals, and could likewise have expected his audience's familiarity with them. Thus, though he may have had only inherited information and cultural memories of Israel's grand New Year festival, it is very possible he had first-hand experience of a similar processional New Year festival which likewise celebrated the chief warrior storm-god's victory over his serpentine foe. If no longer celebrated at the Jerusalem temple as it had been during the monarchy, New Year festivals such as the *Akītu* at Palmyra likely provided some phenomenological context for Mark's first century audience.

Date

Like other apocalyptic writers, particularly Daniel, Mark was probably writing at a time of intense political tension and uncertainty. Scholarly consensus places the first gospel's composition just around the time of the first Jewish war with Rome, which raged from 66 to 74 CE.[8] It was during this conflict that the simmering tensions between Jews and Romans finally erupted into all-out war, ultimately leading to the destruction of the Jewish Temple. Generally speaking, it was a time

---

[6] Ted Kaizer, *The Religious Life of Palmyra: A Study of the Social Patterns of Worship in the Roman Period*, Oriens et Occidens (Stuttgart: Steiner, 2002), 200.

[7] Joel Marcus, *Mark 1-8: A New Translation with Introduction and Commentary*, 2 vols., The Anchor Bible (New York: Doubleday, 2000), 33-7. Marcus argues that "[i]n view of [the] evidence, the theory of Syrian provenance seems to be the strongest one available" (36). Cf. Helmut Koester, *Introduction to the New Testament*, 2 vols., Hermeneia (Philadelphia: Fortress Press, 1982), vol. 2, 167: "It is not known where the Gospel of Mark was written—probably not in Rome, where it is often located because of its Latinisms and its relationship to Peter. It is better to assume that Mark was written in a major metropolis of the east where various lines of fully-developed traditions had intersected. Antioch or another city of the Syrian west coast fulfill these conditions" (167). For discussion of the debate over Syrian provenance, see John Donahue, "The Quest for the Community of Mark's Gospel," in *The Four Gospels, 1992: Festschrift Frans Neirynck*, ed. F. Neirynck and Frans van Segbroeck (Leuven: Leuven University Press, 1992), 823-8.

[8] Adela Yarbro Collins, *Mark: A Commentary*, Hermeneia (Minneapolis: Fortress Press, 2007), 11.

rife with apocalyptic expectation. Many saw in this conflict, as Daniel had seen in the revolt against the Seleucids, the final battle of the end of days. In such a context (probably only a year before the Roman destruction of the Temple in 70 CE), Mark wrote his account of Jesus' ministry.[9] It should not be surprising then that Mark's chief interest is to depict Jesus as the divine warrior in the final apocalyptic war.

If written in 69 CE, Jesus' crucifixion would have been less than forty years before the time of Mark's composition, and in the apocalyptic discourse in Chapter 13, the Markan Jesus declares, "Truly I tell you, this generation will not pass away until all these things have taken place" (v. 30). The things to which Jesus is referring presumably includes, in addition to the horrors of the end-times, his second coming as the triumphant Son of Man. Given the events taking place in Palestine, it would seem then that Mark expected his return very soon, perhaps any minute. His return would be the climactic conclusion to the cosmic war.

For Mark, however, the first phase of that war had been inaugurated by Jesus' earthly ministry nearly forty years earlier. Boyd is quite correct in asserting then that "the thematic unity of Christ's ministry (as well as that of his disciples and the early postapostolic church) becomes fully intelligible only against the backdrop of a warfare worldview."[10] This apocalyptic war is articulated in terms of the combat myth, and the enemies are those of the combat myth.

Genre

Assuming that Mark is indeed drawing from mythic material to compose and structure his gospel, we are presented with important questions about the nature of his work, particularly with regard to historicity. To what extent is Mark's composition biography, and to what extent is it apocalyptic myth? While there may seem to be a tension between these two forms of narrative, such incongruities are likely far more jarring to moderns than to Mark's initial audience. We have already seen how the combat myth was, even from the earliest times, frequently utilized to articulate events occurring in historical time and space. The ancient Israelites only emphasized this aspect,

---

[9] Ibid., 14.
[10] Boyd, *God at War*, 19.

articulating, for example, the "historical" event of the miracle at the Red Sea in terms of the "mythic" language of the *Chaoskampf* tradition. Certainly for Mark, his gospel is "myth" insofar as it communicates "ultimate reality"[11]—namely the salvific work of Jesus through his battle with Satan. But it is not only myth in the word's most basic sense, for his narrative is more than symbolic storytelling, and many of the deeds of Jesus are certainly not beyond the means of ordinary human language to express. Like the Greek writers of *historia*, then, he is narrating human events in human time. Mark's gospel is thus an historical account expressed in terms of apocalyptic myth.

Indeed, Norman Perrin refers to Mark as an "apocalyptic drama,"[12] while, in her extensive commentary on Mark, Collins observes:

> The author of Mark has taken the model of biblical sacred history and transformed it, first, by infusing it with an eschatological and apocalyptic perspective and, second, by adapting it to Hellenistic historiographical and biographical traditions.[13]

Elsewhere she suggests that "[a]lthough the Gospel of Mark is not history in the rational, empirical Greek sense or in the modern critical sense, it seems to have been such in an eschatological or apocalyptic sense and in the intention of the author."[14] Thus, we might say that Mark is writing apocalyptic biography, or even *biography as apocalypse*.

This blend of mythology and biography is what allows Mark to cast Jesus as both the messianic divine warrior and the carpenter from Nazareth. Forsyth highlights this blending of historical narrative and cosmic myth well when he writes:

> ...[T]he link is clear between the explicit war language of the apocalyptic writings themselves and the general context into which Mark, and the other synoptic writers, place the daily activity of Jesus. The link is a narrative, the Christian legacy from the ancient combat myth but now transformed to history

---

[11] For a discussion of myth and history in these terms, see Batto, *Slaying the Dragon*, 11.

[12] Norman Perrin and Dennis Duling, *The New Testament, an Introduction: Proclamation and Parenesis, Myth and History* (San Diego: Harcourt Brace Jovanovich, 1982), 237.

[13] Collins, *Mark*, 1.

[14] *Is Mark's Gospel a Life of Jesus?: The Question of Genre*, The Père Marquette Lecture in Theology (Milwaukee: Marquette University Press, 1990), 148.

or legend, in which Jesus plays the role of hero and liberator of his people from the depredations of, now even possession by, the powers of evil.[15]

If indeed Mark is writing "a particular kind of history, which may be called a narration of the course of the eschatological events,"[16] and the central eschatological event was God's battle with Satan, then Mark is narrating the ministry of Jesus as the historical realization of God's battle with Satan. In Mark, the apocalyptic combat myth is thus expressed in historical terms, and history is articulated via the framework of the combat myth. While there is a kind of innovation here, as Collins suggests, it is hardly unprecedented. Such application of the myth should not be surprising to us, since it was just this kind of use that characterized the combat myth genre throughout the history of Israel, and indeed, throughout the history of the ancient Near East. History and myth are expressed in terms of the other.

---

[15] Forsyth, *The Old Enemy*, 287.
[16] Collins, *Is Mark's Gospel a Life of Jesus?: The Question of Genre*, 148. Cf. *Mark*, 42-4.

CHAPTER 5
PREPARING THE WAY: MARK'S PROLOGUE

Before turning to Jesus' specific battles with Satan, Sea, and Death, our introductory concerns lead us to consider the prologue of Mark's gospel (1:1-11), for it is here that the author sets out the very core of his message and the framework for the rest of his narrative. Indeed, Rikki E. Watts has stressed the importance of Mark's prologue for understanding the entire gospel's message and structure.[1] He has shown that, in keeping with the literary customs of ancient literature by which a prologue was expected to present the principal concerns of the entire work at the beginning, *the introductory verses of Mark's gospel are programmatic*. Watts writes:

> Taken together with Mark's apparent awareness of contemporary literary techniques (e.g. his use of chiasm and hinge structures), these factors suggest that he also understood the importance of his prologue. In literary antiquity the role of the prologue was, by convention, to provide 'an indication of what is to be said so that hearers can know beforehand what the work is about'.[2]

Citing Donald Earl's study on ancient literary prologue conventions,[3] he then notes, "So widespread was this convention that whether you were dealing with 'history, epideictic oratory, philosophical dialogue, political treatise or whatever, your first sentence had to announce what you were writing'."[4] If Mark does indeed place this traditional emphasis on his opening, then one should expect it to reveal much about the broader concerns and message of the evangelist.

Indeed, I shall argue that, with his prologue, Mark introduces the fundamental relationship between Jesus' ministry and the combat myth—a relationship which will fundamentally informs the rest of the work. Compositionally, this prologue is made up of three components: (1) the title of the work (v. 1),[5] (2) the scriptural epigraph (vv. 2-3), and

---

[1] Rikki E. Watts, *Isaiah's New Exodus in Mark* (Tübingen: Mohr Siebeck, 1997), 53-136.

[2] Ibid., 54. The concluding citation is from Aristotle's *Rhetoric* 1414b.

[3] Donald Earl, "Prologue-Form in Ancient Historiography," *ANRW* 1.2 (1972): 856.

[4] Watts, *Isaiah's New Exodus in Mark*, 55.

[5] For Mk 1:1 as the work's title, see e.g., Collins, *Mark*, 130-2; Marcus, *Mark 1-8*, 143; Pheme Perkins, *The New Interpreter's Bible 8*, 12 vols. (Nashville: Abingdon Press, 1994), 527.

(3) the scene of baptism and election of Jesus as Son of God (vv. 4-11). Each of these components serves, in fact, to cement the connection between Jesus and the divine warrior of the combat myth tradition.

The Title: Proclamation of Victory

Because of its prevalence in Christian history, the term "good news" (*euangelion*) found in the title of Mark has become so commonplace that it does not immediately strike a modern reader as remarkable. Indeed, the word was common already in the early church. Paul uses it frequently in his letters to refer to the core of the Christian message, as do other authors of the New Testament.[6] Such usage has continued to the present day, such that the English derivative "gospel" itself is generally understood as the whole Christian message of salvation and redemption in its broadest terms. One is thus tempted to assume that it means here just what it has meant through extensive Christian usage: the saving work of Jesus Christ through his death and resurrection. While this is true in some respects, this crucial word seems, in fact, to have drawn its original semantic power from its associations with the Hebrew combat myth tradition.

This idea of a "good report," "good news" or "glad tidings" (all of which I shall use interchangeably) has rich and ancient origins, many of which we have in fact already noted. The roots of the term can be observed even in the ancient Canaanite mytho-cultic literature from Ugarit—which, of course, had parallels in ancient Israel. In this context, the "good news" refers specifically to Baal's victory over the forces of Chaos and the construction of his palace/temple demanded by his consequent kingship. So Anat joyously proclaims El's decree:

> Adolescent Anat laughed,
> She raised her voice and declared:
> "Receive the good news, O Baal,
> Good news I bring to you!
> 'Let a house be given you like your brothers',
> A court, like your kin's.
> Call a caravan into your house,

---

[6] Rom 1:1-2, 9, 15, 17; 11:28; 15:16, 19-20; 16:25; 1 Cor 1:17; 4:15; 9:12, 14, 16, 18, 23; 15:1-2; 2 Cor 2:12; 4:3-4; 8:18; 9:13; 10:14, 16; 11:7; Gal 1:7, 11; 2:2, 5, 7, 14; 4:13; Eph 1:13; 3:6-7; 6:19; Phil 1:7, 12, 14, 16, 27; Col 1:5-6, 23; 1 Thes 1:5; 2:2, 4, 8-9; 3:2; 2 Thes 1:8; 2:14; 2 Tim 1:8, 10-11; 2:8; Philemon 1:13; 1 Pet 1:12, 4:6; Rev 14:6.

Wares inside your palace.
Let the mountains bring you abundant silver,
The hills, the choicest gold.
And build the house of silver and gold,
The house of purest lapis lazuli.'"[7]

Likewise, Sigmund Mowinckel observes:

> The term 'glad tidings' (*bšrt*) was already used in Ugarit about the announcement that Baal had again become alive, and in the same terms the cultic festival [of Tabernacles] announced to Israel the appearance of Yahweh as king and his enthronement.[8]

That is, Baal had defeated the forces of Chaos and was now resurrected, thus able to bring again the life-giving autumnal rains. This was celebrated as "good news" (*bšwrh*) at the New Year festival where Baal, perhaps ritually enthroned, was praised as king over the cosmos for returning fertility to the land. The earliest use and thus the most basic context for the term lies therefore in the cultic rites of the New Year festival and its celebration of the *Chaoskampf*.

As Mowinckel intimates, the same was true in the Hebrew tradition, where the act of "reporting the good news" was signified by the cognate Hebrew verb *bśr*. Such, for example, is the word's meaning in the Hebrew psalms recited at Yahweh's enthronement during the Feast of Tabernacles. The people would joyously proclaim the good news of Yahweh's victories over the chaos-monsters and his consequent accession to kingship over the cosmos. Used in this context, both at Ugarit and Israel, the verb *bśr* means, "To report the good news of the divine warrior's victory over the forces of Chaos at the New Year festival." In the Greek of the Septuagint, however, this word is consistently translated by the verb *euangelizomai*. Thus, for Greek-speaking Jews in the apocalyptic period—when (as we have seen) the combat myth and its cultic significance were still widely appreciated—the semantic associations of *bśwrh* would have been carried by the Greek word *euangelion*.

However, this "good news" takes on new significance with the rise of apocalypticism. As we have seen, the apocalyptic worldview was largely developed out of late prophecy's cosmic aggrandizement of the traditional New Year festival. Mowinckel summarizes this idea

---

[7] *CTA* 1.4.v.25-35 = Smith, *The Ugaritic Baal Cycle Vol. 1*, 539.
[8] Mowinckel, *The Psalms in Israel's Worship*, 142.

well, drawing attention to the influence of Deutero-Isaiah and positing that, in later Jewish thought after the Babylonian Captivity,

> [t]he salvation to come is looked upon as an enthronement day of Yahweh with cosmic dimensions—such in short is the substance of the prophecy of re-establishment and later also of eschatology. That was how Deutero-Isaiah preached it (Isa. 52.7), and he gave the tone to later prophecy. He largely imitates the forms and ideas of the psalms of enthronement and harvest in order to express what was at hand: the victory of Yahweh over all hostile powers and his taking possession of the world empire, with the renewal of the covenant with his chosen people and its royal house, and with endless happiness and greatness for his worshippers.[9]

We have considered these developments already. Of particular importance here, however, is the way in which Deutero-Isaiah appropriates the traditional language of the festival—specifically this term, the "good news"—to articulate his message of cosmic restoration. So in Isaiah 52:7-8, for example, we read:

> How beautiful upon the mountains
>> are the feet of *the herald of the good news* (*mĕbaśśēr*),
>> *who announces peace,*
> *the herald who reports good news* (*mĕbaśśēr ṭôb*),
>> *who announces salvation,*
>> who says to Zion, "Your God has become king!"
> Listen! Your sentinels lift up their voices;
>> together they sing for joy;
> For in plain sight they see
>> the return of Yahweh to Zion.

The imagery of the festival is clear. For those suffering in captivity, the prophet promises that God will soon reveal himself to his people for all to see—just as they had witnessed the cultic epiphany of his ark going in procession to the Temple. So too, employing the traditional language of the festival, the prophet infuses new cosmic significance to "reporting the good news." Yahweh is again victorious again over the forces of Chaos (here understood as oppressive Babylon). This is the "salvation" of Israel, the "good news" of the enemy's defeat. Kingship of Yahweh consequently follows. Thus, with all else about the Near Year, the "good news" is aggrandized in Deutero-Isaiah's vision of restoration. Notably, the Septuagint translates this passage with the Greek verb *euangelizomai*.

---

[9] Ibid., 189-90.

This same idea informs Isaiah 40:3-5 and 9-10, where the prophet links the traditional processional epiphany of the festival and the cosmic procession at the promised restoration:

> A voice cries out:
> "In the wilderness, clear the Road of Yahweh!
>   Make straight in the desert a processional way for our God!
> Every valley shall be lifted up,
>   and every mountain and hill be made low;
> the uneven ground shall become level,
>   and the rough places a plain.
> Then the glory of Yahweh shall be revealed,
>   and all people shall see it together,
>   for the mouth of Yahweh has spoken."
> …Ascend a high mountain,
>   O herald of good news (*mĕbaśśeret*) to Zion;
> lift up your voice with strength,
>   O herald of good news (*mĕbaśśeret*) to Jerusalem,
>   lift it up, do not fear;
> say to the cities of Judah,
>   "Behold your God!"
> *See*! Lord God comes with might,
>   and his arm rules for him. (Is 40:3-5, 9-10a)

Here the herald reporting the good news of Yahweh's victory is the herald of the New Year procession. As we have seen, the priestly herald was to cry out to the people, "Prepare the Road of Yahweh!" at the festival and ensure a clear path for the cultic objects of the procession. Like Isaiah 52, the glad tidings are announced by this messenger in celebration. In the Septuagint, this herald is called *ho euangelizomenos*—"the good news reporter" or "the messenger of the good news." As we shall see presently, these very verses from Isaiah 40 form the core of Mark's scriptural epigraph.

Following these developments of late prophecy into apocalypticism, and keeping in mind the significance of the combat myth and New Year festival in that emerging worldview, it is clear to see how the "good news" would have been understood in such a context. By the first century CE, a claim to "report the good news" would have been a pregnant expression of apocalyptic fulfillment. It would have signified that Yahweh *had* defeated the Devil, that cosmic reflex of the chaos-monster. The apocalyptic battle had been waged—and won.

Thus, the idea of the "good news" sees three distinct stages in its semantic development: 1) In the traditional mytho-cultic context at

Israel and perhaps at Ugarit too, it was the announcement of the processional herald at the New Year festival of the storm-god's victory over the chaos-enemies and consequent enthronement as king. 2) In late Hebrew prophecy it was the cosmic aggrandizement of this idea: announcement of Yahweh's victory over Israel's oppressors and the impending procession along a cosmic *via sacra* to his new Temple, where the god would then reign as king over the world forever. 3) Finally, in Jewish apocalypticism, it is the announcement of Yahweh's victory over the forces of the Devil, resulting in his eternal kingship over the resurrected and re-purified righteous.

It is in this final sense, as the apocalyptic reflex of the traditional "good news," that we are to understand Mark's "good news of Jesus Christ" (*euangelion Iēsou christou*).[10] Thus, with the very title of his work, Mark is boldly proclaiming his theological message: Jesus Christ is the divine warrior who has come and won victory in battle against the Devil. By calling his work by this name, he sets the tone for the rest of his work: this is to be a chronicle of war. So, on these connotations and associations of the word *euangelion*, Joel Marcus notes:

> Both in Deutero-Isaiah and elsewhere the term and its cognates are associated with military victory (see e.g. Philostratus *Life of Apollonius of Tyana* 5.8; Isa 40:9-10; 41:25-27), a nuance that Boring[11]...captures nicely when he translates *euangelion* as "good news of victory from the battlefield."[12]

Perhaps, then, a better translation of Mark's title might be: "The Beginning of the Good News of Jesus Christ's Victory from the Battlefield." Such would capture the essence of the word, anyway.

That this is but the beginning, however, must not be overlooked, since Mark calls it only such. This is just *hē archē*, the outset or start, suggesting that the cosmic war is only begun in the ensuing account of Jesus Christ's ministry. Yet how are we to understand this? What marks his ministry as preliminary or incomplete? What remains to be finished after Jesus' battles with Satan, Sea, and Death? For elucidation on this point, consider another text which depicts Jesus as the divine

---

[10] Watts, *Isaiah's New Exodus in Mark*, 96-9 and esp. 167-8, makes a similar conclusion in drawing the connection between the *euangelion* of Jesus and that of the Yahweh-Warrior in Deutero-Isaiah.

[11] M. Eugene Boring, *Mark: A Commentary*, New Testament Library (Louisville: Westminster/John Knox Press, 2006), 30.

[12] Marcus, *Mark 1-8*, 146.

warrior *qua* the apocalyptic combat myth: the Book of Revelation. There we saw the earthly ministry and sacrificial death of Jesus beginning, but not concluding, the apocalyptic conflict. It is by the blood of the Lamb that the Dragon is fought and cast down from heaven. But, once cast down, his power actually increases over the earth. It is not until the *second* coming of Jesus that the Dragon is ultimately vanquished. In Revelation, then, Jesus' earthly ministry does parallel a spiritual battle with the Dragon: such is the beginning of the good news. The conclusion is the End itself.

Such a schema was probably not idiosyncratic to the author of Revelation and his immediate audience, but rather representative of broader Christian conceptions of the church and its position in history at the close of the first century CE. Many Christians, who indeed understood themselves to be living after Jesus' ministry yet before the cosmic Day of Yahweh, would have viewed their days as the historical interim between the inauguration and the culmination of this great battle. Jesus began the battle with the Dragon; the final conclusion would come at the imminent End.

Such seems to be the theological perspective indicated by Mark's title: The *Beginning* of the Good News. Indeed, as we shall see in the following chapter, Mark seems to affirm the general progression of Revelation with its various stages of apocalyptic war. These considerations, however, shall be presented in due course. For now, at least, we have considered Mark's title and found that within its six Greek words a whole theological vision is expressed. The work Mark presents is to be a chronicle of the outset of the apocalyptic war. Jesus is the divine warrior and has proved victorious, at least in an initial way, over the forces of the Devil.

The Epigraph: Heralding the Sacred Way

Recalling Watts's observation that the prologue and in particular the first sentences of ancient works were programmatic, it is revealing indeed that Mark quotes Deutero-Isaiah from the very outset of his work. In fact, Mark's epigraph is an amalgamation of two scriptural passages: Malachi 3:1 and Isaiah 40:1,[13] yet Mark credits only Isaiah.

---

[13] Many commentators also see Exodus 23:20 in Mark's epigraph. This may be questionable, however, since it is in fact Malachi who has imbedded this reference into *his* composition. The allusion then is Malachi's, not Mark's. Nevertheless, it is worth

The reason for this single attribution has long been a source of debate, leading many scholars to see it as a simple error.[14] However, when we appreciate the influence of Deutero-Isaiah on apocalyptic eschatology, the single attribution to Isaiah becomes clear. Mark would have it explicit that Isaiah's message—the prophet's revaloration of the New Year festival—is indeed central to his own. As the chief prophet of cosmic rejuvenation *qua* the combat myth and its cultic enshrinement, the tradition of Isaiah is the prophetic lineage in which Mark most directly wishes to stand.

Despite this explicit emphasis on Isaiah, however, both of the passages he quotes are in fact rooted in the imagery of the New Year:

Malachi 3:1-2 = Mark 1:2	**Isaiah 40:3-5 = Mark 1:3**
<u>See, I am sending my messenger to prepare the Way before me</u>, and the Lord whom you seek will suddenly come to his Temple. The messenger of the covenant in whom you delight—indeed, he is coming, says Yahweh of Hosts.	<u>A voice cries out: "In the wilderness prepare the Way of Yahweh, make straight in the desert a processional road for our God</u>. Every valley shall be lifted up, and every mountain and hill be made low; the uneven ground shall become level, and the rough places a plain. Then the glory of Yahweh shall be revealed, and all people shall see it together, for the mouth of Yahweh has spoken."

Thus, while the attribution is limited only to Isaiah, *both passages share a crucial conceit: they both employ the imagery of the New Year festival, at which Yahweh, as the victorious divine warrior, processes up his Sacred Way to the Temple.* Since we have already considered at length Deutero-Isaiah's utilization of this traditional material, a few observations must be made about Malachi—namely, his reasons for employing the imagery of the New Year festival and why Mark includes him in his crucial epigraph.

In her commentary on Malachi, Beth Glazier-McDonald insightfully notes the prophet's use of mytho-cultic imagery, astutely identifying the "Way" of 3:1 with the processional road traveled by

---

noting for the broader appreciation of the New Year festival's presence in Mark's quoted material, that the verse occurs immediately after a list of Yahweh's festival commandments, specifically the Feast of Tabernacles in v. 16. Any significance in this proximity is questionable.

[14] See e.g., Bart D. Ehrman, *Misquoting Jesus: The Story Behind Who Changed the Bible and Why* (New York: HarperSanFrancisco, 2005), 94-5.

Yahweh at the autumn New Year festival.[15] Thus, the prophet's description of Yahweh as "the Lord whom you seek" recalls the epiphanic nature of the procession, when the people would *see* Yahweh in the form of his ark passing by them. This, Glazier-McDonald claims, is mirrored in Enthronement Psalm 24, where the people likewise seek Yahweh on his day of epiphany.[16] Furthermore, Malachi's use of *ādōn* ("lord") highlights Yahweh's kingship, emphasizing the cultic "Day of the Lord" motif.[17] His coming against the wicked and the sorcerers recalls his coming against the chaos-waters in battle, and is described in the same terms.[18] Thus, Malachi, like Deutero-Isaiah before him, employs the festival as a metaphor for spiritual regeneration/re-purification.

Interestingly, Glazier-McDonald—entirely outside the context of Markan considerations—also notes that Malachi 3:1 is in "striking parallel" to Isaiah 40:3,[19] the other text Mark quotes. However, her analysis of this connection stops at simple recognition; no explanation or further comparison is presented. The reason should be clear to us, however: both are drawing from a common font of tradition, the New Year festival, as a potent metaphor for their prophetic message. Though writing at different times and for different purposes, they share a common set of ideas and images drawn from the cultic celebration. Given the popularity and importance of the festival, these images would have been well-known—cultural givens whose metaphorical use could be broadly appreciated.

Thus, though both make use of the festival's imagery, their specific concerns cause them to emphasize different aspects of the tradition. Deutero-Isaiah, concerned with Babylon's subjugation of Israel and the hope of her restoration, focuses on the divine warrior component of the festival, with its victory over the chaos-enemy and the consequent rejuvenation. Malachi, on the other hand, has a rather narrower concern. Writing after the Temple has been rebuilt, his message seeks to address the ritual impurity of the people and the cultus, which he feels to be in a state of serious breach. Thus, in his call to reform, *Malachi employs instead the festal image of the Temple's re-*

---

[15] Beth Glazier-McDonald, *Malachi: The Divine Messenger*, SBL Dissertation Series (Atlanta: Scholars Press, 1987), 136-42.
[16] Ibid., 141.
[17] Ibid., 142.
[18] Ibid., 155-9.
[19] Ibid., 136.

purification and general ablution of the people. In this ritual, we recall, the ark of Yahweh would leave the Temple so that the purification could take place. This purification complete, the ark would then return along the Sacred Way for reinstallation, where the cultic offerings would once again be pure and efficacious. All of this is present in Malachi's metaphor:

> See, I am sending my messenger to prepare the Way before me, and the Lord whom you seek will suddenly come to his Temple. The messenger of the covenant in whom you delight—indeed, he is coming, says Yahweh of Hosts. But who can endure the Day of his coming, and who can stand when he appears? For he is like a refiner's fire and like fullers' soap; he will sit as a refiner and purifier of silver, and *he will purify the descendants of Levi* and refine them like gold and silver, *until they present offerings to Yahweh in righteousness. Then the offering of Judah and Jerusalem will be pleasing to Yahweh as in the days of old and as in former years.* (Mal 3:1-4)

Thus, Malachi envisions a figure who will officiate the ritual purification of the priests and people. This figure he poetically describes in terms of the priestly herald of the New Year festival, who prepared the Sacred Way for Yahweh on "the Day of the Lord"—that time of annual renewal and ablution of the people.

Thus, in both Isaiah 40 and Malachi 3, the processional herald of the New Year festival plays a key role. This was the messenger of Yahweh who, proclaiming the "good news" of the god's victory over Chaos, cleared the Sacred Way for the great cultic procession. In Malachi's vision, which reflects the priestly identity of the original herald and thus his key role in the ablution process, this herald is the leader of the great purification.

Like other aspects of the festival, this messenger figure too seems to have been the object of cosmic aggrandizement in apocalyptic speculation. In this sense, the herald of the festival comes to have an eschatological reflex in a great purifying figure who shall come at the cosmic New Year to facilitate, as it were, the Great Re-purification. Indeed, in Malachi, this awaited figure is presented as a second Elijah. One reason for this identification of the cosmic herald as an apocalyptic Elijah becomes intelligible when considered against the background of similar apocalyptic speculation. Elijah was one of only two figures mentioned in the Hebrew Bible to have ascended directly to Heaven before death. The other was Enoch, of whom prolific use was made by apocalypticists, engendering a whole literature around the figure (including the book *1 Enoch*, which we briefly examined). These figures, because of their special ascension, were believed to have had privileged access to the workings of the Divine Council. Moreover, their purity was evinced by their special admittance to the Heavenly Court. Thus, it is understandable that apocalyptic speculation employing a typology of the New Year festival would posit the emphatically pure yet still-human Elijah in the mediating role of Yahweh's herald.

As Mark implies from the outset of his gospel (1:6) and states explicitly elsewhere (9:11-13), John the Baptist is indeed the second, apocalyptic Elijah. Indeed, as Mark's epigraph is immediately followed by the appearance of John the Baptist and his preparatory work for Jesus, the association is clear from the beginning: *John the Baptist is the apocalyptic reflex of the New Year festival's herald, readying the eschatological Sacred Way for the divine warrior Jesus.* Malachi 3 looks to a great purifying herald who shall refine the people and the cult; so John washes the people and mediates their reformation. Isaiah 40 looks to Yahweh's "coming with strength" down this Sacred Way; so John speaks of Jesus, saying "the Stronger One is coming" (*erchetai ho ischuroteros*). Indeed, even the idea of Jesus *following* John, albeit temporally and not spatially, admits comparison to John as leader of the procession, standing at the head of the great eschatological New Year.

However, John himself acknowledges that his purification is not the ultimate cleansing. He washes with mere water; Jesus shall cleanse by the very Spirit of God. This acknowledgement is important, not least because it sets up the expectation of another, final purification performed by Jesus. That event must wait, however, until the final chapters of Mark's gospel. Indeed, with this acknowledgement, *Mark sets up an expectation which intimates the very structure of his gospel: John has prepared the Way; now Jesus must walk it up to the Temple and completely purify the cultus and the people.* The Sacred Way now leads from John to crucifixion.

Indeed, when we examine the structure of the Mark's gospel, this progression is precisely what we find. Most scholars recognize a tripartite structure to the Gospel of Mark, with the two key breaks around 8:21 and 11:1.[20] Joel Marcus's simple outline is representative of this consensus:

> I. 1:1-15 – PROLOGUE
> II. 1:16-8:21 – **ACT I**: Jesus' Early Ministry
>   A.   1:16-3:6 FIRST MAJOR SECTION – Honeymoon and Beginning of Opposition
>   B.   3:7-6:6a: SECOND MAJOR SECTION – The Struggle Intensifies
>   C.   6:6b-8:21: THIRD MAJOR SECTION – Feasts
> III. 8:22-10:52 – **ACT II**: FOURTH MAJOR SECTION – "On the Way"
> IV. 11-1-15:47 – **ACT III**: Jerusalem Ministry
>   A.   11:1-13:37: FIFTH MAJOR SECTION – Teaching
>   B.   14:1-15:47: SIXTH MAJOR SECTION – Dying
> V. 16:1-8: EPILOGUE[21]

Thus, after a brief prologue (variously defined by commentators), Part I narrates Jesus' ministry around the Sea of Galilee; Part II depicts Jesus' activities on the way to Jerusalem; and Part III tells of his teaching and death in Jerusalem. A brief epilogue narrates his resurrection. The most basic schema might therefore read simply: 1) Sea of Galilee Ministry, 2) The Way, 3) Jerusalem Ministry.

However, while Part II serves to link Jesus' ministries in Galilee and Jerusalem, it is hardly a mere transitional bridge. Rather, scholars recognize it as a significant, deliberately-crafted part of Mark's gospel with a core, unifying theme: *the Way*. J. M. Swartley's analysis was seminal in structural studies of Mark and the evangelist's use of the "Way."[22] His key findings are well summarized by Watts:

> [Swartley] begins by noting that several scholars have confirmed the literary integrity of Mark's 'Way'/'journey' section, namely 8:21/8:27 – 10:45/11:1, citing its three triads consisting of passion predictions (8:31; 9:31; 10:32), the disciples' failure to understand (8:32-33; 9:32; 10:35-41), and subsequent teaching (8:32-38; 9:35-37;10:42-45). Other unifying themes are: an increasing focus on both Jesus' disciples and their discipleship via the passion predictions on his messiahship, the Christological declarations in the bracketing 'healing of the blind'

---

[20] Cf. Watts, *Isaiah's New Exodus in Mark*, 123-4. Watts surveyed sixty-one representative analyses of Markan structure and concludes that "even in the face of differing organising rubrics there is substantial agreement as to the major Markan literary divisions," 123.

[21] Marcus, *Mark 1-8*, 64.

[22] W. M. Swartley, "The Structural Function of the Term 'Way' (Hodos) in Mark's Gospel," in *The New Way of Jesus: Essays Presented to Howard Charles*, ed. William Klassen (Newton: Faith and Life Press, 1980).

narratives (8:22-30 and 10:46-52), the recurring use of the [Son of Man] title, and the transfiguration scene. Finally, there is Mark's redactional use of ὁδός. As Swartley notes, this term appears seven times in the 'Way' section, frequently in key contexts and in conjunction with imperfect verbs (8:27; 9:33, 34; 10:17, 32, 46, 52). Markan redactional intent is suggested in that of these instances Matthew has only two parallels (both with aorists: 20:17b, roughly par. to Mk 10:32; 20:30 par. to Mk 10:46) and Luke merely one (18:35 par. Mk 10:46). This is in stark contrast to the seven occurrences in Mark outside of this section (1:2f; 2:23; 4:4, 15; 6:8; 8:3; 11:8; 12:14) five of which are paralleled in both Matthew and Luke.[23]

Thus, the middle section of Mark constitutes a distinct literary unit with its own complex organization, the most important features of which emphasize 1) the disciples' misunderstanding of Jesus' identity/role, and 2) the "Way" they are traveling to Jerusalem.[24]

Of scholars writing on Markan structure since Swartley, Rikki E. Watts offers the most insightful reading in his book *Isaiah's New Exodus in Mark*. According to Watts, the idea of a "New Exodus" is a key motif in Deutero-Isaiah, who articulates his vision of Restoration from exile via an Exodus typology: just as Yahweh led the Israelites out of Egypt into the Promised Land, so shall he now lead them out of Babylon back to Zion. Thus the motif follows the progression:

A) Yahweh's deliverance of his exiled people from the power of the nations and their idols;
B) the journey along the 'Way' in which Yahweh leads his people from their captivity among the nations;
C) arrival in Jerusalem, the place of his presence, where Yahweh is enthroned in a gloriously restored Zion.[25]

Bringing together numerous strands of evidence, Watts argues that Mark means to depict Jesus as the divine warrior leading Israel out of captivity (from Satan's forces) in terms of the form of Isaiah's "New Exodus" motif. Thus Watts argues that Mark's tripartite structure mirrors the above three-fold progression of Isaiah's "New Exodus":

---

[23] Watts, *Isaiah's New Exodus in Mark*, 124-5.
[24] See also Werner H. Kelber, *Mark's Story of Jesus* (Philadelphia: Fortress Press, 1979), 43-56; Joel Marcus, *The Way of the Lord: Christological Exegesis of the Old Testament in the Gospel of Mark*, T & T Clark Academic Paperbacks (London: T & T Clark International, 2004), 12-47; *Mark 8-16: A New Translation with Introduction and Commentary*, The Anchor Bible (New York: Doubleday, 2009), 589-92.
[25] Watts, *Isaiah's New Exodus in Mark*, 135.

<table>
<tr><td align="center">Isaiah</td><td align="center">Mark</td></tr>
<tr><td>A) Yahweh's deliverance of his exiled people from the power of the nations and their idols
B) the journey along the 'Way' in which Yahweh leads his people from their captivity among the nations
C) arrival in Jerusalem, the place of his presence, where Yahweh is enthroned in a gloriously restored Zion</td><td>A) Jesus delivers his people from Satan's forces around the Sea of Galilee

B) the journey along the 'Way' to Jerusalem

C) arrival in Jerusalem, where Jesus is crucified</td></tr>
</table>

Watts's analysis is most astute, and he is indeed correct about Mark's dependence on Deutero-Isaiah and the prophet's three-fold progression. However, while he recognizes this crucial link between Mark and Isaiah, Watts's analysis of Deutero-Isaiah is incomplete, since he fails to appreciate the true nature of the original progression in Deutero-Isaiah: *it is based upon the combat myth and the New Year festival*. For Deutero-Isaiah, the defeat of Babylon mirrored the defeat of the chaos-monster, the Sacred Way Yahweh's processional way, and the arrival in Jerusalem the installation/enthronement of the ark in the Temple:

<table>
<tr><td align="center">New Year Festival</td><td align="center">Isaiah</td></tr>
<tr><td>A) Yahweh's deliverance of his people from the powers of Chaos and destruction

B) the journey along the Way, over which Yahweh leads his people in glad procession
C) arrival in Jerusalem, the place of his presence, where Yahweh is enthroned in a re-purified Temple</td><td>A) Yahweh's deliverance of his exiled people from the power of the nations and their idols;

B) the journey along the 'Way' in which Yahweh leads his people from their captivity among the nations
C) arrival in Jerusalem, the place of his presence, where Yahweh is enthroned in a gloriously restored Zion</td></tr>
</table>

Watts's failure to appreciate the New Year typology in Deutero-Isaiah is typical of commentators' consideration of the Exodus motif as a *sui generis* motif rather than an adaptation of the original combat myth pattern. Once one appreciates the underlying role of the combat myth, however, various other resonances in texts like Deutero-Isaiah can be heard which vastly improve our understanding of their theological message. So it is with Mark.

Despite Watts's failure to appreciate this crucial mythic/cultic pattern, his investigations are immensely fruitful for this study, for we see that Mark is not drawing upon an Exodus typology inherited from

Deutero-Isaiah, but rather a combat myth/New Year festival typology inherited from the prophet (both directly, and mediated through apocalyptic developments):

New Year Festival	Mark
A) Yahweh's deliverance of his people from the powers of Chaos and destruction	A) Jesus delivers his people from Satan's forces around the Sea of Galilee
B) the journey along the Way, over which Yahweh leads his people in glad procession	B) the journey along the 'Way' to Jerusalem
C) arrival in Jerusalem, the place of his presence, where Yahweh is enthroned in a re-purified Temple	C) arrival in Jerusalem, where Jesus is enthroned at his crucifixion after re-purifying the Temple

Thus the eschatologized combat myth/New Year festival is fundamental to the general outline and structure of Mark. Rendered somewhat basically, Mark's structure thus appears like this:

> *Prologue* (1:1-11): Heralded and Elected
> **PART I: THE SEA** (1:12-8:21): Battles Satan and the Sea itself around the Sea of Galilee
> **PART II: THE WAY** (8:22-13:37): Victorious, leads procession up the Way to the Temple/Jerusalem, which he re-purifies[26]
> **PART III: ZION** (14:1-15:47): Enthroned on the cross, battles Death.
> *Epilogue* (16:1-8): Victorious and Resurrected

Thus, Watts's observations about the traditionally programmatic nature of the prologue and the Gospel of Mark hold true, as it is undeniably significant that Mark's two scriptural citations both allude to the processional road of Yahweh at the New Year festival. While both Isaiah and Malachi originally drew on the image of the processional road for different reasons, their common aggrandizement of the festival—that key font for apocalyptic imagery—explains Mark's utilization of their prophecies in his scriptural epigraph. By quoting these passages at the outset, Mark is signaling that his "good news of Jesus Christ" will fulfill these prophecies, as Jesus shall defeat the forces of Chaos and then walk the eschatological processional way to a re-purified Temple for enthronement. In this way, the combat myth and its key cultic expression provide Mark the very structure for his narrative.

---

[26] For setting the terminus of this section at 13:37 and not 10:52 (like Marcus and others), see Chapter 8.

As we have seen, the Red Sea was connected with the chaos-waters from Israel's earliest poetic traditions. Interestingly, however, it is not only the Red Sea that is depicted in these terms. For while the Israelites exit Egypt by crossing the Red Sea, they enter Canaan by crossing the Jordan River:

> For Yahweh your God dried up the waters of the Jordan for you until you crossed over, as Yahweh your God did to the Red Sea, which he dried up for us until we crossed over, so that all peoples of the earth might know that the hand of Yahweh is mighty, and so that you may fear Yahweh your God forever.[27]

In this sense, Yahweh's control over the waters—both the Red *Sea* (Heb. *Yām*) and the Jordan *River* (Heb. *Nāhār*)—parallel Baal's victories over Sea (Yamm) and River (Nahar). So Psalm 114 paints the Red Sea and the Jordan River as the defeated enemies of the Exodus *Chaoskampf*:

> When Israel went out from Egypt,
>> the house of Jacob from a people of strange language,
> Judah became God's sanctuary,
>> Israel his dominion.
> The Sea looked and fled;
>> the Jordan turned back.
> The mountains skipped like rams,
>> the hills like lambs.
> Why is it, O Sea, that you flee?
>> O Jordan, that you turn back?
> O mountains, that you skip like rams?
>> O hills, like lambs?
> Tremble, O earth, at the presence of Yahweh,
>> at the presence of the God of Jacob,
> who turns the rock into a pool of water,
>> the flint into a spring of water.

The poetic parallelism here clearly echoes that of Sea and Judge River from the Ugaritic texts.[28] Moreover, while Psalm 114 echoes the ancient combat myth generally, it is specifically the literary traditions

---

[27] Josh 4:23-4.
[28] Cf. Cross, *Canaanite Myth and Hebrew Epic*, 139.

related to the New Year festival's ritual enthronement of the storm-god which the poet recalls. Compare the psalmist's taunting of Sea and River to the scene of Baal's enthronement from Ugaritic tradition:

> Baa[l] gave forth his holy voice.
> Baal repeated the is[ssue of (?)] his [li(?)]ps,
> His ho[ly (?)] voice covered (?) the earth,
> [At his] voice…the mountains trembled.
> The ancient [mountains?] leapt [up?],
> The high places of the ear[th] tottered.
> The enemies of Baal took to the woods,
> The haters of Hadd to the mountainsides.
> And Mightiest Baal spoke:
> "O Enemies of Hadd, why do you tremble?
> Why tremble, you who wield a weapon against the Warrior?
> Baal looked forward;
> His hand indeed shook,
> The cedar was in his right hand.
> So Baal was enthroned in/returned to his house.[29]

In both texts, the mountains leap at the god's power and the trembling ones are taunted for their fear of the victorious divine warrior. In Psalm 114, it is the Sea and the River who flee—those enemies of the combat myth who would cowardly submit at the god's *mighty voice*. So was the combat myth adapted to articulate Yahweh's workings at the Exodus *and* entry into Canaan.[30] In addition to the Red Sea, the Jordan River was also portrayed in Jewish tradition as the personified chaos-waters which Yahweh controls and divides—parallel to Judge River in the Ugaritic combat myth.[31]

With such semantic resonances, it is worth considering whether the Jordan River ought to be read in such a light at Jesus' baptism. Indeed, both scholarly and religious readers have traditionally done so. So Eliade, for example, considering the symbolism of Christian baptism in light of the combat myth, writes that

---

[29] *CAT* 1.4.vii.29-42 = Smith and Pitard, *The Ugaritic Baal Cycle Vol. 2*, 650.

[30] Dahood maintains that Psalm 114 primarily concerns Yahweh's entrance into Canaan. This would strengthen its connection to the Conquest in addition to the Exodus. He takes the Sea here, however, to refer to the Dead Sea and not the Red Sea. See Dahood, *Psalms*, 133-7.

[31] This association may be reflected in later Jewish folklore, which posited that Leviathan drinks from a tributary of the Jordan River, which flows into the ocean through a secret channel. On this, and other later beliefs about the chaos-monsters, see Robert Graves and Raphael Patai, *Hebrew Myths: The Book of Genesis*, 2nd ed. (London: Cassell, 1965), 47-53.

into the Christian valorization of the waters there enter certain new elements connected with a "history," specifically with sacred history. First of all, there is the valorization of baptism as a descent into the abyss of the waters for a combat with the marine monster. This descent has a model—Christ's descent into the Jordan, which was at the same time a descent into the Waters of Death.[32]

He then cites Cyril of Jerusalem, who, even in the fourth century, retained the mythological significance of Jesus' baptism. Cyril posits:

According to Job, the dragon Behemoth was in the Waters and received the Jordan into his jaws. Now, since the heads of the dragon must be broken, Jesus, having gone down into the Waters, bound the Strong One, so that we should have the power to walk on scorpions and snakes.[33]

Here the theologian explicitly links Satan with the Dragon of the *Chaoskampf* while simultaneously recalling both the *binding* and the *trampling* motifs of the combat myth—all in commentary on Jesus' baptism in the Jordan.

Of course one may counter that the scene can hardly be called a combat, since Jesus is not battling the River but merely passing through it at his baptism. However, we have seen the combat myth tradition employed in just this way to articulate the Exodus. In the song from Exodus 15, for example, God does not battle the Sea, but miraculously divides it so his people can cross. The same is true of the Jordan itself: God does not battle the Jordan, but miraculously divides it so his holy ark can cross. Though there is no battle, both the Red Sea and the Jordan crossings are intimately connected with the Hebrew combat myth. The miraculous work of God was common in both. The same is likely true here: Jesus does not battle the Jordan, but passes through it—or, one might say, *divides* it.

Allowing for this broader perspective, there are some intriguing parallels which bear consideration:

(1) As we shall see in Chapter 8, Mark depicts Jesus in terms of the Ark of the Covenant on the processional Way to Jerusalem for enthronement. Granting this, one may see Mark setting up such an interpretation with Jesus' "passing through" the Jordan (i.e., his

---

[32] Eliade, *The Sacred and the Profane: The Nature of Religion*, 133.

[33] Jean Daniélou, *Bible et Liturgie: La Thâeologie Biblique des Sacraments et des Fãetes D'aprâes les Páeres De L'eglise*, Les Orandi (Paris: Editions du Cerf, 1951), 58.

154

baptism). Of course Yahweh, in the form of his ark, passed through the Jordan on the way into Canaan; this passage inaugurated the Conquest. So does Jesus' baptism in the Jordan inaugurate the final, eschatological Conquest—that of Satan's forces over the world.

(2) Jesus is described as "going up from the water" (*anabainōn ek tou hydatos*). That the divine warrior would "go up from the water" matches well the traditional terminology of the festival, as Yahweh, after defeating the chaos-waters, would "go up" (*'ālâ*) the processional way in the form of his ark to the Temple. The Septuagint translates *'ālâ* in these passages with the Greek word *anabainō*. Thus, if Mark were seeking association with the combat myth, he is certainly using the right terminology.

(3) As soon as Jesus begins ascending from the water, the heavens are torn apart (a typical apocalyptic motif) and Yahweh's voice issues from the heavens, declaring, "You are my beloved son; in you I delight" (v. 11). This election is articulated via an allusion to Psalm 2—a psalm celebrating the Davidic king's enthronement:[34]

> Why do the nations conspire,
>   and the peoples plot in vain?
> The kings of the earth set themselves,
>   and the rulers take counsel together,
>   against Yahweh and his anointed, saying,
> "Let us burst their bonds asunder,
>   and cast their cords from us."
> He who sits in the heavens laughs;
>   Yahweh has them in derision.[35]
> Then he will speak to them in his wrath,
>   and terrify them in his fury, saying,
> "I have set my king on Zion, my holy hill."
> I will tell of the decree of Yahweh:
> He said to me, "*You are my son;*
>   *today I have begotten you.*
> Ask of me, and I will make the nations your heritage,
>   and the ends of the earth your possession.
> You shall break them with a rod of iron,
>   and dash them in pieces like a potter's vessel."

---

[34] In fact, Tremper Longman and Daniel G. Reid, *God Is a Warrior*, Studies in Old Testament Biblical Theology (Grand Rapids: Zondervan, 1995), 94, point out: "At least one scroll from Qumran (4QFlor 1:10-11 [4Q174]) interprets Psalm 2 in terms of eschatological conflict, with the enraged nations arrayed around the Lord and his messiah seen as the forces of Belial set against the elect of Israel."

[35] Mark Smith sees a parallel with Yahweh's scoffing here and the taunts of Baal at his enthronement. See Smith and Pitard, *The Ugaritic Baal Cycle Vol. 2*, 678.

> Now therefore, O kings, be wise;
>   be warned, O rulers of the earth.
> Serve Yahweh with fear,
>   with trembling, kiss his feet,
> or he will be angry, and you will perish in the way;
>   for his wrath is quickly kindled.
> Happy are all who take refuge in him.

When the enemy nations conspire against him, the king, by means of Yahweh, utterly conquers them. The king thus derives his power ultimately from Yahweh. With God's words, Mark is clearly connecting Jesus' baptism with the ancient Davidic king's election and enthronement.

Therefore, in addition to painting Jesus as the divine warrior, Mark also depicts him as the delegate of Yahweh, the awaited messiah. He thus draws on the enthronements of both Yahweh and king, simultaneously highlighting Jesus' divinity and his messiahship. Both of these kings, the heavenly and the earthly, were warriors who established order and defeated Israel's enemies. Indeed, both had power over the chaos-forces, Sea and River, as we noted in consideration of Psalm 89. Here, at enthronement, Yahweh grants to the new king both recognition as his son and powers over the chaos-waters:

> ...I will set his hand on Sea
>   and his right hand on Rivers.
> He shall cry to me, 'You are my Father,
>   my God, and the Rock of my salvation!'
> I will make him the firstborn,
>   the highest of the kings of the earth. (Ps 89:25-27)[36]

So the political theme has its apocalyptic reflex in Mark.

Thus, following John (the processional herald), Jesus enters the Jordan (traditionally associated with the chaos-waters), passes through/*divides* them via baptism (cf. the ark), "goes up from the waters" (as the ark would "go up" the processional way after defeated the chaos-waters), and as the heavens open, a mighty voice declares Jesus the son of God (in language from a Davidic enthronement psalm which likewise grants powers to subdue the chaos-waters).

Furthermore, that the spirit (or its descent) is described as a dove may also point to a connection between the Jordan and the chaos-

---

[36] Cf. Smith, *The Ugaritic Baal Cycle Vol. 1*, 109.

waters. Joel Marcus posits that, of the possible interpretations for this comparison of the Spirit with a dove,

> the most plausible is the theory that the dove is meant to echo Gen 1:2, where the spirit soars, birdlike, over the waters. This theory is supported by *b. Hag.* 15a, in which the Spirit's hovering over the primeval waters is compared with a dove's brooding over its young...[37]

This further emphasizes the Jordan as the raging waters, as "The Beginning of the Good News of Jesus Christ" mirrors the traditional "in the beginning," when Yahweh battled the chaos-waters at Creation (cf. Jn 1:1). The baptism of Jesus thus stands in a new Creation typology. The original battle of cosmogony has its apocalyptic reflex in the origin of Jesus' ministry: his baptism.

Mark sets all of these resonances in a narrative whose progression strongly resembles a scene from the apocalyptic *Testaments of the Twelve Patriarchs*. In this text we find a description of the arrival of the eschatological messiah-priest:

> When vengeance will have come upon them from the Lord, the priesthood
>   will lapse
> And then the Lord will raise up a new priest
> to whom all the words of the Lord will be revealed.
> He shall effect the judgment of truth over the earth for many days.
> And his star shall rise in heaven *like a king...*
> *The heavens will be opened,*
> *and from the temple of glory sanctification will come upon him,*
> *with a fatherly voice*, as from Abraham to Isaac.
> And the glory of the Most High shall burst forth upon him.
> And the spirit of understanding and sanctification
> shall rest upon him [in the water].
> ...And *Beliar shall be bound by him.*
> And he shall grant to his children the authority *to trample on wicked spirits.*[38]

The phrase "in the water" was presumably added by a later Christian interpolator who recognized the similarities between this scene and Mark 1.[39] The dependence goes the other way, however, and Mark is likely drawing upon this passage in crafting Jesus' own messianic election. If so, it is certainly significant that this poetic passage draws on the traditional combat myth motifs of *binding* and *trampling* the

---

[37] Marcus, *Mark 1-8*, 160.
[38] *T. Levi* 18:1-3a, 6-7, 12 in OTP 1.794-5.
[39] OTP 1.795, note c.

apocalyptic chaos-enemy Beliar. By extension, it is Jesus who will fulfill this eschatological hope.

Moreover, it is notable that the *Testaments* link the opening of the heavens and sanctification coming "from the temple." If we are to take Jesus' "going up" from the waters as reminiscent of the ark's ascent to the temple, this would provide an additional connection: Heaven is the ideal Temple, which—when the sky is torn apart—directly sends down its sanctification in the form of the Spirit. Jesus' "going up" then would in fact be towards the Heavenly Temple, which opens for this representative of Yahweh just as the Temple gates had opened for the ark.

Finally, another apocalyptic text with clear combat myth associations is also potentially at work in Jesus' baptism: Daniel 7. There, the "one like a son of man" receives kingship from the Ancient of Days after the destruction of the chaos-monster. So here, Jesus, self-styled the "Son of Man" in Mark, is declared "son" by God after coming up from the Jordan.

All of these elements provide a basis for seeing Mark's depiction of Jesus' baptism as an apocalyptic reflection of the traditional combat myth. Granting the connection, the rest of the event follows the progression expected from the combat myth: Jesus shows his power at the Jordan, "goes up" from the waters, is met by sanctification from the Heavenly Temple (via the dove) and receives kingship from Yahweh. So we have (1) miracle at the River, (2) ascent towards the Temple, (3) conference of kingship/enthronement The progression is that of the combat myth.

From the outset, then, Mark appears to be weaving a tapestry of various *Chaoskampf* allusions. In his prologue, Mark sets the stage for the coming conflict, casting Jesus as the eschatological divine warrior who will indeed travel the processional Way for enthronement once he has defeated the evil forces that threaten Israel. As the ark processed through the Jordan, so does Jesus. Now must begin the Conquest of Canaan—here the eschatological Conquest which will rid the world of the evil forces of Chaos. These evil forces take three principal forms in Mark's gospel: Satan, Sea, and Death. We shall now turn to Jesus' victory over these cosmic enemies, beginning with his battles against the ultimate villain, Satan himself: the Dragon.

CHAPTER 6
BATTLING SATAN

Contesting in the Desert (Mk 1:12-13)

In startling brevity, Mark here narrates the inauguration of the great apocalyptic battle. Here we see Jesus, freshly invested as the divine warrior, head into the desert for the first confrontation with the Devil. Ernest Best observes that, "according to Jewish demonology the desert is one among other places which demons are specially supposed to inhabit."[1] We have also seen how, in the apocalyptic reflex of the combat myth's *scattering* motif, the desert becomes the prison abode for the temporarily defeated chaos-rebel.[2] That Jesus' is powerfully compelled into the desert as his very first act suggests a divine warrior keen to face the cosmic enemy. With the advent of Jesus' ministry, the time for battle has arrived at last.

However, the desert/wilderness had other potent associations in Jewish literature. Indeed, its connection specifically with the wanderings of the Exodus tradition would likely have been paramount for Mark's audience.[3] That Mark is alluding to this traditional association becomes virtually explicit when Jesus' duration there is reckoned at forty days, thereby echoing the forty years of Israel's wanderings. Mark is thus clearly employing an Exodus typology, the implication being that Jesus is beginning a New Exodus. The first rescued Israel from the oppression of Egypt, the second shall rescue her from the oppression of the Devil.

Indeed, some recent works have emphasized this portrayal of Jesus' ministry *qua* the Exodus-Conquest tradition.[4] They recognize Jesus' mission as the divine warrior chiefly against the backdrop of a "New Exodus," in which Jesus is the new Moses-Joshua figure. Leading Israel out of bondage to Satan as Moses did from Egypt, he then enters the Promised Land to rout the enemy forces of the Devil

---

[1] See Ernest Best, *The Temptation and the Passion: The Markan Soteriology*, 2nd ed., Monograph Series / Society for New Testament Studies (Cambridge: Cambridge University Press, 1990), 5, esp. n. 3.

[2] See, e.g., *KTU* 1.83:9-13; Ps 74:12-17; Ezek 29:5.

[3] Jeffrey B. Gibson, *The Temptations of Jesus in Early Christianity*, Journal for the Study of the New Testament Supplement Series (Sheffield: Sheffield Academic Press, 1995), 60-62.

[4] See e.g., Longman and Reid, *God Is a Warrior*; Watts, *Isaiah's New Exodus in Mark*.

just as Joshua defeated the Canaanites. Jesus is thus indeed the divine warrior—specifically the divine warrior of Israel's Exodus and Conquest.

Such an interpretation is not incorrect, only incomplete. We have seen divine warfare represented throughout the ancient Near East chiefly via the combat myth genre. The divine warrior was the storm-god who slew the chaos-monsters, thereby ensuring rejuvenation. So it was in Israel as well. *Only as a secondary adaptation does the combat myth come to frame the uniquely Israelite tradition of the Exodus.* Ancient Israelites made use of the common mythic pattern to articulate that story, but this does not mean that the Exodus and Conquest then provide the foundational context for the divine warrior. Quite the contrary: they remain adaptations, albeit ancient and authoritative by the first century, of the older mythic pattern. The more basic association of the divine warrior was with the primordial battle with Chaos, and this continues long after the divine warrior motif is connected with the Exodus and Conquest. Indeed, the demonstrable primacy of the combat myth in the development of apocalypticism argues a secondary role for eschatologization of the Exodus-Conquest tradition.

Thus, the divine warrior theme is essentially rooted in the *Chaoskampf*, which, because of its political theme, was applied to Israel's various historical situations. Such was the case with the Exodus and Conquest, as we see in the earliest poetic traditions of the Hebrew Bible such as Exodus 15. The themes of God's control over the waters, defeat of an oppressive gentile enemy, and the consequent creation and establishment of Israel's national identity (i.e., its cosmogony) all found natural expression in the combat myth. Mowinckel summarizes the conflation of ideas well when he writes:

> [I]t is understandable that Creation and the rise of Israel should become one: Creation reaches its climax in the rise of Israel, i.e. the *election*, manifesting itself in the escape from Egypt. Egypt becomes the chaotic monster Rahab and the Reed Lake becomes the primeval ocean, Tehom (Isa. 30.7; Ex. 14.48); and just as in the beginning Yahweh 'divided' the waters, so did he also divide the waters of the Reed Lake for his people. Quite logically the thought would also arise that through this 'creative act' on the part of Yahweh, he became king of Israel.[5]

---

[5] Mowinckel, *The Psalms in Israel's Worship*, 154.

This distinction concerning the basis of the divine warrior tradition is an important one. If the divine warrior is understood only in relation to the Exodus-Conquest, his more fundamental roots in the combat myth pattern are lost. Rather, seeing Mark as continuing the trend of eschatologizing the combat myth, the Exodus-Conquest typology becomes intelligible within his broader apocalyptic message. Like the ancient writers, this adaptation is secondary; the root remains the *Chaoskampf*. When we recognize this, the emphasis on a "New Exodus" in Mark is diminished for the broader message of Mark's gospel: the apocalyptic combat myth. The resonances of the Exodus remain, of course, but in their proper relationship to the larger theme of divine warfare, understood more fundamentally as God's battles with the forces of Chaos. This said, we can now analyze Mark's Exodus-Conquest typology in its proper context.

As we saw in our examination first of the ancient Hebrew combat myth and then with regard to Jesus' baptism, the Jordan River was sometimes seen as the raging waters of the *Chaoskampf*. In the association of the Exodus with the combat myth, the Jordan River was parallel to the Red Sea just as Judge River was parallel to Prince Sea in the traditional myth. With such semantic overtones, it is significant that Jesus' baptism in its waters is his first action in the gospel narrative. Indeed, when we consider (1) the Jordan's resonances as chaos-waters in the New Exodus-Conquest, (2) Jesus' forty-day trial in the desert, and (3) the Sea of Galilee as his immediate destination afterwards (where he defeats the forces of Satan), it appears as though Mark is reversing the progression of the original Exodus-Conquest tradition:

Yahweh	Jesus
1) Defeat Enemies at the Sea	1) Jordan River
2) Wilderness for 40 years	2) Wilderness for 40 days
3) Jordan River	3) Defeat Enemies at the Sea

This reversal forms a kind of chiasma of sacred history, and is not uncommon for eschatological reflexes of traditional material (cf. *Urzeit wird Endzeit*). Moreover, such a structure in Mark essentially correlates the Exodus *Chaoskampf* with the Conquest battles, as the battles which succeed the Israelites' Jordan crossing match in sequence the battles around the Sea of Galilee.

Mark's application of Exodus typology as a variant of the combat myth tradition is thus one means by which the author sets Jesus in the role of apocalyptic divine warrior. Specific vocabulary and idioms he employs to describe this first conflict cement the connection. Because so many crucial implications of the scene hinge on a proper interpretation of these specific terms, I shall consider them now in some depth. These include 1) the nature of Satan's "testing," 2) nuances of the conjunction "and" (especially in Mark), 3) the identity of the "Beasts," 4) the relationship of Jesus being "with" the Beasts, and 5) the nature of the assistance provided by the angels:

1) Once in the wilderness, Jesus is tested by Satan, whom he must defeat before the eschatological Promised Land, the New Eden of Yahweh's re-Creation, can be entered. The nature of the battle, however, is not the kind of outright warfare that we see between Michael and Satan, for example, in Revelation 12. Rather, Jesus is "tested by Satan" (*peirazomenos hypo tou Satana*). Though perhaps ambiguous now, the word *peirazō* would have held definite connotations for Mark's audience.[6] Examining the word's application in Classical and Hellenistic literature, the Septuagint, pseudepigraphal writings, and finally its importance in the New Testament, Jeffrey Gibson defines it as the act of "being probed and proved, *often through hardship and adversity*, in order to determine the extent of one's worthiness to be entrusted with, or the degree of one's loyalty or devotion to, a given commission and its constraints."[7] Thus we find Jesus engaged in a struggle to prove his mettle against the Accuser and show that he is fit to take up the role for which he has just been invested: the messianic divine warrior. Therefore, while *peirazō* means "to test" in this way, C. S. Mann is essentially correct in the implications of this struggle when he writes in his commentary on Mark, "The verb *peirazō* ought to be understood in the sense of 'to wage war on'—the first engagement in the eschatological conflict."[8] Joel Marcus similarly observes that, with the word *peirazō*, "the emphasis…is on the implacable hostility between the two combatants."[9] Thus, to Mark's audience there was no confusion about what was occurring: Jesus was engaged in battle with the cosmic rebel Satan.

---

[6] Gibson, *The Temptations of Jesus*, 54-56.
[7] Ibid., 56-57; emphasis mine.
[8] C. S. Mann, *Mark: A New Translation with Introduction and Commentary*, The Anchor Bible (Garden City: Doubleday, 1986), 203.
[9] Joel Marcus, *Mark 1-8: A New Translation with Introduction and Commentary*, 2 vols.Ibid. (New York2000), 167.

This somewhat periphrastic approach to describing cosmic warfare may seem curious until one appreciates its literary import. For, by staging the battle as a "test" or "trial," Mark both sets up the battle *and* links the opponent with the cosmic rebel of the combat myth. We have seen how, with the theological developments of the apocalyptic period, Leviathan comes to represent the Devil—the Serpent from the combat myth is Satan himself. After texts such as *The Life of Adam and Eve*, this equation of Satan and serpent fuses with another serpent from Hebrew tradition: the serpent who tempts Eve in the garden.[10] With this association, remarks Forsyth, the words Devil and Satan come to "imply the whole apocalyptic combat myth. The tempter is the cosmic adversary."[11] By having Satan "test" Jesus, Mark recalls the testing of the serpent in the garden.[12] With the word *peirazō*, Mark affirms this association and establishes Satan again as the Serpent—and, by extension, the chaos-monster, the Dragon.[13]

2) Having set up the battle and the identity of the opponent, Mark leaves his audience (if only for a moment) in suspense. Though in narrative time the exposition lasts but a short time, the sense of the narrative itself has Jesus contesting with Satan *for over a month*. There is, it seems, a kind of stalemate in the desert battle. For forty days Jesus has fought the Devil—with no decisive result.

The conclusion of the conflict must follow, and indeed it does. The hinge word is the conjunction *kai*, whose most basic meaning is simply "and." However, the Greek conjunction is more versatile and dynamic than our English "and." Depending on context, it may have a concessive sense and be better translated as "but." Mark uses the word in its concessive sense frequently throughout his gospel.[14] I believe such a rendering fits better here than "and," since, having created the tension of uncertainty with the battle's exposition, the author quickly resolves it with the battle's conclusion: Jesus battled Satan for forty

---

[10] Cf. *Apocalypse of Abraham* 23:7 and *Apocalypse of Moses* 17:1.

[11] Forsyth, *The Old Enemy*, 232, 233.

[12] Best, *The Temptation and the Passion*, 6. Though the resonances of an Exodus/Conquest typology seem more apparent than, as Best argues, an Adam/Paradise typology, his insight is still valid in connecting Satan's temptation of Jesus with the serpent's temptation in the garden given the *Chaoskampf* resonances.

[13] This connection between the tempting serpent and the Dragon may also be at work in Rev 12:9: "And the Great Dragon was cast down, *the ancient Serpent*, who is the Devil and Satan, who leads the whole world astray" (Cf. Aune, *Revelation*, vol. 2, 696-7).

[14] The NRSV, for example, translates *kai* as "but" in 1:25; 3:12; 4:17, 19, 38; 5:4, 19; 6:19, 21; 9:18; 12:3, 12, 19; 14:55, 59; and 16:11.

days—*but* was eventually victorious! The way Mark expresses this victory is itself idiomatic, and is explained below.

3) The word Mark uses for Beasts here is *thēria*. While the word can essentially refer to wild animals of any kind, Mark seems to be employing the term in a far more specific sense—namely, the mythological sense. We have seen that this Greek word—either translating the Hebrew, or in original composition—can refer not just to beasts, but to the *Beasts* (as it were) of the *Chaoskampf* tradition. For example, in the Septuagint's Greek translation of Psalm 68, the chaos-monsters which Yahweh rebukes are called *thēria*, while it is *thēria* that arise out of the Sea in Theodotion's translation of Daniel 7. In Revelation 13—an original Greek composition—the author uses *thēria* to refer to the Beasts which rise out of the sea and land as chaos-monsters. This final case is particularly instructive, for here the Beasts (*thēria*) are clearly the helpers of the Dragon (*drakōn*), standing in the subordinate relationship of Leviathan to Yamm or Tiamet's monstrous helpers to the draconic sea goddess herself.

Mark seems to be employing the term here in the same sense—as helpers of Satan, whom he has already equated with the great Serpent/Dragon through the *testing* of Jesus. Satan is the Dragon, his demonic helpers are the Beasts. This relationship explains quite well, I believe, the otherwise vexing presence of *thēria* in this encounter. Some have erroneously seen a return to the pre-Fall serenity of Paradise, with Jesus in harmony with the wild animals in a kind of Adam typology. The clear antagonism between Satan and Jesus makes this idea tenuous indeed, however, and Ernest Best rightly counters this theory of the beasts, arguing (if somewhat vaguely), "That they signify evil is the more probable interpretation; the beasts are congruent with Satan and the desert, all of them suggesting the evil with which Jesus must contend."[15] This general sense of congruity becomes focused and fixed when we see them as the helper Beasts to the chief Dragon of the combat myth.[16]

4) Most translations of Mark render the phrase *ēn meta tōn thēriōn* in strictly literal terms: "he was with the Beasts." However, one

---

[15] Best, *The Temptation and the Passion*, 8. Likewise William L. Lane, *The Gospel According to Mark: The English Text with Introduction, Exposition, and Notes* (Grand Rapids: Eerdmans, 1974), 61.

[16] Collins remarks that Mark "pits Jesus, the Spirit of God, and the angels, on the one hand, against Satan, wild animals, and (it is implied) demons, on the other" in Collins, *Mark*, 153.

must appreciate the Greek idiom Mark employs here, since it turns out that the two words *ēn meta* can imply a great deal. Indeed, with these words, Mark signals the shift from forty days of stalemate to the final overpowering of the Devil and his forces. Jesus is not *meta* "with" the Beasts, he is *meta* "over/after/above" them.

In his book *The Temptations of Jesus in Early Christianity*, Gibson notes that the construction *ēn meta* can signify subordination and mastery over something.[17] He writes:

> In the LXX, μετά with some form (especially ἦν) of the imperfect of εἰμί is used in many of its instances to signify the subordination of one man or group to another, and bears or implies the specific meaning 'to be under the (military) command of'.[18]

Therefore, to say that Jesus *ēn meta* the Beasts actually suggests that he "had mastery over the Beasts"—a sense one could translate by the English idiom "was over" (e.g., "he is king *over* you"). While this subordination of the Beasts does not suggest military command (as Gibson interprets it, *qua* an Adam typology), it does imply a general sense of command and power over something. Here it signifies, after the turn "but" (*kai*), that Jesus has proven powerful over Satan and his helper Beasts.

5) Jesus, however, does not accomplish this feat alone. Rather, the role of the angels is critical. Indeed, their importance is hardly captured by the NRSV translation of *diakoneō* as "they waited on him." The verb suggests the giving of aid or assistance but, to be sure, they are not aiding him in the way a servant might wait on a hungry master, but rather as an army contingent or group of lesser commanders might aid a general. Longman and Reid are correct then in their assessment that

> we should consider the possibility that the angels of Mark 1:13 are not simply emissaries of heavenly hospitality, but in their assistance (*diakoneō*) provide strategic counsel to Jesus the divine warrior at a crucial moment of eschatological warfare.[19]

---

[17] Gibson, *The Temptations of Jesus*, 66 n. 93.

[18] Ibid., 66. For examples of this usage in the LXX, Gibson offers Gen 8:1; 34:5; Num 14:23; Judg 14:11; 1 Sam 13:2; 14:21, 23; 22:2; 2 Sam 3:22; 23:9; 1 Kgs 11:40; 2 Kgs 25:25; 1 Chron 11:13; Neh 2:12; Jer 33:24; 48:2; Est 2:20, as well as others.

[19] Longman and Reid, *God Is a Warrior*, 97.

Indeed, because their assistance is mentioned just at the moment of victory, after forty days of Jesus struggling (presumably alone) with Satan, their aid may be interpreted as critical indeed. It may prove the decisive factor in Jesus' victory over the forces of the Devil. Indeed, just as *kai* can have a concessive sense ("but"), it can also suggest result ("for/because"). Rendered thus, it may be that Jesus proves victorious "*because* the angels aided him."

With these terminological considerations out of the way, we can step back again from the specifics and appreciate the compact excitement in the progression of these two verses from Mark:

> And immediately the Spirit drives him out into the desert. And he was in the desert forty days being tested by Satan.
> But he was [powerful] over the Beasts, for the angels aided him.

So we see the determined divine warrior, thrust into action by the Holy Spirit to begin his ministry with the cosmic confrontation. In the desert, Jesus struggles to prove himself against Satan. For forty days, the two contend. Then, at last, aided by the armies of heaven, Jesus proves victorious over Satan and his helpers, the chaos-monsters.

Finally, it is remarkable that this scene seems to have been composed within the framework of a psalm with clear *Chaoskampf* imagery: Psalm 91.[20] The address to the righteous in Psalm 91 articulates Yahweh's protection of his faithful clearly in terms of combat myth imagery: the faithful shall prove victorious over evil just as Yahweh defeated the forces of Chaos. This mythological aspect is even more pronounced in the Septuagint version:

> No evils will come upon you,
>   and no scourge shall come near your dwelling-place.
> Because *he will command his angels in regards to you,*
>   to guard you in all your ways.
> They shall bear you up on their hands,
>   lest you ever strike your foot against a stone.
> *You shall tread on the asp and the basilisk,*
>   *and trample on the lion and the dragon.* (vv. 10-13, LXX)

The configuration of adversarial Beasts and administering angels is the same as in Mark. Moreover, these evil Beasts are envisioned as the chaos-monsters of Israel's combat myth—mythical serpents including

---

[20] Gibson, *The Temptations of Jesus*, 67.

the deadly basilisk, as well as the dragon (*drakonta*) himself. Their mode of destruction is likewise that of the combat myth: *trampling* of the body.[21] That this psalm frames Jesus' desert struggle with Satan is made explicit in the accounts of Matthew and Luke. There, in the Q material which both of those gospels share, Satan himself speaks and quotes from Psalm 91.

Thus, while the two verses that narrate Jesus' first engagement with Satan are concise, they are brimming with significance and suggestion. Jesus has thus defeated Satan. The crucial victory has been won and the reassertion of Yahweh's kingship is at hand. Indeed, such is the expected progression from the combat myth, and so we read in Mark in the following verses (14-15):

> Now (after John was arrested), Jesus came to Galilee, reporting the good news of God, and saying, "The time is fulfilled, and the Kingdom of God has come near! Repent, and believe the good news!"

Satan and his Beasts have been subdued, meaning the would-be usurper king—the cosmic rebel—is defeated and Yahweh shall now once again become king over the cosmos. The traditional *Chaoskampf* theme of kingship is thus here clearly evident, as Jesus himself now proclaims that the Kingdom of God (*hē basileia tou theou*) is bearing down. Indeed, now it is Jesus himself who proclaims the "good news" of his own victory.

Muzzling the Raging Demon (Mk 1:21-28)

Having defeated Satan and the Beasts in the desert, Jesus now begins his ministry proper by turning his attention to the Sea—that is, the Sea of Galilee. As the setting for almost half of Mark's gospel, this is the epicenter for nearly all of his succeeding battles with the remnant forces of the Devil. Indeed, the Sea of Galilee and its environs shall prove the crucial eschatological battlefield, as Jesus' victories there will allow him to process along the Way up to the Temple/Jerusalem for enthronement. The Dragon himself may be subdued, but his helpers

---

[21] Ps 91 was also associated with exorcism of evil spirits at Qumran, another example of apocalyptic Judaism's linking of the combat myth with the defeat of evil spirits. See Géza Vermès, *The Complete Dead Sea Scrolls in English*, Penguin Classics (London: Penguin Books, 2004), 316; Collins, *Mark*, 151.

still possess the territory. To rout them and annex the area for the Kingdom of God, Jesus now enters enemy territory and there initiates the New Conquest.

As his first act in this Conquest, Jesus enters the synagogue at the coastal town Capernaum and there proclaims his message. Mark is not specific about his message here, but one may presume it is essentially the same as the message Jesus proclaims in verse 14: the "good news," the report of Satan's defeat. We might therefore imagine that Jesus has triumphantly entered the synagogue and decisively declared that Satan's rule has ended and that the Kingdom of God is now come. Such an audacious message would certainly fit with the response he receives, as those in the congregation are immediately struck by his authority/power (*exousia*). Jesus' message is indeed quite unlike the theologizing of the scholars; it is a bold announcement of victory, while he himself exhibits the true command of an agent of power: the "Stronger One" prophesied by John the Baptist.

Indeed, this power quickly finds an opportunity for dramatic demonstration when an "unclean spirit" in possession of a man in the synagogue stands up and opposes Jesus directly. This is the first mention of a polluted or unclean spirit in Mark's gospel—entities which, we shall soon see, come to play a key part in Jesus' ministry as the chief antagonists of the divine warrior. Given their importance it is pertinent to recall that their origins are to be found in the apocalyptic combat myth. As the survey of Part One showed, an influential idea attested by and/or stemming from the Enochic literature posited that they arose from the slain Giants born to the rebellious Watcher angels. Most of them were destroyed, but a portion was left on earth to do the work of the Devil—that is, to take humans captive in the cosmic battle by possessing them or making them sick. Only on the cosmic Day of Yahweh, the "Day of the great conclusion" (1 Enoch 16:1-2), would these oppressive spirits be subdued. For Mark, that era was clearly inaugurated by Jesus' ministry. Thus, opposed by just such a spirit in the synagogue, the expectations for Jesus are clear: a battle must ensue.

And so it does. After the engagement with Satan and the Beasts in the wilderness, this is the next skirmish in the apocalyptic battle.[22] The demon recognizes it as such and asks Jesus, either in terror or a taunting hubris, "Have you come to destroy us?" Being a spirit, the

---

[22] In his commentary, Marcus, *Mark 1-8*, 186, titles this event "The Opening Battle," which is of course something of a misnomer since the desert temptation was Jesus' first true confrontation with Satan.

demon knows Jesus is the divine warrior—information unknown and indeed continually misunderstood by the human beings around Jesus. Thus it proclaims, "I know who you are: the Holy One of God!" With this assertion, the demon reveals both its recognition that the moment is one of confrontation, as well as its very weapon in that confrontation. Ancient understandings of magic and exorcism posited that to know someone's name was to have power over them.[23] So the spirit's knowledge of Jesus' identity is the very source of the its power to oppose him. Thus Collins argues that "the speech, because of its special knowledge about Jesus, is dangerous. The spirit's speech is an attack, and it must be met with a counterattack."[24]

Remarkably, Mark then describes the battle in language and imagery that clearly echo the Hebrew combat myth: Jesus responds to this threat with a *rebuke*. The evangelist is thus unmistakably employing the combat myth's *mighty voice* motif—specifically called the *rebuke* (*g'r*) in the Hebrew myths—by which the storm-god would threaten and terrorize the chaos-monsters into submission and thereby establish order. Thus, if there were any doubt, Mark here unambiguously presents Jesus as the apocalyptic divine warrior who subdues the forces of the Devil just as Yahweh subdued the forces of the Sea.

In his article "The Terminology of Mark's Exorcism Stories," H. C. Kee appreciates these resonances with the traditional combat myth, noting that the *rebuke* was key to Yahweh's battles with Sea and even appears in the Ugaritic texts within the context of Baal's struggle for kingship.[25] Kee therefore notes that it "is linked thus philologically as well as conceptually with older Semitic usage,"[26] and even posits that the word *g'r* is

> a technical term for the commanding word, uttered by God or by his spokesman, by which evil powers are brought into submission, and the way is thereby prepared for the establishment of God's righteous rule in the world.[27]

---

[23] Collins, *Mark*, 169-173; Longman and Reid, *God Is a Warrior*, 98.

[24] Collins, *Mark*, 173.

[25] *CAT* 1.2.ii.24.

[26] Howard Clark Kee, "The Terminology of Mark's Exorcism Stories," *NTS* 14 (1968): 237.

[27] Ibid., 235.

It is thus remarkable that Mark uses the verb *epitimaō* for "rebuke," as this is the Greek equivalent of the Hebrew *g'r*, and is used in the Septuagint to translate *g'r* in passages describing Yahweh's battles with the raging Sea:[28]

<table>
<tr><td align="center">MASORETIC TEXT</td><td align="center">SEPTUAGINT</td></tr>
<tr><td align="center">Psalm 18:15</td><td align="center">Psalm 17:16</td></tr>
<tr><td>Then the channels of the Sea were seen, and the foundations of the world were laid bare at your rebuke (migga'ărātkā), O Lord, at the blast of the breath of your nostrils.</td><td>And the founts of the Waters were seen, and the foundations of the world were exposed at your rebuke (epitimēseōs), O Lord, at the blasting of the breath of your anger.</td></tr>
<tr><td align="center">Psalm 104:6-7</td><td align="center">Psalm 103:6-7</td></tr>
<tr><td>You cover it with the Deep as with a garment; the Waters stood above the mountains. At your rebuke (ga'ărātkāmin) they flee; at the sound of your thunder they take to flight.</td><td>The deep, like a cloak, is his covering: the waters will stand on the mountains. At your rebuke (epitimēseōs) they will flee; at the voice of your thunder they will become afraid.</td></tr>
<tr><td align="center">Psalm 106:9</td><td align="center">Psalm 105:9</td></tr>
<tr><td>He rebuked (wayyig'ar) the Red Sea, and it became dry;</td><td>And he rebuked (epitimēsen) the Red Sea, and it was dried up…</td></tr>
<tr><td align="center">Job 26:11-13</td><td align="center">Job 26:11-13</td></tr>
<tr><td>The pillars of heaven tremble, and are astounded at his rebuke (migga'ărātô). By his power he stilled the Sea; by his understanding he struck down Rahab. By his wind the heavens were made fair; his hand pierced the fleeing Serpent.</td><td>The pillars of heaven were passive and astonished at his rebuke (epitimēseōs). Hehas put down the Sea with his might, and crippled the sea-monster with his skill. The barriers of heaven fear him, and by a command he has slain the rebel Dragon.</td></tr>
</table>

So Mark uses the specific terminology of the Hebrew *Chaoskampf* to directly relate Jesus' exorcism with Yahweh's battle with the Sea. What Kee fails to emphasize, however, is that only apocalyptic aggrandizement of the combat myth renders this allusion fully intelligible.

However, the *mighty voice/rebuke* is by no means the extent of traditional *Chaoskampf* imagery employed by the evangelist here, for,

---

[28] Ibid., 238. The following table is not exhaustive. Longman and Reid, *God Is a Warrior*, 100, note that the use of *epitimaō* here signals Jesus as the divine warrior subduing his enemy, but do not emphasize the word's original context in the Hebrew combat myth.

having rebuked the spirit, Jesus then orders it to be bound in a muzzle
(*philōthēti*: "Be muzzled!"). With this command, Mark proceeds to
make obvious use of the traditional *binding* motif from the combat
myth as well. Like Ninurta and the Stone Things, the Storm-God and
the Serpent, Marduk and Tiamet, Yahweh and Leviathan, Raphael and
Azazel, and the messiah and Beliar, so Jesus binds the demon.

Indeed, as we have seen, being bound *with a muzzle* was the
particular fate of the defeated chaos-monster in the Ugaritic and
Israelite combat myths. So Anat and Tunnan (Dragon):

> [Anat] sets a muzzle on Tunnan.
> She binds him on the heights of Lebanon[29]

and Yahweh and Sea:

> The Lord said: "I stifled the Serpent, muzzled the Deep Sea." (Ps 68:23)[30]

With this, Mark evinces clear and intimate familiarity with the
traditional Hebrew combat myth since, though the *binding* motif was
employed in apocalyptic transformations of the combat myth, *no extant
apocalyptic text speaks specifically of this as binding with a muzzle.*
This is a unique and telling detail in Mark's employment of combat
myth imagery comparable to other apocalyptic texts. For, as
apocalyptic authors reveal their intimacy with combat myth traditions
through mention of archaic details (e.g., the Isaianic Apocalypse's
poetic traditions evinced at Ugarit, Daniel's "Canaanite" configurations
for Yahweh and the son of man, Revelation's specification of seven
heads for the chaos-monster Leviathan, etc.), so does Mark here. There
can be no mistake that he is making use of the ancient myth, and in the
process revealing intimate knowledge of its traditional contours.

The evangelist continues to characterize the evil spirit as the
raging Sea in his description of the demon's final subjugation. In the
Hebrew Bible, Yahweh's weapon is indeed his rebuking thunder, but
the Sea also roars and cries out in its tempestuous rage. Indeed, the
roaring of Sea is perhaps its principle characteristic when mentioned in
the context of the *Chaoskampf*. Despite the roaring of the Sea,

---

[29] *KTU* 1.83:9-10 = Pitard, "The Binding of Yamm: A New Edition of the Ugaritic Text
KTU 1.83," 273. Cf. CAT 1.3.iii.38-40.
[30] Cf. Dahood, *Psalms*, 131 (see Chapter 2 for notes on this translation).

however, Yahweh's roar (his *mighty voice*) is mightier, and so he subdues the chaos-waters. Thus Enthronement Psalm 93:

> The Rivers have lifted up, O Yahweh,
>> the Rivers have lifted up their voice;
>> the Rivers lift up their roaring!
> But mightier than the voices of many Waters,
>> than the waves of Sea,
>> is Yahweh on high. (Ps 93:3-4)

Likewise, Isaiah 17:12-13:

> Ah, the thunder of many peoples,
>> they thunder like the thundering of the Sea!
> Ah, the roar of nations,
>> they roar like the roaring of mighty Waters!
> The nations roar like the roaring of many Waters,
>> but he will *rebuke* them, and they will flee far away,
> chased like chaff on the mountains before the wind
>> and whirling dust before the storm.

The image is also attested at Qumran, already transformed here into an apocalyptic metaphor:

> The torrents of Belial burst through into Abaddon, and *the plotters from the deep make an uproar with the noise of those who belch forth slime.* The earth *shouts* out, because of the disaster which comes about in the world, and all its plotters *scream*. All who are upon it behave as if mad, and they melt away in the gr[ea]t disaster. *For God thunders with the roar of His strength and His holy dwelling roars forth in His glorious truth.* Then the heavenly hosts shall *raise their voice* and the everlasting foundations shall melt and quake. The war of the heroes of heaven shall spread over the world and shall not return until an annihilation that has been determined from eternity is completed. Nothing like this has ever occurred.[31]

In all such passages, the Sea roars and rages with its own thunder, but the thunder of Yahweh (his rebuke) proves more powerful, and the chaotic waters are thereby subdued. In just the same way, the evil spirit opposes Jesus by crying out (*anekraxen*) and roars with a great voice (*phōnēsan phōnē megalē*) like the thundering of mighty waters, and then, when he is repulsed, convulses (*sparaxan*) like the stirred-up

---

[31] 1QH^a Col. XI (Col. III + Frg. 25) lines 32-36 = Parry and Tov, *The Dead Sea Scrolls Reader*, 25.

waters. The rebuke of the divine warrior proves mightier, and so the evil spirit is vanquished.

The consequence of victory over the unclean spirit is the same for Jesus as it was for Yahweh or Baal or Marduk or Ninurta: his power is confirmed and his authority is recognized. For the storm-gods of the ancient Near East, this meant that a temple was built and the god was enthroned as king over the cosmos.[32] In Mark, we read that

> they were all amazed, and consequently discussed amongst themselves, saying, 'What is this? A new teaching—with authority (*exousian*)! Even the unclean spirits he commands, and they listen to him (*hypakouousin autō*)!' And his report (*hē akoē*) then went out everywhere into the whole surrounding region of the Galilee.

This conclusion is noteworthy for a number of reasons. First, *hypakouousin autō* is often translated "they obey him."[33] More literally, however, it means "they listen to him." The sense is the same in English. The distinction is important, however, because the idea of listening goes back to heeding the voice of the divine warrior, which is the means by which God ultimately defeats his enemies—be they demons or the raging waters. Yahweh speaks his thunderous voice, and the chaos-waters listen.

Secondly, Jesus' victory over the demon causes word of him to spread, and his *akoē* (translated "news" or "report") is carried everywhere. This use of *akoē* is significant since we noted that "to report good news" (*euangelizomai*) has roots in the combat myth tradition and refers to the warrior god's victory over his chaos-enemies. These are the resonances Deutero-Isaiah is drawing upon when he uses the term to recall Yahweh's epiphany at the New Year Feast of Tabernacles. Thus, in the Septuagint translation of Isaiah 52:6-7, we find that *euangelizomai* takes a direct object: *akoē*:

> I stand by like a season upon the mountains,
>> like the feet of one gladly reporting the news of peace (*euangelizomai akoēn eirēnēs*),
>> as one reporting news that is good,
> because I will make heard your salvation,
>> saying, "O Zion, your God shall reign!"

---

[32] Such a fate also awaits Jesus, as we shall see in Chapter 8.
[33] As in, e.g., the NRSV, NASB, KJV, NIV, ESV, ASV.

Such a conclusion to Jesus' exorcism is quite fitting. As the New Year celebrants gladly reported (*euangelizomai*) Yahweh's victory over the chaos-monsters as the news (*akoē*) of peace, so in Mark's glad report (*euangelion*) does the news (*akoē*) of Jesus spread into the region after his defeat of the forces of evil.

Indeed, we seem to have in Mark 1:21-28 a fairly complete and independent combat myth, even if only one battle in a larger war. In addition to the apocalyptic reflexes of the *Chaoskampf*'s traditional themes (which indeed underlie every combat in Mark and shall therefore be specifically addressed only when warranted), we find striking use of its traditional imagery, as Mark employs both the *mighty voice* and *binding* motifs in the context of battle.

Looking at its relationship to Forsyth's schema, we find: (1) *Lack/Villainy*: Satan and his evil forces have taken control of the cosmos generally and a man in the synagogue in particular. (2) *Hero emerges/prepares to act*: Jesus emerges from Nazareth and (3) *Donor/Consultation*: is baptized by John the Baptist, at which time he receives the Holy Spirit. (4) *Journey*: Jesus arrives in Capernaum and teaches at the synagogue. (5) *Battle*: An unclean spirit, possessing the man in the synagogue, opposes Jesus, roaring at him and attempting to gain power over him. (Functions 6-9 are absent here, as Forsyth noted they sometimes are.[34]) (10) *Victory*: Jesus binds/muzzles the demon, then casts it out. Function 11 is not present. (12) *Triumph*: The report of Jesus' authority and power is proclaimed throughout the region.

Binding Satan (Mk 3:22-27)

As his report spreads and his ministry continues with dramatic healings, Jesus gains both followers and opponents. Indeed, his very success is then used against him as the religious scholars point to his victorious exorcisms as evidence for complicity with the Devil. Jesus' response then, beyond merely chiding their faulty logic, reveals that his conception of the apocalyptic war he is waging stems from cosmic transformations of the combat myth.

First he demands, "How is Satan able to cast out Satan?" The question is instructive as it unequivocally shows Jesus' equation of the possessing demons with the rule of Satan. Thus, to battle unclean

---

[34] Forsyth, *The Old Enemy*, 446.

spirits is, by extension, to battle the Devil himself, as such spirits are merely extensions of the Devil's power. The evil forces fight as a unified front. This is reinforced by his second telling remark: "If a kingdom is divided against itself, that kingdom is not able to stand." Here, Jesus insinuates that Satan indeed has a kingdom (*basileia*) just as God has a kingdom. As we have seen, such an apocalyptic configuration of contesting kings/kingdoms derives from the aggrandizement of the traditional combat myth, in which *kingship*—and specifically accession to kingship via success in battle—was a central theme. So the theme of kingship had its apocalyptic reflex, the importance of which appears early in Mark with Jesus' proclamation of the good news and the imminent coming of the Kingdom of God. So here, in the context of Jesus' battles with Satan's helpers, the fundamental question is about kingship: who will have power over the cosmos—who will be king?

Having thus alerted his audience yet again to his *Chaoskampf* typology, Mark reiterates the identity of Jesus as the divine warrior with clear imagery from the combat myth's political theme. Thus the defeat of Satan is described again in terms of the *binding* motif. Jesus says, "But no one can go into the house of a strong man (*tou ischyrou*) to plunder his things unless he first bind the strong man, and then he will plunder his house." While referring to Satan as "the strong man" emphasizes the power of his opponent, it also reminds the reader of Jesus' own identity as "the stronger man" (*ho ischyroteros*) whom John the Baptist hailed in 1:7. The Devil is mighty, but Jesus is might*ier*. With these resonances, one may be led to recall Psalm 93, an Enthronement Psalm of the New Year festival, with its similar complex of ideas (e.g., the kingship of Yahweh, the might of the chaos-enemy and the greater might of Yahweh):

> Yahweh has become king! he is robed in majesty;
> > Yahweh is robed; he is girded with strength.
> He has established the world; it shall never be moved.
> > Your throne is established from of old;
> > you are from everlasting.
> The Rivers have lifted up, O Yahweh,
> > the Rivers have lifted up their voice;
> > the Rivers lift up their roaring!
> But mightier than the voices of many Waters,
> > than the waves of Sea,
> > is Yahweh on high.
> Your decrees are very sure;
> > holiness befits your House,

O Yahweh, forevermore.

Just as Yahweh exercised his superior might over the Sea by binding it, so the stronger Jesus binds Satan the strong man. Mark here uses the Greek *deō*, "to bind," which was the common term used in Greek renderings of the combat myth tradition and its later transformations (e.g., of Leviathan's binding in Job 40:21, 24 [LXX], the binding of Beliar *T. Levi* 18:12, and the binding of the Dragon/Satan in Rev 20:2). Indeed, the implication is that Jesus *has bound* Satan already, since, as Jesus says, only once the strong man is bound can one plunder or despoil his things. Since Jesus is speaking in defense of his exorcisms, the plunder he is referring to can only mean the people possessed by Satan whom he is taking away from the Devil. Such are those "captives" from the apocalyptic combat myth in the *Testaments of the Twelve Patriarchs*. So *Testament of Dan* 5:10-11:

> He will make war against Beliar;
> He will grant the vengeance of victory as our goal.
> *And he shall take from Beliar the captives, the souls of the saints...*

or *Testament of Zebulun* 9:8:

> And thereafter the Lord himself will arise upon you, the light of righteousness with healing in his wings. *He will liberate every captive of the sons of men from Beliar*, and every spirit of error will be trampled down.

Both metaphors highlight the martial component: Jesus frees the captives/prisoners of war taken by Beliar/Satan the way a man plunders and takes spoils in a time of war. The *Testaments* clearly articulated this cosmic restoration and salvation in terms of the combat myth; so too does Mark. Thus, like the other warrior gods in the ancient combat myths, Jesus must bind his enemy before he can take back what the rebel has usurped.

Finally, this scene gives strong confirmation that Mark shares an important theological conception most clearly expressed in Revelation, which posits that the defeat of the Devil shall not occur in one single confrontation, but rather in successive stages. So, in that text, we see the Devil decisively defeated in heavenly battle, only to continue his antagonism on the earth. Later, the Devil is indeed *bound*, only to be released for a thousand years. Only after these defeats is he captured again and cast into the flames. The specific progression is not as critical as the idea of *stages of defeat*. The apocalyptic war against the rebel shall see various victories, the final triumph reserved for the true end of time.[35]

Such, I argued, was the sense of Mark's title: "The *Beginning* of the Good News of Jesus Christ." That it is just *hē archē*, the outset or start, suggests that the cosmic war is only begun in the ensuing account of Jesus Christ's ministry. Moreover, it is within this framework that I have interpreted the first and only true confrontation Jesus has with Satan: the testing in the desert. Taking that confrontation as the decisive first victory most fully explains Jesus' own proclamation of the "good news," of a victory already won against the enemy. Jesus' own message of victory and the coming Kingdom of God suggest that he has *already* battled Satan and subdued him (in the desert), but that this was only the first stage in the grand apocalyptic victory.

With Jesus' remarks on the binding of the strong man, Mark gives us still greater cause to accept this interpretation. Jesus is liberating the captives of the Devil, he is taking back the souls from Satan—things impossible, by his own admission, had not the Devil already been bound. However, Mark has not presented Jesus as having bound Satan, only as having proved victorious against him in a scene clearly articulated in terms of an ancient combat myth typology. This scene took place *in the desert*, which, we recall, is the same resting-place of the subdued and *bound* chaos-monster. When we recall that Satan's principle offensive against Jesus is described as a test or tempting, thereby linking him with the Serpent in apocalyptic speculation, the whole "binding of the Serpent" image from the traditional combat myth is evident. It therefore seems that the specific means of Jesus' great initial victory is revealed: as one might expect of the divine warrior, *he has bound the tempter Serpent in the desert*. Though this binding has only subdued the Devil, it has at the least incapacitated him, such that now Jesus is able to rout the rest of the Devil's helpers who still occupy the land destined for the Kingdom of God.

Drowning Satan's Legion in the Sea (Mk 5:1-20)

Just as he had with the first demoniac in the synagogue, so Mark here portrays the Gerasene demoniac as the raging Sea which the divine

---

[35] Cf. also Lk 10:18.

warrior Jesus must subdue.[36] So the enemy likewise rages, shouting (*krazōn*) day and night upon the mountains. The demoniac is in a perpetual state of disruption and, like the demoniac in Mark 1, roars in irresistible might. Here, moreover, the demoniac is explicitly encountered in close proximity to the Sea itself, heightening the connection with Chaos and the traditional unruly Waters. Likewise, the demoniac's residence among the tombs, apart from highlighting his uncleanness, may also parallel the chaos-enemy's associations with "the Pit." As the term in Hebrew usage was equated with death and Sheol (and, incidentally, the miry *waters* of death[37]), the demoniac's habitation in tombs metaphorically links him with the realm of Death. In this way Mark has taken a symbolic/mythic motif and converted it into an historical one, making the cosmic Pit the earthly tombs. Finally, about the binding with chains, Mark uses the typical word *deō* again— the verb often used for the binding of chaos-enemies.[38]

Association with the chaos-enemy of the combat myth is cemented when we consider the scriptural passage from which Mark is likely drawing: Enthronement Psalm 68 from the New Year festival.[39] Mowinckel calls this "a typical procession psalm for the new year festival" and notes its "identification of the actual and potential enemies of Israel with the chaotic powers."[40] Indeed, as noted at the conclusion of "The Combat Myth in Hebrew Cult" in Chapter 2, the psalm is brimming with traditional combat myth imagery. So we see (in addition to imagery of the storm theophany which permeates the psalm): the *scattering* of Yahweh's enemies (v. 1), the announcement

---

[36] The theme of chaos permeates the scene. Perkins, *The New Interpreter's Bible 8*, 582, writes, "The ominous signs of social and religious chaos attached to this story are as dramatic as the storm at sea that attended the crossing." He points to the Gentile setting and the demoniac's condition, which is akin to a wild animal's. The man's dwelling in the tombs and the herd of swine add further layers of social breakdown and impurity.

[37] See Nicholas J. Tromp, *Primitive Conceptions of Death and the Nether World in the Old Testament* (Rome: Pontifical Biblical Institute, 1969), 66-71.

[38] Marcus, *Mark 1-8*, 343, notes that the inability of anyone to bind the demoniac recalls the Strong Man parable. "The implication," writes Marcus, "is that the possessed man in our passage derives his supernatural strength from the Strong Man, Satan." Likewise, Perkins, *The New Interpreter's Bible 8*, 585, notes, "This story is a dramatic illustration of Jesus' earlier claim that his exorcisms represent the binding of Satan (3:27). Its allusions to the OT, to cosmological myths, to powerful experiences of impurity and chaos, and to the political powers of the time have stretched the story beyond the normal elements of an exorcism."

[39] Robert A. Guelich, *Mark 1-8:26*, Word Biblical Commentary (Dallas: Word Books, 1989), 277.

[40] Mowinckel, *The Psalms in Israel's Worship*, 152.

of the "good news" (v. 11), a triumphal procession of captives (vv. 17-18) in the New Year procession to the Temple (vv. 24-7), allusion to Yahweh's victory over Death (v. 20), the *muzzling* of the Serpent and the Sea (v. 22),[41] the *rebuke, trampling,* and *scattering* of the chaos-monsters (v. 30), and Yahweh's *mighty voice* (v. 33). Specifically, Mark seems to be drawing on a Septuagint-like rendering of verse 6, which reads:

> God settles the solitary in a house, leading forth the shackled in strength,
> likewise the rebels dwelling in tombs.

This translation, while capturing the essence of the Hebrew, has also introduced some significant novelties for interpretation. Compare the Masoretic:

MASORETIC (68:6)	SEPTUAGINT (67:7)
God gives the desolate a home to live in;	God settles the solitary in a house,
he leads out the prisoners to prosperity,	leading forth the shackled in strength,
but the rebellious live in a parched land.	likewise the rebels who dwell in tombs.

The most obvious departure from the Masoretic text is the reference to tombs (*taphois*), which is unique to the translation. If Mark is alluding to this passage then, it is from the Septuagint version (or one of similar rendering) that he is drawing.

Interestingly, the Greek introduces novel ambiguities for translation. So, for example, the prisoners (here called *pepedēmenous* = lit. "those having been bound," from *deo*) are led *en andreia*, where *en* can mean "in," "into," or even "with." Thus, the bound may be "led *into* strength" (that is, into prosperity), or "led *in* strength," as in triumph. This latter interpretation is aided by the translation of *kôšārôt* (Heb. "prosperity, strength") as *andreia* (Gk. "strength, manliness"). Thus, while retaining its core sense of divine justice and salvation, the wording of the Greek facilitates an interpretation which assimilates the leading of the bound in verse 7 with the image of the triumphal procession of captives that follows in verse 18 (19 in the Septuagint). In this reading, while led in submission to the gloating power of the divine warrior, the rebels themselves are ultimately redeemed and settled—even those who once dwelled in tombs. The sense the verse acquires in

---

[41] So Dahood, *Psalms*, 131; Miller, "Two Critical Notes on Psalm 68 and Deuteronomy 33," 240 and n. 3. For a critique of this reading, see Day, *God's Conflict*, 113-19.

the later Greek interpretation has Yahweh leading his New Year procession of captives, but ultimately in order to redeem them.

Such a reading fits very well with Mark's program. Now, at the cosmic New Year inaugurated by Jesus' subdual of Satan, the rebels "dwelling in tombs" are brought into the victorious procession of Jesus—the evil being extinguished while the rebel himself is redeemed. Jesus' battle and defeat of the demons is thus articulated against the background of the New Year procession—apt foreshadowing for the coming "Way" section and its climax of the triumphal entry. But this procession is ultimately redemptive, as those who had once opposed the divine warrior as rebels are now saved. Jesus redeems the persons Satan himself had taken captive.

Having established the demoniac's connections with the rebellious raging Sea, Mark's specification of his location "on the mountains" likely serves his narrative as more than just superfluous detail. As we have seen, one form of the Hebrew *Chaoskampf* seems to have echoed elements of the Mesopotamian myth of Ninurta and the Azag Demon, where the chief concern after the chaos-monster's defeat was the waters' accumulation on the mountaintops. Because of this, Ninurta created an irrigation system and thereby set the proper boundaries for the waters. Likewise, in the traditional Hebrew version, Yahweh subdues the rebellious waters on the mountains with his mighty rebuke, frightening them to flee to their proper boundaries:

> *...the Waters stood upon the mountains.*
> *At your rebuke they flee;*
>   *at the sound of your thunder they take to flight.*
> They rose up to the mountains, ran down the valleys
>   to the place that you appointed them.
> You set a boundary that they may not pass,
>   so that they might not again cover the earth. (Ps 104:4b-9)[42]

So in Mark we find the raging demons roaring on the tops of the mountains, waiting to be subdued and put in their right place by Jesus. In this way, Jesus' removal of the unclean spirits from their improper location (i.e., the man on the mountains) to their proper setting (i.e., the pigs and then the Sea) mirrors the progression of the old combat myth: at the rebuke of the divine warrior, the raging demons descend from the

---

[42] Cf. the orderly separation of the earth from the Waters in Gen 1. A similar idea may underlie Ps 46:2-3.

mountain into the properly contained Sea below. So might the demons never again cover the earth after their battle with Jesus.

For, to be sure, the confrontation between Jesus and the demoniac is a battle, narrated as an intense back-and-forth struggle. When Jesus arrives, the demoniac runs to him and, like the first demoniac and the roaring Sea, shouts at him with a great voice (*kraxas phōnē megalē*). He then pleads, "What is there between me and you, Jesus—Son of the Most High God? I abjure you by God: do not torture me!" As in the confrontation with the demon in the synagogue, ancient conceptions of magic power are crucial for appreciating this scene as one of combat— of attack and counter-attack. Collins notes that

> [t]he verb ὁρκίζω ("to make one swear, bind by an oath," "abjure") … [is] usually used by the exorcist to force the demon to depart from the possessed person. The demon's use of the term signifies his resistance to Jesus and that a struggle is taking place between them.[43]

However, the demon's abjuration, though narrated first, is actually *not* the first offensive of the encounter. Rather, it comes as a response to Jesus' earlier demand that the demons exit the man (mentioned afterwards as a kind of parenthetical explanation). This suggests that Jesus' initial attempt to exorcize the demons proved unsuccessful, leaving the demons in their former position and powerful to challenge Jesus with their own abjurations.

In his *second* attempt after his initial failure, Jesus moves to the device of overpowering an enemy by means of knowledge of their identity. Indeed, the demons themselves had just employed this technique when they addressed him as "Jesus—Son of the Most High God." As this had not worked in the attack of the synagogue demoniac, however, so does it fail on Jesus here. Jesus, however, asks the demon (apparently thinking it to be just one), "What is your name?" The demons' response reveals that they are not one but *many* demons, and that their collective name is "Legion."

With this confession, the story takes on clear political resonances, for "legion" was a Latin word (*legio*) signifying a few thousand Roman soldiers. Because the Romans were the subjugating power then occupying Israel, some scholars have taken this admission of the demons to reveal the story's central theme: a condemnation of Rome by

---

[43] Collins, *Mark*, 268.

linking the demonic forces with Rome.[44] Indeed, we have found this to be a typical device of apocalyptic writers who, inheriting the traditional tendency to politicize the combat myth, aggrandize the historical element to equate the evil, dominating, Gentile forces with the forces of the Devil. The association of political enemy with chaos-monster became, in apocalyptic transformations of the myth, associations of the political enemy with the Dragon himself. It is in just this vein that Mark employs the *political* reflexes of the apocalyptic combat myth here. By naming the demons Legion, Mark stands clearly in the apocalyptic *Chaoskampf* tradition.

However, this should not obfuscate the essential core of the struggle. To interpret Mark as articulating concerns of a fundamentally political nature (as some have done) is to exaggerate the historical reflex of the myth at the expense of the broader themes of the apocalyptic combat myth. Indeed, Collins rightly concludes that, though there are secondary political overtones to the story—and indeed "[i]t would be a culturally logical step for the audience to link the kingdom of Satan with Rome and the healing activity of Jesus with the restored kingdom of Israel"[45]—nevertheless it is "more likely that the earliest audiences would have read the story of the Gerasene demoniac in connection with the theme of the battle between Jesus and Satan."[46] As the puppet-master of oppressive nations, Satan's power is the true source of Rome's power, and thus Satan, not Rome, is the ultimate enemy. Rome is a helper Beast; Satan is the Dragon.

Eventually, Jesus is able to subdue the demons by accepting their request that they not be sent out of the country but rather into a nearby herd of swine. Collins observes that this was actually a means of trickery on the part of Jesus:

> The demons, according to the narrative, did not foresee that the pigs would rush into the sea and drown. They wanted to stay in the district of the

---

[44] See, e.g., Ched Myers, *Binding the Strong Man* (Maryknoll: Orbis Books, 1991), 192-4; John Dominic Crossan, *Jesus: A Revolutionary Biography* (San Francisco: HarperSanFrancisco, 1994), 99-102.

[45] Collins, *Mark*, 270.

[46] Ibid., 269-70. This is true partly because "legion" was not a word which referred exclusively to Roman soldiers, but also because the earthly political situation ultimately mirrored the battles between the heavenly powers. Likewise, Marcus notes, "It is not clear if Mark himself is a party to such anti-Roman sentiments, but the portrayal of Jesus as the conqueror of a legion of demonic foes fits the overall Markan concept of the Messiah as God's holy warrior." See Marcus, *Mark 1-8*, 352.

Trickery, we have seen, was often the means to victory by the divine
warriors of ancient Near Eastern combat myths. So, for example, after
being defeated by Illuyankas, the Storm God holds a banquet at which
he intoxicates Illuyankas, thereby allowing an easy slaying of the
serpent. Likewise, when Ninurta's arrows prove ineffective against
Anzu, the god enlists the aid of the trickster god Ea, who hatches a plot
that ultimately proves effective against Anzu. In the Ugaritic texts, it
appears that Baal tricks Mot into eating his own brothers before their
decisive confrontation.[48] It is possible that such elements may have
found their way into Jewish conceptions of the combat myth, and were
transmitted along with other *Chaoskampf* themes, but we cannot know
for sure.[49]

After Jesus outwits the demons, they hurtle down the cliff-ledge
into the Sea, recalling how, at Yahweh's rebuke,

> [the Waters] rose up to the mountains, ran down the valleys
>> to the place that you appointed them.
> You set a boundary that they may not pass,
>> so that they might not again cover the earth. (104:8-9)

So the demons, which used to cry out on the tops of the mountains (v.
5), are now, after the divine victory, sent down the steep bank (*kata tou
krēmnou*) into the Sea—the place which the Lord (Jesus) has assigned.
Pheme Perkins insightfully notes (with allusion to the preceding event
in Mark's gospel): "The storm at sea has evoked the mythic cosmology
of the divine warrior's victory over the chaos monster (4:35-41).
Although the demons try to avoid being driven out of the country, they
wind up in the sea (the waters of chaos), where they belong."[50]

Finally, besides recalling the descent of the raging Waters from
the combat myth generally, the drowning of the demons also recalls the
most important *specific* adaptation of the myth: the drowning of

---

[47] Collins, *Mark*, 271. Cf. Marcus, *Mark 1-8*, 345, 352.

[48] Moor, *An Anthology of Religious Texts from Ugarit*, 96. Cf. ns. 466 and 352.

[49] The motif of tricking the chaos-monster may lie behind Job 41:5 and potentially Ps
104:26.

[50] Perkins, *The New Interpreter's Bible 8*, 584. Similarly, Longman and Reid, *God Is a
Warrior*, 116, note the connection with the storm at sea, suggesting, "The spirits are
banished to the watery corpse of a cosmic foe that Jesus has only recently subdued."

Pharaoh's men in the Red Sea at the Exodus.[51] We have already seen how Mark's combat myth typology has led him to portray Jesus as leading a New Exodus and Conquest. That he causes the enemies of God to be drowned in the Sea obviously works within this conceit. Here, as in the Exodus story, the divine warrior is not defeating the Sea itself, but rather employing it as a tool for his defeat of an enemy. Again, Mark's Exodus typology becomes fully appreciable only in the context of the combat myth and divine warfare.

Having thus analyzed the story, key elements of the traditional combat myth are obvious. Notably, the *political* theme of the myth in its apocalyptic reflex is paramount, as Mark, like so many apocalyptic writers before, situates the cosmic battle in the historical context of Israel's oppression by a Gentile overlord.

Traditional imagery too is employed, most notably the *binding* motif, but also the *scattering* motif, as the defeated demons are cast down and strewn upon the Sea.

Finally, in narrative terms, we have again a fairly complete combat myth: (1) *Lack/Villainy*: Satan's demons have taken control of a man. Though once bound, the demoniac has burst his chains and now rages wildly, harming both himself and the community. (2) *Hero emerges/prepares to act*: Jesus emerges from Nazareth and (3) *Donor/Consultation*: is baptized by John the Baptist, at which time he receives the Holy Spirit. (4) *Journey*: Jesus crosses the Sea and arrives in the region of the Gerasenes. (5) *Battle*: The man possessed by unclean spirits approaches Jesus to oppose him. (6) *Defeat*: Jesus' initial attempt to overpower the demoniac by command fails. (7) *Enemy ascendant*: The demoniac then tries to assert control over Jesus by traditional magical rites. (8) *Hero recovers*: These fail on Jesus. (9) *Battle rejoined*: Now Jesus demands to know the spirit's name. (10) *Victory*: Overpowered, the spirits reveal their name, then beg to be sent into the swine instead of out of the country. Jesus casts the spirits into the pigs, which then plummet off the bank into the Sea to drown. Function 11, the punishment of the enemy, is not present, since Jesus appears not to do as the spirits had feared, which is to torture them. (12) *Triumph*: The news of what Jesus has done is reported by the healed demoniac and increases his reputation.

---

[51] See, e.g., *God Is a Warrior*, 116; Marcus, *Mark 1-8*, 348-9.

As we have encountered often in the ancient Near Eastern myths, the chaos-enemy is usually aided by "helpers": lesser powers, often monstrous as well, who serve as underlings and allies to the principal adversary of the divine warrior. Like henchmen of the criminal mastermind, help is always needed by the cosmic rebel to fulfill his or her plans of chaos and destruction. Therefore these "helpers" play a critical supporting role in the combat myth genre. Azag had his Stone Things, Tiamet her various draconic beasts, Yamm his dragon Litan, and Yam his Rahab/Leviathan.

Without doubt, Jesus' principal enemy in Mark's gospel is the Dragon himself, Satan—the lord of this world. It is to destroy Satan and his kingdom that Jesus has come as the divine warrior. Thus we understand Jesus' exorcisms and healings as smaller skirmishes in this broader war. The unclean spirits are but the armies of Satan—indeed, his legions (cf. Mk 5:9). As such, they are the most obvious examples of Satan's supporting forces. However, the demons/unclean spirits are not the only allies of Satan in the cosmic war. Though it is indeed a spiritual war Jesus is waging, the actors need not be only spiritual entities. As the possessions and illnesses in the gospel make abundantly clear, the spiritual realm is hardly divorced from the material. Quite the contrary: the unseen, spiritual state of affairs has its direct influence on human beings. Satan's power, his kingly rule, is not simply a metaphysical reality, it is physical—experienced tangibly by those on earth. The realities "on the ground" mirror those in the heavens. Such a perspective is, as we have seen, core to apocalypticism. So it is in Daniel, where world empires are merely puppet regimes of the true lord of the world, Satan. The earthly battles between the righteous and the unrighteous are in fact shadows of the cosmic spiritual war being waged above. Spiritual enemies have earthly counterparts. So it is in Mark as well.

The Satanic enemies of Jesus thus far examined have been entirely spiritual: unclean spirits, or their Leader himself. However, Jesus' opposition has a terrestrial, human component too. In Mark, they are as equally ubiquitous as their supernatural counterparts, and in fact pose more of an immediate threat to Jesus and his ministry than the largely toothless demons. In many ways this should not be surprising, for these human enemies are by definition powerful. As we have seen, the apocalyptic perspective held Satan to be the ruler of the world through the evil human rulers of the nations. To be in a position of power, then, meant one was at the very least an abettor of the Enemy, and at worst a co-conspirator. If Satan maintained his control over the earth, it was done through his earthly minions: those in positions of power who kept the oppressive status quo and facilitated his evil designs.

Given this perspective, it is no surprise that, in Mark, Satan's human allies are those in positions of power: the elite, the rulers and the authorities. Thus, the evil Gentile overlords, the Romans, fill out part of this rank. Though, as we saw in the *Testaments of the Twelve Patriarchs* and the literature from Qumran, Mark also paints the Jewish authorities with this brush. In fact, it is the Jewish authorities—those political (Herod/the Herodians), but more so those religious (the scribes, the Pharisees, and the Temple priests/elders)—whom Mark seems to target with the greatest vitriol.[52]

These authorities are *never* portrayed positively. In fact, they are described in every instance as being in opposition to Jesus—arguing with him, or testing him, or plotting to kill him. Indeed, apart from the unclean spirits, they constitute Jesus' chief opposition, countering and questioning him at every turn, and ultimately seeking to destroy him:

Herod/Herodians

3:6	Pharisees conspire with Herodians how to kill him
6:14-29	Portrayed as archetypal wicked ruler, Herod kills John the Baptist
8:15	Jesus warns: Beware the leaven of Pharisees and Herod
12:13	Pharisees and Herodians challenge Jesus on issue of taxes to Caesar

Scribes

2:16	The "scribes of the Pharisees" challenge him for eating with sinners
7:1-12	Jesus attacks them for "traditions of men" and Korban
10:33	Jesus predicts: Son of Man to be handed over to chief priests/scribes

---

[52] *Mark 1-8*, 192, citing Dieter Lührmann, "Die Pharisäer und Die Schriftgelehrten Im Markusevangelium," *ZNW* 78 (1987): 182, notes that "the scribes are terminologically linked with the theme of authority throughout Mark's narrative (see 1:22; 2:6, 10; 3:15, 22; 11:27, 28, 29, 33). ...[This] places them , in Mark's dualistic universe, on the side of Satan."

11:17-18	Chief priests and scribes like den of robbers; they seek to kill him
11:27-8	Chief priests and scribes question Jesus' authority
12:1-12	Jesus levels his parable of the wicked tenants against them
14:1	They conspire with the chief priests to kill Jesus
14:43	They send mob to arrest Jesus, along with the chief priests and elders
14:53-65	Jesus tried before them as well as chief priests and elders
15ff.	They bring him to Pilate, accuse him, mock him, etc.

Pharisees

2:16	The "scribes of the Pharisees" criticize him for eating with sinners
2:24	They challenge Jesus about eating grain on the Sabbath
3:6	They conspire with Herodians to kill Jesus
7:1	They challenge Jesus on hand washing
8:11	They demand a sign from Jesus
8:15	Jesus warns: Beware the leaven of Pharisees and Herod
10:2	They try to test Jesus with questions about divorce
12:1-12	Jesus levels his parable of the wicked tenants against them
12:13	They and the Herodians challenge Jesus on issue of taxes to Caesar

Chief Priests

11:18	Chief priests and scribes seek to kill him
14:1	They seek to kill him with scribes
14:43	They send mob to get Jesus, along with scribes and elders
14:53-65	Jesus tried before them and scribes and elders
15ff	They bring him to Pilate, accuse him, mock him, etc.

While serving as the most active and powerful source of opposition to Jesus after Satan, Mark makes their Satanic connections clear. For example, we saw how, in Jesus' first battle with Satan in Mark 1:12-13, the Devil is said to "test" (*peirazō*) him, a word Mann interprets in its Markan context as 'to wage war on.'"[53] Accepting the connotative significance of this word, it is certainly revealing that the Pharisees also "test" (*peirazō*) Jesus in 8:11 and 10:2, as do the Herodians with the Pharisees in 12:15. As allies of Satan, their

---

[53] Mann, *Mark: A New Translation with Introduction and Commentary*, 203.

confrontations with Jesus are described in the same terms, their "testing" likewise linking them with the tempting Serpent.[54] Indeed, the connection is explicit in the other synoptic gospels: in Matthew 23:33, Jesus denounces them as "snakes" and a "brood of vipers," while Luke places a similar defamation on the lips of John the Baptist in Luke 3:7.

Joel Marcus astutely notes that this association of the scribes with Satan is anticipated already at Jesus' first battle with the demons. Indeed, the tension between Jesus and the scribes is

> foreshadowed at the beginning of the exorcism in 1:21-28, where the evangelist contrasted Jesus' authoritative teaching with the instruction of the scribes; that may have already been a hint to perceptive hearers that, for Mark, the scribes were on the side of Satan. This juxtaposition between 1:16-45 and 2:1-3:6 drives the point home: though routed for the moment by Jesus' exorcisms and healings, the demons now counterattack through human instruments, perhaps with special fierceness because they know that Jesus has been sent to destroy them and their time is short (see 1:24; cf. Rev 12:12). This counterattack takes the form of arguments with the scribes and Pharisees...

Thus we may see the opposition of the scribes/Pharisees as not only mirroring the demonic opposition, but indeed as *part of* that opposition. They are the allies of Satan in opposing Christ, and it follows that, if Christ is to defeat Satan and inaugurate the Kingdom of God, he must likewise defeat the religious authorities as helpers in Satan's cause.

The importance of these authorities as agents of Satan comes to be of key significance after Jesus arrives in Jerusalem. There, as we shall see, Jesus challenges them head-on in a series of conflicts which further links them with the forces of evil. It is through this equation of the religious authorities with the unclean spirits/forces of Satan that Mark, by showing their defeat, intimates Jesus' purification of Jerusalem in terms of the ancient New Year festival ablutions. Moreover, their actions directly lead to Jesus' torture and crucifixion, and thereby help the forces of Chaos and evil assume their greatest dominance over the cosmos. Indeed, the climax of the crucifixion, described and understood in cosmic terms, most clearly indicts the political and religious authorities as the instruments of Satan in the far greater spiritual war of the apocalypse. However, these arguments must wait for more in-depth treatments in Chapters 8 and 9.

---

[54] Longman and Reid, *God Is a Warrior*, 117-8, remark: "It appears that Mark uses *peirazō* as a leitmotif to alert his readers to the ultimate source of the mounting conflict leading Jesus to the cross."

CHAPTER 7
BATTLING SEA

Concluding the previous chapter, I noted that Satan, as chief antagonist in Mark's gospel, is aided by helpers, such as the political and religious leaders, who serve as his agents and instruments in maintaining his hegemony over the world. Indeed, their power and eminence reflects the backwards state of affairs in a world where the Devil is king. The regime of justice and peace that Yahweh would implement is stymied by Satan's grip, which twists and distorts the perfection of God's creation to its terrifying inverse. Thus, wicked men rule where the just ought to, sickness pervades where there should be health, and death conquers where the righteous should live.

It is within this context of a world turned upside-down that one must read the so-called "nature miracles." Jesus, as the rejuvenating divine warrior, sets out on his mission to restore the fallen world by defeating Satan, thereby ushering in the fertility and abundance of God's Kingdom. The ancient motif of agricultural rejuvenation at the New Year festival becomes transformed via apocalypticism into the vision of cosmic rejuvenation at the End. So Jesus marches through Israel, waging war on the forces of Chaos which have disrupted God's perfect world.

Apart from battling Satan and his demonic forces (whose struggle and defeat are portrayed *like* the raging Sea's), Mark also depicts Jesus subduing the Sea itself. Nature, like all else under Satan's dominance, has become distorted and corrupt—working evil rather than harmony for the righteous, and the Sea, Yahweh's old enemy, serves as the chief representative of Satan's allies in Nature. So, in the articulation of Christ's eschatological rejuvenation, the motif of the raging Sea returns as the paramount expression of Chaos and disorder in a cosmos under evil kingship. Jesus' victories over the Sea represent Mark's most explicit use of the *Chaoskampf* tradition and most obvious theological application of the combat myth: Jesus is the divine warrior, sanctioned and empowered by God himself to bring about the world's radical transformation. No destructive power shall be spared. He is the messianic figure of salvation, who has come on the cusp of the cosmic New Year to finally deliver Israel from all the powers of Chaos, and slay the Dragon in the Sea.

To be sure, the Sea plays a pivotal role in the Gospel of Mark. It is the home-base, the hub around which the entirety of the first part of

Mark's narrative revolves. So Elizabeth Malbon writes in *Narrative Space and Mythic Meaning in Mark* that the Sea "becomes the focal point for the first half of the narrative" and that Mark in fact draws special attention to the Sea: "the Markan emphases at this point does illustrate clearly the density of Markan references to events on the sea. The reader is reminded insistently of this special location when it occurs in the narrative."[1] The Sea then is not merely a neutral backdrop for the first of Mark's three parts, but an important conceptual setting whose context is emphatically reiterated and whose connotations are richly suggestive.

That such connotations are important to Mark is evidenced by his choice of terminology for the Sea of Galilee. Indeed, scholars have noted his rather imprecise use of the word "sea" (*thalassa*) for what should be more accurately called a "lake" (*limnē*). For example, Josephus refers to the same body of water as "Lake Gennesar" (*Gennēsar hē limnē*), while Luke likewise calls it Lake Gennesaret (*hē limnē Gennēsaret*) in his gospel.[2] For Mark to use the word "sea" then suggests that he is seeking to draw upon all the connotative and literary implications of that word. Malbon perceptively observes:

> Biblical imagery, particularly in the Psalms but also in Genesis 1 and the Book of Job, frequently portrays the sea as chaos that only the Lord can order or reorder, a threat that only divine power can securely control. At this point it is clear that Markan application of the term *thalassa*, "sea," rather than *limnē*, "lake," to the Lake of Galilee serves well its narrative and theological purposes. Though *limnē* is more geographically precise, the more ambiguous *thalassa* is rich in connotations from the Jewish Scriptures. The Markan Gospel presupposes this connotation of the sea as chaos, threat, danger...[3]

By calling it the "Sea" of Galilee, then, Mark is cueing his audience into its host of *Chaoskampf* associations. This is not just a body of

---

[1] Elizabeth Malbon, *Narrative Space and Mythic Meaning in Mark* (San Francisco: Harper and Row, 1986), 62, 54.

[2] Collins, *Mark*, 156.

[3] Malbon, *Narrative Space and Mythic Meaning in Mark*, 100. Cf. Eugene LaVerdiere, *The Beginning of the Gospel: Introducing the Gospel According to Mark*, 2 vols. (Collegeville, Minn.: Liturgical Press, 1999), 42. In her commentary, Collins sees the use of *thallasa* as coming more from a proposed Semitic linguistic background of the author. However, though she does not think the mythological connotations are the primary reason for such terminology, she does concede that "the use of the word certainly evoked those traditions," Collins 2007, 157.

water, this is the raging Sea, the chaos-waters that Yahweh must subdue. This is Yamm.

Indeed, there are grounds more relative than this for linking Mark's Sea of Galilee with the destructive chaos-waters of the combat myth. Malbon notes that, in the gospel's myriad references to the sea, only two do not signal topographical points of reference, but are instead found within the parables and teachings of Jesus. In these contexts, the "sea" serves a more metaphorical function and sheds light on the implicit qualities it holds for Mark. These references are found in Mark 9:42 and 11:23:

Mark 9:42	Mark 11:23
And whoever causes one of these little ones who believes in me to sin, it would be better for him if a great millstone were hung around his neck and he were cast into the Sea.	Amen I say to you, that whoever says to this mountain, "Be taken up and cast into the Sea," and if he does not doubt it in his heart, but believes that what he says will happen, it will be done for him.

Malbon concludes that "[b]oth of these hypothetical and hyperbolic statements of the Markan Jesus disclose an assumption that the sea is a powerful agent of destruction ...[and] a threatening entity."[4] In each case, the Sea spells destruction for whatever enters it. The sense of the Sea then in these passages is one of annihilation and ruin. Such negative connotations fit well with all that we have so far examined about the traditional waters of Chaos. So Malbon concludes, "Non-topographical applications enrich the reader's understanding of the connotative value of topographical terms"[5] and evince an understanding of the Sea as a force of evil that is elsewhere taken for granted by Mark.

From all of this, we may conclude that: (1) The Sea plays a pivotal role in Mark, acting as the "focal point" of the first part of the gospel. It is mentioned repeatedly, even redundantly—an emphasis which draws attention to its important associations. (2) The use of the term "Sea" for the "Sea of Galilee" is actually rather imprecise, and its use signals that Mark is utilizing the term "Sea" primarily for its mythical resonances. (3) The correlation between the "Sea" and the chaos-waters is implied in the Markan Jesus' parables. In both cases where the word is used metaphorically and not geographically, it is understood as a negative, hostile, and destructive force. Such

---

[4] Malbon, *Narrative Space and Mythic Meaning in Mark*, 58-59.
[5] Ibid., 59.

characterization fits with traditional conceptions of the Sea, and affirms what other lines of evidence suggest: that Mark is making use of the Sea within a *Chaoskampf* typology.

The Sea in Mark is thus clearly a menacing force—a threat and, in fact, an enemy. Because Satan is in control of the world, and his rule is the source of corruption in the world, one may assume that this menacing nature of Sea owes to the Devil. Sea, we might say, is a helper of Satan in his evil kingdom now corrupting and distorting God's creation.[6] Thus far in our investigation, Jesus has not yet confronted the Sea directly the way Yahweh did in the primordial past. Yet such a showdown is all but demanded if Jesus is truly the eschatological savior.

Muzzling the Raging Sea (Mk 4:35-41)

Despite the crucial role of the combat myth in Mark's gospel, it is principally this passage (and often this passage only) which commentators acknowledge as alluding to the Hebrew *Chaoskampf* tradition. No doubt this is because its resonances with the older myth are so obvious. Indeed, it is by far the most direct and explicit representation of Jesus as the divine warrior who subdues the raging Sea. As Boyd has succinctly put it, "It is as though Yahweh is, in the person of Jesus Christ, once again confronting his archenemy Yamm in the chaotic and threatening waves of the Sea of Galilee."[7]

The scene opens with Jesus suggesting to his disciples a journey across the Sea to the opposite shore. They consequently disembark, accompanied, we are told, by a few other boats as well. Just then, however, arises "a great tempest of wind" (*lailaps megalē anemou*) and "the waves crashed into the boat" so that the boat fills with water. Like an angry dragon roused from its slumbers, the Sea has suddenly turned into the familiar destructive entity from Israel's mythic traditions. Lake Gennesar is now the raging Sea, the Deep, the roaring Waters.

The villain thus established, familiarity with the traditional narrative leads us to expect the emergence of the hero now: Jesus will rise up and defeat the chaos-enemy. But far from jumping into action, Jesus is asleep on a cushion in the stern of the boat! Commentators

---

[6] In the traditional myth, the Dragon is the helper of Sea. Here, Sea is the helper of the Dragon.

[7] Boyd, *God at War*, 207.

have approached this interesting detail with various interpretations. Comparisons are often made with the story of Jonah and the mention made of his sleeping in the tempest-rocked boat.[8] Alternatively, Bernard Batto has proposed that the scene mirrors an ancient Near Eastern motif of the sleeping god who can rest because his authority is assured.[9] The similarities with Jonah are compelling, given that prophet's own struggles with a giant sea-monster, and Mark may indeed be nodding to that story. Similarities with ancient Near Eastern gods is also fitting, since Jesus is here standing in the role of the ancient Near Eastern divine warrior. However, as Jesus' authority is hardly assured at this point in Mark's narrative, with many battles still ahead (including his own crucifixion), this association is less convincing. Indeed, I propose a different explanation.

In "Developments of the Hebrew Combat Myth" in Chapter 2 I examined the most crucial application of the myth in wake of the Babylonian Captivity. Appealing to the ancient battle to provoke God to action, writers recalled the "wonders of old" (e.g., Ps 77:11), the mighty deeds Yahweh did in primordial time and so might do again. For them, *it was as though Yahweh had fallen asleep* and needed to be roused to action. Indeed, Collins has recognized this basic connection in Mark, noting:

> The depiction of Jesus sleeping, being awakened by the disciples, and then stilling the storm is reminiscent of a motif in the Hebrew Bible that involves the metaphor of God being roused from sleep by the people in order to deliver them by performing a mighty deed.[10]

Collins fails to note, however, that this mighty deed was *Yahweh's defeat of the chaos-monsters*. So Psalm 74:

> Your foes have roared within your Holy Place;
>> they set up their emblems there.
> …How long, O God, is the foe to scoff?
>> Is the enemy to revile your name forever?
> Why do you hold back your hand;
>> why do you keep your hand in your bosom?
> Yet God my King is *from of old,*
>> working salvation in the earth.

---

[8] See Collins, *Mark*, 260, and n. 20 on 259.
[9] Bernard Frank Batto, "The Sleeping God: An Ancient Near Eastern Motif of Divine Sovereignty," *Biblica* 68 (1987): 153-77.
[10] Collins, *Mark*, 260.

> You divided Sea by your might;
> you broke the heads of the Dragons in the waters.
> You crushed the heads of Leviathan;
> you gave him as food for the people in the wilderness. (vv. 74:4, 10-14)

Here the psalmist laments the roaring of Yahweh's enemies in his desecrated Temple. It is as though the thunderous Sea, in its clamorous uproar, now rages in the Holy Place of God. But Yahweh has not come yet to re-purify it as was done during the New Year, so the psalmist recalls the way he broke the heads of the dragons in the water in petition—that he might do so again. It is in this vein that Deutero-Isaiah writes in chapter 51:

> *Awake, awake*, put on strength,
> O arm of Yahweh!
> *Awake, as in days of old,*
> the generations of long ago!
> Was it not you who cut Rahab in pieces,
> who pierced the Dragon?
> Was it not you who dried up Sea,
> the Waters of the Great Deep;
> who made the depths of Sea a road
> for the redeemed to cross over?
> So the ransomed of Yahweh shall return,
> and come to Zion with singing;
> Everlasting joy shall be upon their heads;
> they shall obtain joy and gladness,
> and sorrow and sighing shall flee away.
> I, I am he who comforts you;
> why then are you afraid of a mere mortal who must die,
> a human being who fades like grass?
> You have forgotten Yahweh, your Maker,
> who stretched out the heavens
> and laid the foundations of the earth.
> You fear continually all day long
> because of the fury of the oppressor,
> who is bent on destruction.
> But where is the fury of the oppressor? (Is 51:9-14)

Surely this is what Mark has in mind by depicting Jesus asleep in the cabin. Indeed, this is the message of his entire gospel: if God had been asleep before, he is awake *now*, and will finally slay the dragons in the water—all the chaos-enemies: Satan, Sea, and Death. To stress this point, Mark emphasizes Jesus' waking. Verse 38 says that the disciples "woke him up" (*egeirousin auton*), and then, "having been woken up" (*diegertheis*), he addresses the raging Sea. The second participle is seemingly gratuitous, but serves Mark's theological message in highlighting what is going on. God's people have been suffering for centuries; this is the moment, the time of Jesus' ministry, when God has finally woken up and heard his people's calls to defeat the chaos-monsters. The question, "Teacher, do you not care that we are perishing?" is the question Jews had been asking of God for generations. The Markan Jesus now answers that question once and for all. His response to his disciples at the close of the scene, "Why are you afraid?" seems a direct reference to Isaiah 51, where Yahweh himself asks, "Why then are you afraid?" and derides his people for their fear and lack of faith. The calming of the storm in Mark, then, is a clear and dramatic enactment of Deutero-Isaiah's promise: Yahweh has awoken, slain the Dragon—why did you doubt?

After being awoken, Jesus now steps up to battle the raging Sea. As H. C. Kee has observed, he does this in the same way that Yahweh had in the Hebrew Bible: by his thunderous *rebuke* (*epitimaō*).[11] As we recall, this was the traditional means by which Yahweh brought the chaos-waters into submission:

<table>
<tr><td align="center">MASORETIC TEXT</td><td align="center">SEPTUAGINT</td></tr>
<tr><td align="center">Psalm 18:15</td><td align="center">Psalm 17:16</td></tr>
<tr><td>Then the channels of the Sea were seen, and the foundations of the world were laid bare at your rebuke (migga ʿărātkā), O Lord, at the blast of the breath of your nostrils.</td><td>And the founts of the Waters were seen, and the foundations of the world were exposed at your <u>rebuke</u> (epitimēseōs), O Lord, at the blasting of the breath of your anger.</td></tr>
<tr><td align="center">Psalm 104:6-7</td><td align="center">Psalm 103:6-7</td></tr>
<tr><td>You cover it with the Deep as with a garment; the Waters stood above the mountains. At your rebuke (ga ʿărātkāmin) they flee; at the sound of your thunder they take to flight.</td><td>The deep, like a cloak, is his covering: the waters will stand on the mountains. At your <u>rebuke</u> (epitimēseōs) they will flee; at the voice of your thunder they will become afraid.</td></tr>
<tr><td align="center">Psalm 106:9</td><td align="center">Psalm 105:9</td></tr>
<tr><td>He rebuked (wayyig ʿar) the Red Sea, and it became dry;</td><td>And he <u>rebuked</u> (epitimēsen) the Red Sea, and it was dried up...</td></tr>
</table>

---

[11] Kee, "The Terminology of Mark's Exorcism Stories," 232-46.

<table>
<tr><td align="center">Job 26:11-13</td><td align="center">Job 26:11-13</td></tr>
<tr><td>The pillars of heaven tremble, and are astounded at his rebuke (migga 'ărātô). By his power he stilled the Sea; by his understanding he struck down Rahab. By his wind the heavens were made fair; his hand pierced the fleeing Serpent.</td><td>The pillars of heaven were passive and astonished at his <u>rebuke</u> (epitimēseōs). He has put down the Sea with his might, and crippled the sea-monster with his skill. The barriers of heaven fear him, and by a command he has slain the rebel Dragon.</td></tr>
</table>

So Jesus rebukes the tempest wind and then, remarkably, *speaks to* the Sea (*eipen tē thalassē*), commanding it be silent and *bound in a muzzle* (*Siōpa! Pephimōso!*). Thus, like Yahweh, he uses his *mighty voice* to bring the Sea into obedient submission, while binding with a muzzle was the fate of the defeated chaos-monster in the Ugaritic and Israelite combat myths. In fact, the same progression of rebuking and muzzling was used on the demoniac in Mark 1. Here, they are found in a situation more at home to their origins in the combat myth. Yahweh rebuked and bound the Sea with a muzzle; so too does Jesus.

Throughout the engagement, the Sea is treated as a personal agent, an entity to which Jesus can speak and give command. It is not merely a natural geographical location, it is a being—Yamm, the raging Sea personified. Indeed, James Edwards observes that the verb *phimoō* here

> occurs in the second person singular, as though Jesus were addressing a personal being. Its unusual perfect passive imperative form indicates that the condition shall persist, that is, 'Be still, and stay still.'[12]

This second observation is also intriguing as Mark implies that Jesus' battles with the Sea will be the ultimate, end-all confrontation. Finally the End has approached in Mark, and the forces of Chaos are meeting their final defeat.

Finally, *Chaoskampf* passages like Psalm 89:9-10 lie palpably behind the Markan calming of the storm:

> You rule the raging of the Sea;
> *when its waves rise, you still them.*
> You crushed Rahab like a carcass;
> you scattered your enemies with your mighty arm.
> The heavens are yours, the earth is also yours;
> the world and all that is in it—you have founded them.

---

[12] James R. Edwards, *The Gospel According to Mark*, The Pillar New Testament Commentary (Grand Rapids: Eerdmans, 2002), 150.

Immediately after Jesus rebukes the wind and speaks to the Sea, the wind ceases and there is a great calm (*ekopasen ho anemos kai egeneto galēnē megalē*). The Sea has been bound by the divine warrior. It lies defeated, muzzled so it cannot speak—subdued by Jesus' mighty rebuke.

Again, much of this language we have already seen in the exorcism accounts, where Jesus rebukes and muzzles the unclean spirits. Mark is thus presenting as essential equivalents both Satan/his demonic forces and the raging Sea. The demons are presented in terms of the chaos-waters, but the chaos-waters are equally understood as demonic in nature. In this we get a clear sense of Mark's perspective: the world is overwhelmed—indeed, invaded—by evil forces of Chaos and destruction. Satan, the Sea, and the powers of Death are all forces that threaten the lives and well-being of the righteous. Jesus is defeating them all.

The episode concludes with the disciples in awe. They wonder to themselves, "Who indeed is this that even the wind and the Sea listen to him (*hypakouei autō*)?" As in the combat myths, the defeat of the chaos-forces spells the proclamation (or here the pondering) of the hero's power and authority. As before, the chaos-enemies are said to "listen to him." This is what the unclean spirits did when Jesus rebuked the demoniac in 1:27. In both cases they highlight Jesus' victory by means of his *mighty voice*. Like Yahweh, Jesus thunders his rebuke and the chaos-waters listen—cowering in defeat, *bound* by the divine warrior.

Eating the Chaos-Monsters at the Messianic Banquet (Mk 6:30-44)

Here, in the account of the feeding of the four thousand, we find Mark subtly—though strikingly—alluding the eschatological banquet at which the two chaos-monsters, Leviathan and Behemoth, were to be eaten by the righteous. The scene thus casts Jesus as the victorious divine warrior who has defeated the chaos-monsters and now celebrates his triumph with a kingly feast—at which his foes serve as the main course.[13] With this miracle, then, Mark employs the apocalyptic transformation of a traditional topos from the combat myth—one in

---

[13] Cf. Marcus, *Mark 1-8*, 410-11.

which *the defeated chaos-monster is divided and scattered, its body serving as nourishment in a once-barren place.*

To recall our survey from Part One, we saw that the roots of this topos lie far back in ancient Near Eastern myth, specifically in the *dividing/scattering* motif. So Ninurta "*scattered* [Azag] over the mountain" and "strewed it like flour."[14] More importantly, though, it was the fate of the chaos-enemies in the Ugaritic material, as when Anat slew and scattered the Dragon in the desert:

> She sets a muzzle on Tunnan.
> She binds him on the heights of Lebanon.
> "Toward the desert (*or*: Dried up), shall you be scattered, O Yamm!
> To the multitude of *ḫt*, O Nahar!
> You shall not see (or: Indeed shall you see); lo! you shall foam up!"[15]

She also tears Mot to pieces and scatters him like grain, whereupon he is eaten by birds.

In the Hebrew material, there are many instances of Yahweh *dividing* and/or *scattering* the chaos-enemies.[16] Indeed, the Exodus tradition owes much to this motif, as both the Red Sea and Jordan River crossings are articulated in its terms.[17] But we also find the specific topos in which the divided chaos-monster is scattered *as nourishment in the desert*. So Psalm 74, whose petition to Yahweh recalls:

> You *divided* the Sea by your might;
>   you broke the heads of the Dragons in the Waters.
> You crushed the heads of Leviathan;
>   you *gave him as food for the creatures of the wilderness*. (vv. 13-14)

This topos is particularly pronounced in the mythically-charged political execrations of Isaiah and Ezekiel. So Isaiah 14's king of Babylon (who would unseat Yahweh and enthrone himself on Zaphon like the cosmic rebel) is "cast out…like loathsome carrion," while Ezekiel 29:3-5 is even more explicit in linking the Egyptian Pharaoh with the scattered Dragon:

> I am against you,

---

[14] Jacobsen, *The Harps That Once*, 249-50.
[15] *KTU* 1.83:9-13 = Pitard, "The Binding of Yamm: A New Edition of the Ugaritic Text KTU 1.83," 273.
[16] See, e.g., Ps 18:14, 68:30, 89:10, 144:5-7.
[17] As, e.g., Ex 14:21, 15:8-10; Neh 9:11; Ps 78:13, Ps 136:13; Is 63:12.

> Pharaoh king of Egypt,
> the great Dragon sprawling
>   in the midst of its channels,
> saying, "My Nile is my own;
>   I made it for myself."
> I will put hooks in your jaws,
>   and make the fish of your channels stick to your scales.
> I will draw you up from your channels,
>   with all the fish of your channels
>   sticking to your scales,
> *I will fling you into the desert,*
>   you and all the fish of your channels;
> you shall fall in the open field,
>   and not be gathered and buried.
> *To the animals of the earth and to the birds of the air*
>   *I have given you as food.*

Likewise 32:2-5:

> You consider yourself a lion among the nations,
>   but *you are like a Dragon in the Seas*;
> you thrash about in your streams,
>   trouble the water with your feet,
>   and foul your streams.
> Thus says Yahweh God:
>   In an assembly of many peoples
>   *I will throw my net over you*;
>   and I will haul you up in my dragnet.
> I will throw you on the ground,
>   *on the open field I will fling you*,
> *and will cause all the birds of the air to settle on you,*
>   *and I will let the wild animals of the whole earth gorge themselves with*
>   *you.*
> I will *strew your flesh on the mountains*,
>   and fill the valleys with your carcass.

All of these passages evince an underlying tradition in which Yahweh, having defeated the Dragon, scattered its corpse in the desert to serve as food/carrion.

Such strains of the combat myth, once domesticated within Jewish thought, later provided material for apocalyptic authors as they identified the Dragon with the Devil. So Yahweh has Satan "cast onto earth" from Heaven in *The Life of Adam and Eve*,[18] while in *1 Enoch* this expulsion is even more clearly linked to the *scattering* motif, as the

---

[18] 14:3-16:1 in OTP 1.262.

rebel Azazel is *bound* and then *cast into the desert*.[19] The aspect of nourishment is not lost, though, as it shows up in the Book of Revelation, when the birds gorge themselves on the bodies of the defeated helpers of the Beast (Rev 14:19-21).

Elsewhere, however, the motif informs an apocalyptic tradition in which the chaos-monsters shall themselves sustain the righteous as food at the eschatological banquet. So *4 Ezra* 6:49-52:

> Then you kept in existence two living creatures; the name of one you called Behemoth and the name of the other Leviathan. And you separated one from the other, for the seventh part where the water had been gathered together could not hold them both. And you gave Behemoth one of the parts which had been dried up on the third day, to live in it, where there are a thousand mountains; but to Leviathan you gave the seventh part, the watery part; and *you have kept them to be eaten by whom you wish, and when you wish.*

That these chaos-monsters will be eaten specifically at the messianic banquet is made clear in *2 Baruch* 29:4:

> And it will happen that when all that which should come to pass in these parts has been accomplished, the Anointed One will begin to be revealed. And Behemoth will reveal itself from its place, and Leviathan will come from the sea, the two great monsters which I created on the fifth day of creation and which I shall have kept until that time. And they will be nourishment for all who are left.

In this apocalyptic transformation, two aspects of the ancient combat myth are combined: the *dividing/scattering* of the chaos-monster, and the victorious warrior god's triumphal feast after slaying the chaos-monster. Such feasts occur, for example, after Baal's slaying of Yamm[20] and Mot,[21] and likely reflect a cultic reality—namely, the New Year festival. For the ancient Israelites, such was the mythological significance of the Feast of Tabernacles—a feast and public celebration of Yahweh's victory over the chaos-monsters. In Jewish apocalypticism, however, the Feast of Tabernacles itself is transformed into the eschatological celebration of Yahweh's victory over the forces of the Devil. *The New Year festival becomes the eschatological banquet.* It is in the context of this apocalyptic feast that the chaos-monsters are consumed. So Day:

---

[19] 1 Enoch 10:4-6a.
[20] *CAT* 1.3.1 2-22.
[21] *CAT* 1.4 vi 38-59.

> It is wholly in keeping with the view that the eschatological banquet in Judaism…had its origin in the banquet following Yahweh's and ultimately Baal's victory over the unruly sea and the chaos-monsters…[I]t is specifically the chaos-monsters Leviathan and Behometh which are to be devoured at the messianic banquet.[22]

It is within this tradition, Micah Kiel has argued, that Mark describes Jesus' miraculous feeding of the people in the desert.[23] Mark offers us the first hint of this when he emphasizes the role of the fish in his narrative. For when Jesus asks, "How many bread loaves do you have?" the disciples answer, "Five—*and two fish*," offering more information than was requested and thereby drawing attention to the two fish.[24] Recognizing this emphasis, Kiel infers that a "helpful step in understanding the role of fish in Mark is to examine the traditions gathered around the fish as a symbol within Judaism."[25] This line of inquiry leads him to Leviathan and "the creation battle, in which God enters the chaotic primordial waters and slays a mythical beast."[26] He notes:

> The fish was associated with Leviathan, God's primordial adversary. At the very least, one can observe a trajectory that extends from the OT reflections on chaos, Leviathan, and primordial waters, to the idea of the mythical beast being food for the righteous, as seen in *2 Baruch, 4 Ezra, 1 Enoch*, and *Tobit*. By the first century, this trajectory found expression in the apocalyptic tradition in which fish represented both threat and opportunity. The great fish/monster Leviathan tried to assert chaos but in the end is thwarted, with the righteous tasting the victory.[27]

Though the presence of fish alone is hardly enough to link the miracle to the combat myth, the setting *in the desert* helps cement the association, since the desert was indeed the place where the body of the

---

²² Day, *God's Conflict*, 150. Cf. "Miracles and Miracle Stories" in Joel B. Green, Scot McKnight, and I. Howard Marshall, *Dictionary of Jesus and the Gospels* (Downers Grove: InterVarsity Press, 1992), 559.
²³ Micah Kiel, "The Apocalyptic Significance of Mark's First Feeding Narrative (6:34-44)," *Koinonia* 18 (2006): 93-114.
²⁴ Kiel, "The Apocalyptic Significance of Mark's First Feeding Narrative (6:34-44)," 94.
²⁵ Ibid., 99.
²⁶ Ibid., 99.
²⁷ Ibid., 103.

chaos-monster was scattered and eaten.[28] Thus, an eschatological banquet in the desert is fitting. In fact, the placement of the feeding narrative itself within Mark's gospel may signal its connection with the combat myth, since the calming of the storm and the healing of the Gerasene demoniac occur in close proximity. In this way, says Kiel, the sea calming episode foreshadows the messianic banquet:

> The threat from the churning waters is cast as the chaotic waters of creation, which creates the possibility that Leviathan, up to his old tricks, lurks in the deep, causing the chaos, a subtle anticipation of the fish that will arrive on the scene in 6:38.[29]

In short, he says, "The chaos that asserted itself when Jesus crossed the lake (4:35-41) has been pulled from the water and lies supine and at Jesus' mercy (6:38, 41)."[30] Kiel could also have noted the close proximity to the miracle of Jesus' treading upon the Sea (see below), which follows immediately after the feeding narrative at 6:45. So the feeding narrative is bounded by two other stories that paint Jesus as the conquering divine warrior defeating the Sea.[31]

With the apocalyptic significance of the miracle clear enough, we see that Mark narrates the event as an instance of Jesus *dividing* and *scattering* the fish. Verse 41 reads:

> Taking the five loaves and the two fish, he looked up to heaven, and blessed and *broke* the loaves, and *gave* them to his disciples to *distribute* to the people; and he *divided* the two fish among them all.

In fact, Jesus' actions here are so similar to Psalm 74, Mark may be alluding to that text as the very "script" for the event:

> You *divided* the Sea by your might;
> >you *broke* the heads of the Dragons in the Waters.
> You crushed the heads of Leviathan;
> >you *gave him as food for the creatures of the wilderness*. (vv. 13-14)

---

[28] Kiel overlooks this connection, however, linking the setting instead with Israel's camps in the desert after the Exodus. Ibid., 109.

[29] Ibid., 108.

[30] Ibid., 110.

[31] However, this also complicates the function of the feeding narrative here. If indeed the raging Sea has not been totally subdued, how then can Jesus celebrate the final victory banquet? Perhaps this event is but a foreshadowing of the greater victory to come, and thus the greater banquet: the Eucharist. For connections with this feeding narrative and the Eucharistic meal, see Marcus, *Mark 8-16*, 410-11.

Though not in precisely the same order, the basic elements are the same in each:

Yahweh	Jesus
divided the Sea	*divided* (*emerisen*) the fish
broke the heads of the dragons	*broke* (*kateklasen*) the bread
gave them	*gave* (*edidou*) them to the disciples
as food in the wilderness	as food in the wilderness

So the primordial battle becomes the eschatological banquet itself, the Feast of Tabernacles the cosmic New Year feast, and Jesus filling the role as the messianic divine warrior.

Treading upon the Sea (Mk 6:45-52)

The immediate aftermath of the miraculous feeding suggests that the event should be read as a *type* of the eschatological banquet, but not the banquet itself. For the cosmic New Year festival can only be celebrated after the forces of Chaos are completely subdued. Clearly in Mark's own time, this was not the case. Jesus' ministry was only "the beginning of the good news," so any true eschatological banquet would be premature if narrated in Mark's gospel.

Indeed, just after the feast in the desert, Jesus sends his disciples ahead of him—toward Bethsaida, across the Sea—only to find that the raging Sea has not yet been fully subdued. An adverse wind (*ho anemos enantios*) rises up and effectively halts their journey. The disciples strain against the wind with their rowing, but make no progress. Such winds are a common element in scenes depicting the raging Sea. We saw, for instance, the great tempest of wind (*lailaps megalē anemou*) that arose when the disciples were tossed on the waters before. But the tempestuous winds were clearly part of combat myth imagery. So Daniel 7:2:

> I, Daniel, saw in my vision by night the four winds of heaven stirring up the great sea, and four great Beasts came up out of the Sea, different from one another...

The apocalyptic *Testaments* make similar use of the wind associated with the chaotic Sea:

> Those who rule shall be like sea monsters,
> swallowing up human beings like fish.
> Free sons and daughters they shall enslave;
> houses, fields, flocks, goods they shall seize.
> ...*Like a whirlwind* shall be the false prophets:
> They shall harass the righteous.[32]

Thus, Collins' critique may be too fastidious when she asserts that calling this event a "storm at sea" would be an overstatement (given there is no explicit mention of a "storm," only an adverse wind).[33] We may still detect the theme of the chaos-waters here given the correlation between unruly winds and the raging Sea. The enemy thus introduced, we now expect the intervention of the divine warrior.

And indeed, he comes. Seeing the disciples so struggling, Jesus makes his way to them by *treading upon the Sea* (*peripatōn epi tēs thalassēs*). With this remarkable act, Jesus literally walks in the footsteps of Yahweh, who trampled the Sea at his great victory in primordial time. So Psalm 77:

> When the Waters saw you, O God,
> when the Waters saw you, they were afraid;
> the very Deep trembled.
> ...Your way was through the Sea,
> your path, through the mighty Waters;
> yet your footprints were unseen. (vv. 16, 19)

We find the same motif in Job:

> [Yahweh] alone stretched out the heavens
> and *trampled the waves of the Sea*;
> ...God will not turn back his anger;
> the helpers of Rahab bowed beneath him. (Job 9:8, 13)

And again, in Habakkuk 3:

> Was your wrath against River, O Yahweh?
> Or your anger against River,
> or your rage against Sea,
> When you drove your horses,
> your chariots to victory?
> You brandished your naked bow,
> sated were the arrows at your command.

---

[32] *T. Judah* 21:7, 9.
[33] Collins, *Mark*, 333.

> …You *trampled* the Sea with your horses,
> churning the mighty waters. (vv. 8-9a, 15)

In a similar way, the *trampling* motif of the combat myth was poetically employed to describe Yahweh and his people crossing over the Sea towards the Promised Land. So Deutero-Isaiah uses the myth here:

> Was it not you who cut Rahab in pieces,
> who pierced the Dragon?
> Was it not you who dried up Sea,
> the Waters of the Great Deep;
> who made the depths of Sea *a road*
> for the redeemed to cross over? (Is 51:9c-10)

John Paul Heil offers a thorough examination of all the above texts in his extensive analysis of Jesus' sea-walking miracle.[34] He recognizes their relationship with the combat myth tradition and the motif of Yahweh's defeat of the forces of Chaos. Considering their relation to the sea-walking miracle, Heil concludes, "By walking on the sea Jesus reveals himself as the Son of God endowed with absolute power of dominance over the ungodly power of the waters of chaos."[35] However, because Heil focuses just on the trampling of the Sea, he does not speak to other mythological resonances with the combat myth. For example, Psalm 91, which we saw Mark using in the opening battle between Jesus and the Devil, includes the assurance:

> You will tread on the lion and the adder,
> the young lion and the serpent you will trample under foot. (v. 13)

The Septuagint translates this verse with imagery even more at home in the *Chaoskampf* tradition, replacing "adder" with the mythological serpentine beast "basilisk" (*basiliskon*) and aggrandizing the serpent to "dragon" (*drakonta*). This emphasizes the mythical implications of the passage, and shows how the forces of evil were being linked with the dragon of the combat myth in Second Temple Judaism. Thus the *Testaments of the Twelve Patriarchs*:

---

[34] John Paul Heil, *Jesus Walking on the Sea: Meaning and Gospel Functions of Matt. 14:22-33, Mark 6:45-52, and John 6:15b-21*, Analecta Biblica (Rome: Biblical Institute Press, 1981).
[35] Ibid., 108.

> And thereafter the Lord himself will arise upon you, the light of righteousness with healing in his wings. He will liberate every captive of the sons of men from Beliar, and *every spirit of error will be trampled down.*[36]

Likewise *T. Levi 18:12*:

> And Beliar shall be bound by him.
> And he shall grant to his children the authority *to trample on wicked spirits.*

Given the apocalyptic perspective of Paul specifically and the early church generally, it is no surprise that the same image is found in the New Testament:

> The God of peace will shortly crush Satan under your feet. (Rom 16:20)

Or 1 Corinthians 15:24:

> Then comes the end, when he hands over the kingdom to God the Father, after he has destroyed every Ruler and every Authority and Power. For he must reign until he has *put all his enemies under his feet.* The last enemy to be destroyed is Death.

All of these texts convey a common understanding of the role of the combat myth *trampling* motif. At the End, God will trample upon his enemies—the sources of illness and destruction which are the wicked spirits of the Devil. He will even put Death under his feet. For Mark's gospel then, Jesus is clearly fulfilling this eschatological expectation. In Mark 6, this is literally the raging Sea swept by the powerful wind. Read metaphorically, however, it also symbolizes the central goal of his entire ministry. All of Jesus' exorcisms and healings find a kind of poetic embodiment in the reenactment of the ancient myth of Yahweh trampling the waters.

Heil and others have persuasively argued that, fundamentally, the sea-walking miracle functions as an *epiphany*. This accounts for why Jesus "wished to pass by them" (*ēthelen parelthein autous*) since, in the theophanies to Moses and Elijah, Yahweh is said "to pass by" before them (*parelthein*).[37] Also common are the assurances against being afraid, and certainly the expression of the divine name hinted at with

---

[36] *T. Zeb* 9:8.
[37] Collins, *Mark*, 334.

Jesus' proclamation "I AM I" (*egō eimi*). The sea-walking miracle works essentially then as an epiphany story—though one in which the disciples fail to recognize his true identity.

This is particularly notable, as we have seen that *the procession and enthronement of Yahweh at the Feast of Tabernacles acted as the chief ritual epiphany in Israelite cult.* The transfer of Yahweh's ark was the time when all Israel *saw* Yahweh, no longer hidden within the Holy of Holies but moving in procession to the celebration of thronging spectators. Indeed, the image of Yahweh would then literally be seen to "pass by" his people as the ark made its way to its sacred destinations. This was the "Day of the Lord," which later writers interpreted as the eschatological day of God's judgment over the earth. So Jesus appears to his disciples in epiphanic glory in the same context of victory over the chaos-forces.

However, in keeping with Mark's continually subverted depiction of Jesus' divine identity (considered in greater detail in Chapter 9), the disciples do not recognize him for who he is, but rather fear he is a ghost. The concluding remark "and they were utterly astounded, for they did not understand about the loaves" refers back to the feeding miracle, which occurred immediately prior, and also represented Jesus' victory over the chaos-forces. Their failure to understand *that* event, portrayed as the eschatological banquet, means they cannot comprehend this most recent epiphany of Jesus or its significance. In both stories, Jesus is presented as the dominant victor over Chaos. Both the banquet and the epiphanic procession were celebrations of Yahweh's victories over the raging Sea and its dragon. In Jesus' ministry, however, the significance of these events is not comprehended by his followers.

This theme of misunderstanding Jesus' identity as the victorious divine warrior is pervasive in Mark. The irony of the gospel is that, after being urged for centuries to take action and fight the forces of Chaos, God is finally doing so—but no one recognizes it. This idea is intimately related to another central notion in Mark: the re-interpretation of messiahship. All of these elements—ironic reversal, misunderstanding, and reinterpretation of the "Son of Man"—play a crucial role, as we shall see, in Jesus' climactic struggle in Jerusalem and his battle against Death.

CHAPTER 8
THE COSMIC NEW YEAR FESTIVAL

Up to this point, Jesus' ministry has been characterized by a series of battles with the demonic forces that rule the world—with the Dragon (Satan himself), his helpers, and the raging Sea. But Jesus has met all of these challengers and defeated them soundly. And so, with Jesus' victory established, we come to Mark's middle section—his "Way" section. Jesus has defeated the Sea and the Dragon and can now process to his Temple along the Sacred Way for enthronement.[1] So Mark's middle section serves as the Sacred Way itself: the road connecting Jesus' battles around the Sea with his glorious triumph in Jerusalem. The cosmic New Year, that apocalyptic transformation of the combat myth's cultic setting, is about to be ushered in by Jesus, the messianic divine warrior.

To briefly review, the Feast of Tabernacles was the annual harvest festival of the ancient Israelites which had as its central cultic theme the Hebrew combat myth. In this sense it was akin to other ancient Near Eastern New Year festivals. So, for example, the combat myth about the Hittite Storm God and the dragon Illuyankas served as "the text of the Purulli (Festival),"[2] the annual Hittite New Year festival celebrated each spring.[3] Only at this sacred time could the statue of the storm-god residing in the temple be brought out and wheeled on an ox-drawn carriage in procession to its special cult shrine.[4] Similarly, the combat myth in the *Enûma Eliš* was a central liturgical element in the Babylonian *Akītu* festival—the twelve-day Babylonian New Year celebration. On the fifth day, in keeping with the festival's theme of rejuvenation, the priests would purify the temple of any pollution, while the kingship was likewise renewed. On either the eighth or ninth day of the festival came the great procession, when the statues of the gods would pass through the streets of the city on jeweled chariots in great pomp and fanfare. On their way from the main gate of the Esagila, along Marduk's processional street and through the Ishtar Gate, singers, dancers, and musicians would accompany them.[5] The

---

[1] This much is recognized by Longman and Reid, *God Is a Warrior*, 119-24.

[2] Hoffner and Beckman, *Hittite Myths*, 11, A i 1.

[3] Bryce, *Life and Society*, 195.

[4] Burney, *Historical Dictionary of the Hittites*, 86.

[5] Bidmead, *The Akītu Festival*, 96.

gods would then be kept in the special suburban cult shrine, the *bīt akīti*, before ultimately returning to their usual temple residences.

The ancient Feast of Tabernacles was dedicated to rejuvenation, as Yahweh had proven victorious over the Chaos forces of death and sterility. So the Temple was re-purified and the Davidic covenant renewed.[6] Then on the seventh day, the central cultic act was performed: the procession of the ark from its suburban cult shrine to the re-purified Temple, accompanied by singers, dancers, and musicians. Enthroned, Yahweh was proclaimed king over the cosmos for defeating the dragon.

The myth and its festival eventually became a potent framework for apocalypticists to articulate their hopes that Yahweh would triumph over the Devil and usher in a cosmic New Year. And so it is, I shall now argue, that Mark portrays Jesus' journey to Jerusalem precisely in terms of this traditional Israelite ritual. Like Yahweh, Jesus has defeated the raging Sea and battled the Dragon (Satan). Now he may "go up" to Jerusalem, leading his processional train along the Sacred Way to the Temple for enthronement.

On the Sacred Way (Mk 8:27-10:52)

In both thematic and structural ways, Jesus' procession along the Way begins at 8:27. Here Mark enters on his second main section, the "Way" section. With the exception of a final exorcism (9:14-29), Jesus' battles are over and now he sets out with his disciples "on the Way."[7] As we recall from Part One, to "go up" to Jerusalem was cultic terminology used to describe pilgrimage and ritual procession to the Temple on the *měsillâ*, the ascending paved road.[8] Moreover, as we saw in Chapter 5 in the context of Jesus' baptism, to "go up" (Heb. *'ālâ*) was translated as *anabainō* in the Septuagint. So too in Mark, who at 10:32-33a makes it explicit that Jesus is now indeed "going up" to Jerusalem as at Tabernacles:

---

[6] Mowinckel, *The Psalms in Israel's Worship*, 126, 130.

[7] Longman and Reid, *God Is a Warrior*, 117, observe: "After Mark 9:38 and continuing on through the Passion narrative, there are no references to Jesus' or anyone else's carrying on combat with demons. But the theme of conflict does not disappear; rather, it is carried on between Jesus and the Jewish authorities…" That is, just after Jesus begins his procession to Jerusalem, his battles with spiritual entities have ended, and his enemy takes on a different form: that of the authorities.

[8] Mowinckel, *The Psalms in Israel's Worship*, 171. Cf. Tidwell, "No Highway," 251-69.

<blockquote>
And they were on the Way going up to Jerusalem (*anabainontes eis Hierosolyma*), and Jesus was leading them, and they were amazed, and those following were afraid. And taking the Twelve alongside again, he began to say to them the things about to happen to him: "Behold, we are going up to Jerusalem (*anabainomen eis Hierosolyma*)..."
</blockquote>

This passage is remarkable for a number of reasons. First, it specifies the setting as "on the Way," continuing the section's unifying theme. Secondly, Mark notes that they are "going up to Jerusalem," the (almost technical) phrase for ritual procession such as occurred at the Feast of Tabernacles. Mark seems to be drawing special attention to the phrase, as Jesus uses the expression in both verse 32 and 33. Finally, Jesus is said to be "leading them" (*proagōn autous*) while the twelve disciples all follow (*akolouthountes*), just as though Jesus were indeed at the head of a procession, leading his twelve disciples up to Jerusalem.

Such a configuration no doubt recalls the tradition of the New Year procession wherein the Davidic king would lead the twelve tribes to the Temple:

<blockquote>
Your *solemn processions are seen*, O God,
    the processions of my God, my King, into the Sanctuary—
the singers in front, the musicians last,
    between them girls playing tambourines:
"Bless God in the great congregation,
    Yahweh, O you who are of Israel's fountain!"
There is Benjamin, the least of them, in the lead,
    the princes of Judah in a body,
    the princes of Zebulun, the princes of Naphtali. (Ps 68:24-27)
</blockquote>

Likewise Psalm 122, one of the Songs of Ascent, which even specifies a ritual enthronement in the Temple as the conclusion of the sacred procession:

<blockquote>
I was glad when they said to me,
    "Let us go to the House of Yahweh!"
Our feet are standing
    within your gates, O Jerusalem.
Jerusalem—built as a city
    that is bound firmly together.
To it the tribes go up, the tribes of Yahweh,
    as was decreed for Israel,
to give thanks to the name of Yahweh.
For there the thrones for judgment were set up,
    the thrones of the house of David. (vv. 1-5)
</blockquote>

Finally, Jesus comes to the outskirts of Jerusalem—to Bethany, on the Mount of Olives (11:1). Here the procession begins in earnest. Until this point, various people have been intersecting with Jesus "on the Way" (e.g., the rich young ruler ran up to Jesus on the Way, but left it sadly [10:17-31]; the blind Bartimaeus was alongside the Way before Jesus healed him, then joined on the Way [10:46-52]). Now, however, at the dramatic transition to Mark's third section, the entire city of Jerusalem joins in with Jesus on the processional Way. The Way that began in Galilee after Jesus' victory over Satan and Sea has finally arrived at Zion, and now heads directly for the Temple itself.

Excursus: The Sacred Way and the Mount of Olives

Before moving on, however, it is necessary to appreciate an important detail to which Mark emphatically draws our attention: Jesus enters Jerusalem and the Temple *from the Mount of Olives*. To appreciate the implications of this seemingly minor detail one must know what Mark and his audience would have known: *the Sacred Way of the New Year festival led from the Mount of Olives, down into the Kidron Valley, and then up to the Temple Mount, entering the Temple complex through the east gate.*

While biblical sources do not state this route explicitly, considerable evidence corroborates it. As we have seen, there would have been a fixed processional path in ancient Jerusalem by which Yahweh's ark traveled to the Temple during festive processions. This was the *mĕsillâ*, the paved "road that ascends," and some scholars have conjectured about its route. Mowinckel, for example, has argued that

> [o]n the basis of the story told in 2 Sam. 6 as to how David took Yahweh's ark to Jerusalem, we may guess that…it ran on the outside (to the east) of, or through the royal castle and into the temple court through the eastern gate.[9]

Such is the evidence from 2 Samuel 6, anyway, which Mowinckel and many others take more or less as the "script" for the ritual.

However, if we accept that descriptions of ark transference in the Hebrew Bible may be interpreted as "foundation texts" for the annual

---

[9] Mowinckel, *The Psalms in Israel's Worship*, 171.

ritual, then other texts may also reflect the procession. Indeed, Michael Goulder has argued that

> just as 2 Samuel 6 is often (and correctly) understood to echo an annual procession of the ark to the Jerusalem Temple, so the account of David's ascent of the Mount of Olives in 2 Samuel 15 should be understood as the pattern of an annual mourning procession.[10]

In 2 Samuel 15, David leads a fleeing group out of the city of Jerusalem and up the Mount of Olives during Absalom's insurrection—an event which, according to Johannes C. de Moor, would have occurred at the New Year.[11] Indeed, *following David comes the ark*, taken from the city by the high priests Abiathar and Zadok and carried up the mountain. Once there, David orders its return to the city, saying that he shall see it again if found worthy by Yahweh. The priests obey and the ark is returned.

Goulder hypothesizes that this story echoes an *annual New Year procession up the Mount of Olives*, positing Psalms 51-72 as liturgical texts for such a procession. As many of these psalms deal with issues of sin and repentance, he suggests that

> the Prayers were chanted liturgically in a procession one day in the autumn festival at Jerusalem. ...Like king, like people: each year brought its catalogue of troubles, no doubt in just punishment for national sin; but each New Year it was possible to hope, through the liturgy, that atonement had been made for the past, and that a time of peace, prosperity and hegemony lay ahead.[12]

Though Goulder bases his theory of this event on sometimes dubious connections between the Psalms and the life of David, the core of his argument is compelling for other reasons. Such a procession of repentance fits well, for instance, with the themes of the New Year festival. As Mowinckel argues—and as parallels from the *Akītu* and *Purulli* New Year celebrations support—the Israelite harvest festival was a time of general ablution and, by extension, forgiveness of sins.[13]

So, as the ark was removed from the Temple for the its annual purification, the people would have followed it on its way to its

---

[10] M. D. Goulder, *The Prayers of David (Psalms 51-72)*, Journal for the Study of the Old Testament. Supplement Series (Sheffield: JSOT Press, 1990).

[11] Moor, *New Year with Canaanites and Israelites*, 16-17.

[12] Goulder, *The Prayers of David (Psalms 51-72)*, 28-29.

[13] Mowinckel, *The Psalms in Israel's Worship*, 127-8.

temporary shelter: *a suburban cult shrine on the Mount of Olives*. Indeed, 2 Samuel 15 supplies us with additional evidence that this shrine was in fact on the Mount of Olives, as verse 32 says that, after his ascent up Olivet, "David came to *the summit where God was worshipped*." This is supposedly the first mention in the Hebrew Bible of a place on Olivet devoted to the worship of Yahweh.[14] However, if this refers to the House of Obed-Edom—the place where the ark would have been kept every year for some period (and thus constituted a significant place of worship)—this is simply another reference to that cultic site.

As the procession moved to Olivet and the people were called to reflect upon their own need for re-purification, they may have indeed sung hymns such as Psalm 51 (as Goulder suggests):

> Have mercy on me, O God,
> according to your steadfast love;
> according to your abundant mercy
> blot out my transgressions.
> Wash me thoroughly from my iniquity,
> and cleanse me from my sin.
> For I know my transgressions,
> and my sin is ever before me. (vv. 1-3)

As a time of ablution for the year's impurities, such hymns fit well with the themes of restoration and rejuvenation.[15] Indeed, David's remark on Olivet is intriguing in this light. He declares,

> If I find favor in the eyes of Yahweh, he will bring me back and let me *see* both [the ark] and his dwelling place. But if he says, 'I have no pleasure in you,' behold, here I am, let him do what seems good to him. (2 Sam 15:25-6)

Such a declaration reads nearly like a liturgical formula, since the ablution on Olivet would have been necessary for the *epiphany* of the enthronement of the ark within the Temple (i.e., the *seeing* of the ark in the Temple). Thus Psalm 24:3-4:

> Who shall ascend the hill of Yahweh?

---

[14] So *ABD*, "Olives, Mount of," 13.

[15] Likewise, this purification ritual may be related to the purification sacrifice of the red heifer (Num 19:1-10), which tradition holds took place on the Mount of Olives just opposite the eastern gate of the Temple (*Para* 3.6-7). However, these connections are admittedly quite conjectural.

> And who shall stand in his Holy Place?
> Those who have clean hands and pure hearts,
>> who do not lift up their souls to what is false,
>> and do not swear deceitfully.

At some point, when the ancient New Year festival was broken into its constituent parts, *this part of the festival dedicated to ablution became the Day of Atonement* (Tishri 10), between New Year's Day proper (Tishri 1) and the Feast of Tabernacles (beginning Tishri 15). Indeed, this correlation raises its own corroborative evidence for the location of the processional way, since, on the Day of Atonement, the "scapegoat" was led from the Temple "into the wilderness" (Lev 16:10). Tidwell's analysis of topographical associations with the processional way recognizes a

> collocation of *mĕsillâ* and a city's 'wilderness' (*midbār*), the eastern rain-shadow side of the hill or mound on which the city stood or that part of a city's 'field' that was grazing land, (Josh. Viii 15, 24; Judg. xx 42-7; 2 Sam. ii 24; Isa. xl 3).[16]

The Temple stood on Mount Moriah, whose eastern side led down into the Kidron Valley toward the "wilderness" of the Mount of Olives. So 2 Sam 15:23, where David escapes Absalom's insurrection by fleeing there:

> The whole country wept aloud as all the people passed by; the king crossed the Wadi Kidron, and all the people moved on toward the wilderness (*midbār*).

This would suggest a *mĕsillâ* on the eastern side of Mount Moriah, which led toward the Mount of Olives. That the scapegoat was led to the Mount of Olives over the *mĕsillâ* fits well with our understanding of processional purification rites at the festival. In fact, another more rare purification rite, the sacrifice of the Red Heifer, complements these findings. The heifer was sacrificed on the Mount of Olives, and the Mishnah (*Para* 3.6) explicitly refers to a "ramp" or "causeway" (*'wšym*) from the Temple Mount to the Mount of Olives, upon which the priests would lead the heifer for the sacrifice. Such a causeway (if we are to trust the tradition) was presumably the *mĕsillâ* itself (or a temporary structure built thereon).

---

[16] Tidwell, "No Highway," 262.

This time of atonement and ablution would have been the context for one crucial New Year event: the re-purification of the Temple.[17] As we saw, it was during the ancient Near Eastern New Year festivals that the gods would leave their temples to be housed in temporary suburban cult shrines while their principal temples were cleansed of the year's impurity. During the *Akītu* this temporary structure was the *bīt akīti*, or "*Akītu* house"; during the *Purillu*, the *ḥesti* house (located to the *east* of Hattussa). So, in Jerusalem, the ark would exit the Temple and stay at the *House of Obed-Edom* to the east, just outside the city, while the Temple was cleansed. Moreover, it should be noted that "house" usually means "temple" when describing the abode of a god, or even smaller tent-shrine structures which housed the ark before Solomon's Temple (e.g., Josh 6:24). Here it no doubt carries such a significance. The House of Obed-Edom thus served as Israel's suburban cult shrine, and, because the Kidron Valley served as the eastern boundary of the city proper,[18] the House of Obed-Edom must have been beyond it—that is, on the Mount of Olives.[19]

As for the account of the ark's travel to and return from Olivet in 2 Samuel 15, it seems to be deliberately evoking the tradition of the New Year festival procession. Though set in the unique context of Absalom's rebellion, this passage may have reflected an annual ritual. But why this connection of David's flight from Jerusalem with the enthronement procession of the New Year festival? On a literary level, such an echo is entirely fitting. On New Year's day, David's kingship

---

[17] Mowinckel, *The Psalms in Israel's Worship*, 126-30.

[18] Cf. 1 Kgs 2:37.

[19] While this is a novel theory, the Mount of Olives is intriguingly referred to as "the traditional goal of the New Year's ark procession" in John Barton and John Muddiman, *The Oxford Bible Commentary* (Oxford: Oxford University Press, 2001), 537, though no evidence is offered to support this assertion. Mowinckel, however, has posited that the shrine lay to the *west* of the city, presumably based on the location of Kiriath-jearim, the site from which the ark is initially taken in 2 Samuel 6 on its first journey to Jerusalem, which indeed lies to the north-west. However, even 2 Samuel 6:10 says that, after Uzzah illicitly touched the ark, David "took it aside" (*wayyaṭṭēhû*) to the House of Obed-Edom. The new direction is unspecified, and, while this does not prove an eastern location for the site, it does mean that a western one is not demanded (as Mowinckel would assume). However, the place of "Uzzah's breach" would have to have been fairly close to the city if "he took it aside" meant he moved it to the *opposite* side of the city. It is noteworthy then that P. Kyle McCarter's asserts "Uzzah's Breach" was probably a hole in Jerusalem's city wall itself. See P. Kyle McCarter, *II Samuel: A New Translation with Introduction, Notes, and Commentary*, The Anchor Bible (Garden City: Doubleday, 1984), 170. Thus, if the ark were at the very walls, then taking the ark "aside" validates *any* cardinal direction.

has *lapsed* and stands in need of renewal—an occasion which Absalom, the presumptive heir, uses as the opportunity for his accession. David is thus depicted following the processional road out of the city, as the author of the account, like Hebrew authors and prophets throughout the ages, draws on the cultic ceremony so fraught with significance.

Or else, interpreting the passage slightly differently, the connection went the other way. As commonly occurs, stories are created to explain enigmatic rituals whose original purpose is forgotten or obscured. Therefore, just as 1 Samuel 6 serves as the "script" for the procession, so 2 Samuel 15 may serve in part as an etiological elucidation of its route. That the story was indeed etiological in some way is supported by a strikingly comparable account of an earlier flight of David—not from Absalom, but from Saul. In 1 Samuel 20, Jonathan warns David that Saul will try to kill him, and so David flees to Nob— a sacred high place apparently on Olivet (cf. Is 10:32). Interestingly, the cult shrine there houses "bread of the Presence": holy bread which the priests set before the face of Yahweh. Yet only the ark serves as the presence of Yahweh, and such holy bread is found only one other place: in the tabernacle before the Ark of the Covenant.[20] Moreover, the priests officiating there are the descendants of Eli, former priest of the ark at Shiloh. The story is thus elucidated if we see Nob as part of/identical to the suburban cult shrine which housed the ark during Tabernacles.[21] Finally, Abiathar is the son of Ahimelech, the high priest of Nob. When Saul later slays the priests of Nob, Abiathar comes into David's service as a priest of the ark. He is in fact the same priest who leads the ark in procession up Olivet in 2 Sam 15.[22] Thus, the two stories exist as a kind of "doublet" in which David flees Jerusalem and heads to the cult site on Olivet; both involve Abiathar, the high priest of the ark. Perhaps they constitute two separate etiologies for the route of the *mĕsillâ*. Whatever their source, however, both traditions have the Mount of Olives as the location of a suburban cult shrine to which David fled.

---

[20] Cf. Ex 25:30, Lev 24:5-9.

[21] Whether such a shrine existed at the time of David is dubious, as it seems instead like a retroactive projection of later cultic realities *after* the Temple had been built.

[22] It is intriguing that Abiathar and Ahimelech were often confused in the tradition. For example, 2 Sam 8:17 refers to "Ahimelech the son of Abiathar, which contradicts 1 Sam 23:26 and 30:7, which have Abiathar as the son of Ahimelech (see *ABD*, "Abiathar," 13). Such confusion may be related to their shared roles as officiating priest of the ark in the processional way etiologies. Interestingly, even Mark himself gets confused in 2:26, where Jesus calls Abiathar the priest at Nob whereas 1 Sam 21:1 says it was Ahimelech.

Whether such stories should be read as "foundation texts" or simply stories which allude to existent cultic traditions as a literary device, they provide additional evidence that the ark would leave the Temple through the eastern gate to stay for a time in a suburban cult shrine on the Mount of Olives. There it would remain while the Temple was re-purified for the coming year. The people may have followed, and—in keeping with the festival's concern for ablution—sung hymns of repentance and sought God's forgiveness. After the time of ablution was over, however, the procession would commence its festive celebration, following the ark now from the Mount of Olives back down into the Kidron Valley and then up to the Temple through the eastern gate, where the ark would once again be installed.

Further evidence for this comes from 1 Kings 1. There we read that David's imminent death leads his son Adonijah to proclaim himself king and assemble the components of a procession: a chariot, and men to run in front of him (v. 5). Notably, the priest of the ark, Abiathar, is said to follow him.[23] All these Adonijah leads to a feast he holds east of the city and beyond the Kidron, where

> Adonijah sacrificed sheep, oxen, and fattened cattle by the Serpent's Stone, which is beside En-rogel, and he invited all his brothers, the king's sons, and all the royal officials of Judah, but he did not invite Nathan the prophet or Benaiah or the mighty men or Solomon his brother. (vv. 9-10, ESV).

The occasion for this feast is most likely the New Year,[24] as that was the usual occasion for a king's accession and enthronement—and, as de Moor notes, the time when would-be usurpers arose.[25] One assumes that, despite the fact David is still living, Adonijah has taken the opportunity of the auspicious day to jumpstart his reign.

With Adonijah having declared himself king and already celebrating his feast just outside the city, Solomon, as would-be heir, is forced to act fast and ready a counter-feast to that of his older brother. He and his mother plot with David, and devise an alternative coronation event, which is promptly acted upon:

---

[23] Thus Adonijah has men in front and men behind him (taking Joab and Abiathar's "following" in a literal sense as well). As we shall see, the designations "those in front" and "those behind" were typical in descriptions of cultic processions.

[24] Moor, *New Year with Canaanites and Israelites*, 17-18.

[25] Ibid., 16-18, and n. 224 on 17.

> So the priest [of the ark] Zadok, the prophet Nathan, and Benaiah son of Jehoiada, and the Cherethites and the Pelethites, *went down* and had Solomon ride on King David's mule, and led him to Gihon. There the priest Zadok took the horn of oil from the tent and anointed Solomon. Then they blew the trumpet, and all the people said, "Long live King Solomon!" And all the people *went up following him, playing on pipes and rejoicing with great joy*, so that the earth quaked at their noise. (1 Kgs 1:38-40)

This counter-coronation causes Adonijah to lose his audience of supporters at his own feast, allowing Solomon to consolidate power and forcing Adonijah to retract his claim to the throne.[26]

This story is revealing for our consideration of the processional route. Adonijah, at the New Year, leads a coronation procession from Jerusalem to the Serpent's Stone near En-rogel, the "Spring of the Trampler." The precise location of these landmarks has long eluded scholars, but they were certainly *east of the city*, along the Kidron. Remarkably, Tidwell intimates that Jerusalem's Sacred Way is implied here:

> The Old Testament portrait of ancient Israel's "road that ascends" consistently maintains an unbreakable bond between *mᵉsillâ* and sacred sites, specifically the tabernacle/tent/Ark-sanctuary cities...[such as] Jerusalem ([e.g.] *1 Kings i 9, En-Rogel and [the Serpent's Stone]*...). ...In fact, the evidence suggests that the "road that ascends"...was on certain festival occasions, notably at Sukkot, a significant part of *a sacred way whose two termini were the temple within the city and a natural sacred site outside the city walls*.[27]

If we connect Tidwell's dots here, we find that Jerusalem's *měsillâ* in David's time would have run from the city, down through the Kidron Valley to the east, and connected with En-Rogel and the Serpent's

---

[26] While it is true that this story describes the enthronement procession of an earthly king and not that of Yahweh, it is still helpful for illuminating the procession of the ark, since the religious and political (re)enthronements were connected, and would have occurred on the same day. Other commentators have likewise noted the connection with the ark procession. So Brent Kinman, *Jesus' Entry into Jerusalem: In the Context of Lukan Theology and the Politics of His Day*, Arbeiten Zur Geschichte des Antiken Judentums und des Urchristentums (Leiden: E.J. Brill, 1995), 60: "Indeed, it is possible that the ark narrative underlies 1 Kgs 1 and that the coming of Solomon and Zion's king was tantamount to a re-enactment of the ark ceremony. The chief differences in these stories have to do with the specific person and manner of transport (a mule for Yahweh's agent, the king; the priests for Yahweh, coming symbolically in the ark), although one may see general links between the accounts even in these 'differences.'"

[27] Tidwell, "No Highway," 263; emphasis mine.

Stone. However, since En-rogel is listed as a boundary marker between the tribes of Judah and Benjamin (cf. Josh 15:7), it is usually located to the south-east of the City of David—too southerly for a *měsillâ* connecting the Temple Mount and Olivet. During David's reign, however, and presumably dating back to its days as a Canaanite city, En-rogel and the Serpent's Stone may indeed have served as the *měsillâ*'s terminus. Presumably, when Solomon built the Temple to the north, on Mount Moriah, the processional way of the city accommodated its new cultic center, and the terminus likewise shifted northward.

This is remarkable, since comparative data from ancient Hittite and Emarite practices strongly support the hypothesis that the Serpent's Stone once served as the processional way's terminus. At Hattusa, the processional way extended from the temple within the city to the sacred *ḫuwasi* stone outside the city.[28] Likewise, at Emar, during the *zukru* festival, the storm-god Dagan was led in procession from his temple to the sacred "standing stones." These were holy stones which were anointed for the festival and the coming of the god. Once arrived, a feast would commence and the priestess of the storm-god would be enthroned, after which the storm-god returned in procession to his temple. Similar religious standing stones existed in ancient Israel and were called *maṣṣēbôt*.[29] Richard Hess notes that these resemble both the *ḫuwasi* stones of the Hittites, and the sacred standing stones of Emar.[30] The Serpent's Stone was probably just such a stone,[31] and may too have been associated with the processional way. Indeed, the name of the landmark suggests a connection with the combat myth. The festival celebrated Yahweh's defeat of Leviathan, the "twisty Serpent"—a *Chaoskampf* resonance highlighted by its proximity to En-Rogel, the "Spring of the Treader/Trampler" (also called "Dragon's

---

[28] Ibid., 263-4.

[29] Richard S. Hess, *Israelite Religions: An Archaeological and Biblical Survey* (Grand Rapids: Baker Academic, 2007), 198-200.

[30] Ibid., 116.

[31] Though the specific term *maṣṣēbāh* is not used to refer to the Serpent Stone, this does not mean it was not in fact a *maṣṣēbāh*. According to Elizabeth C. LaRocca-Pitts, *Of Wood and Stone: The Significance of Israelite Cultic Items in the Bible and Its Early Interpreters*, Harvard Semitic Museum Publications (Winona Lake: Eisenbrauns, 2001), 222-4, there are various instances in which stones that function as *maṣṣēbôt* are not designated as such. She also presents "evidence that seems to support the theory that [the Dueteronomistic Historian] is intentionally avoiding the term *maṣṣēbāh* for monuments which are approved of."

Spring" in Neh 2:13). Such names may reflect Yahweh's treading of the chaos-waters.

A *měsillâ* is twice intricately connected with sacred stones in the Bible. One such remarkable passage is 1 Samuel 6:11-15, which indeed show a sacred stone as the terminus of a *měsillâ*:

> [The Philistines] put the ark of Yahweh on the cart, and the box with the gold mice and the images of their tumors. The cows went straight in the direction of Beth-shemesh along a processional way (*měsillâ*), lowing as they went; they turned neither to the right nor to the left, and the lords of the Philistines went after them as far as the border of Beth-shemesh. Now the people of Beth-shemesh were reaping their wheat harvest in the valley. When they looked up and saw the ark, they went with rejoicing to meet it. The cart came into the field of Joshua of Beth-shemesh, and stopped there. *A large stone was there*; so they split up the wood of the cart and offered the cows as a burnt-offering to Yahweh. The Levites took down the ark of Yahweh and the box that was beside it, in which were the gold objects, and *set them upon the large stone*. Then the people of Beth-shemesh offered burnt-offerings and presented sacrifices on that day to Yahweh.

This passage very likely reflects cultic realties related to the New Year procession: the ark of the covenant travels a processional way during Israel's harvest. The presence of the ark precipitates great rejoicing as at the New Year celebration, and the ark comes to rest at a large stone (probably a *maṣṣēbāh*) at the end of the *měsillâ*. The Israelites then set the ark upon the stone—suggesting its cultic significance—and sacrifice to Yahweh. The Serpent's Stone may have served a similar function.[32]

Returning to 1 Kings 1, we read that Solomon, not to be outdone by Adonijah's feast, also leads a coronation procession into the Kidron Valley, to the spring of Gihon—which was evidently within earshot of the Serpent's Stone, though not visible to it (1 Kings 1:41). Included in his processional train is Zadok, the *other* priest of the ark. Finally, the

---

[32] There is archeological evidence to support such practices. At Tel Dan, for example, a small stand supporting *maṣṣēbôt* is located just outside the city gate. A road once led from this stand of *maṣṣēbôt* outside the city all the way to the temple/high place at the acropolis, where one of the Golden Calves of Jeroboam once stood (1 Kgs 12:29). The king had erected these and instituted a rival Feast of Tabernacles (12:32), at which he sacrificed on the altar. It is very possible that the Golden Calf itself was processed from the high place down to the stand of *maṣṣēbôt* and then back again to the high place at this rival Feast of Tabernacles. Conversations in 2012 with Ross Voss, the site's principal excavator, have assured me of this conclusion.

trumpet is blown[33] and all the people proclaim "Long live King Solomon!" Then they all "go up" (*'ālâ*) in procession behind Solomon back to Jerusalem, dancing and playing music at great volume (the ground itself quakes!). The scene is thus reminiscent of David's earlier procession in 2 Samuel 6, when the ark was first transferred to Jerusalem, accompanied by dancers and singers. Hearing the celebration, Adonijah wonders at its meaning when Abiathar's son (and thus the herald of the processional way) enters. Adonijah asks him about it, saying, "Come in, for you are a worthy man and surely you *report good news* (*wĕṭôb tĕbaśśēr*)" (v. 42). But for Adonijah, the news is not good: Solomon, not he, will be king.

Such is the evidence gleaned from narrative accounts such as 1 and 2 Samuel and 1 Kings. However, the New Year procession was, as we saw earlier, frequently employed as metaphor in the prophetic and poetic literature of ancient Israel. Many instances of this have already been examined in some depth, including Deutero-Isaiah's vision in which Yahweh's processional way extends from Jerusalem all the way to Babylon—in the *east*. Similarly, Ezekiel's visions present a crucial reflex of the New Year festival which links the processional way with the Mount of Olives. The prophet writes of Yahweh's glory riding upon his chariot-throne, which leaves the Temple through the east gate and stops on the Mount of Olives:

> And the glory of Yahweh ascended from the middle of the city, and stopped on *the mountain east of the city*. (Ezek 11:23)

Then, after the fiery purgation/purification of Jerusalem in his absence, Yahweh returns to his Temple from the east:

> Then he brought me to the gate, *the gate facing east*. And there, *the glory of the God of Israel was coming from the east*; the sound was like the sound of mighty waters; and the earth shone with his glory. The vision I saw was like the vision that I had seen when he came to destroy the city, and like the vision that I had seen by the river Chebar; and I fell upon my face. As the glory of Yahweh *entered the Temple by the gate facing east*, the spirit lifted me up, and brought me into the inner court; and the glory of Yahweh filled the temple. (Ezek 43:1-5)

---

[33] An act which Moor, *New Year with Canaanites and Israelites*, 16, notes is a "New-Year's rite." Cf. Enthronement Psalm 47:5: "God has *gone up* (*'ālâ*) with a shout, Yahweh with the sound of a trumpet."

The prophet is describing the return of Yahweh to Jerusalem from Babylon, where his people were captives. Like Deutero-Isaiah, however, he is no doubt drawing upon the traditional route of the Sacred Way to describe this departure from and return to the Temple. Such would have been the most obvious inspiration for the vision. The glory of God leaves the Temple and rests on the Mount of Olives. In his absence, the city is purged, which in turn allows Yahweh and his people to return—Yahweh's glory doing so again through the east gate into the now-re-purified Temple.[34]

The same metaphor is employed by Second Zechariah, who, in keeping with the nature of Jewish apocalyptic eschatology, describes the New Year festival in cosmic dimensions. First comes the sack of Jerusalem: the impurities of the Gentiles taking over the holy city of God. Women are raped and the houses are looted. In short, the city has become utterly profaned and polluted. However, finally Yahweh "goes forth" (presumably from his Temple) as the divine warrior to stand upon Olivet:

> On that day his feet shall stand on the Mount of Olives, which lies before Jerusalem on the east. (Zech 14:4a)

The mountain then splits in two, and all the people in Jerusalem exit the city through the road created by the fissure—the cosmic Sacred Way of the apocalypse. With the people gone, Yahweh swoops down into the city and purges it of the evil occupiers. Abundance and fertility are then restored and Yahweh reassumes his place to become king over the cosmos (v. 9). All those who remain, Jew and Gentile, then "go up" annually to celebrate the Feast of Tabernacles. Those who do not shall see no rain.

So Zechariah mirrors the cultic practices of the Feast of Tabernacles to narrate his apocalyptic vision. Though an apocalyptic aggrandizement of the festival, it still maintains the core events: (1) the city is polluted, (2) the people exit the city to the east towards (in this case *through*) the Mount of Olives, (3) Yahweh too leaves the city from his Temple and stays upon the Mount of Olives, (4) the city is purged of impurities, (5) Yahweh and the people return to the city to celebrate the Feast of Tabernacles, (6) abundance, fertility, and rain follow.

---

[34] Cf. Ezekiel use of the ark procession's imagery with the ark's capture by the Philistines in 1 Sam 4:21-22, where the ark's theft is described as "the glory of Yahweh departing from Israel."

Thus Deutero-Isaiah, Ezekiel, and Second Zechariah all employ the metaphor of the enthronement procession in their visions, while 1 Samuel 21-22, 2 Samuel 15, and 1 Kings 1 likewise reflect the procession in some way. All of this evidence points to a housing of the ark to the east, on the Mount of Olives, during the New Year festival. The ark would leave the Temple through the east gate and travel down into the Kidron Valley, where the *měsillâ* stopped at the Serpent's Stone, then up the Mount of Olives. In its absence, the Temple would be re-purified. The people followed in its wake and likewise asked for ablution and forgiveness from Yahweh. After the Temple had been re-purified, the ark would then be taken from the House of Obed-Edom on the Mount of Olives back down the Kidron Valley, then, with the people behind, "go up" (*'ālâ*) the Sacred Way to be reinstalled in the Temple for Yahweh's ritual enthronement.

The Enthronement Procession of Jesus (Mk 11:1-11)

At last, Jesus' procession has arrived at the Mount of Olives and now begins the procession proper—down into the Kidron and then up to the Temple. Remarkably, however, the significance of the combat myth in Jesus' "triumphal entry" has gone (almost) entirely unappreciated by scholars and exegetes.[35] Yet the scene presents us with perhaps Mark's most powerful utilization of the ancient myth and its associated cultic practice from ancient Israel. Here Jesus enters Jerusalem just as Yahweh did, when his ark, traveling in procession up the Sacred Way, would enter the Temple for enthronement during the

---

[35] Paul Duff recognizes the Markan Jesus as the triumphing divine warrior in Paul Brooks Duff, "The March of the Divine Warrior and the Advent of the Greco-Roman King: Mark's Account of Jesus' Entry into Jerusalem," *JBL* 111 (1992): 51-71. However, he makes the faulty connection with Greco-Roman victory processions instead of the Jewish enthronement procession. On the other hand, the section "Cultic Contexts and Connotation of 'the Way'" in Timothy C. Gray, *The Temple in the Gospel of Mark: A Study in Its Narrative Role*, Wissenschaftliche Untersuchungen Zum Neuen Testament. (Tübingen: Mohr Siebeck, 2008), 16-19, insightfully (though briefly) draws the connection between Jesus' triumphal entry and the enthronement festival, but fails to appreciate its apocalyptic significance, or, for that matter, its crucial structural and thematic significance in the work of Mark as a whole. Similarly, Kinman, *Jesus' Entry into Jerusalem: In the Context of Lukan Theology and the Politics of His Day*, 58-60, recognizes in passing the procession of the ark as a probable context for the description of Jesus' entry in Luke, but likewise misses the broader significance of this connection.

Feast of Tabernacles. Sea and Dragon are defeated, and now the divine warrior can come to his temple as king over the cosmos.

Indeed, having shown that the route of the Sacred Way connected the Temple Mount to the Mount of Olives, we can see Mark planting seeds of this expectation as he sets up the correlation with the ancient festival. So, when Jesus approaches the traditional origin of Jerusalem's Sacred Way, Mark seems to linger on the detail, stressing, "When they draw near to Jerusalem—to Bethphage, and Bethany—towards the Mount of Olives..." There can be no doubt in the mind of Mark's audience: Jesus is about to traverse the traditional Sacred Way of the divine warrior as he "goes up" to Jerusalem. Though this route has been noted by exegetes, its immense historical and cultic significance have been all but ignored. So Perkins, for example, blandly but symptomatically remarks, "The road in question leads from the Mount of Olives (v. 1*a*) to the Temple (v. 11*a*)," and that is all.[36] To be sure, such a road existed in the first century CE and no doubt occupied the place of the more ancient *mĕsillâ* from the past.[37]

Having thus established that Mark means to portray Jesus' "triumphal entry" in terms of the Tabernacles procession, we should not be surprised to find that the description of the entry is strikingly reminiscent of the ancient festival. For instance, it seems to have been common practice to lay one's cloak on the ground at the coronation of a new king. So 2 Kings 9:13:

> [Jehu said,] "Thus says Yahweh, I anoint you king over Israel.'"
> Then hurriedly they all took their cloaks and spread them for him on the bare steps; and they blew the trumpet, and proclaimed, "Jehu is king."

As we have seen, the accession of a new king usually occurred at the time of the New Year harvest festival, when the monarchy was renewed. Such a practice would likely have taken place then during the enthronement of Yahweh himself. Indeed, the phrase "Jehu is/has become king!" is identical to the proclamation "Yahweh is/has become king!" in Enthronement Psalms 93 and 96. The act is thus unquestionably connected to the assumption of kingship, which was the consequence of Yahweh's victories over the Sea.

---

[36] Perkins, *The New Interpreter's Bible 8*, 658.

[37] Indeed, even today one can see the large sealed "Golden Gate" on the eastern wall of the Temple Mount, which dates to the sixth century CE. It stands more or less where the gate would have been in the time of Herod.

In addition to the laying down of cloaks, the literary description of celebrants and their distribution in the procession may also be modeled on the traditions of the enthronement ritual. Enthronement Psalms make reference to two distinct groups of processors: namely, those "in front" and "those behind." So Psalm 68:24-25:

> Your solemn processions are seen, O God,
> >   the processions of my God, my King, into the sanctuary—
> > *the singers in front, the musicians last,*
> >   between them girls playing tambourines.

Compare also 2 Samuel 6:3-5, a "foundation text" for the ritual:

> They carried the ark of God on a new cart, and brought it out of the house of Abinadab, which was on the hill. Uzzah and Ahio, the sons of Abinadab, were driving the new cart with the ark of God; and Ahio went *in front of the ark*. David and all the house of Israel were dancing before Yahweh with all their might, with songs and lyres and harps and tambourines and castanets and cymbals.

Here we find the ark proceeding to songs and celebration, with a description of Ahio "in front," though none are explicitly mentioned as following behind.[38] Elsewhere, the allotment of "those ahead" and "those behind" is more explicit, albeit in a context of war and not celebration:

> When Joshua had spoken to the people, the seven priests carrying the seven trumpets before Yahweh went forward, blowing their trumpets, and the ark of Yahweh's covenant followed them. *The armed guard marched ahead of the priests who blew the trumpets, and the rear guard followed the ark.* (Josh 6:8-9)

While such descriptions may simply be a periphrastic way of expressing processional marches, their regularity and frequency suggest a more traditional source: they may have been engrained in oral formulae about such processions. This is corroborated by modest evidence of similar descriptions about other ancient Near Eastern New Year processions. So, for example, the Assyrian king Sennacherib describes the scene he has had depicted on the copper doors of the *bīt akīti as*:

---

[38] As we saw, the role of the Sacred Herald was probably played by the son of the high priest. This is likely the significance of Ahio's position "in front of the ark."

> [a] figure of Assur, going to battle against Tiamat, carrying the bow, on his
> chariot holding the 'weapon of the storm' (*abubu*), and Amarru, who goes
> with him as charioteer…I engraved upon the gate, (besides) *the gods who
> march in front and the gods who march behind him…*[39]

If such formulae for the description of celebrants in the New Year's
procession were common, they may lie behind Mark's own
formulation:

> And those walking ahead and those following behind cried out, "*Hosanna!*"
> (Mk 11:9)

It is striking that Jesus' transportation and the ark's are also the
same. Transporting the ark required a ritually pure means—a carrier not
yet used for ordinary purposes. Its use was sacred and so could not
have any association with the profane. Thus, when David and the
people transport the ark to the Temple, "They carried the ark of God *on
a new cart*" (2 Sam 6:3). Similarly, when the Philistines had captured
that precious object, they sent it back on a "new cart" drawn by
unyoked (and thus ritually pure) cattle:

> Now then, get ready *a new cart* and two milch cows that have never borne a
> yoke, and yoke the cows to the cart, but take their calves home, away from
> them. Take the ark of Yahweh and place it on the cart, and put in a box at
> its side the figures of gold, which you are returning to him as a guilt
> offering. Then send it off, and let it go its way. (1 Sam 6:8-9)

Based on these and similar descriptions of the ark's transfer, it seems
safe to assume that, during the New Year's enthronement procession,
the ark would have been borne upon a "new cart" drawn by cattle that
were ritually-pure—that is, cattle not already used for any other profane
purpose. And so it is that, in Mark, Jesus is transported to the Temple
upon a donkey *that has not yet been ridden by anyone else*. In
preparing for his entrance, Jesus commands his disciples:

> Go into the village ahead of us, and then as you are coming into it you will
> find a donkey tied up, *upon which no person has yet sat*. Untie it and bring it.
> (Mk 11:2)

---

[39] Quoted in Henri Frankfort, *Kingship and the Gods: A Study of Ancient Near Eastern
Religion as the Integration of Society & Nature*, Oriental Institute Essay (Chicago:
University of Chicago Press, 1948), 327.

Such will serve Jesus as his unprofaned form of transportation into Jerusalem.

With this introduction of the donkey, however, Mark is also weaving in the tradition of Zechariah 9:9, whose messianic vision proclaimed:[40]

> Rejoice greatly, O daughter Zion! Shout aloud, O daughter Jerusalem! Lo, your king comes to you; triumphant and victorious is he, humble and riding on a donkey, on a colt, the foal of a donkey.

To be sure, Second Zechariah is also drawing heavily upon the enthronement procession at the Feast of Tabernacles. We saw, for instance, that in the New Year Sukkot procession described in 1 Kings 1, Solomon proceeds along the *měsillâ*'s Sacred Way *upon a mule*. Its seems to have been customary at the New Year enthronement for the king to "go up to Jerusalem" upon a donkey. No doubt this is the tradition Second Zechariah is recalling, given that author's clear application of the *Chaoskampf* tradition and the Divine Warrior Hymn. Indeed, Paul Hanson posits a direct basis on the combat myth pattern, noting,

> Zechariah 9 is a paradigm example of the prophetic adaptation of the league- royal cult ritual pattern. Here its structure breaks down as follows:
>
> Conflict – victory (1-7)
> Temple secured (8)
> Victory shout and *procession (9)*
> Manifestation of Yahweh's universal reign (10)
> Salvation: Captives released (11-13)
> Theophany of Divine Warrior (14)
> Sacrifice and banquet (15)
> Fertility of restored order (16-17)[41]

As we can see from this schema, Hanson posits verse 9 as Zechariah's transformation of the traditional procession element from the combat myth pattern. The king's entrance on the donkey is thus equated with the King's coming at the enthronement procession. So it is in Mark. But the addition of the donkey's "newness," the fact that no one has yet ridden it, is not found in Zechariah. This is the creation of Mark (or his

---

[40] Matthew makes Mark's connection explicit when he writes in 21:5 that "this took place to fulfill what had been spoken through the prophet," and then quotes Zech 9:9.
[41] Hanson, *The Dawn of Apocalyptic*, 315-16.

source) to highlight the connection between Jesus' entry and that of the triumphant divine warrior, who was represented by the conveyance of his holy ark on an unprofaned cart drawn by unprofaned cattle.[42]

The connection with Jesus' entry and the New Yew harvest festival becomes virtually explicit with the mention of "leafy branches" in 11:8. As Mark's Jewish (or even God-fearing) audience would have been well aware, Leviticus 23 commanded how the Festival of Tabernacles should be celebrated, declaring:

> On the fifteenth day of this seventh month, and lasting seven days, there shall be the Festival of Booths to Yahweh.
> …On the first day you shall take the fruit of majestic trees, branches of palm trees, boughs of leafy trees, and willows of the brook; and you shall rejoice before Yahweh your God for seven days. (vv. 33, 40)

So in Mark, while some herald Jesus' enthronement by laying down their cloaks, "others cut leafy branches from the fields" and sing hymns. This is precisely how the ancient Israelites would have celebrated the coming of Yahweh's ark along the processional way, and even in the first century would have been an obvious allusion to the celebration of Tabernacles.

However, such hymn-singing was also an important part of Sukkot and the enthronement procession, for we possess a whole collection of Enthronement Psalms that served as its liturgy. One such important hymn, which was sung at the procession of Yahweh's ark to his Temple, was Psalm 118:

> *Save us, we beseech you, O Yahweh!*
>   O Yahweh, we beseech you, give us success!
> Blessed is the one who comes in the name of Yahweh.
>   We bless you from the House of Yahweh.
> Yahweh is God,
>   and he has given us light.
> Bind the festal procession with branches,
>   up to the horns of the altar. (vv. 25-27)

Apart from the evidence of the psalm itself—which speaks of Yahweh's victories over Israel's enemies, calls for the "Gate of Righteousness" to be opened so the celebrants may enter, and speaks of

---

[42] The connection between the newness of the donkey and ritual purity/sacred purpose is also made by Boring, *Mark: A Commentary*, 518.

binding the festal sacrifice with leafy branches—Mowinckel also observes that the Mishna connects it to the Feast of Tabernacles and petitions for rain. "There is absolutely no reason," he concludes, "to reject the tradition in the Mishna Sukka IV.5 that Ps. 118 belonged to the feast of Tabernacles."[43]

Remarkably, Mark places Psalm 118 in the mouths of those accompanying Jesus' procession to the Temple (Mk 11:9). In so doing, he explicitly links Jesus' entry into Jerusalem/the Temple with Yahweh's procession into Jerusalem/the Temple. He even maintains the Aramaic phrase, "*Hosanna*!" for "Save us, we beseech you!" Perhaps, by the first-century CE, the *Hosanna* cry had already become a liturgical call that was part of the popular celebration of the Festival of Booths, and so Mark does not feel the need to translate the term. So it was, for example, at the Hittite *Purulli* festive procession, when "[v]arious cultic calls [were] made by designated performers and attendants—'aha!', 'kasmessa!', 'missa!'."[44] "*Hosanna*!" may have been a similar cultic call in the Israelite tradition. Indeed, Psalm 89:15 speaks of a "festal shout," which may have been this very exclamation.

At last, the climactic moment comes: the procession concludes as Jesus arrives at the Temple. Everything in Mark's narrative up to this point has thoroughly associated Jesus with the triumphant divine warrior—fresh from his battle with the forces of Chaos and the Sea, proceeding to his temple amid celebration and hymn-singing—to ascend his Temple throne and be proclaimed king over the cosmos. But Mark's account takes a very unexpected turn:

> And he came into Jerusalem, into the Temple, and, looking around at everything—(it was already quite late)—went out to Bethany with the Twelve. (Mk 11:11)

Having arrived at the Temple, Jesus simply looks around and goes back to Bethany! Mark's audience is left hanging, their expectations frustrated. Where is his enthronement? Where is his triumphant declaration as king over the cosmos?

Many commentators have noted the anticlimactic nature of the moment and mused over its significance.[45] Collins's analysis, however, gets at the core of the issue:

---

[43] Mowinckel, *The Psalms in Israel's Worship*, 120.
[44] Bryce, *Life and Society*, 190.
[45] Collins, *Mark*, 520; Marcus, *Mark 8-16*, 780.

<blockquote>
This verse is anticlimactic because the honor paid to Jesus in the preceding verses leads the audience to expect his installation as king. Mark frustrates this expectation for several interrelated reasons. …Mark portrays his kingship ironically in chaps. 11-15. Second, Mark redefines the role of the messiah. When Peter identifies Jesus as the messiah in 8:29, Jesus explains that messiahship involves suffering, death, and resurrection (8:31). Jesus cannot be enthroned as a king in the usual sense during his earthly lifetime because of this destiny of suffering and death.[46]
</blockquote>

Indeed, it is no accident or some awkward result of Mark's source redaction. This frustration of expectations is a deliberate move by Mark as part of his entire theological program. As we shall see, the Markan Jesus proposes a radical reinterpretation of messiahship and the role of the divine warrior. In the following chapter "Victory over Death," we shall at last see Jesus' enthronement. It will not be in the Temple, however—but on the cross.

The Re-purification of the Temple/City (Mk 11:12-13:36)

Having demonstrated that Jesus' triumphal entry is indeed portrayed in terms of the Sukkot enthronement procession, we find that succeeding events in Mark's narrative are significantly illuminated when considered through this cultic lens. Indeed, I shall argue that the entire remainder of Mark's gospel likewise follows the progression of the eschatologized New Year festival, wherein the Temple and Jerusalem are cleansed of pollutants/evil and the new era ushered in by the victorious divine warrior.

We have seen that temple re-purification was an important part of ancient Near Eastern New Year festivals. This is not surprising, given that such festivals celebrated rejuvenation and rebirth, marking new beginnings and returns to earlier, unpolluted states of existence. Thus, the ritual impurities which had accumulated throughout the year were expunged, and the temple cleansed for the coming year ahead. Mowinckel has argued that a similar purification of the Israelite Temple took place at the Feast of Tabernacles.[47] Scriptural evidence for this hypothesis is ample. We read, for instance, that Solomon's Temple was first consecrated at the Feast of Tabernacles—an important datum

---

[46] Collins, *Mark*, 520.
[47] Mowinckel, *The Psalms in Israel's Worship*, 126, 130.

in itself, but also illuminating because subsequent re-consecrations
would have operated as ritual repetitions of the first.[48] The persistence
of such a ritual tradition is in fact evidenced by a passage in 1
Maccabees, which details events over half a millennium after
Solomon's initial purification.[49] Here, after defeating their Greek
overlords who had polluted the Temple, the Jews re-purify and
rededicate it *during the Feast of Tabernacles*. Indeed, there is even a
celebratory procession, complete with song and leafy branches:

> On the twenty-third day of the second month, in the one hundred seventy-
> first year, the Jews entered [the Temple] with praise and palm branches, and
> with harps and cymbals and stringed instruments, and with many hymns
> and songs, because a great enemy had been crushed and removed from
> Israel. (1 Macc 13:51)

In 2 Maccabees 10:6-7, this connection with Sukkot is explicit:

> They celebrated it for eight days with rejoicing, *in the manner of the
> Festival of Booths…*
> Therefore, carrying ivy-wreathed wands and beautiful branches and also
> fronds of palm, they offered hymns of thanksgiving to him who had given
> success to *the purifying of his own Holy Place*.

In metaphorical terms, this same Temple re-purification furnished
Amos, Ezekiel, Malachi, and Zechariah with the poetic imagery for
their theological programs of redemption. It provided the perfect
metaphor for God's return to a sinful people—a return predicated on
the people's repentance and ablution, which had been sought yearly on
procession to the Mount of Olives. As we have seen, ideas about the
apocalypse arose largely out of eschatologized notions about these very
ritual practices. The End will come when Yahweh repeats his victory
over Chaos and his consequent enthronement in a re-purified Temple
occurs in epic and universal terms.

So Second Zechariah uses the idea of Yahweh's future
eschatological victory and purgation of impurity, going beyond
Deutero-Isaiah and raising the expectation of Israel's restoration to
truly apocalyptic proportions. Here, what had been the *Temple's*
purification during Yahweh's absence on the Mount of Olives

---

[48] Ibid., 127.
[49] Even if one rejects the antiquity of traditions presented in the DtrH, seeing them as
retroactive projections of later practice back into the time of Solomon, there is still a
continuity of a few *centuries* from a post-exilic redaction to the Maccabean period.

Zechariah now turns into the eschatological cleansing of the *entire city*. The prophet concludes with the establishment of Yahweh's kingship: the expected end to the New Year festival, and even the Gentile nations are said to come up to Jerusalem every year for the celebration of that very Feast of Tabernacles.

It has long been noted that Mark draws upon Second Zechariah in crafting Jesus' entry into Jerusalem.[50] It is thus no accident that Jesus' cleansing of the Temple immediately follows his triumphal entry from the Mount of Olives. This is clearly the progression of the New Year cultus, taken up and eschatologized by apocalyptic authors from Second Zechariah to Mark. Indeed, this progression may be yet another reason for the abrupt and awkward end to Jesus' entry. For, if Mark is in fact following that pattern, one should expect Jesus to be enthroned now in the Temple. Instead, the event ends with an anticlimax, as Jesus simply looks around and leaves. Why? The Temple and the city have not been purified yet.

Traditionally, this required the presence of Yahweh to *leave* the Temple and rest on the Mount of Olives. This is precisely what happens in Mark. Jesus, still serving in his role as Yahweh's embodied presence (i.e., the ark) leaves the Temple and heads to Bethany, a village on the Mount of Olives. Joel Marcus considers the etymology of this place name, writing: "Nehemiah 11:32 mentions a place called 'Ănānyāh, apparently on the Mount of Olives; this could also have been called bêt Ănānyāh = 'the house of Ananiah,' that is, Bethany."[51] Thus, Bethany is "the house of Ananiah." In fact, the context of this reference in Nehemiah 11 may also be significant, since it appears within a list of villages just to the east of Jerusalem. Intriguingly, Ananyah is listed immediately after Nob, which, we have seen, may have been the location of the cult site on the Mount of Olives that was identified with the House of Obed-Edom. This suggests a close geographical proximity to a site already evidenced to have connections with an ark shrine. This is potentially significant since it would mean that, after departing from the Temple, Jesus stays in the "house of Ananiah" just as the ark stayed in the House of Obed-Edom, if not (at some point) in the "house of Ananiah" itself.

---

[50] For bibliography, see Duff, "The March of the Divine Warrior and the Advent of the Greco-Roman King: Mark's Account of Jesus' Entry into Jerusalem," 65, esp. n. 44.
[51] Marcus, *Mark 8-16*, 771.

The following day, Jesus returns to the Temple in order to enact the actual purgation and purification of sin that must take place at the eschatological Feast of Tabernacles:

> And they come into Jerusalem. And going into the Temple, he began to cast out the buyers and sellers in the Temple, and the tables of the money-changers and the seats of the pigeon-buyers he overturned, and was not letting anyone carry things through the Temple. (Mk 15:15-16)[52]

Here, Mark's borrowing from apocalyptic transformations of Tabernacles is clear—specifically in his use of Second Zechariah. For in that prophetic text we read, in the last line of Zechariah 14, "And there shall no longer be traders in the house of Yahweh on that day." So the Markan Jesus is clearly fulfilling here the apocalyptic prophecy of Second Zechariah. Interestingly, Mark here uses the verb *ekballō* ("to drive out")—the same word he uses when Jesus exorcizes unclean spirits. So Mark equates what is going on in the Temple with the workings of the unclean spirits.[53] The traders possess the Temple as the unclean spirits possessed men. In exorcizing them, Jesus cleanses the Temple from spiritual uncleanliness as he healed the possessed from unclean spirits. Such a connection should come as no surprise. As noted earlier, Temple purification was intimately related to exorcism.[54] Eliade observed that "[a]lmost everywhere the expulsion of demons, diseases and sins coincide—or at one time coincided—with the festival of the New Year." In Mark's eschatological New Year's enactment, Jesus' exorcisms—both of the people and the cultic site—find thematic harmony.

However, while Jesus' re-purification is most dramatically rendered in the scene of the Temple's cleansing, it ultimately

---

[52] Admittedly, while a progression based on the New Year festival helps to elucidate the otherwise anticlimactic ending to the procession, Jesus' presence in and then departure from the Temple creates its own problems. The original purpose of the ark's departure was to facilitate the re-purification of the Temple by others (presumably the priests). Why then does Jesus both leave *and* fulfill the purification himself? Mark is drawing on the eschatologized imagining of the festival such as is found in Second Zechariah and other prophets. Thus, while he may be maintaining the traditional practice of removing the ark to Olivet in his depiction, he clearly seeks to employ those later understandings of the festival in which Yahweh himself, as the divine warrior, swoops down in his might to re-purify the city. The result is perhaps illogical, but the message is clear: Jesus is the divine warrior as Yahweh was.

[53] Marcus, *Mark 8-16*, 782.

[54] Bidmead, *The Akītu Festival*, 72.

transcends that specific locale. Like the divine warrior in the apocalyptic transformations of the festival, Jesus seeks in fact to cleanse the *entire city*. To do this, he must contend with the enemies of God who still inhabit it. In Zechariah 14, these are the Gentile nations who have descended upon Jerusalem; in Malachi 3, these are the corrupt priests, as well as those who oppress the widow and orphan, liars, and the like. In Mark, these are the chief priests and the scribes: the helpers of Satan continuously struggling with Jesus throughout the gospel.

Indeed, the rest of chapter 11 and the entirety of chapter 12 are dedicated to Jesus' confrontations with these powerful enemies. In this section of Mark, contentious discourse is presented as satanic attack and divine counter-attack. So the chief priests and scribes challenge Jesus' authority (11:27-33), the Pharisees and the Herodians challenge him on paying taxes to Caesar (12:13-17), the Sadducees challenge him on the resurrection of the dead (12:18-27), a scribe challenges him on which is the greatest commandment (12:28-34). Similarly, Jesus challenges the scribes' interpretation of the messiah (12:35-7), and warns his audience to beware of the scribes (12:38-40). Even those passages not narrating a verbal jousting between Jesus and these groups clearly serve to comment on the failures of the authorities. Thus the story of the withered fig tree, which is interwoven with the Temple cleansing (11:12-14 and 11:20-25), serves as a condemnation on the Temple and the religious authorities. Their stewardship has not borne fruit, and so it will be cut down. Likewise, the parable of the wicked tenants (12:1-12) is a clear attack on the religious authorities who have not only failed to tend to God's vineyard, but in fact have become his enemies and seek to kill him. For this, God will destroy them. Finally, the humble offering of the widow which closes the chapter (12:41-44) stands as a clear contrast to the rich and hypocritical religious authorities, who, for all their wealth and power, have yet failed to be obedient to God. In all of these accounts, Jesus is understood as battling the evil occupying forces of God's Temple. Indeed, we have seen that the chief priests "test" (*perazō*) him here, and so stand in for Satan as the adversaries of the divine warrior. But Jesus defeats them all, and Perkins astutely notes, "From a narrative point of view, Mark may intend readers to recognize that Jesus has taken over the area that his opponents claimed for their own."[55] The Kingdom of God again controls the field: Jerusalem.

After these battles with the religious authorities, the thirteenth chapter of Mark presents Jesus' apocalyptic discourse. Here, he foretells the total destruction of the Temple: not one of its stones will be left atop the other after God enacts his Final Judgment. In images and motifs entirely at home in apocalyptic visionary language, Jesus proceeds to describe *the final and complete purification of the city*. This discourse looks forward to the true apocalyptic transformation of the cosmos, of which Jesus' triumphal entry and Temple cleansing were the historical realizations.

Thus, Mark depicts the Temple re-purification *literally* in 11:15-19. Then, following the eschatological transformation of the re-purifying ritual (as envisioned for example in Zechariah 14 and Malachi 3), he *figuratively* depicts the eschatological battle with the evil and corrupt occupying forces in 11:27-12:44. Finally, Mark concludes with a full-blown *visionary* account of the End, at which time the Temple will be totally destroyed and God will complete the restoration and rejuvenation of his people. So he represents the re-purification of the Temple in three ways, each of increasing intensity. From 11:15 to 13:37 we find a literal, figurative, and then mythic depiction of Israel's re-purification.

This purification completed, Mark fulfills the prophetic words he placed at the very beginning of his gospel: the introductory citation, blending Malachi 3 and Isaiah 40, which harkens back to the procession at the New Year festival. For Mark, these texts were still salient, as the Temple workings were still seen to be corrupt and the Jewish people still under the control of a foreign Gentile power—no longer Babylon, but Satan and his helpers. From the outset, then, Mark had set up the expectation that Jesus would be the eschatological representative of the Lord who would finally come to his Temple along the processional way after slaying the forces of Chaos and re-purify Israel. In Mark 11, this expectation is fulfilled.

---

[55] Perkins, *The New Interpreter's Bible 8*, 659. Cf. Seán Freyne, *Galilee, Jesus, and the Gospels: Literary Approaches and Historical Investigations* (Philadelphia: Fortress Press, 1988), 59-60.

In his article "No Time for Figs,"[56] Charles W. F. Smith applies a critical eye to the long-held assumption that Jesus' entry into Jerusalem begins a week-long ministry in that city, one which ultimately climaxes with his resurrection during Passover. This configuration is largely based on Mark 14:1, which reads, "It was two days before the Passover and the festival of Unleavened Bread..." Assuming Jesus had entered Jerusalem in chapter 11 *in order to celebrate Passover*, he would have entered on Sunday, been crucified on Friday, and risen again on Sunday.[57] However, Smith concludes, "In the text itself the evidence that Mark describes a week can be found only by looking for it."[58] Indeed, nowhere does Mark say that Jesus' entry into Jerusalem (as described in chapter 11) is to celebrate Passover. In fact, there is no reason to link the chronological context of 14:1 in any way to the events that have occurred since 11:1.

Once free from this assumption, new and significant possibilities arise. Could Jesus' triumphal procession—modeled so clearly on the traditional Tabernacles procession—have taken place during *that festival*? Indeed, all we have thus far examined seems to imply as much. The "going up" terminology, James and John's expectations of enthronement, the origin from Olivet, the royal procession, the Hosanna shouts, the leafy branches, the destination of the Temple, its consequent re-purification, the battles with the occupying evil authorities in Jerusalem—all of these otherwise disparate elements form a coherent and unified complex once set against the backdrop of Tabernacles. When we lose the assumption that all of this occurs during Passover week—of which the text itself offers no notion—then a Tabernacles setting indeed seems most likely.

Smith offers an additional strand of evidence with his analysis of the fig-tree parable (which bookends Jesus' "cleansing of the Temple" at 11:12-14 and 11:20-25). The parable, he says, if taken in its assumed context of Passover, is incomprehensible. Why does Jesus go to the fig-tree expecting fruit if it is springtime—in Nisan, the month of Passover? When he doesn't find any, why does he curse the tree for not bearing fruit, since *no* fig trees would be bearing fruit in that month? Regardless of historical veracity, and even if meant only for its

---

[56] Charles W. F. Smith, "No Time for Figs," *JBL* 79 (1960): 315-27.
[57] Cf. Marcus, *Mark 8-16*, 767-71.
[58] Smith, "No Time for Figs," 316.

metaphorical application, the basic sense is confused if read in a springtime context. Only a fall setting, indeed a Tabernacles setting, makes this event intelligible.[59] Only then would Jesus' frustration be justified. The statement "For it was not the time for figs" in 11:13 is therefore, according to Smith, most likely a later editor's gloss, who (for similar reasons as modern exegetes) also misunderstood the context as occurring near Passover.[60]

Indeed, a Tabernacles setting illuminates other aspects of chapters 11 and 12 as well. In the parable of the wicked tenants, for example, Jesus' response to the wicked religious authorizes is told as a parable about a vineyard at harvest-time. A man planted a vineyard with a winepress and left it to tenants; then, at the appropriate time (*tō kairō*; i.e., the season of harvest), he sent his servants—and finally his own son—to collect the yield. Since the son in the parable is presumably Jesus himself coming to the wicked tenants (Jerusalem and the Temple), we may infer that Jesus too has come to Jerusalem and the Temple at harvest-time. Thus Smith rightly concludes, "The allusions embedded in Mark 11 1—12 12 provide the narrative as a whole with a means of interpretation which comes to life when we place it against its Tabernacles background."[61]

Given that Mark never connects Jesus' triumphal entry and the Passover, and that both the fig-tree story and the parable of the wicked tenants are considerably elucidated if read against a harvest-time context, it seems most likely that *the Markan Jesus in fact celebrates his triumphal enthronement procession during the Feast of Tabernacles itself.* With this, it becomes all but impossible to deny that Mark is crafting his "apocalyptic biography" of Jesus as an impressive, eschatological transformation of the Feast of Tabernacles. In it, Jesus is the divine warrior who ascends to the Temple from the Mount of Olives in a triumphant enthronement procession, having defeated the Satanic forces of Chaos, Sea and Dragon.

But of course Jesus cannot yet be enthroned as king, for his central salvific deed is not yet done. True, Jesus has left the vicinity of the Sea and has defeated the foes that occupied it, as well as the Sea itself. For this, he can enter Jerusalem like a triumphing victor. But one last enemy remains—Death, the "final enemy" from the combat myth progression, which he must defeat before he can finally receive his

---

[59] Ibid., 316-17.
[60] Ibid.
[61] Ibid., 317.

kingship. Indeed, though he has made his triumphant procession to the Temple and cleansed it, his final enthronement awaits him not there, but at Golgotha. Jesus is in Jerusalem for his last combat, one which will soon take place on the cross.

CHAPTER 9
BATTLING DEATH

Even for the earliest Christians, Jesus' death represented a kind of paradox: his victory lay in his defeat, his glory in his suffering.[1] Such a perspective arose out of a radical re-imagination of the messiah and his role. While traditionally understood as political and militaristic—to be filled by an eschatological warrior who would literally overpower and destroy Israel's enemies (political or spiritual)—early Christians radically reinterpreted the role of the messiah in light of Jesus' historical ministry. And, to be sure, the crucifixion posed the greatest challenge in this regard.[2]

Mark was certainly a crucial link in this process of reinterpretation. He, more than any other evangelist, highlights the apparent defeat of Jesus (e.g., his disciples' continuous failure to understand his mission and identity, the agony of the cross, the seemingly tragic final words "My God! My God! Why have you forsaken me?" etc.). Indeed, since William Wrede's hypothesis about the Markan Jesus' "messianic secret,"[3] the failure of the people to recognize Jesus as the true messiah has itself been recognized as a crucial theme in Mark. If nothing else, this theme allowed for an early explanation of why Jesus, far from receiving immediate and total acceptance by his people, was in fact arrested and condemned to death. No doubt the people were simply looking for a different kind of messiah.

The *true* messiah (Mark has Jesus knowingly tell his disciples) must, contrary to traditional notions, suffer and die. The first we hear of this concept is in chapter 8—coming, in fact, right at the outset of Mark's "Way" section:

> And Jesus and his disciples came to the villages of Caesarea Philippi. And, on the Way, he asked his disciples, saying to them, "Who do the people say I am?" And they spoke to him, saying, "John the Baptist; and others, Elijah; and others, one of the prophets." And he asked them, "But who do *you* all think I am?" In reply, Peter says to him, "You are the messiah." And he ordered them not to tell anyone about him. And he began to teach them that it was necessary for the Son of Man to suffer much and to be rejected by the

---

[1] As, e.g., Jn 12:23-24.

[2] Cf. 1 Cor 1:23.

[3] Put forward in William Wrede, *Das Messiasgeheimnis in Den Evangelien* (Göttingen: Vandenhoeck & Ruprecht, 1901).

So Mark sets about redefining the role of the messianic divine warrior. The traditional "Son of Man," who slew the Beast in Daniel 7 and thereby received dominion from the Ancient of Days, is here envisaged as a victim, a man of sorrows rejected and killed by the religious authorities.

Peter, however—apparently quite disturbed by this notion of the messiah—rebukes (*epitiman*) Jesus. Interestingly, the scene then plays out like other instances of Jesus encountering opposition. Peter has raised up his voice in challenge to Jesus, but Jesus rebukes him back (*epetimēsen*) and calls him "Satan," as if subduing him with his mighty voice just as he had the demons and raging Sea. To argue for the traditional notion of the messiah is to think in human terms, and even to be in league with the Devil. It is as though, through Peter, Satan is testing Jesus again as he had in the wilderness. As before, Jesus overcomes the wiles of Satan, this time by his commanding *rebuke*.

Jesus reiterates his novel conception of the messiah twice more in in the "Way" section, at 9:30-32 and 10:32-34. In this way, the Markan Jesus redefines the Son of Man figure from Daniel 7, particularly the mode of his salvific, conquering act. To be the Son of Man—that is, to slay the Beast, to be the Baal-like cloud-rider and receive everlasting dominion from the El-like Ancient of Days—Jesus must die and rise again in Jerusalem. It is as though the Markan Jesus conceives of the Son of Man in terms of the *entire* combat myth progression—not just the battle with the Dragon/Beast, but also (even *principally*) with Death. Indeed, this final battle is now the most salient: to be the Son of Man is to succumb to Death, and return from it victorious.

Enthronement on the Cross (Mk 15:16-32)

As we have seen, Jesus' battles with Satan/Sea in the Galilee and with Death in Jerusalem are linked together by Mark's central "Way" section. This middle section is broadly based on the Sacred Way, and is itself concluded by a processional entry into Jerusalem modeled explicitly on the Tabernacles enthronement procession. Though traditionally this procession ended with the enthronement of Yahweh (the ark) within the Temple, in Mark the procession ends abruptly as an anti-climax. Jesus, entering the Temple, simply looks around and then leaves. There is no enthronement, no proclamation of "Jesus has become king!" the way the Enthronement Psalms declare, "Yahweh has become king!" There are only frustrated expectations. Why?

I have already suggested one reason: as in the traditional progression of the ritual, Jesus must first *leave* the Temple before its re-purification can take place. However, this but delays the expected enthronement; it does not obviate it. The expectation, though frustrated, remains. Jesus must be enthroned. And indeed, after cleansing the Temple and battling the occupying evil in Jerusalem, *he is*—not in the Temple, but on the cross. True to the reinterpretation of the Son of Man's role, the eschatological divine warrior does not take his throne and kingship in the expected manner. To think he would is but to think human things, not the things of God. Mark has offered us a new set of expectations—that the divine warrior will only gain true victory once he has been killed and brought back to life. He thus delays the consummation of the procession until Jesus' crucifixion: the true messiah's glory.

As setup to this final assumption of kingship, Mark narrates the anointing of Jesus at Bethany (14:3-9)—an event permitting multiple interpretations. The one explicitly offered by Jesus is that, "She has anointed my body beforehand for its burial" (v. 8), thus foreshadowing his crucifixion. However, given that Jesus' crucifixion is also his enthronement, one is permitted another reading: *she is anointing Jesus as king*. So Death and royal glory are again equated. Finally (and admittedly most dubious), we have already noted that "Bethany" means "House of Ananiah," and may have been traditionally related to another "house" which stood near the summit of Olivet: the House of Obed-Edom. If Mark is indeed aware of this tradition, his explicit setting of the anointing "in the house" (*en tē oikia*) of Simon the Leper would be a telling emphasis. Having considered the whole *měsillâ* complex (which linked the House of Obed-Edom and the ancient Israelite "Serpent's Stone"), as well as the similarities of this Serpent's Stone with Hittite *ḫuwasi* stones and Emarite sacred stones, it is remarkable that both the Hittite and Emarite sacred stones were ritually *anointed* as part of festive processions of the storm-god. In the Hittite case, we know this practice occurred specifically during the New Year. If we may take such evidence as attesting a more widespread Levantine practice, then perhaps the Serpent's Stone was similarly anointed as part of the ancient Israelite New Year procession.[4] However, this hypothesis, though enticing, probably exceeds beyond what the evidence will safely bear. Nevertheless, I consider it here for the sake of thoroughness.

At last, though, Mark gives his audience the (un)expected conclusion to the events begun in chapter 11: the coronation and proclamation of Jesus as king. However, this comes not from the Jews in celebration, but mockingly from the Roman soldiers in derision:

> And the soldiers led him inside the palace (which is the praetorium), and they call together the whole cohort. And they dress him in a purple robe and, having woven an acanthus crown, put it on him. And they began to greet him, "Hail, king of the Jews!" And they were beating his head with a stick and spitting on him and, bending their knees, did homage to him. And when they had mocked him, they stripped him of the purple robe and dressed him with his cloak. And they lead him out to crucify him. (Mk 15:16-20)

This is the true assumption of Jesus' kingship in Mark's radical new schema of expectations for the Son of Man. This is his earthly acquisition of dominion, presented as a stark inversion of its cosmic archetype from Daniel 7:

> I saw one like a son of man
>   coming with the clouds of heaven.
> And he came to the Ancient of Days
>   and was presented before him.
> To him was given dominion
>   and glory and kingship,
> that all peoples, nations, and languages
>   should serve him.
> His dominion is an everlasting dominion
>   that shall not pass away,
> and his kingship is one
>   that shall never be destroyed. (Dan 7:13b-14)

So the Roman soldiers, in mocking Jesus, ironically declare what the reader—but no one else in Mark's gospel—already knows: he is the King. The mocking salute to Jesus, "Hail, King of the Jews" is Mark's

---

[4] Perhaps to sanctify it as the rest/stand for the ark as is in 1 Sam 6:11-15. This configuration would have placed the trampled "Serpent" beneath the feet of Yahweh (the ark being understood as his footstool). Cf. the cast-metal "Sea" said to grace Solomon's Temple in 1 Kgs 7:23-6, and Yahweh being "enthroned over the Flood" (Ps 29:10).

functional equivalent of "Jesus has become king!" in the traditional sense as pronounced in the Enthronement Psalms.

Now, as Jesus' is removed to Golgotha for execution, Mark seems to echo scenes from the Hebrew Bible which depict the transportation of the ark into the Temple. He writes, "And they carry him to Golgotha place, which means 'The Place of the Skull.'" Some commenters have noted the peculiar usage of the Greek verb *pherō* here, usually translated into English as "brought."[5] While the word itself can be translated variously depending on context, its most basic sense is "*to bear* or *carry* a load."[6] So Collins notes that scholars such as William Campbell and T. E. Schmidt have, each for their own purposes, respectively translated the verb more literally as "to carry" or "to bear." In fact, Schmidt suggests that the bearing of Jesus recalls how Roman military leaders were borne in triumphal processions. Perhaps, however, Mark is echoing a different kind of triumphal procession: the bearing of Yahweh's ark to his Temple for enthronement.

We saw this same theme at work in Jesus entry procession, but the idea is more subtle here since it hinges on allusive syntax. So we find that the transfer of the ark to the Temple is twice described in the Hebrew Bible in quite similar terms:

2 Samuel 6:17 (LXX)	1 Kings 8:6 (LXX)
And they <u>carry</u> the ark of the Lord, and set it in its *Place*…	And the priests <u>carry</u> the ark to its *Place*…
kai <u>pherousi</u> tēn kibōton tou Kyriou kai anethēsan autēn eis ton <u>topon</u> autēs…	*kai <u>eispherousin</u> hoi hiereis tēn kibōton eis ton <u>topon</u> autēs…*

Sigmund Mowinckel believes these passages were ritual "scripts" for the enthronement procession at the Feast of Tabernacles. Concerning the first he writes that

> this story hardly deals with something that happened just once, but rather with a 'legend', *reflecting fixed cultic custom*, the rite of a festal day: from a house outside the temple precincts the festal procession with Yahweh's ark probably used to proceed at the festival of harvest, new year and enthronement, which was also the festival for the consecration of the Temple.[7]

---

[5] As in the NRSV, NASB, KJV, NIV, ESV. The ASV retains the verb's historical present tense, "bring."

[6] LSJ, s.v. φέρω.

[7] Mowinckel, *The Psalms in Israel's Worship*, 215.

The similar account in 1 Kings is modeled after this first procession and thus served as another account of the enthronement ritual.[8]

By comparison, Mark 15:22 reads:

And they <u>carry</u> him to Golgotha *Place*, *kai <u>pherousin</u> auton epi ton Golgothan*
which means "The *Place* of the Skull." *<u>topon</u>, ho estin methermēneuomenon*
  Kraniou <u>Topos</u>

The similarity of the passages is clear. All use the historical present of the verb *pherō*[9] in third-person plural, and emphasize the destination of the holy object as a particular "Place" (*topos*). Though, even if these similarities are purely coincidental (as, admittedly, the specific words are rather common), certainly the image of Jesus (the physical presence of Yahweh on earth) being *carried* by a group who seek to enthrone him (upon the cross) would signal a clear enough parallel with the bearing of the ark for enthronement in the Temple.

After Jesus is carried to Golgotha Place, he is finally crucified. Mark clearly presents this as Jesus' glorious enthronement, as various aspects of his depiction suggest:

> Now it was the third hour, and they crucified him. And an inscription of his charge had been written overhead: "The King of the Jews." And two criminals are crucified with him, one on his right and one on his left. (Mk 15:25-28)

First, the kingship of Jesus is emphasized by the placard, "The King of the Jews." One would expect a throne as the proper place for a triumphant king, but the reinterpretation of the divine warrior that the Markan Jesus proposed earlier in the gospel demands that one see his cross as his glory. Second, and more importantly, the detail that Jesus is crucified between two bandits, one on his right and one on his left, makes the connection with enthronement all but explicit. The configuration recalls the request made by James and John in chapter 10 to be enthroned with Jesus on his right and left at the glorious apocalyptic End:[10]

> And James and John, the sons of Zebedee, come to him, saying to him, "Teacher, we wish it that you might do what we ask of you." And he said to them, "What do you wish me to do for you?" And they said to him, *"Grant*

---

[8] Ibid., 127.
[9] Or, in 1 Kings 8:6, *eispherō*.
[10] Collins, *Mark*, 748.

> *to us that we might sit, one on your right and one on your left, in your glory."* But Jesus said to them, "You do not know what you are asking. Are you able to drink the cup which I drink, or to be baptized in the baptism with which I am baptized?" And they said to him, "We are able." And Jesus said to them, "The cup which I drink you will drink and the baptism with which I am baptized you will be baptized, *but to sit at my right or at my left is not mine to grant, but is for those for whom it has been prepared."* (Mk 10:35-40)

This request, says Collins, "presupposes that Jesus will be enthroned as king and judge of the new age as God's agent."[11] Indeed, that Jesus' enthronement was imminent apparently seemed obvious to James and John: after all, their request comes as the disciples are "on the Way, going up to Jerusalem" with Jesus leading them in procession (v. 32), who himself emphasizes, "See, we are going up to Jerusalem" after which he refers to himself as the Son of Man (v. 33). Taking this enthronement of Jesus for granted, the sons of Zebedee ask to sit on either side of him in his impending glory.

But, as Jesus' response makes clear, this request is based on faulty, traditional notions of the divine warrior's enthronement. Jesus replies, "You do not know what you are asking. Are you able to drink the cup which I drink, or to be baptized in the baptism with which I am baptized?" Perkins makes the connection here between Jesus' baptism of suffering with the chaos-waters, noting, "Old Testament references to water overwhelming the sufferer in lament psalms may have provided the origin for this metaphor (Pss 42:8; 69:3)."[12] Indeed, Psalm 42 contrasts the overwhelming chaos-waters with the joy of the Feast of Booths:

> These things I remember,
>   as I pour out my soul:
> how I went with the throng,
>   and led them in procession to the House of God,
> with glad shouts and songs of thanksgiving,
>   a multitude keeping Festival.
> ...[Yet] Deep calls to deep
>   at the thunder of your cataracts;
> all your waves and your billows
>   have gone over me! (vv. 4, 7)

---

[11] Ibid., 495.

[12] Perkins, *The New Interpreter's Bible 8*, 653. Cf. Marcus, *Mark 8-16*, 747, who notes: "In nonbiblical Greek, words of the bapt- group are used figuratively for the immersion of the people in various sorts of evils ... and in the OT and Jewish texts water and flood imagery are deployed in a similar way (see e.g., Ps 42:7; Isa 43:2; 1 QH 11[3]:28-36)."

Psalm 69 also recalls the mythological background of the overwhelming waters:

> Do not let the Flood sweep over me,
>   or the Deep swallow me up,
>   or the Pit close its mouth over me" (v. 15)

That Mark had this verse in mind when writing of the crucifixion is evidenced by Mark 15:36, where the soldiers offer Jesus sour wine—an allusion to Psalm 69:21: "They gave me poison for food, and for my thirst they gave me vinegar to drink." If we take Perkins' suggestion seriously (which we should), we see that Mark is making yet another connection between Jesus' battle with Death on the cross and the *Chaoskampf* tradition. His death is baptism in the overwhelming chaos-waters.

In any event, Jesus assures them that they are truly ignorant of what it means to be enthroned with him. His enthronement will be on his cross. His enthronement is his death. James and John, like Peter before, have their minds not on the things of God but on the things of men. They are working within traditional notions of kingship, power, authority, and the Son of Man—which Jesus again, using this opportunity, attempts to redefine:

> And hearing this, the ten began to be annoyed with James and John. So calling them to himself, Jesus says to them, "You know that the ones recognized to rule over the Gentiles have power over them and [that] their great men exercise their authority over them. But it is not so among you all, but whoever might wish to be great among you shall be your servant, and whoever might wish to be first among you shall be the slave of all. For indeed, the Son of Man did not come to be served but to serve, and to give his life as a ransom for all. (Mk 10:41-5)

So Jesus denies their request. They do not understand what it takes to be enthroned as Jesus understands enthronement, and so will not be on his right or left in his glory. Instead, this position of "glory" is taken by the two robbers, for whom it has been prepared. Collins summarizes all of this succinctly:

> Finally, this portrayal of Jesus' crucifixion between two robbers reprises the request of James and John in 10:37… The evocation of the earlier text in the account of the crucifixion elaborates the ironic portrayal of Jesus as king that already characterized Mark's source. Jesus hangs on a cross with a

placard announcing his kingship, but James and John are not with him. Because of their fear of suffering and death, they abandoned him and the places of honor are filled by men who are unworthy.[13]

So Mark *directly* connects Jesus' crucifixion with the rising expectation of his enthronement.

Another element to do so is the structuring of the crucifixion itself around Psalm 22. Surprisingly, though it has long been recognized that Psalm 22 is at work in Mark 15, no commentators have investigated its links with enthronement, and the significance this might play in Mark's crucifixion-enthronement paradigm. It is clear that the casting of lots for Jesus' clothing is based on Psalm 22:18, and that the motif of mockers shaking their heads at him is based on Psalm 22:7. More powerfully, however, the very *first* words of Psalm 22 are the very *last* words of the Markan Jesus: "My God, My God, why have you forsaken me?" And yet, for all this, overlooked are the psalm's words immediately following this cry, which refer to Yahweh enthroned:

> My God, my God, why have you forsaken me?
> > Why are you so far from helping me, from the words of my groaning?
> O my God, I cry by day, but you do not answer;
> > and by night, but find no rest.
> *Yet you are holy,*
> > *enthroned (yôšēb) on the praises of Israel.*
> In you our ancestors trusted;
> > they trusted, and you delivered them. (vv. 1-4)

Though the speaker of the psalm—and now Jesus himself—cries out in desperation and abandonment, the following verse rings through with a vision of hope, an adversative realization of Yahweh's power in the face of life's suffering: "*Yet* you are holy, *enthroned* on the praises of Israel." Jesus appears to be abandoned in his crucifixion, but surely an audience conversant in the psalms could not help but hear this hopeful answer echoing in their heads to the psalmist's plight. It is as though salvation itself were transposed upon this scene of despair, victory beaming simultaneous with defeat—in short, a masterful stroke for an author keen to show glory in suffering, and a divine warrior crucified.

---

[13] Collins, *Mark*, 748.

Having considered Jesus' crucifixion within the typology of Yahweh's New Year enthronement, let us now step back for a moment to consider the ways in which Mark foreshadows this event with other scenes of "enthronement." For with Jesus upon the cross we have in fact our *third* (and final) instance of Jesus' "enthronement" in Mark's gospel. Two earlier events, described partially in terms of enthronement, have foreshadowed this climax: the baptism (1:9-11), and the transfiguration (9:2-13).

The baptism I have already analyzed at some length in Chapter 5. There I noted (1) the Jordan River's connection with the chaos-waters, (2) Jesus' "passing through" them via his baptism as a reflection of the ark's crossing, (3) Jesus' "going up" from the water in terminology reminiscent of the festival, (4) reception of Sonship from God in language mirroring a psalm of royal enthronement (which is steeped in *Chaoskampf* imagery), and (5) possible allusion both to the *Testament of Levi* (which connects the election of the messiah with the apocalyptic transformation of the combat myth binding motif), and to Daniel 7. All of these elements contribute to the epiphany of God's glory to the people below as he proclaims the election of his Son. The heavens are rent, the Spirit of God descends, and a voice speaks from the sky declaring Jesus the Son of God. Such is Jesus' first "enthronement" over the waters of Chaos, his first presentation with the reins of kingship. Still, it is only partial, the typology of enthronement latent and most subtlety employed compared to the other two events.

The *baptism* clearly stands as the first enthronement sequence, the *crucifixion* as the last. The middle event occurs at the very core of Mark's gospel, the "*transfiguration*":

> And after six days, Jesus takes with him Peter and James and John and brings them up a high mountain by themselves. And he was transformed in front of them, and his clothing became exceedingly gleaming-white such as no fuller on earth would be able to bleach them. And Elijah and Moses appeared to them, and they were conversing with Jesus. And in reply, Peter says to Jesus, "Rabbi, it is good for us to be here. Let us make three tabernacles, one for you, and one for Moses, and one for Elijah." (For he did not know what to reply, for they were afraid.) And there was a cloud overshadowing them, and a voice came from the cloud: "This is my beloved son; listen to him!" And all of a sudden, looking around, they no longer saw anyone but Jesus alone with them. (Mk 9:2-7)

While this event evinces clear associations with the Feast of Tabernacles, Harold Riesenfeld was the first to appreciate its connections with the enthronement ritual specifically. Rightly seeing it as eschatological reflex of the autumnal ritual, he concludes that "la Transfiguration soit en liaison directe avec la fête juive des Tabernacles" and is "incompréhensibles, si l'on ne tient pas compte de deux faits essentiels: l'interprétation messianique de l'Ancien Testament et les conceptions eschatologiques qui se cristallisaient autour du culte contemporain."[14]

First, the setting—both temporal and geographical—are insightful. Mark gives the geographical context a few verses earlier, saying that Jesus and his disciples "went out into the villages of Caesarea Phillippi" (8:27).[15] It is presumably from the arrival in this area that Mark reckons the six day count mentioned in 9:2.[16] Temporally, this would place the transfiguration seven days after the setting out "on the Way" in 8:27. Now, as Mowinckel has argued, the ritual enthronement of Yahweh most likely took place on the seventh day of the New Year festival.[17] So in Mark, the transfiguration occurs on the seventh day after Jesus left behind the defeated Sea and set out upon the processional way.

Since Mark has noted no change of location, it seems fair to assume that Jesus is still in the villages of Caesarea Phillippi. On the day of the transfiguration, Mark says that Jesus took the disciples up a high mountain (*oros hypsēlon*). While he is not specific as to which mountain this is, certainly *the* high mountain dominating the landscape was (and still is) Mount Hermon—a site long connected with the

---

[14] Harald Riesenfeld, "Jésus Transfiguré, L'arriére-plan récit évangélique de la Transfiguration de Notre-Seigneur," (PhD, Université d'Uppsala, 1947), 304-5.

[15] This verse is particularly significant, since it begins Mark's "Way" section after the framing story of the blind man's healing (whose parallel is found in Blind Bartimeus' healing at the conclusion of the journey in 10:46-52); the verse contains the first instance of the word *hodos* "way" in the "Way" section.

[16] There are no other temporal indicators mentioned between the two events, and the brief events noted in between—Peter's confession of Jesus as the messiah (which actually occurs "on the Way" and thus not even in Caesarea Phillippi itself), and Jesus' subsequent teaching—do not require more than one day to have transpired. Moreover, the temporal setting Mark supplies here is unique: it is the only temporal context the author gives in his entire Gospel before the Passion narrative (cf. Eduard Schweizer, *The Good News According to Mark* (Richmond: John Knox Press, 1970), 181. This would suggest that Mark is providing this detail for a reason. So Marcus, *Mark 8-16*, 631, notes, "'After six days,' then, is unusual, and it probably has some sort of symbolic resonance."

[17] Mowinckel, *The Psalms in Israel's Worship*, 124.

dwelling of the Canaanite Gods. Some scholars have even connected it with Mount Zaphon—Baal's holy mountain,[18] where the storm-god's palace was constructed and where he was enthroned after defeating Yamm. If Mark is indeed assuming Hermon as the mountain of the transfiguration, it is certainly a fitting site for the event.[19]

Time and location both hinting at enthronement, other elements confirm this expectation. So, while not using the typical language of cultic procession (*anabainō*), Jesus does "bring up" (*anapherō*) his disciples to a mountain (= Temple mount).[20] Once there, the divine transformation and ensuing supernatural activity clearly work within the genre of epiphany,[21] which is significant given that the enthronement procession had served as Yahweh's chief festal epiphany in ancient Israel. So Mark says that a cloud overshadowed them,[22] from which a voice declares, "This is my beloved son; listen to him!" These highlight the epiphanic nature of the transfiguration, and indeed present it as a kind of storm theophany.[23] God's words, "This is my beloved son" mirror those he declared at Jesus' baptism. In this way, Mark is clearly drawing a parallel between the two events. Indeed, both foreshadow Jesus' final enthronement, when the centurion (not God) will assert, "Truly this man was the Son of God" (15:39). Both also recall the enthronement scene in Daniel 7, when the Son of Man rides upon the clouds, defeats the Beast, and receives kingship from the Ancient of Days in the throne-room. So Perkins notes that, at the transfiguration, "the predicted glory of the coming Son of Man (8:38) is

---

[18] See e.g., John C. L. Gibson et al., *Ugarit, Religion and Culture: Essays Presented in Honour of Professor John C.L. Gibson*, Ugaritisch-Biblische Literatur (Münster: Ugarit-Verlag, 1996), 180. It should be noted, however, that the more popular view identifies Zaphon with Mount Casius further north.

[19] This is another argument for Syrian provenance, since, if Mark was first written in Syria for a Syrian audience, these ancient mythological associations with Mount Hermon would have been all the more potent.

[20] Our earlier observation on the Greek word *pherō* (in the context of formulaic descriptions of ark transference) may thus be pertinent here as well.

[21] See e.g., Perkins, *The New Interpreter's Bible 8*, 630.

[22] On the Sukkot associations with the overshadowing cloud, as well as other Tabernacles connections with the transfiguration, see Marcus, *Mark 8-16*, 1115-17.

[23] Recall how Yahweh rode the clouds as the storm-god advancing to battle the chaos-waters. It was his mighty *voice* which subdued them. Here we encounter both. That God commands the disciples, "Listen to him!" (*akouete autou*) may indeed recall how the rebuked demons listened to Jesus. In 1:27, the amazed crowd remarks, "Even the unclean spirits he commands, and they listen to him (*hypakouousin autō*)!'" Likewise, the amazed disciples remark at 4:41, "Who indeed is this that even the wind and the Sea listen to him (*hypakouei autō*)?" The root *akouō* ("to listen") is the same in each.

anticipated by the shining white garments of Jesus (9:3)."[24] Indeed, if we take the "high mountain" as Mount Hermon, the connections with Daniel 7 are even more striking, since, as we saw, the author of Daniel 7 was clearly drawing upon "Canaanite" mythological conceptions (the Ancient of Days = El, Father of Years; the Son of Man riding upon the clouds = Baal, Rider of the Clouds).

The most obvious connection with the Tabernacles enthronement festival, however, is Peter's suggestion, "Let us make three tabernacles, one for you, and one for Moses, and one for Elijah" (v. 5). Recognizing all of the associations with the Tabernacles enthronement festival, Peter suggests that they construct three tabernacles (*skēnas*)[25] on the mountain. Peter himself understands the scene within the typology of the Feast of Tabernacles, and so suggests constructing booths in which to stay.[26] Moreover, the specific presence of Moses and Elijah play into the enthronement motif. As we have seen, Elijah was named by the prophet Malachi as the herald of the eschatological enthronement procession. Mark himself quotes this prophecy in his epigraph. To meet Elijah then "on the Way" to Jerusalem, in the very eschatological enthronement procession he was prophesied to herald, gives a clear indication of what is happening. As for Moses, Joel Marcus notes, "The first postbiblical trajectory in the presentation of Moses that is relevant for the Markan transfiguration narrative has to do with Moses' enthronement at Mount Sinai."[27] Indeed, already in the second century BCE, Moses was understood to have been *enthroned* by God, and even

---

²⁴ Perkins, *The New Interpreter's Bible 8*, 630.

²⁵ See e.g., Lev 23:42 (LXX).

²⁶ The parenthetical note that immediately follows in Mark's narrative (which asserts that Peter says this because he was afraid and did not know what to say) must not mean that Peter is completely confused at the scene. Quite the contrary: he appreciates the clear enthronement context. The note may simply show that Peter still has human conceptions of the enthronement of Jesus (cf. 8:32-33). He relates it to a religious festival with its booth-dwelling traditions, and fails to appreciate the extraordinary imminence of the deity himself. As we saw, Jesus repeatedly seeks to redefine the Son of Man and his enthronement, as he does in fact immediately after this scene in 9:9-10. Till the end, Peter, James, and John (cf. 10:35-45) fail to appreciate the radical enthronement for which Jesus is destined. However, the parenthetical note may not be original, but a gloss by a later editor who did not appreciate the Tabernacles associations, just as the (same?) potential glossator did not with the parable of the fig tree. So Marcus, *Mark 8-16*, 638, notes that "it is likely that in the pre-Markan narrative, which lacked 9:6, [Peter's suggestion] was regarded as appropriate."

²⁷ *The Way of the Lord: Christological Exegesis of the Old Testament in the Gospel of Mark*, 84.

shared in God's kingship.[28] His appearance with Jesus may highlight the enthronement motif in this way.

Thus we have three "enthronements": baptism (1:9-11), transfiguration (9:2-13), and the crucifixion (15:16-32). Remarkably, each of these three occur within the three distinct sections of Mark. The baptism opens Jesus' ministry around the Sea in the first section, the transfiguration occurs just after Jesus has set out on the Sacred Way in the second "Way" section, and the third comes as the dramatic conclusion to the gospel in the third section. Thus it is clear that, in each, Mark means to highlight the enthronement motif, structuring his gospel such that each of his parts contains one "enthronement." The first two, however, essentially serve to foreshadow the final, true enthronement of Jesus upon the cross.

Defeat and Victory on the Cross (15:33-39)

There seems to be only one—though crucial—example of Jesus defeating the forces of Death in Mark's gospel, and that is his resurrection.[29] This victory is his final and conclusive one, and in this respect parallels Yahweh's defeat of Death (and so, indirectly, Baal's defeat of Death). Thus, what E. Theodore Mullen says of the Canaanite combat myth is also relevant here:

> The progression in the myth is logical. To insure the fertility and stability of the cosmos, [the storm-god] must first make the universe secure from Yamm and the chaotic forces of the sea. Next he must overcome the forces of death and sterility, an equally important conflict.[30]

In a similar sense, Jesus must first make the universe secure from Satan and the chaotic forces of the Sea. Next he must overcome the power of Death.

---

[28] Ibid., 84-5.

[29] Other possible instances of victory over Death do occur in the gospel. In 5:21-43 Jesus is believed to raise a girl from the dead. His claim, however, that "the child is not dead but sleeping," allows for different understandings of this event. The healing of the boy in 9:14-29 is a slightly less ambiguous example, though still vague in its significance. In both of these stories, then, it may be that no one is actually resurrected. For an alternative interpretation, see *Mark 1-8*, 370-3.

[30] Mullen, *The Divine Council in Canaanite and Early Hebrew Literature*, 75-76.

We have already dealt with the use of "Canaanite" imagery in Jewish apocalypticism, noting that the ancient Israelites shared many Canaanite conceptions of the combat myth which were transmitted all the way down to the first century CE and beyond, perhaps via the traditional continuity of Tabernacles cultus. Across the centuries, ancient Hebrew texts show a conception of Death much akin to the Canaanite deity. In that continuing tradition, he remained the insatiable devourer. Proverbs 27:20 declares that "Sheol and Abaddon are never satisfied"—figures clearly personified in Job 28:22: "Abaddon and Death say, 'We have heard a rumor of it with our ears.'" Indeed, evidence shows that they were still appreciated as personified divine beings *in apocalyptic literature of the first century CE*. Revelation 9, for example, describes Abaddon as a netherworldly king and fallen angel:

> And the fifth angel blew his trumpet, and I saw a star that had fallen from heaven to earth, and he was given the key to the shaft of the bottomless pit; he opened the shaft of the bottomless pit, and from the shaft rose smoke like the smoke of a great furnace, and the sun and the air were darkened with the smoke from the shaft. Then from the smoke came locusts on the earth, and they were given authority like the authority of scorpions of the earth. *…They have as king over them the angel of the bottomless pit; his name in Hebrew is Abaddon*, and in Greek he is called Apollyon. (Rev 9:1-3, 11)

Thus, mythic conceptions of Death—specifically those from the combat myth—were demonstrably maintained well into the apocalyptic period. Such texts evince a much vaster, living mythology than is immediately apparent in the Hebrew Bible—one which likely included a battle between Yahweh and Death. So John J. Collins asserts:

> There can be no doubt that many more mythological traditions were transmitted in Second Temple Judaism than are now extant in the Hebrew Bible. Glimpses of such traditions can be seen in [Isaiah 24-27], which alludes to Leviathan (27:1); *the destruction of Môt, or Death* (25:8); and an enigmatic punishment of the host of heaven (24:21-23).[31]

Indeed, the combat myth between Yahweh and Death seems to have gained great prominence in the apocalyptic period—no doubt due, at least in part, to the growing inclusion of an afterlife in Jewish theology. Belief in resurrection, and thus the ultimate destruction of Death's power, began in the apocalyptic period and is one of the

---

[31] Collins, *Daniel*, 293.

theological features distinguishing it from older Jewish religion. It is no surprise then that we find the mythic combat with Death employed by apocalyptic writers—especially those of the New Testament. So Paul alludes to it, for example, in 1 Corinthians 15:

> But in fact Christ has been raised from the dead, the first fruits of those who have died. For since death came through a human being, the resurrection of the dead has also come through a human being; for as all die in Adam, so all will be made alive in Christ. But each in his own order: Christ the first fruits, then at his coming those who belong to Christ. *Then comes the end, when he hands over the kingdom to God the Father, after he has destroyed every Ruler and every Authority and Power. For he must reign until he has put all his enemies under his feet. The last enemy to be destroyed is Death.* (vv. 20-26)

Death is here the "last enemy" (*eschatos echthros*), just as he was in the traditional progression of the combat myth.[32] Moreover, Death's position beneath the feet of Yahweh may recall his fate in the combat myth, as he too was probably trampled. So Albright's translation of Habakkuk 3:12-13:

> In fury you trod upon the Earth, in anger you trampled nations.
> You came forth to save your people, to save your anointed.
> You crushed the head of wicked Death, destroying him tail-end to neck.[33]

Paul continues his mythological allusions for the Corinthians a few verses later:

> When this perishable body puts on imperishability, and this mortal body puts on immortality, then the saying that is written will be fulfilled: "Death has been swallowed up in victory." "Where, O Death, is your victory? Where, O Death, is your sting?" The sting of Death is sin, and the power of sin is the law. But thanks be to God, who gives us the victory through our Lord Jesus Christ. (vv. 54-7)

Here, Paul alludes to two mythic instances of Death in the Old Testament: the Isaianc Apocalypse (25:8), and Hosea 13:14. Both likely reflect the combat between Yahweh and Death. Indeed, Paul refers to Death's defeat as a victory (*nikos*) accomplished through

---

[32] cf. *ABD*, "Warrior, Divine," 879, which notes: "Lying behind this Pauline perspective is the apocalyptic idea that the world is caught in a struggle between divine and diabolical forces which will one day be resolved by the conquest of Chaos and death."
[33] For this translation, see Chapter 2.

Jesus, making Jesus the divine warrior just as Yahweh was. A similar sentiment is found in Romans 5:14 and 17:

> Yet Death was king from Adam to Moses, even over those whose sins were not like the transgression of Adam, who is a type of the one who was to come. ...If, because of the one man's trespass, Death ruled as king through that one, much more surely will those who receive the abundance of grace and the free gift of righteousness rule in life through the one man, Jesus Christ.

Here, Paul takes the allusion further and speaks of Death ruling as king (*ebasileusen*, from *basileus* = "king"), thereby invoking the combat myth's political theme of contested kingship. Like the ancient Mot, Death presumably had a kingdom. In keeping with the apocalyptic mentality, it reigned in fact over all the earth. But Jesus overthrows Death as king to usher in instead the Kingdom of God.

In his book *The Defeat of Death: Apocalyptic Eschatology in 1 Corinthians 15 and Romans 5*, Martinus de Boer succinctly summarizes much of this Pauline conception of Death:

> In both 1 Corinthians 15 and Romans 5...Paul understands the anthropological reality of death in accordance with the traditions of Jewish cosmological apocalyptic eschatology as an inimical, murderous, quasi-angelic power that had held all Adamic humanity in subjection and enslavement. Death is hypostatized as a power external to human beings, which nevertheless exerts and manifests its hegemony over and among human beings... Indeed it must be said that Paul cosmologizes, or 'mythologizes', death for his readers...[34]

Clearly Paul conceived of Death in a mythic sense, or at the very least could express his theological ideas in terms of traditional myth. Either way, his writings reveal that the ancient combat between Yahweh and Death was still alive and salient, particularly for articulating to early Christian communities the salvific work accomplished by Jesus through his death and resurrection.

Nowhere is such a mythological understanding of Death more explicit than in the Book of Revelation. Revelation 20 offers perhaps the strongest evidence that the myth of Yahweh's combat with Death was not only current in the first century CE, but actively serving

---

[34] Martinus C. de Boer, *The Defeat of Death: Apocalyptic Eschatology in 1 Corinthians 15 and Romans 5*, Journal for the Study of the New Testament Supplement Series (Sheffield, England: JSOT Press, 1988), 183.

apocalyptic Christian communities as they sought to articulate the significance of Jesus' death and resurrection. So we find Jesus following the traditional progression of the myth as, after binding the Dragon, he turns his wrath on Death:

> Then Death and Hades were thrown into the lake of fire. This is the second death, the lake of fire; and anyone whose name was not found written in the book of life was thrown into the lake of fire.
> Then I saw a new heaven and a new earth; for the first heaven and the first earth had passed away, and the Sea was no more. (Rev 20:14-21:1)

One particularly striking aspect of this passage is the mention of both Death and Hades, since the Greek word "Hades" frequently translated the Hebrew "Sheol"—another name for Death himself. Thus it is not two different entities cast into the fire here, but *one*: the old enemy from the combat myth—Mot/Sheol, whose epithets are given in poetic parallel (cf. Yamm and Judge River). So Death maintained the mythical resonances he had had when the writers of the Hebrew Bible employed them.[35]

Although this mythology was still potent and accessible to first century authors, Mark clearly does not employ it in an *overtly* mythical way. Such applications of the myth may have suited the apocalyptic vision of John of Patmos, but for Mark (writing apocalyptic biography), portraying Jesus as literally slaying a personified Death—or better, swallowing him—was simply not an option. The manner of presentation should not, however, prevent our recognition of its mythic undertones. That Jesus was understood by Christians to have defeated Death by his crucifixion and resurrection is clear. The manner of this defeat, however, is rather different from direct combat: Jesus defeats Death by overcoming the power of Death—that is, by his resurrection.

---

[35] In fact, pagan sources also indicate that Mot himself was still known and recognized as a deity of death in the first-century. Claiming to translate Sanchuniathon's accounts of ancient Phoenician mythology, Philo of Byblos, quoted by Eusebius in the second century, writes, "And much later, when another child of [Kronos = El] dies—a son of Rhea named Mouth (Μούθ/Μώτ = Mot)—he sanctified him. And the Phoenicians call this one Death and Pluto." See *Praeparatio Evangelica* 1.10.34 in Albert I. Baumgarten, *The Phoenician History of Philo of Byblos: A Commentary*, Études Préliminaires Aux Religions Orientales Dans L'empire Romain (Leiden: Brill, 1981), 215. Memory of Mot as a figure linked with the chaos-forces, specifically the chaos-waters, is also present in Philo's report that "[s]ome say that [Mōt] is slime, others the putrefaction of a watery mixture." (Quoted in *Praeparatio Evangelica* 1.10.1, in ibid., 97.)

For this he must first die. And so, for the first time, Jesus must be *defeated* by the chaos-enemy.

Dominic Rudman offers an insightful analysis of Jesus' death in just these terms. In his article "The Crucifixion as *Chaoskampf*: A New Reading of the Passion Narrative in the Synoptic Gospels," Rudman clearly asserts that "the crucifixion is expressed literarily as a *chaoskampf*, but one in which the powers of chaos are victorious."[36] To argue this thesis, he points to (1) the spread of darkness at the time of Jesus' crucifixion, (2) the motif of the Creator's death, and (3) the tearing of the Temple curtain.[37] I shall consider each of these arguments, and along the way posit additional evidence for seeing the Markan crucifixion as a combat myth in which Jesus is defeated before proving victorious.

In 15:33, Mark writes: "And when the sixth hour came, a darkness came over the whole Earth until the ninth hour." Rudman sees this as a telling detail, signaling the ascension of Chaos in the cosmos:

> Biblical texts strongly associate darkness or night with the forces of chaos. Darkness is synonymous with chaos in the form of non-existence (Job 3,3-6) or crime (Prov 2, 13), and is therefore particularly associated with Sheol — the place where the human essence resides after death (Job 10,21; 17,11-16; Eccl 11,8).[38]

Indeed, there are many other texts Rudman does not cite which solidify this association. Job, for example, proclaims:

> Are not my days few?
>   Cease then, and let me alone, that I may take comfort a little,
> Before I go whence I shall not return,
>   even to the land of darkness and of the shadow of Death;
> The land dark as midnight, the shadow of Death,
>   and Chaos, and where the light is as midnight.
>   (Job 10:20-22, ASV, modified)

---

[36] Dominic Rudman, "The Crucifixion as Chaoskampf: A New Reading of the Passion Narrative in the Synoptic Gospels," *Biblica* 84 (2003): 105.

[37] Longman and Reid, *God Is a Warrior* instead interpret these elements in light of the judgment leveled upon Israel on Day of the Lord. Thus, they reject Christ's death as a defeat in any sense, but maintain a more orthodox view that God is completely powerful throughout.

[38] Rudman, "The Crucifixion as Chaoskampf: A New Reading of the Passion Narrative in the Synoptic Gospels," 104.

Here, Death and Sheol are explicitly linked with Chaos (*wĕlō' sĕdārîm*, lit. "no order") and "deep darkness," where even light is like darkness. Elsewhere in Job, Death and the darkness of the depths of the chaos-waters are equated in poetic parallelism:

> Have you entered into the springs of the Sea,
>   or walked in the recesses of the Deep?
> Have the gates of Death been revealed to you,
>   or have you seen the gates of deep darkness? (Job 38:16-18)[39]

The spread of darkness over the whole land at Jesus' crucifixion thus implies the ascendancy of Death and Chaos as Jesus is defeated. This fits well with the other combat myths we have seen, where the defeat of the storm-god means the ascendancy of death and sterility. In Forsyth's schema, this sequence is expressed in functions 6 and 7, "Defeat" and "Enemy ascendant." Moreover, the spread of unusual darkness is also found in the ancient Mesopotamian combat myths, as when the sun stops and the day turns black as Ninurta battles the Azag, or when darkness covers the mountain as Ninurta battles Anzu.

Darkness is thus associated with Death, but with Chaos more generally. Mark's statement in 15:33 that "a darkness came over the whole Earth" (*skotos egeneto eph' holēn tēn gēn*) may echo Genesis 1:2 (LXX), which says that at Creation "the Earth was formless and uncrafted and darkness covered the deep" (*hē de gē ēn aoratos kai akataskeuastos, kai skotos epanō tēs abyssou*). Rudman misses this connection in his analysis, but such an allusion would be entirely fitting. With Jesus' defeat on the cross, the earth has been plunged back into the state of Chaos that characterized it before Creation. Indeed, this regression into Chaos was fundamental to the ancient Near Eastern conception of the New Year. This was the very reason why the victory of the storm-god was celebrated at the New Year festival, since his victory meant that fertility and life would return after Chaos' defeat. Every year the world regressed into Chaos, and every year at the New Year festival Yahweh's enthronement signaled the defeat of Death and the return of life. So here, before Jesus' life returns at his resurrection, the world is in the trough of death. Chaos has assumed its temporary dominance over the cosmos.

---

[39] Nicholas Tromp provides many more textual examples linking death and darkness in *Primitive Conceptions of Death and the Nether World in the Old Testament*, 140-44.

As shown in Part One, the combat myth was often cosmogonical in nature, given that its central focus was the (re)establishment of an ordered cosmos. The forces of Chaos assert their dominance over the orderly cosmos and its life-bringing storm-god, ultimately to be tamed and destroyed by that resurgent deity. Order is thus reinstated, and out of the Chaos comes the structure of an ordered cosmos, making the myth a story of (re-)Creation. With respect to the crucifixion, Jesus clearly fulfills the role of the divine warrior, traditionally held by Yahweh, the Creator of the world. So Rudman concludes, "The death of this creator figure on the cross is, in a sense, the ultimate victory of Chaos over creation."[40]

Indeed, Mark presents Jesus' crucifixion as a true defeat more than any other evangelist. Apart from his final cry of anguish and abandonment (quoting Psalm 22:1), the only sound Jesus is said to make on the cross is the cry of a great voice. At 15:34, "Jesus shouted with a great voice" (*eboēsen ho Iēsous phōnē megalē*), and at 15:37 (*Iēsous apheis phōnēn megalēn*). Interestingly, this is precisely what the demons were said to do when *Jesus* defeated *them*. Now that Jesus is the one being defeated, it is *his* mighty voice that is not powerful enough to overcome the opposition. God's mighty rebuke is finally not strong enough to conquer the Enemy. In this way, Mark employs the language of spiritual warfare to describe Jesus' battle against Death. Unlike all the battles before, however, Jesus is the one beaten here.[41]

Then Jesus dies—at which moment "the curtain of the Temple was split in two, from top to bottom" (v. 38). Rudman argues that, since the tabernacle was understood as a microcosm of Creation, this is the key moment signifying the triumph of Death and Chaos over Jesus and the orderly cosmos. This interpretation is based on Josephus, who writes that the sanctuary had golden doors before which hung a curtain made of materials that "typified the universe."[42] The rending of this curtain thus signifies a dissolution of the world; Creation has been undone, and Chaos reigns again. Rudman states this succinctly, noting that

---

[40] Rudman, "The Crucifixion as Chaoskampf: A New Reading of the Passion Narrative in the Synoptic Gospels," 105.

[41] cf. Longman and Reid, *God Is a Warrior*, 131: "Jesus...dies at the climax of eschatological battle."

[42] *Bell.* 5.5.4 §212. Cf. Collins, *Mark*, 760.

the establishing and maintenance of boundaries (e.g. against the sea, or death) is crucial to the process of creation and its preservation in the OT. The dissolution of such boundaries could therefore be seen as signifying a victory by the forces of chaos. It is surely significant that this action happens at the precise moment of Jesus' death, when chaos has triumphed and all is despair. At this moment, Jesus' victory remains three days in the future.[43]

However, other significances might also be at play. Overlooked by Rudman and others, for example, is the connection between the rending of the curtain and the allusion to the combat with Death in Isaiah 25:7-8a:

> And he will destroy on this mountain
>> the shroud that is cast over all peoples,
>> the sheet that is spread over all nations;
>> he will swallow up Death forever.

If this is what lies behind Mark's torn curtain, then the shroud or sheet is not so much the symbolic cosmos thrown into total Chaos by the death of Jesus, but a negative element that blocks God's intimacy and connection with his people—one which Jesus' death abolishes. It is precisely at the moment of his death, then, that Jesus is victorious. The shroud is torn, and God has swallowed Death. Given the fundamental paradox of Jesus' crucifixion as discussed at the outset—his victory in defeat, his death which brings life—we may not need to choose between these two seemingly contradictory interpretations.

It is only after Jesus' deposition and burial,[44] in the final lines of the gospel, that we find the climactic assurance of Jesus' total victory over Death. There we read how the women who had been at the crucifixion set out to anoint Jesus' dead body. Mark notes that the time was "early morning, when the sun had risen" (16:2), a detail appreciated by Joel Marcus, who perceptively posits that "the ascent of the sun at Jesus' resurrection reverses the darkness of his crucifixion

---

[43] Rudman, "The Crucifixion as Chaoskampf: A New Reading of the Passion Narrative in the Synoptic Gospels," 107.

[44] In Mark, Jesus' body is requested from the agents of his death (15:43), buried in a tomb (15:46), and mourned by three women—a progression with intriguing echoes of the Ugaritic combat myth with Death. There, Baal's body is retrieved from Death himself by his female consort, Anat, who then mourns and buries him in a pit (*KTU* 1.6.i.10-18). While these similarities likely owe merely to traditional burial customs of the ancient Near East, it is not impossible that a mythic typology is at work even here.

(cf. 15:33)."[45] The ascendancy of Chaos has ended. In Forsyth's schema, this is function 8: "Hero Recovers." And Jesus has indeed recovered. The women find the tomb empty, and an angelic messenger who proclaims: "He has been risen; he is not here." With this declaration, Mark offers his audience the "good news of Jesus Christ," Boring's "good news from the battlefield."[46] Jesus has proven victorious over his enemies—even Death. Longman and Reid note: "There is no question who has won the eschatological battle—even if the reaction of the women is ironically characterized by the archetypal fear that seizes those who encounter Yahweh as the divine warrior. The victim has emerged the victor."[47]

Placing this progression within Forsyth's schema, we have: (1) *Lack/Villainy*: Death, through Satan, has taken control of the cosmos. (2) *Hero emerges/prepares to act*: Jesus emerges from Nazareth. (3) *Donor/Consultation*: Jesus is baptized by John the Baptist, at which time he receives the Holy Spirit. (4) *Journey*: Jesus travels to Jerusalem for his final confrontation. (5) *Battle*: Jesus is crucified. He cries out with a loud voice. (6) *Defeat*: Jesus dies. (7) *Enemy ascendant*: Darkness covers the earth. Satan appears to have won. (8) *Hero recovers*: Jesus returns to life, destroying the power of Death. (9) *Battle rejoined*: History continues; Jesus will come with the clouds of heaven at the End. (10) *Victory*: End-time, parousia. (11) *Enemy Punished*: Satan chained, fire, abyss. (12) *Triumph*: Redemption and New Heaven and Earth.

One could also argue that the Resurrection is itself the "Battle rejoined" and "Victory" in the battle with Death. This is essentially true for Jesus' final battle with Death. For Mark and his audience, however, the final victory still lay in the future. Jesus' victory over Death was just the first-fruits of the coming Harvest. The complete victory over Death would come when *all* of those in Christ would be resurrected. So Mark 13:26-27:

> Then they will see 'the Son of Man coming in clouds' with great power and glory. Then he will send out the angels, and gather his elect from the four winds, from the ends of the earth to the ends of heaven.

---

[45] Marcus, *Mark 8-16*, 1083.

[46] Boring, *Mark: A Commentary*, 30.

[47] Longman and Reid, *God Is a Warrior*, 133.

Or Paul's assurance in 1 Thessalonians that the divine warrior would come again:

> For since we believe that Jesus died and rose again, even so, through Jesus, God will bring with him those who have died... For this we declare to you by the word of the Lord, that we who are alive, who are left until the coming of the Lord, will by no means precede those who have died. For *the Lord himself, with a cry of command, with the archangel's call and with the sound of God's trumpet, will descend from heaven*, and the dead in Christ will rise first. Then we who are alive, who are left, will be caught up in the clouds together with them to meet the Lord in the air; and so we will be with the Lord forever. (1 Thess 4:14, 16-17)

Such are the consequences of Jesus' victory over Death. This is what Mark and his audience were eagerly awaiting and imminently expecting. Only then, when they saw the Rider of the Clouds coming in victory, could they unequivocally proclaim, "Jesus has become king!"

So the typology of the combat myth is complete with Jesus' resurrection. The divine warrior, having slain the Dragon and subdued the raging Sea, made his triumphant procession to the Temple. He was crowned and enthroned, only to face a confrontation with Death—which he loses. So the divine warrior dies, and is tended to in death by female companion as the forces of Chaos gain ascendancy over the cosmos. But their temporary dominance does not last long. The hero recovers, coming back to life to defeat the power of Death. Then his eternal authority is recognized and he indeed becomes uncontested king over the cosmos.

So the ancient mythic pattern, born in the mytho-cultic systems of the ancient Near East, becomes enshrined as Christian gospel—the product of a millennia-long series of transformations from ancient Near Eastern genre to Israelite cultus, Prophetic metaphor, apocalyptic vision, gospel, and, finally, religious creed, alive and thriving today in the 21st century—and beyond.

CONCLUSION

We began our investigation with generic considerations, followed by a brief survey of various ancient Near Eastern combat myths. In terms of plot, these myths narrate the battle between a warrior storm-god and a draconic monster—a battle with thematic significances in the agricultural, cultic, political, and philosophical/theological spheres of human life. Certain details, recurrent enough to warrant the designation of "motif," include the battle tactics of *trampling*, *binding/muzzling*, *dividing/scattering*, as well as the sounding of the divine warrior's *mighty voice*. Having proved victorious over the dragon after a principal setback/defeat, the divine warrior's triumph is celebrated, usually with the construction of the deity's temple and his enthronement as king over the cosmos therein. This mythic celebration mirrored the cultic *Sitz im Leben* of the myths themselves: a New Year festival in which the icons of the gods were processed to and from sacred suburban house-shrines to their principal temples in the city proper. Great music and fanfare accompanied their processions, as the people celebrated the "good news" of rejuvenation brought about by the storm-god's victories over Chaos and death.

The combat myths in the Baal Cycle recovered from Ras Shamra share these elements and cast light on the general mythological traditions of the ancient Levant. There, Baal was the mighty storm-god, who battled the Sea and its Dragon, while his consort, Anat, is likewise said to have *bound/muzzled* the Dragon and *scattered* him in the desert. After his victory with Sea and the Dragon, Baal processes in triumph through the neighboring towns, to be enthroned ultimately within his recently-constructed temple. From there, his *mighty voice* goes forth into the land. However, Death immediately challenges his power. The two battle, and Baal is defeated—mourned and buried by Anat. With the storm-god dead, fertility vanishes and sterility and Chaos gain ascendancy over the land. Finally, however, Baal returns to life to defeat Death and, after victory, is again proclaimed king over the cosmos.

Looking at the Hebrew texts, we can see that these ideas were also present in the mythology and worldview of ancient Israel. Here, the storm-god Yahweh was believed to have battled the Sea and its Dragon, *trampling* its waters and *muzzling* the Dragon. Like Baal, his *mighty voice* is likewise featured, principally to *rebuke* the raging Sea and frighten it back to its proper boundaries. The Israelites also shared the Canaanite conception of Death as the insatiable swallower, and knew a story of his defeat by Yahweh. As in other ancient Near Eastern cultures, these victories were celebrated as "good news" in a cultic New Year festival. For the Israelites, this was the Feast of Tabernacles, which included the ritual procession of Yahweh's ark to his temple from a small house-shrine on the Mount of Olives. During this festival, the Jerusalem Temple was re-purified and Yahweh was re-enthroned as king over his people.

In 587 BCE, however, the Babylonians attacked Jerusalem and destroyed its temple to Yahweh. They deported many Jews to Mesopotamia, where they languished for decades. In their suffering, some recalled Yahweh's primordial battle with the forces of Chaos and implored him to repeat it, this time in a fight against the oppressive Babylonian Empire. Prophets now wrote of Yahweh's processional Sacred Way as a road that would lead them back to a rejuvenated Israel. The New Year festival, with its "good news" of Yahweh's victory over Israel's enemies and his just kingship over the world, became projected into the future with cosmic dimensions.

After the return from Exile, reworking of older religious conceptions continued. Given the disaster of the Captivity and the perceived failures of the new religious and political establishment, salvific hopes continued to be eschatologized, until, completely losing the moors of history, full-fledged apocalyptic visions of a world radically transformed at the end of time came to flourish. Considering the enemy from the combat myth, and perhaps in the context of exposure to foreign traditions, many Jews began to see another supernatural force, antagonistic to Yahweh, at work in the world. Essentially malignant, this force controlled the political empires of the earth. This was the Devil, the supernatural embodiment of Israel's oppressor. But God and his messiah would battle the Devil at the end of time and restore to Israel the glory and power justice demanded. To articulate this conflict, these writers turned to the traditional combat myth pattern, further eschatologizing the myth from the New Year festival to express hopes for Yahweh's ultimate victory and a fully re-purified world. So the Devil becomes the Dragon, a cosmic Leviathan, whose final slaying by the messianic divine warrior would end his oppressive kingship over the Earth, and usher in for the righteous not just a new year, but a New Heaven and Earth.

It was in this apocalyptic context that Jesus of Nazareth carried out his ministry before his execution by the Romans. The early church that arose after his crucifixion, coming out of this milieu, saw him as that messiah—though radically reinterpreted. Divinely commissioned by Yahweh, Jesus battled the forces of Satan, and by his crucifixion defeated Death for all believers. His return was said to be imminent and would conclusively usher in the cosmic New Year, to which all Christians would be resurrected.

As the situation in Roman-occupied Palestine deteriorated, open conflict erupted and apocalyptic expectation grew more rampant. It was at this point that the Gospel of Mark was probably composed. Like others before him, Mark articulated the salvific work of Jesus in terms of the eschatologized combat myth—not with an apocalypse (like John of Patmos), but with an "apocalyptic biography." In it, Jesus is portrayed as the apocalyptic divine warrior, who comes at the End to battle a Devil Mark depicts as the adversaries from the traditional combat myth: Dragon, Sea, and Death.

Following the progression of the ancient combat myth, Jesus' first battles in Mark are with the Dragon (Satan) and the corrupted natural world he rules over, represented by the Sea. These battles comprise the first third of Mark's gospel. In them, Jesus *rebukes* both the demonic forces and the raging Sea with his *mighty voice*—just like Yahweh before him. He declares he has *bound* the strong man, Satan himself, and casts out demons to drown in the Sea. Like Yahweh, he *tramples* the raging waters beneath his feet, and *divides* the symbolic bodies of the chaos-monsters to be eaten by the righteous at the eschatological banquet, thus *scattering* them in the desert.

After these victories over Sea and Dragon, Mark's middle section follows Jesus on "the Way." In terms of the New Year typology, Jesus has defeated the forces of Chaos, and so now must process to the Temple for enthronement. So Mark describes him, leading a procession of his twelve disciples to Jerusalem for the Feast of Tabernacles. Following the traditional route of the Sacred Way, Jesus enters Jerusalem in triumph from the Mount of Olives. Once there, he is borne along in a procession to the Temple as crowds cry the traditional festal shout, sing an Enthronement Psalm, and spread leafy branches like those used at the Tabernacles.

From the Temple, Jesus goes to the suburban house on Olivet, returning the next day to re-purify the Temple, and indeed the entire city of Jerusalem. But his assumption of kingship is delayed until his true enthronement—which, given his radical reinterpretation of the Son of Man and the role of the messiah, is understood as his suffering on the cross. In typical Markan irony then, Jesus is proclaimed king by mocking Roman soldiers, given a crown, and led away to be crucified. Having received his kingship, however, the progression of the ancient combat myth demands that he now battle Death. And so he does. Like Baal before him, though, Death proves victorious in this encounter. Chaos assumes its temporary dominance over the earth and the Enemy is ascendant as darkness covers the earth. Death has won, but his victory will not be final. Indeed, Jesus returns to life, and in so doing proves victorious over the forces of Death.

This is but the beginning of the End, however. Having defeated Death for all believers, Jesus will come again—and soon—whereupon the dead shall rise. At that time, he will be the Rider of the Clouds, the Son of Man who comes and saves the righteous as all the old polluted world is purged away. Then will the cosmic New Year come in full. A New Heaven and a New Earth.

Such is the "good news" of Jesus Christ, and such is the message of Mark—from ancient Near Eastern myth to Christianity's enduring gospel.

BIBLIOGRAPHY

Albright, W. F. "The Psalm of Habakkuk." In *Studies in Old Testament Prophecy*, edited by Harold Henry Rowley. Edinburgh: T. & T. Clark, 1957.

Allison, Dale C. "The Eschatology of Jesus." In *The Encyclopedia of Apocalypticism*, edited by John J. Collins. New York: Continuum, 1998.

Anderson, G. W. "Isaiah XXIV-XXVII Reconsidered." *SVT* 9 (1963): 118-26.

Angel, Andrew R. *Chaos and the Son of Man: The Hebrew Chaoskampf Tradition in the Period 515 BCE to 200 CE*. Library of Second Temple Studies. London: T & T Clark, 2006.

Aune, David Edward. *Revelation*. Word Biblical Commentary. 3 vols. Dallas: Word Books, 1997.

Barton, John, and John Muddiman. *The Oxford Bible Commentary*. Oxford: Oxford University Press, 2001.

Batto, Bernard Frank. *Slaying the Dragon: Mythmaking in the Biblical Tradition*. Louisville: Westminster/John Knox Press, 1992.

———. "The Sleeping God: An Ancient Near Eastern Motif of Divine Sovereignty." *Biblica* 68 (1987): 153-77.

Baumgarten, Albert I. *The Phoenician History of Philo of Byblos: A Commentary*. Études Préliminaires Aux Religions Orientales Dans L'empire Romain. Leiden: Brill, 1981.

Bentzen, Aage. *King and Messiah*. London: Lutterworth Press, 1955.

Best, Ernest. *The Temptation and the Passion: The Markan Soteriology*. Monograph Series / Society for New Testament Studies. 2nd ed. Cambridge: Cambridge University Press, 1990.

Bidmead, Julye. *The Akītu Festival: Religious Continuity and Royal Legitimation in Mesopotamia*. Gorgias Dissertations Near East Series. Piscataway: Gorgias Press, 2002.

Black, Jeremy A., and Anthony Green. *Gods, Demons and Symbols of Ancient Mesopotamia: An Illustrated Dictionary*. London: British Museum Press, 1992.

Blenkinsopp, Joseph. *Isaiah 1-39: A New Translation with Introduction and Commentary*. The Anchor Bible. New York: Doubleday, 2000.

Boer, Martinus C. de. *The Defeat of Death: Apocalyptic Eschatology in 1 Corinthians 15 and Romans 5*. Journal for the Study of the New Testament Supplement Series. Sheffield, England: JSOT Press, 1988.

Boring, M. Eugene. *Mark: A Commentary*. New Testament Library. Louisville: Westminster/John Knox Press, 2006.

Boyd, Gregory A. *God at War: The Bible & Spiritual Conflict*. Downers Grove: InterVarsity Press, 1997.

Bryce, Trevor. *Life and Society in the Hittite World*. Oxford: Oxford University Press, 2002.

Burney, Charles Allen. *Historical Dictionary of the Hittites*. Lanham: Scarecrow Press, 2004.

Clifford, Richard J. "The Roots of Apocalypticism in Near Eastern Myth." In *The Encyclopedia of Apocalypticism*, edited by John J. Collins. New York: Continuum, 1998.

Cohn, Norman. *Cosmos, Chaos, and the World to Come: The Ancient Roots of Apocalyptic Faith*. New Haven: Yale University Press, 1993.

Collins, Adela Yarbro. *The Combat Myth in the Book of Revelation*. Harvard Dissertations in Religion. Eugene: Wipf and Stock Publishers, 1976.

———. *Is Mark's Gospel a Life of Jesus?: The Question of Genre*. The Père Marquette Lecture in Theology. Milwaukee: Marquette University Press, 1990.

———. *Mark: A Commentary*. Hermeneia. Minneapolis: Fortress Press, 2007.

Collins, John J. *Daniel: A Commentary on the Book of Daniel*. Hermeneia. Minneapolis: Fortress Press, 1993.

Cross, Frank Moore. *Canaanite Myth and Hebrew Epic: Essays in the History of the Religion of Israel*. Cambridge: Harvard University Press, 1973.

Crossan, John Dominic. *Jesus: A Revolutionary Biography*. San Francisco: HarperSanFrancisco, 1994.

Dahood, Mitchell. *Psalms*. Garden City: Doubleday, 1966.

Daniélou, Jean. *Bible et Liturgie: La Thâeologie Biblique des Sacraments et des Fãetes D'apráes les Páeres De L'eglise*. Les Orandi. Paris: Editions du Cerf, 1951.

Day, John. *God's Conflict with the Dragon and the Sea: Echoes of a Canaanite Myth in the Old Testament*. University of

Cambridge Oriental Publications No. 35. Cambridge:
    Cambridge University Press, 1985.

———. *Yahweh and the Gods and Goddesses of Canaan*. Journal for
    the Study of the Old Testament. Supplement Series. Sheffield:
    Sheffield Academic Press, 2002.

Donahue, John. "The Quest for the Community of Mark's Gospel." In
    The Four Gospels, 1992: Festschrift Frans Neirynck, edited
    by F. Neirynck and Frans van Segbroeck. Leuven: Leuven
    University Press, 1992.

Duff, Paul Brooks. "The March of the Divine Warrior and the Advent
    of the Greco-Roman King: Mark's Account of Jesus' Entry
    into Jerusalem." *JBL* 111 (1992): 51-71.

Earl, Donald. "Prologue-Form in Ancient Historiography." *ANRW* 1.2
    (1972): 842-56.

Edwards, James R. *The Gospel According to Mark*. The Pillar New
    Testament Commentary. Grand Rapids: Eerdmans, 2002.

Ehrman, Bart D. *Misquoting Jesus: The Story Behind Who Changed the
    Bible and Why*. New York: HarperSanFrancisco, 2005.

Eliade, Mircea. *The Sacred and the Profane: The Nature of Religion*.
    New York: Harcourt, 1959.

Emerton, J. A. "The Origin of the Son of Man Imagery." *JTS* 9 (1958):
    225-42.

Fisher, L. R., and F. B. Knutson. "An Enthronement Ritual at Ugarit."
    JNES 28 (1969): 157-67.

Fontenrose, Joseph. *Python: A Study of Delphic Myth and Its Origins*.
    Berkeley: University of California Press, 1959.

Forsyth, Neil. *The Old Enemy: Satan and the Combat Myth*. Princeton:
    Princeton University Press, 1987.

Foster, Benjamin R. *Before the Muses: An Anthology of Akkadian
    Literature*. 3rd ed. Bethesda: CDL Press, 2005.

Frankfort, Henri. *Kingship and the Gods: A Study of Ancient Near
    Eastern Religion as the Integration of Society & Nature*.
    Oriental Institute Essay. Chicago: University of Chicago
    Press, 1948.

Freyne, Seán. *Galilee, Jesus, and the Gospels: Literary Approaches
    and Historical Investigations*. Philadelphia: Fortress Press,
    1988.

Frost, Stanley Brice. *Old Testament Apocalyptic: Its Origins and
    Growth*. London: Epworth, 1952.

Gibson, Jeffrey B. *The Temptations of Jesus in Early Christianity*. Journal for the Study of the New Testament Supplement Series. Sheffield: Sheffield Academic Press, 1995.

Gibson, John C. L., N. Wyatt, Wilfred G. E. Watson, and J. B. Lloyd. *Ugarit, Religion and Culture: Essays Presented in Honour of Professor John C.L. Gibson*. Ugaritisch-Biblische Literatur. Münster: Ugarit-Verlag, 1996.

Glazier-McDonald, Beth. *Malachi: The Divine Messenger*. SBL Dissertation Series. Atlanta: Scholars Press, 1987.

Goulder, M. D. *The Prayers of David (Psalms 51-72)*. Journal for the Study of the Old Testament. Supplement Series. Sheffield: JSOT Press, 1990.

Graves, Robert, and Raphael Patai. *Hebrew Myths: The Book of Genesis*. 2nd ed. London: Cassell, 1965.

Gray, John. *The Biblical Doctrine of the Reign of God*. T & T Clark, 2000.

Gray, Timothy C. *The Temple in the Gospel of Mark: A Study in Its Narrative Role*. Wissenschaftliche Untersuchungen Zum Neuen Testament. Tübingen: Mohr Siebeck, 2008.

Green, Joel B., Scot McKnight, and I. Howard Marshall. *Dictionary of Jesus and the Gospels*. Downers Grove: InterVarsity Press, 1992.

Guelich, Robert A. *Mark 1-8:26*. Word Biblical Commentary. Dallas: Word Books, 1989.

Gunkel, Hermann. *Schöpfung und Chaos in Urzeit und Endzeit: Eine Religionsgeschichtliche Untersuchung über Gen 1 und Ap Joh 12*. Göttingen: Vandenhoeck und Ruprecht, 1895.

Gurney, O. R. *Some Aspects of Hittite Religion*. The Schweich Lectures. Oxford: Oxford University Press for the British Academy, 1977.

Hamblin, William J. *Warfare in the Ancient Near East to 1600 BC: Holy Warriors at the Dawn of History*. London: Routledge, 2006.

Hanson, Paul. "Jewish Apocalyptic against Its Near Eastern Environment." *RB* 78 (1971): 31-58.

Hanson, Paul D. *The Dawn of Apocalyptic*. Philadelphia: Fortress Press, 1975.

Hauser, Alan J. "Yahweh Versus Death: The Real Struggle in 1 Kings 17-19." In *From Carmel to Horeb: Elijah in Crisis*, edited by

Alan J. Hauser and Russell Inman Gregory, 11-83. Sheffield: Almond Press, 1990.

Heil, John Paul. *Jesus Walking on the Sea: Meaning and Gospel Functions of Matt. 14:22-33, Mark 6:45-52, and John 6:15b-21*. Analecta Biblica. Rome: Biblical Institute Press, 1981.

Hess, Richard S. *Israelite Religions: An Archaeological and Biblical Survey*. Grand Rapids: Baker Academic, 2007.

Hoffner, Harry A., and Gary M. Beckman. *Hittite Myths*. Writings from the Ancient World. 2nd ed. Atlanta: Scholars Press, 1998.

Hollander, Harm W., and Marinus de Jonge. *The Testaments of the Twelve Patriarchs: A Commentary*. Studia in Veteris Testamenti Pseudepigrapha. Leiden: E.J. Brill, 1985.

Horsley, Richard. "The Kingdom of God and the Renewal of Israel: Synoptic Gospels, Jesus Movements, and Apocalypticism." In *The Encyclopedia of Apocalypticism*, edited by John J. Collins. New York: Continuum, 1998.

Jacobsen, Thorkild. *The Harps That Once...: Sumerian Poetry in Translation*. New Haven: Yale University Press, 1987.

Josephus, Flavius. *Jewish Antiquities*. Translated by H. Thackeray. The Loeb Classical Library. 10 vols. Cambridge: Harvard University Press, 1926.

Kaizer, Ted. *The Religious Life of Palmyra: A Study of the Social Patterns of Worship in the Roman Period*. Oriens et Occidens. Stuttgart: Steiner, 2002.

Kapelrud, Arvid Schou. *Baal in the Ras Shamra Texts*. Copenhagen: G.E.C. Gad, 1952.

Kee, Howard Clark. "The Terminology of Mark's Exorcism Stories." *NTS* 14 (1968): 232-46.

Kelber, Werner H. *Mark's Story of Jesus*. Philadelphia: Fortress Press, 1979.

Kiel, Micah. "The Apocalyptic Significance of Mark's First Feeding Narrative (6:34-44)." *Koinonia* 18 (2006): 93-114.

Kinman, Brent. *Jesus' Entry into Jerusalem: In the Context of Lukan Theology and the Politics of His Day*. Arbeiten Zur Geschichte des Antiken Judentums und des Urchristentums. Leiden: E.J. Brill, 1995.

Kloos, Carola. *Yhwh's Combat with the Sea: A Canaanite Tradition in the Religion of Ancient Israel*. Leiden: Brill, 1986.

Koester, Helmut. *Introduction to the New Testament*. Hermeneia. 2 vols. Philadelphia: Fortress Press, 1982.

Lane, William L. *The Gospel According to Mark: The English Text with Introduction, Exposition, and Notes*. Grand Rapids: Eerdmans, 1974.

LaRocca-Pitts, Elizabeth C. *Of Wood and Stone: The Significance of Israelite Cultic Items in the Bible and Its Early Interpreters*. Harvard Semitic Museum Publications. Winona Lake: Eisenbrauns, 2001.

LaVerdiere, Eugene. *The Beginning of the Gospel: Introducing the Gospel According to Mark*. 2 vols. Collegeville, Minn.: Liturgical Press, 1999.

Levenson, Jon. *Creation and the Persistence of Evil: The Jewish Drama of Divine Omnipotence*. San Francisco: Harper & Row, 1988.

Longman, Tremper, and Daniel G. Reid. *God Is a Warrior*. Studies in Old Testament Biblical Theology. Grand Rapids: Zondervan, 1995.

López-Ruiz, Carolina. *When the Gods Were Born: Greek Cosmogonies and the Near East*. Cambridge: Harvard University Press, 2010.

Loretz, Oswald, and Manfried Dietrich. *Mythen und Epen IV*. Gutersloh: Gutersloher Verlagshaus, 1997.

Lührmann, Dieter. "Die Pharisäer und Die Schriftgelehrten Im Markusevangelium." *ZNW* 78 (1987): 169-85.

Malbon, Elizabeth. *Narrative Space and Mythic Meaning in Mark*. San Francisco: Harper and Row, 1986.

Mann, C. S. *Mark: A New Translation with Introduction and Commentary*. The Anchor Bible. Garden City: Doubleday, 1986.

Marcus, Joel. *Mark 1-8: A New Translation with Introduction and Commentary*. The Anchor Bible. 2 vols. New York: Doubleday, 2000.

———. *Mark 8-16: A New Translation with Introduction and Commentary*. The Anchor Bible. New York: Doubleday, 2009.

———. *The Way of the Lord: Christological Exegesis of the Old Testament in the Gospel of Mark*. T & T Clark Academic Paperbacks. London: T & T Clark International, 2004.

McCarter, P. Kyle. *II Samuel: A New Translation with Introduction, Notes, and Commentary*. The Anchor Bible. Garden City: Doubleday, 1984.

McCurley, Foster R. *Ancient Myths and Biblical Faith: Scriptural Transformations*. Philadelphia: Fortress Press, 1983.

Meyers, Carol L., and Eric M. Meyers. *Zechariah 9-14: A New Translation with Introduction and Commentary*. The Anchor Bible. New York: Doubleday, 1993.

Miller, Patrick D. "Israelite Religion." In *The Hebrew Bible and Its Modern Interpreters*, edited by Douglas A. Knight and Gene M. Tucker, 201-37. Philadelphia: Fortress Press, 1985.

————. "Two Critical Notes on Psalm 68 and Deuteronomy 33." *HTR* 57 (1964): 240-43.

Moor, Johannes Cornelis de. *An Anthology of Religious Texts from Ugarit*. Religious Texts Translation Series. Vol. 16, Leiden: E. J. Brill, 1987.

————. *New Year with Canaanites and Israelites*. Kamper Cahiers. 2 vols. Kampen: Kok, 1972.

Mowinckel, Sigmund. *He That Cometh*. New York: Abingdon Press, 1956.

————. *Psalmenstudien*. 6 vols. Oslo: J. Dybwad, 1921-1924.

————. *The Psalms in Israel's Worship*. Oxford: Blackwell, 1962.

Mullen, E. Theodore. *The Divine Council in Canaanite and Early Hebrew Literature*. Harvard Semitic Monographs. Chico: Scholars Press, 1980.

Myers, Ched. *Binding the Strong Man*. Maryknoll: Orbis Books, 1991.

Ollenburger, Ben C. *Zion, the City of the Great King: A Theological Symbol of the Jerusalem Cult*. Journal for the Study of the Old Testament Supplement Series. Sheffield, England: JSOT Press, 1987.

Olmo Lete, Gregorio del. *Canaanite Religion: According to the Liturgical Texts of Ugarit*. Bethesda: CDL Press, 1999.

Page, Hugh R. *The Myth of Cosmic Rebellion: A Study of Its Reflexes in Ugaritic and Biblical Literature*. Leiden: E. J. Brill, 1996.

Pagels, Elaine H. *The Origin of Satan*. New York: Random House, 1995.

Pardee, Dennis, and Theodore J. Lewis. *Ritual and Cult at Ugarit* [in Contains transliterated Ugaritic texts and English translations.]. Writings from the Ancient World. Leiden: Brill, 2002.

Parry, Donald W., and Emanuel Tov. *The Dead Sea Scrolls Reader*. 6 vols. Vol. 5, Leiden: Brill, 2004.

Perkins, Pheme. *The New Interpreter's Bible 8*. 12 vols. Nashville: Abingdon Press, 1994.

Perrin, Norman, and Dennis Duling. *The New Testament, an Introduction: Proclamation and Parenesis, Myth and History*. San Diego: Harcourt Brace Jovanovich, 1982.

Petersen, Allan Rosengren. *The Royal God: Enthronement Festivals in Ancient Israel and Ugarit?* Journal for the Study of the Old Testament Supplement Series. Sheffield: Sheffield Academic Press, 1998.

Pitard, Wayne T. "The Binding of Yamm: A New Edition of the Ugaritic Text KTU 1.83." *JNES* 57, no. 4 (1998): 261-80.

Propp, Vladimir. *Morphology of the Folktale*. Austin: University of Texas Press, 1928.

Riesenfeld, Harald. "Jésus Transfiguré, L'arriére-plan récit évangélique de la Transfiguration de Notre-Seigneur." PhD, Université d'Uppsala, 1947.

Roberts, J. J. M. "Mowinckel's Enthronement Festival: A Review." In *The Book of Psalms: Composition and Reception*, edited by Peter W. Flint, Patrick D. Miller, Aaron Brunell and Ryan Roberts, 97-115. Leiden: Brill, 2005.

Rudman, Dominic. "The Crucifixion as Chaoskampf: A New Reading of the Passion Narrative in the Synoptic Gospels." *Biblica* 84 (2003): 102-07.

Russell, Jeffrey Burton. *The Devil: Perceptions of Evil from Antiquity to Primitive Christianity*. Ithaca: Cornell University Press, 1977.

Schweizer, Eduard. *The Good News According to Mark*. Richmond: John Knox Press, 1970.

Smith, Charles W. F. "No Time for Figs." *JBL* 79 (1960): 315-27.

Smith, Mark S. *The Ugaritic Baal Cycle Vol. 1*. Supplements to Vetus Testamentum,. Leiden: E.J. Brill, 1994.

Smith, Mark S., and Simon B. Parker. *Ugaritic Narrative Poetry*. Writings from the Ancient World. Atlanta: Scholars Press, 1997.

Smith, Mark S., and Wayne Thomas Pitard. *The Ugaritic Baal Cycle Vol. 2*. Supplements to Vetus Testamentum. Leiden: E.J. Brill, 2009.

Stamm, Johann J. "Ein Vierteljahrhundert Psalmenforschung." *Theologische Rundschau* 23 (1955): 1-68.

Swartley, W. M. "The Structural Function of the Term 'Way' (Hodos) in Mark's Gospel." In *The New Way of Jesus: Essays Presented to Howard Charles*, edited by William Klassen. Newton: Faith and Life Press, 1980.

Tidwell, N. L. "No Highway! The Outline of a Semantic Description of Mesillâ." *VT* 45 (1995): 251-69.

Tromp, Nicholas J. *Primitive Conceptions of Death and the Nether World in the Old Testament*. Rome: Pontifical Biblical Institute, 1969.

Vermès, Géza. *The Complete Dead Sea Scrolls in English*. Penguin Classics. London: Penguin Books, 2004.

Volz, Paul. *Jesaia II*. Kommentar Zum Alten Testament. Leipzig: Deichertsche, 1932.

Wakeman, Mary K. *God's Battle with the Monster: A Study in Biblical Imagery*. Leiden: Brill, 1973.

Walton, John H. "The *Anzu* Myth as Relevent Background for Daniel 7?". In *The Book of Daniel: Composition and Reception*, edited by John J. Collins and Peter W. Flint, 69-89. Leiden: Brill, 2001.

Watts, Rikki E. *Isaiah's New Exodus in Mark*. Tübingen: Mohr Siebeck, 1997.

Wrede, William. *Das Messiasgeheimnis in Den Evangelien*. Göttingen: Vandenhoeck & Ruprecht, 1901.

Wright, N. T. *The New Testament and the People of God*. Minneapolis: Fortress Press, 1992.